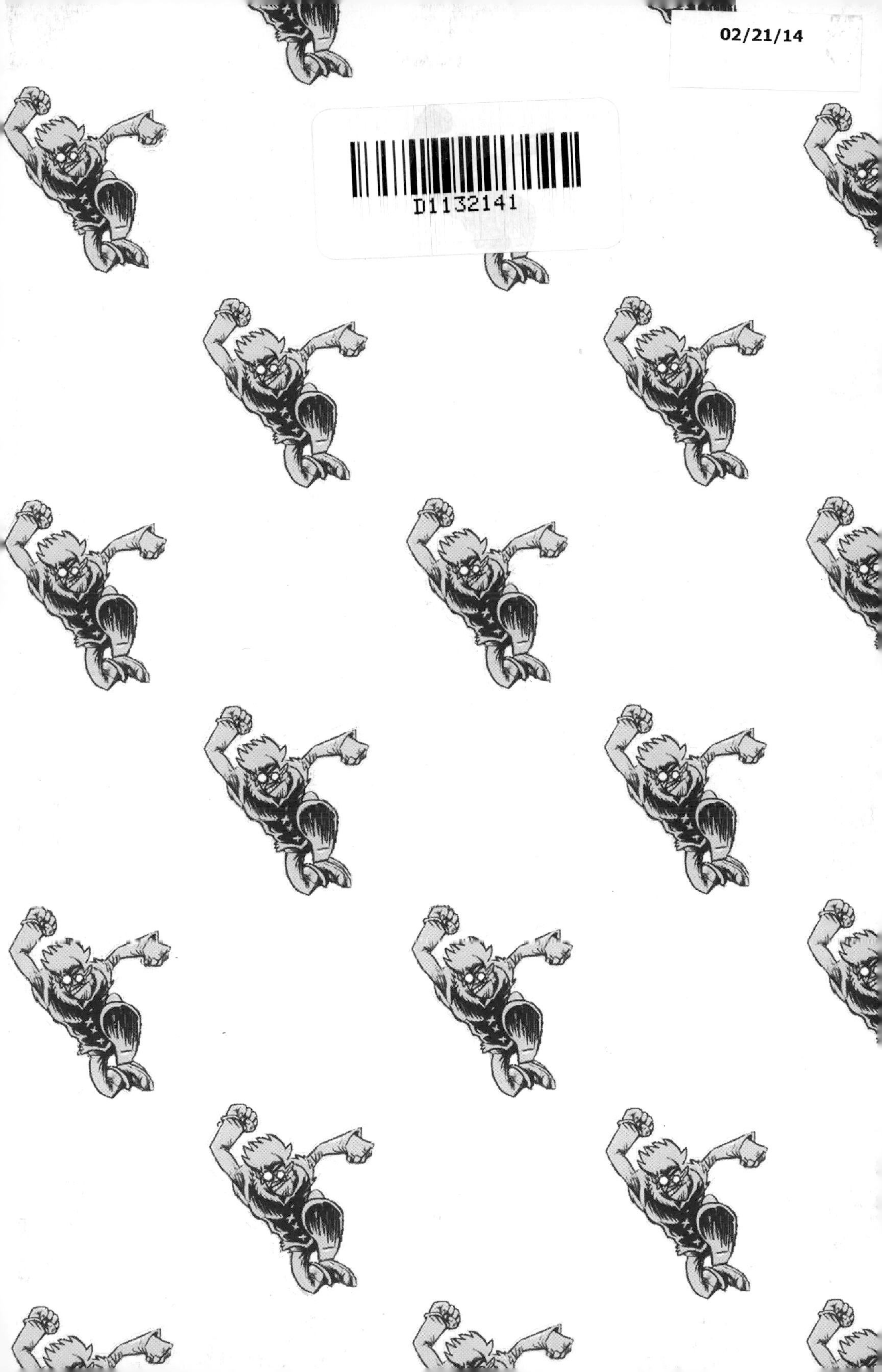

CHERUBS!

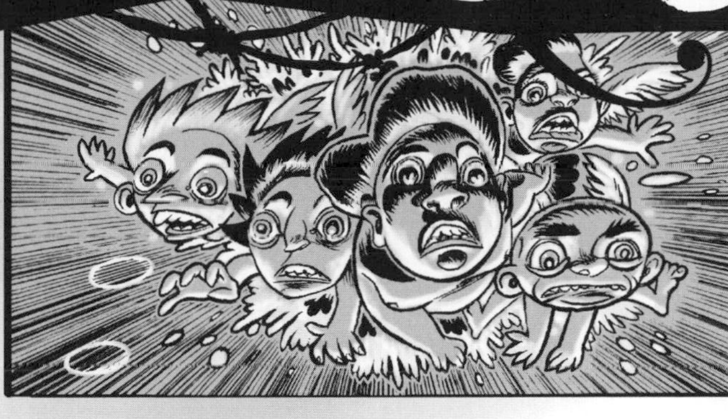

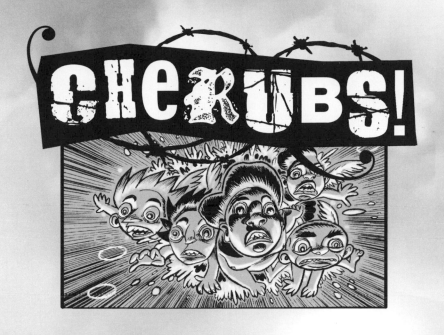

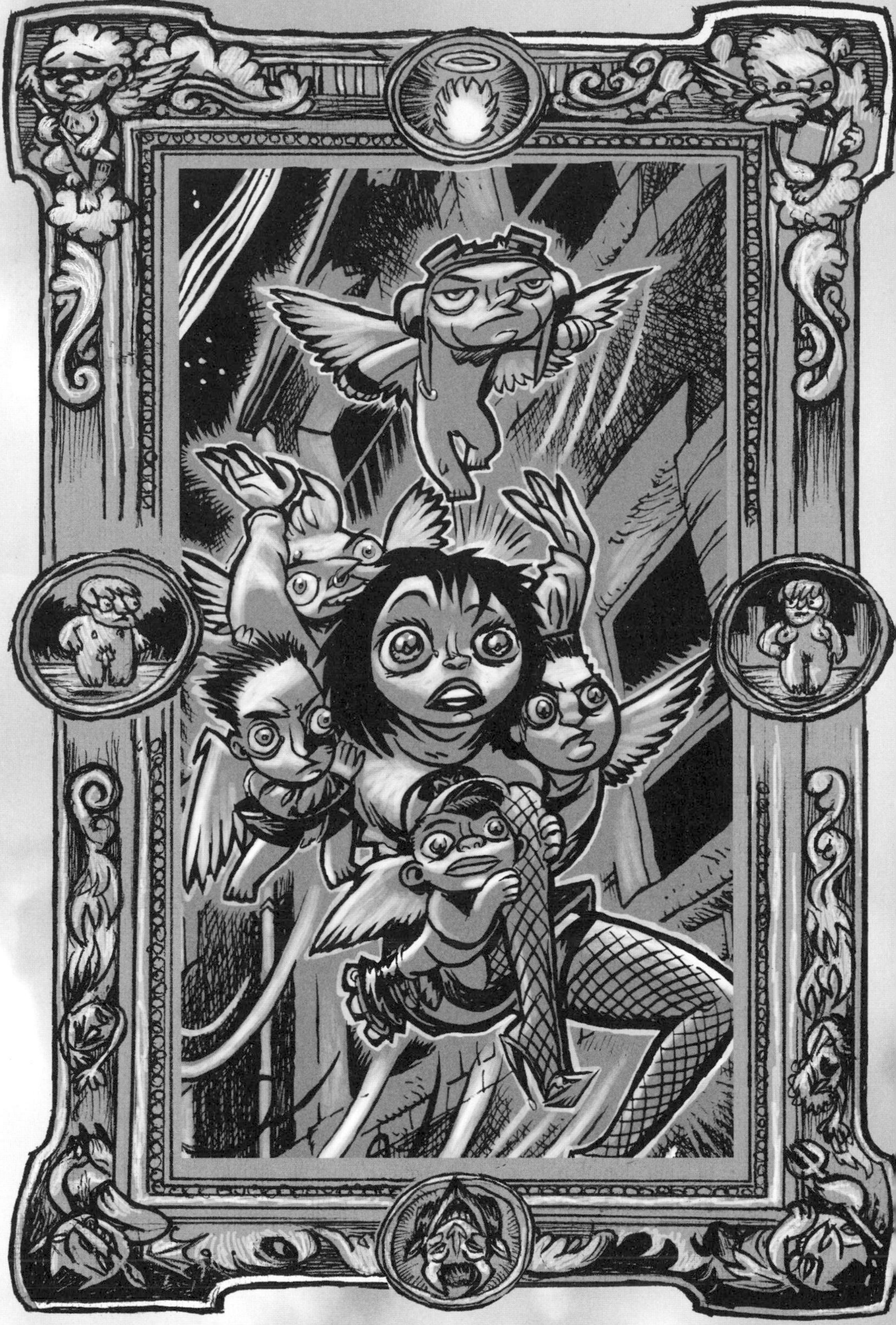

SCRIPT AND LAYOUTS
BRYAN TALBOT

ART
MARK STAFFORD

PAGES 5, 6, AND 31–34
CHOREOGRAPHED AND COWRITTEN BY
MARK STAFFORD

LETTERING
NATE PRIDE

TITLE LOGO
JORDAN SMITH

LATIN ADVISOR
MARY BRANSCOMBE

FOREWORD
MEL GIBSON

AFTERWORD
PAUL POPE

DARK HORSE BOOKS®

PUTTI IN THEIR HANDS

Hi there, ye true holders of the faith (although what you are holding, apart from this book, I have no idea).

To begin with, when you have a name like Mel Gibson, you get some interesting emails and letters.

These range from enquiries about your availability to visit a jail to inspire the prisoners through your powerful understanding of faith, to ones demanding that you cease from making films instantly and suggesting that you are damned whether you do or not.

Of course, I'm not *that* Mel Gibson, but I'll happily send him both the messages of support and the hate mail I've received over the last fifteen years that were intended for him. (. . . and if you are reading this, Mel, can I have your email address as swiftly as possible, please? My inbox is pretty much full.)

This time though, even given that there is a religious theme involved, I knew that the invitation was for me, not the other Mel. I feel honoured to be asked to contribute to this splendid volume that adds so much to the understanding of cherubs in particular and faith in general.

Hmmm . . . well, it sort of adds to it, in that I was left in hopeless giggles, interspersed with evil grins, throughout . . .

Aspects of religion appear in many forms in comics: from the educational and celebratory, like Tezuka's *Buddha*, to the cheerfully willful dismantling or hilarious demolition of some elements of a faith, as is the case in Ennis' *Preacher*. There are also works that aim to convert or to make a faith accessible to a new audience, ranging from the *Manga Bible* in all directions. There is also, in many narratives, the echo of an underlying faith (or myth) that has influenced a creator's thinking, shaping a narrative that may otherwise seem to make no references to any particular religion at all.

Add to that wide-ranging set of approaches and appropriations authorial tones that range from the quietly dignified and studiously explorational to the gleefully savage, and you start getting an idea of a map of the territory of religion in comics.

So where is *Cherubs!* on that map? I've concluded that it is not so much on the map as off it and exploring an entertaining territory somewhere nearby. Furthermore, actually, it doesn't really give a stuff about maps anyway.

Basically, it turns out that "heaven is a place, a place where nothing, nothing ever happens"[1] . . . usually. Although it seems that when something does happen, everything gets complicated and messy very quickly.

That heaven is boring is something I've often suspected, and were I of certain faiths this would leave me with some interesting choices to make. Should I do my best to go to heaven and, despite the benefit of maybe being able finally to sing in tune, go mad from inactivity? Or just ensure myself an afterlife of unrelenting, but probably more intriguing and engaging, agony? This is the kind of dilemma that *Cherubs!* deals with.

To cut to the cherubs themselves, well, they finally stop feeling bored, but the cost is that they find representatives of both heaven and hell are after them. I suspect that if there were a message here (as there isn't anything that offers a more traditionally religious moral) it would be, "Be careful what you wish for; you might get it."

Envisage the Marx Brothers on a high-speed and out-of-control bob-sleigh and you might get a sense of how this narrative unfolds. This is a wild and witty ride, packed with cheerfully blasphemous commentary about small folk with wings dealing with their own reawakened biological functions and appetites.

In addition, they have to come to terms with city life on Earth, with all its many distractions. Whilst they are in pursuit of the truth, they want to catch up on some experiences (preferably entertaining or, at least, interesting) while they are at it.

If it were down to me, I'd want to meet up with the cherubs and their creators in a bar somewhere just after dusk, and see how the night developed.

. . . and, I rather suspect, so would you.

—Dr. Mel Gibson

Comics historian,
Northumbria University
Somewhere near Sunderland, UK

September 2007

---

1. From the song "Heaven" by Talking Heads, which can be found on the album *Fear of Music* (1979). Look, I'm an academic. I have to have a footnote, and a reference, in any piece of writing I do or my brain explodes. In essence, if I didn't do that, things would get messy and I wouldn't like it.

Dedicated to Leo Baxendale, creator of The Bash
Street Kids, *and Dante Alighieri for divine inspiration.*

—BRYAN TALBOT

*Many thanks to Dan Edgely for the demons; Andrew Gaskell for the
photos; Sister Jo for the technology; Anita, Kate, Sarah, and all at the
Cartoon Museum for their patience and support; and Steve Marchant and
Alison Brown for the beer and sympathy. Cheers! Drinks are on Bryan . . .*

—MARK STAFFORD

PUBLISHER
MIKE RICHARDSON

EDITOR (COLLECTION, *CANTICA II*)
CHRIS WARNER

EDITOR (*CANTICA I*)
JOE PRUETT

PUBLICATION DESIGN
ADAM GRANO

This volume includes material previously published as
Cherubs!: Paradise Lost, from Desperado Publishing.

Dark Horse Books
A division of Dark Horse Comics, Inc.
10956 SE Main Street
Milwaukie OR 97222

DarkHorse.com
Bryan-Talbot.com
Hocus-Baloney.com

To find a comics shop in your area, call the Comic Shop Locator Service toll-free at 1-888-266-4226.

First edition: January 2013
ISBN 978-1-59582-984-9

1 3 5 7 9 10 8 6 4 2
Printed in China

CANTICA I

PARADISE LOST

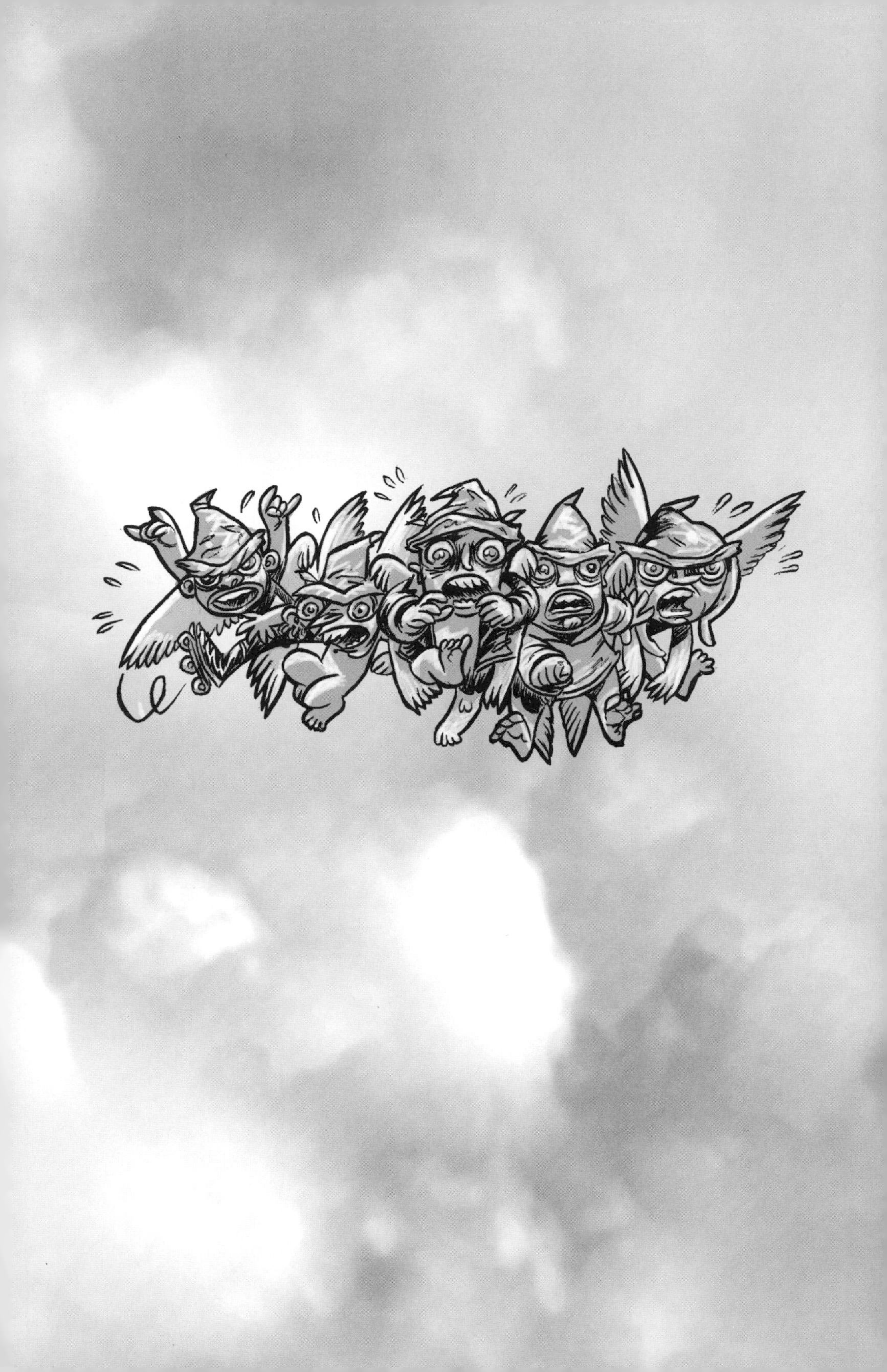

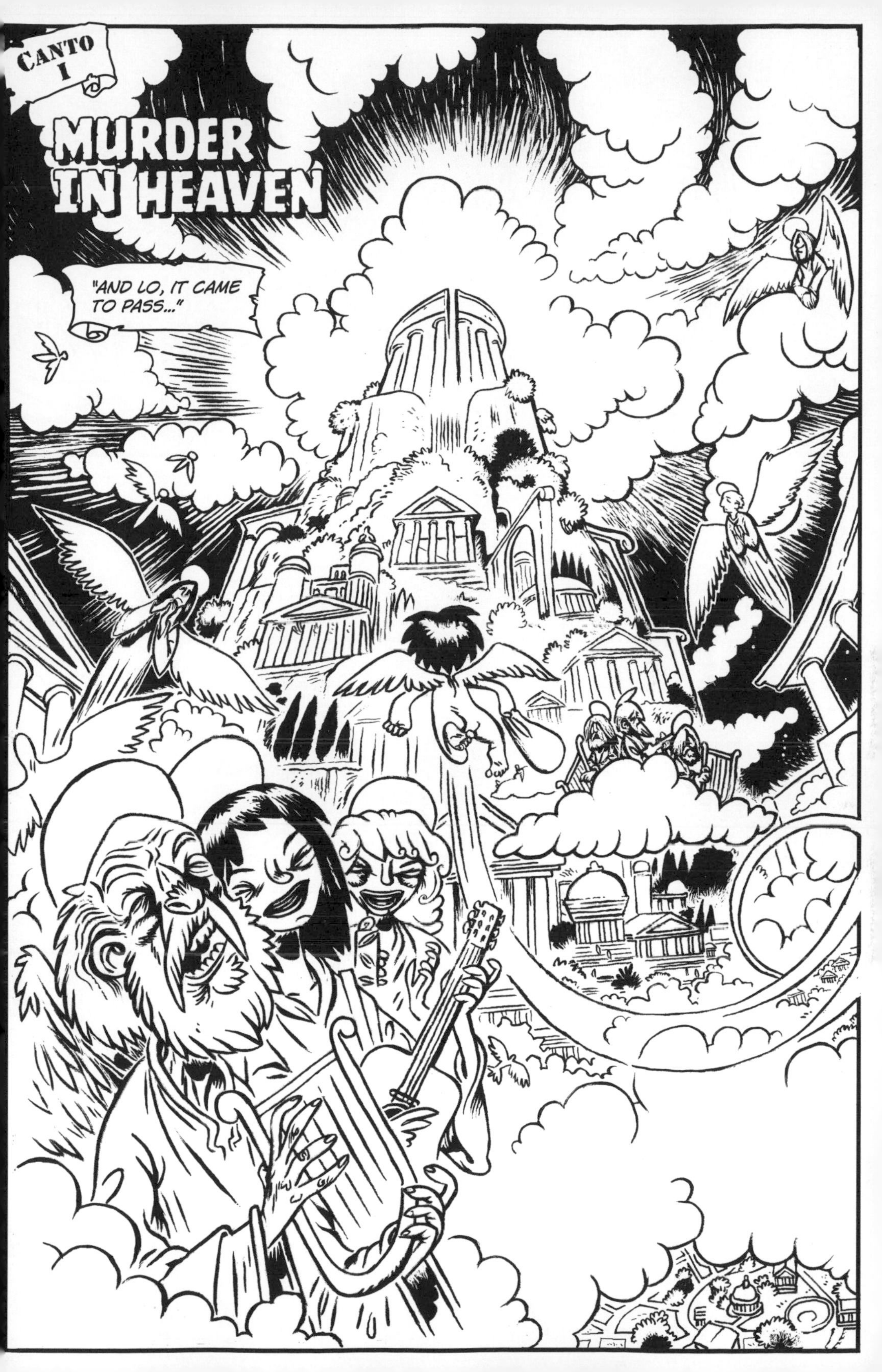
CANTO I
MURDER IN HEAVEN
"AND LO, IT CAME TO PASS..."

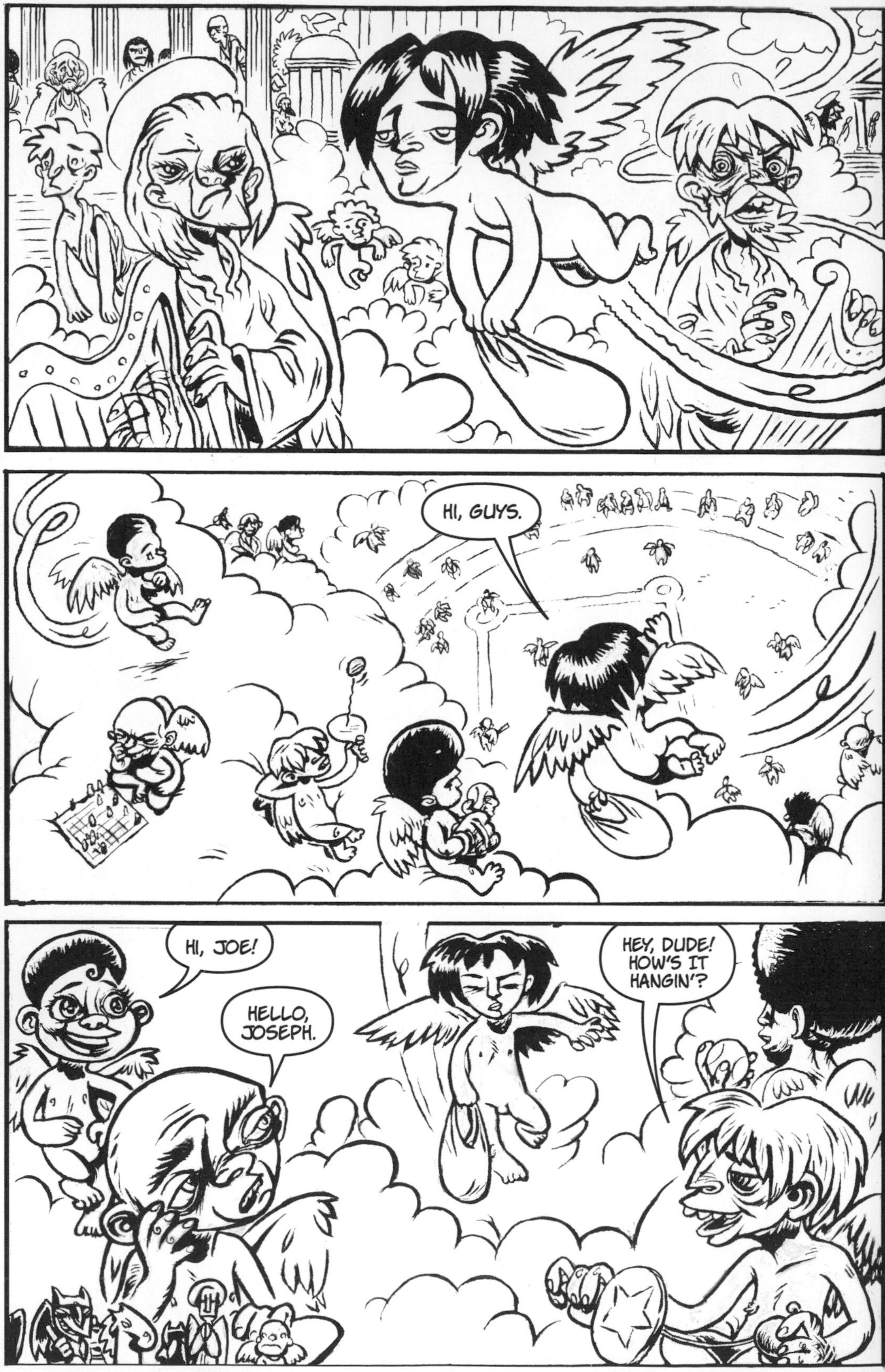
HI, GUYS.
HI, JOE!
HELLO, JOSEPH.
HEY, DUDE! HOW'S IT HANGIN'?

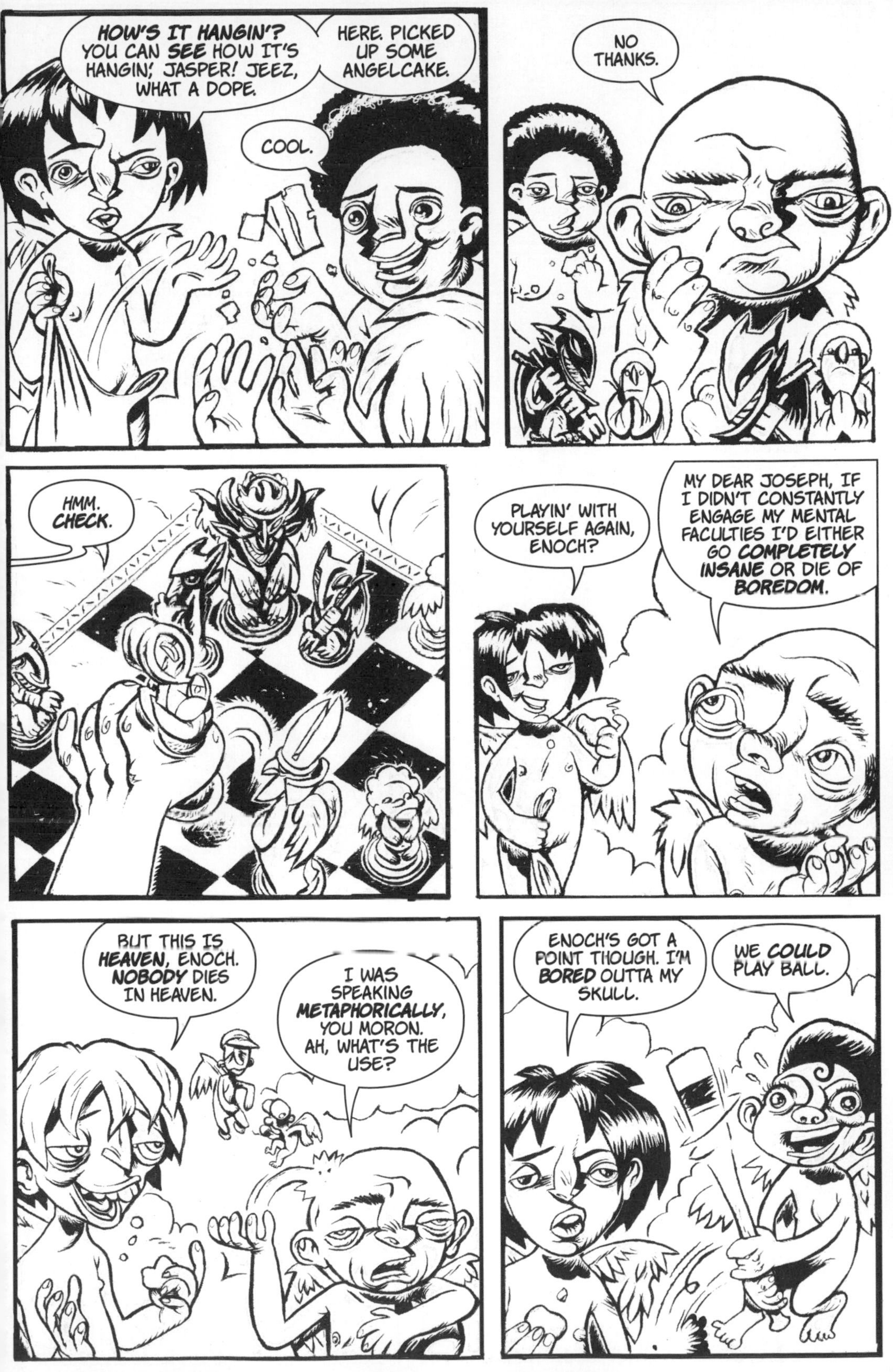
HOW'S IT HANGIN'? YOU CAN SEE HOW IT'S HANGIN', JASPER! JEEZ, WHAT A DOPE.
HERE. PICKED UP SOME ANGELCAKE.
COOL.
NO THANKS.
HMM. CHECK.
PLAYIN' WITH YOURSELF AGAIN, ENOCH?
MY DEAR JOSEPH, IF I DIDN'T CONSTANTLY ENGAGE MY MENTAL FACULTIES I'D EITHER GO COMPLETELY INSANE OR DIE OF BOREDOM.
BUT THIS IS HEAVEN, ENOCH. NOBODY DIES IN HEAVEN.
I WAS SPEAKING METAPHORICALLY, YOU MORON. AH, WHAT'S THE USE?
ENOCH'S GOT A POINT THOUGH. I'M BORED OUTTA MY SKULL.
WE COULD PLAY BALL.

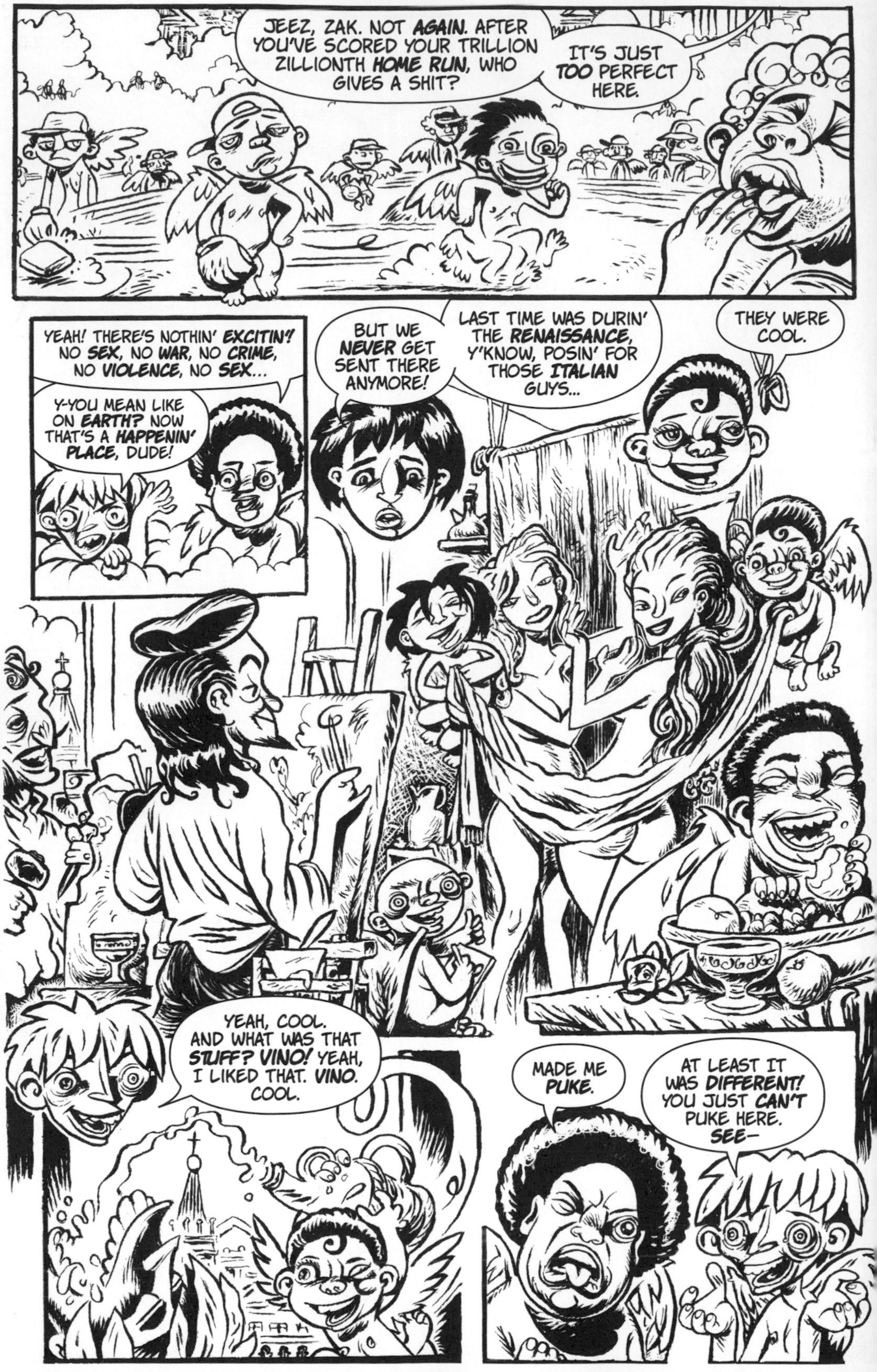
JEEZ, ZAK. NOT AGAIN. AFTER YOU'VE SCORED YOUR TRILLION ZILLIONTH HOME RUN, WHO GIVES A SHIT?
IT'S JUST TOO PERFECT HERE.
YEAH! THERE'S NOTHIN' EXCITIN'! NO SEX, NO WAR, NO CRIME, NO VIOLENCE, NO SEX...
Y-YOU MEAN LIKE ON EARTH? NOW THAT'S A HAPPENIN' PLACE, DUDE!
BUT WE NEVER GET SENT THERE ANYMORE!
LAST TIME WAS DURIN' THE RENAISSANCE, Y'KNOW, POSIN' FOR THOSE ITALIAN GUYS...
THEY WERE COOL.
YEAH, COOL. AND WHAT WAS THAT STUFF? VINO! YEAH, I LIKED THAT. VINO. COOL.
MADE ME PUKE.
AT LEAST IT WAS DIFFERENT! YOU JUST CAN'T PUKE HERE. SEE–

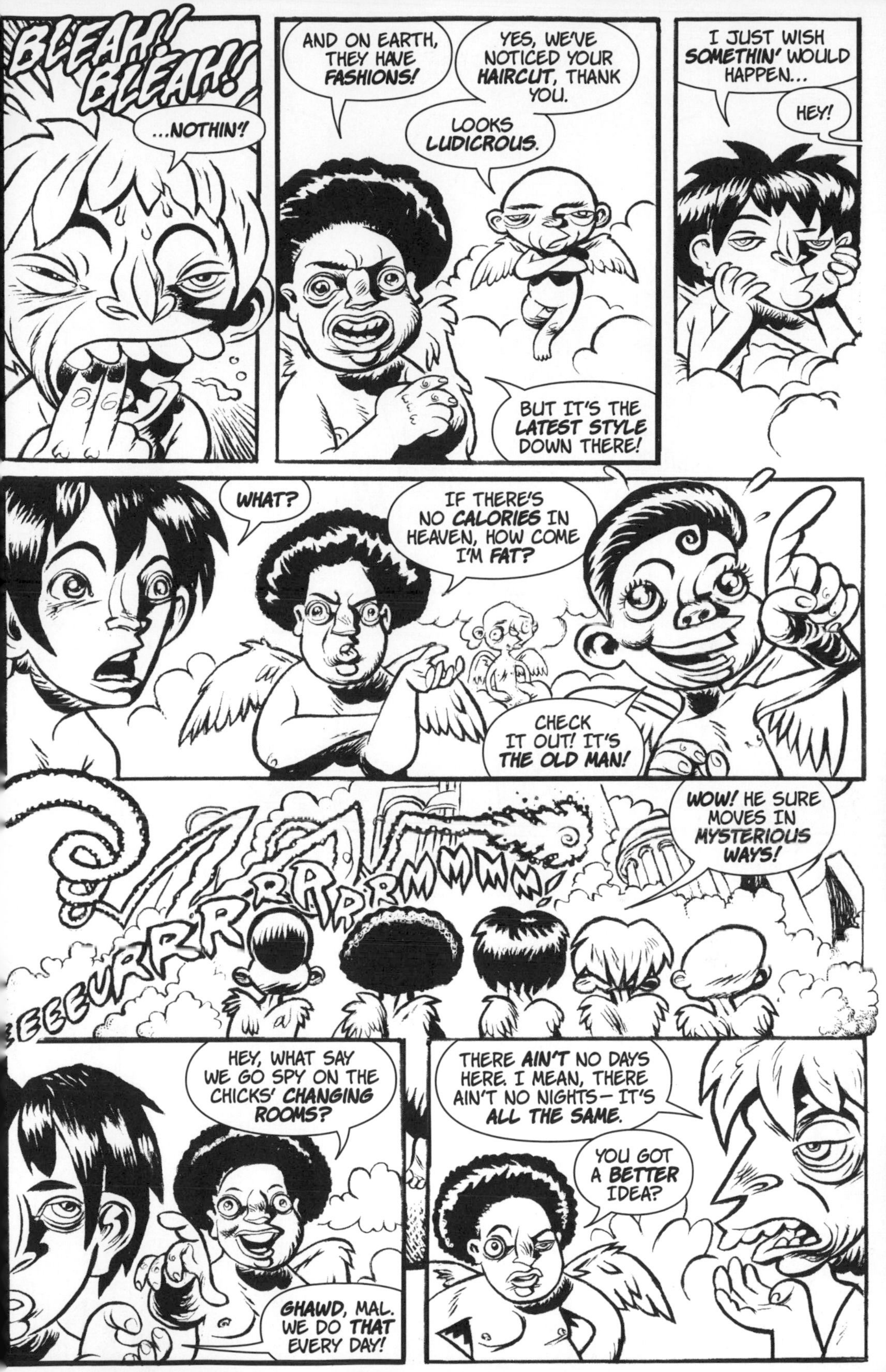
BLEAH! BLEAH!
...NOTHIN'!
AND ON EARTH, THEY HAVE FASHIONS!
YES, WE'VE NOTICED YOUR HAIRCUT, THANK YOU.
LOOKS LUDICROUS.
BUT IT'S THE LATEST STYLE DOWN THERE!
I JUST WISH SOMETHIN' WOULD HAPPEN...
HEY!
WHAT?
IF THERE'S NO CALORIES IN HEAVEN, HOW COME I'M FAT?
CHECK IT OUT! IT'S THE OLD MAN!
EEEEURRRRRRRRRRRMMMMMN!
WOW! HE SURE MOVES IN MYSTERIOUS WAYS!
HEY, WHAT SAY WE GO SPY ON THE CHICKS' CHANGING ROOMS?
GHAWD, MAL. WE DO THAT EVERY DAY!
THERE AIN'T NO DAYS HERE. I MEAN, THERE AIN'T NO NIGHTS— IT'S ALL THE SAME.
YOU GOT A BETTER IDEA?

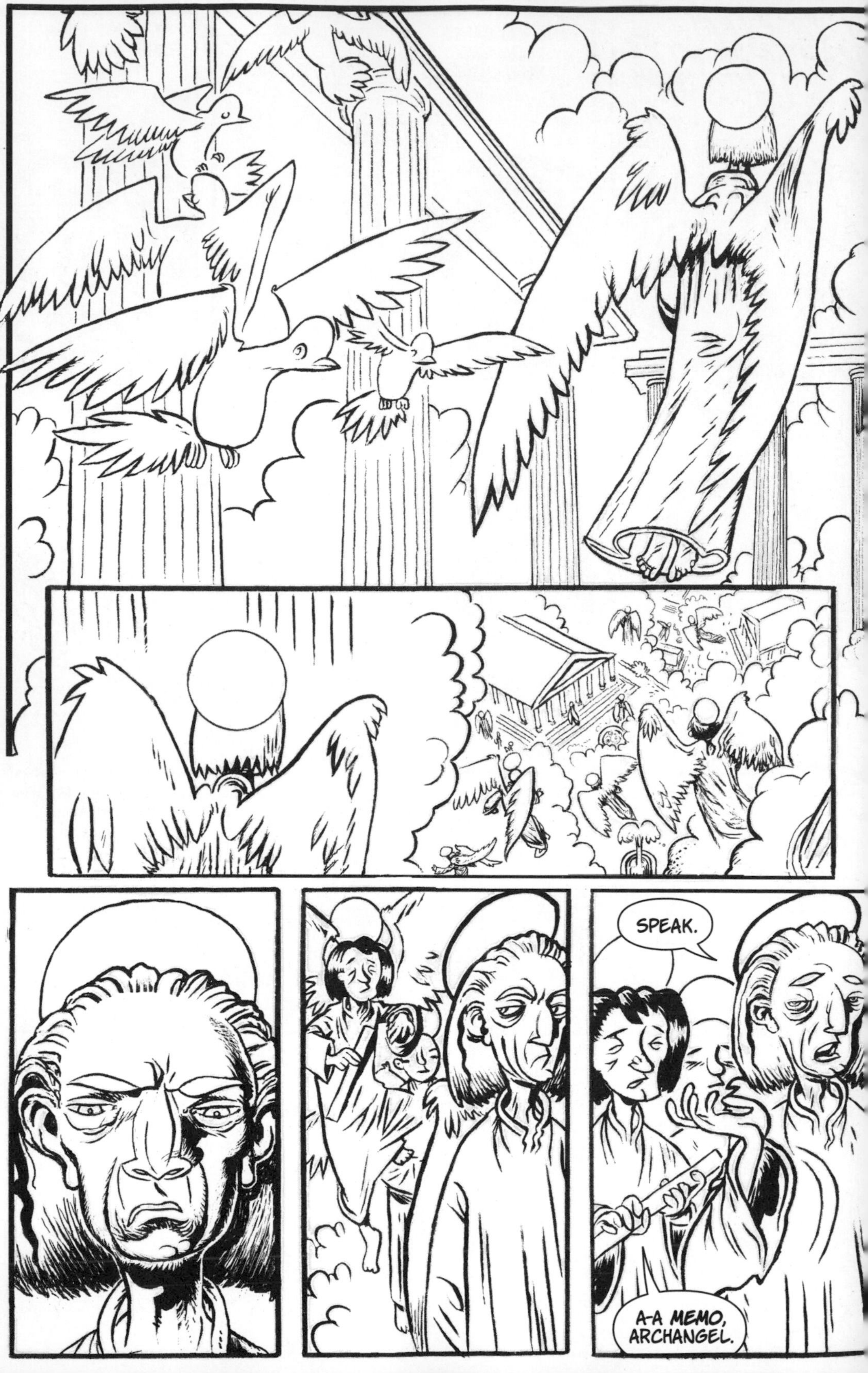
SPEAK.
A-A MEMO, ARCHANGEL.

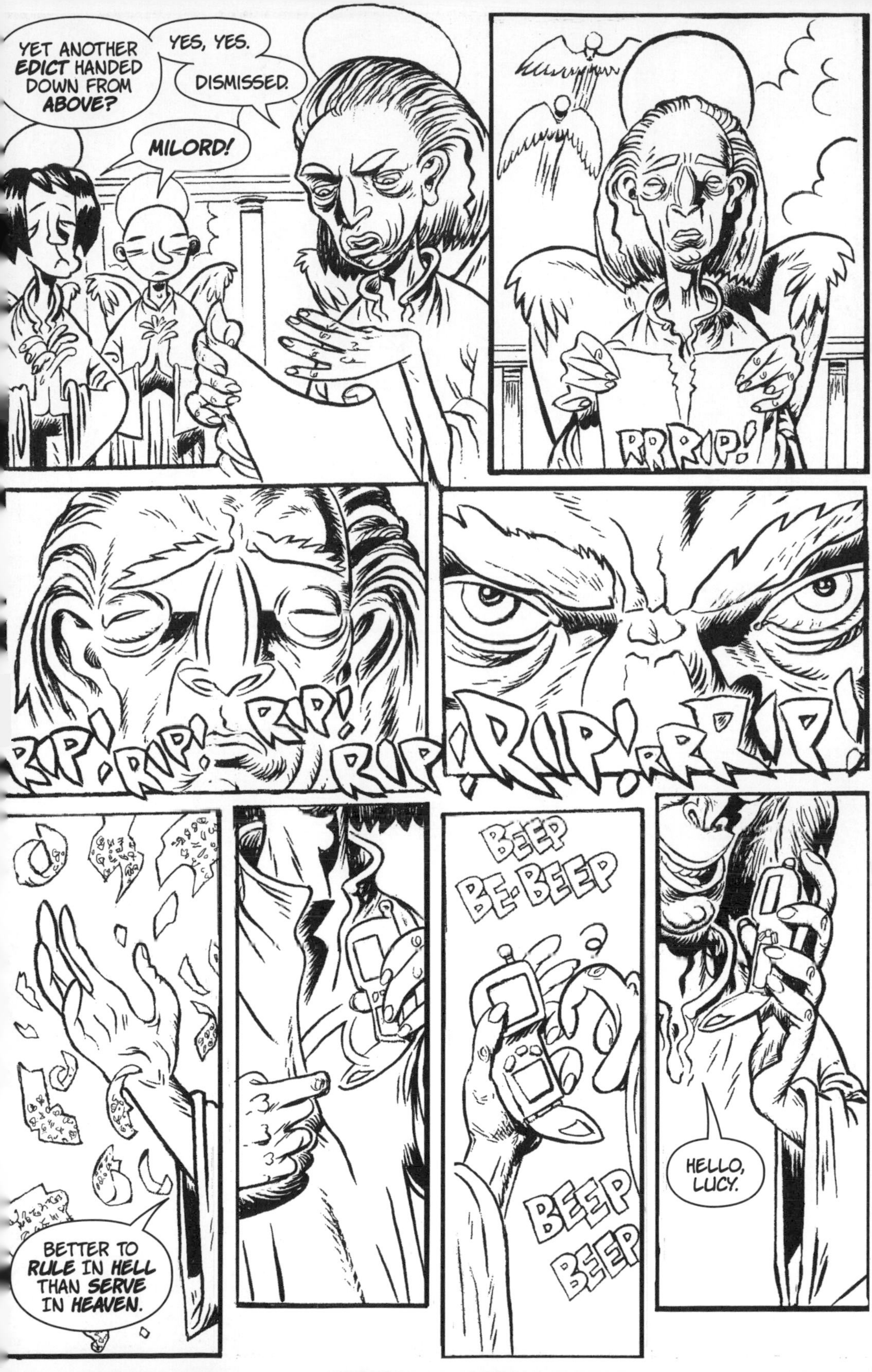
YET ANOTHER EDICT HANDED DOWN FROM ABOVE?
YES, YES.
DISMISSED.
MILORD!
RRRIP!
RIP! RIP! RIP! RIP!
RIP! RRRIP!
BETTER TO RULE IN HELL THAN SERVE IN HEAVEN.
BEEP BE-BEEP
BEEP BEEP
HELLO, LUCY.

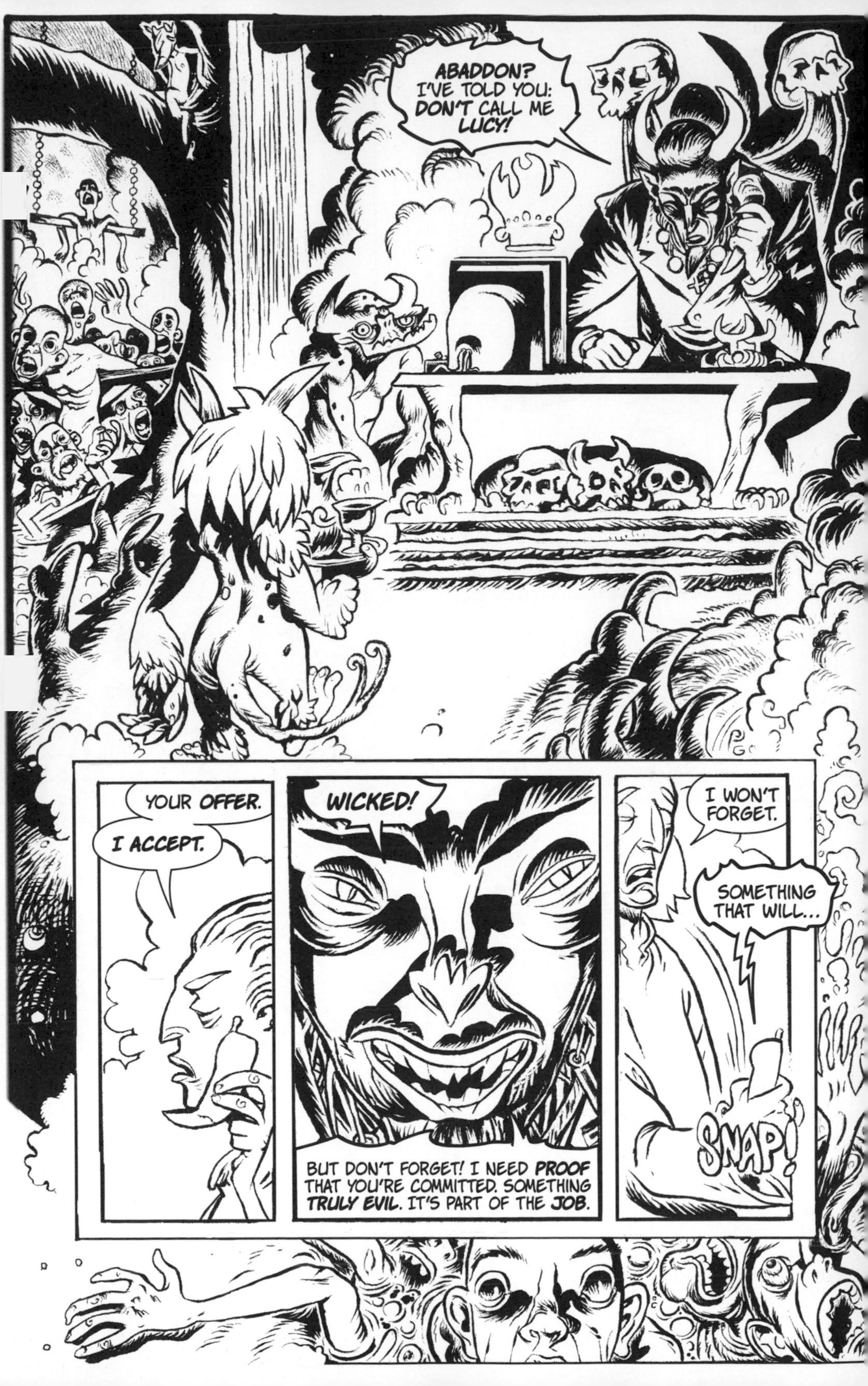
ABADDON? I'VE TOLD YOU: DON'T CALL ME LUCY!
YOUR OFFER.
I ACCEPT.
WICKED!
BUT DON'T FORGET! I NEED PROOF THAT YOU'RE COMMITTED. SOMETHING TRULY EVIL. IT'S PART OF THE JOB.
I WON'T FORGET.
SOMETHING THAT WILL...
SNAP!

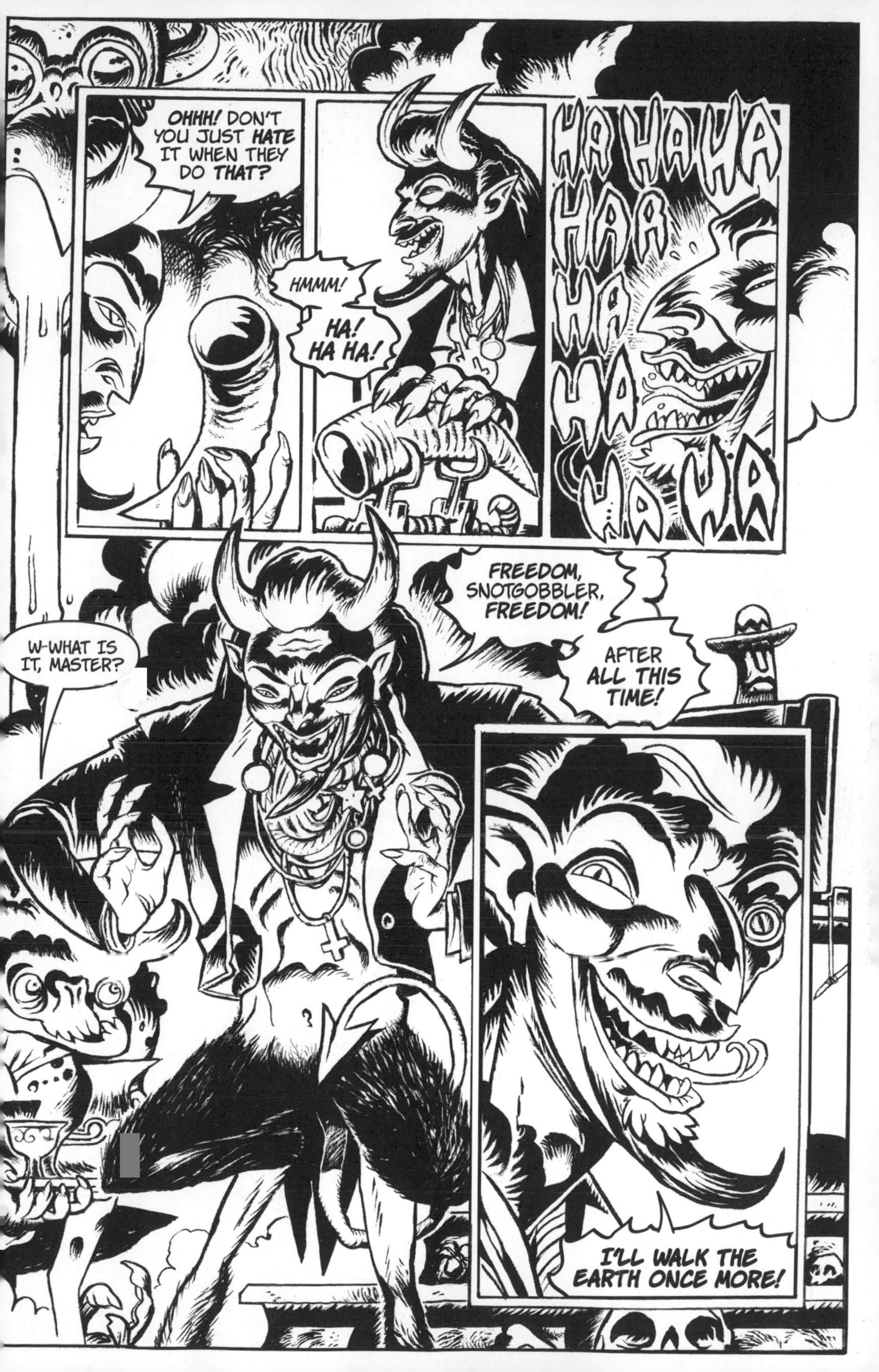
OHHH! DON'T YOU JUST HATE IT WHEN THEY DO THAT?
HMMM!
HA! HA HA!
HA HA HA HA HA HA HA HA HA
FREEDOM, SNOTGOBBLER, FREEDOM!
W-WHAT IS IT, MASTER?
AFTER ALL THIS TIME!
I'LL WALK THE EARTH ONCE MORE!

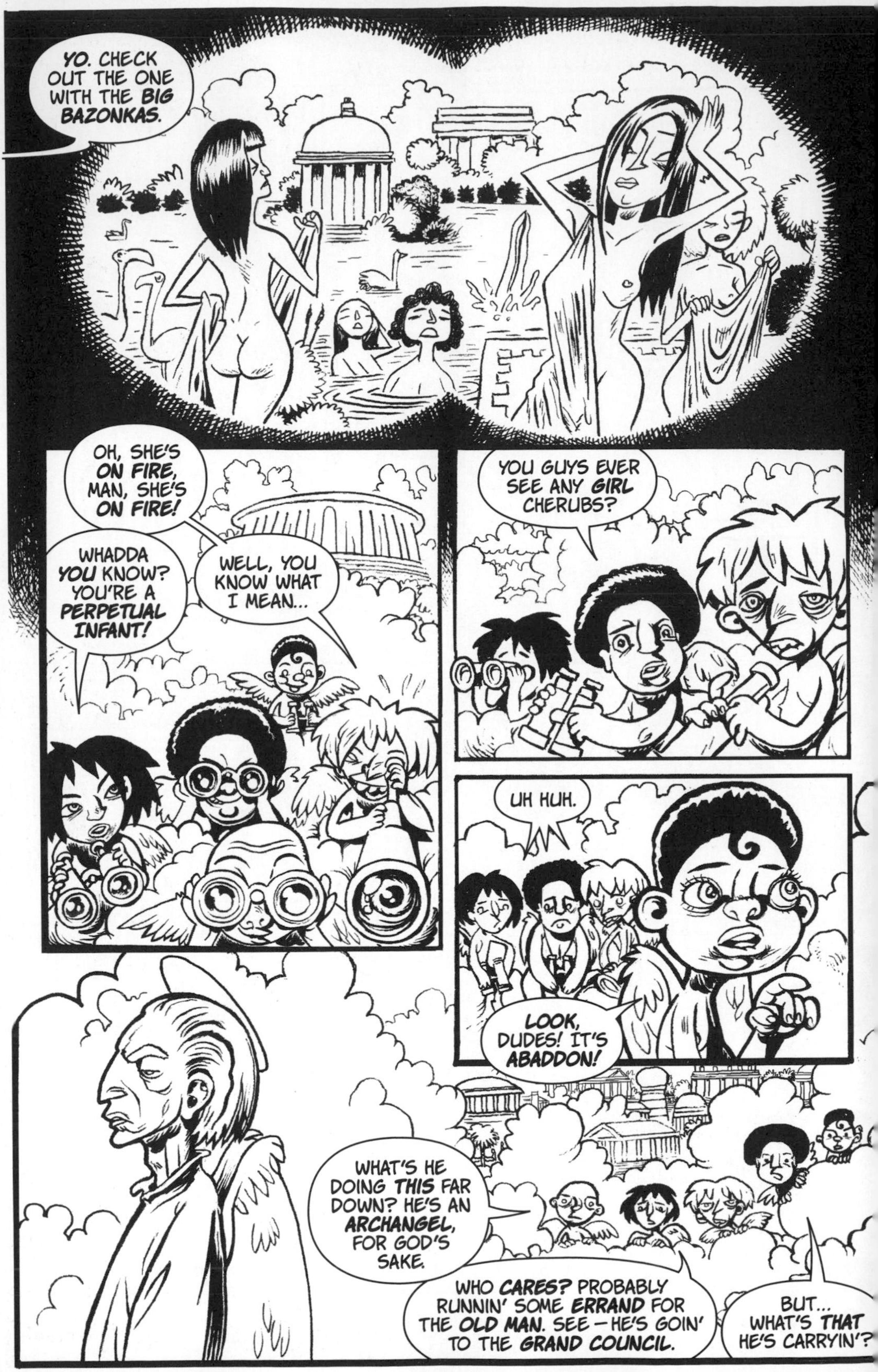
YO. CHECK OUT THE ONE WITH THE BIG BAZONKAS.
OH, SHE'S ON FIRE, MAN, SHE'S ON FIRE!
WHADDA YOU KNOW? YOU'RE A PERPETUAL INFANT!
WELL, YOU KNOW WHAT I MEAN...
YOU GUYS EVER SEE ANY GIRL CHERUBS?
UH HUH.
LOOK, DUDES! IT'S ABADDON!
WHAT'S HE DOING THIS FAR DOWN? HE'S AN ARCHANGEL, FOR GOD'S SAKE.
WHO CARES? PROBABLY RUNNIN' SOME ERRAND FOR THE OLD MAN. SEE—HE'S GOIN' TO THE GRAND COUNCIL.
BUT... WHAT'S THAT HE'S CARRYIN'?

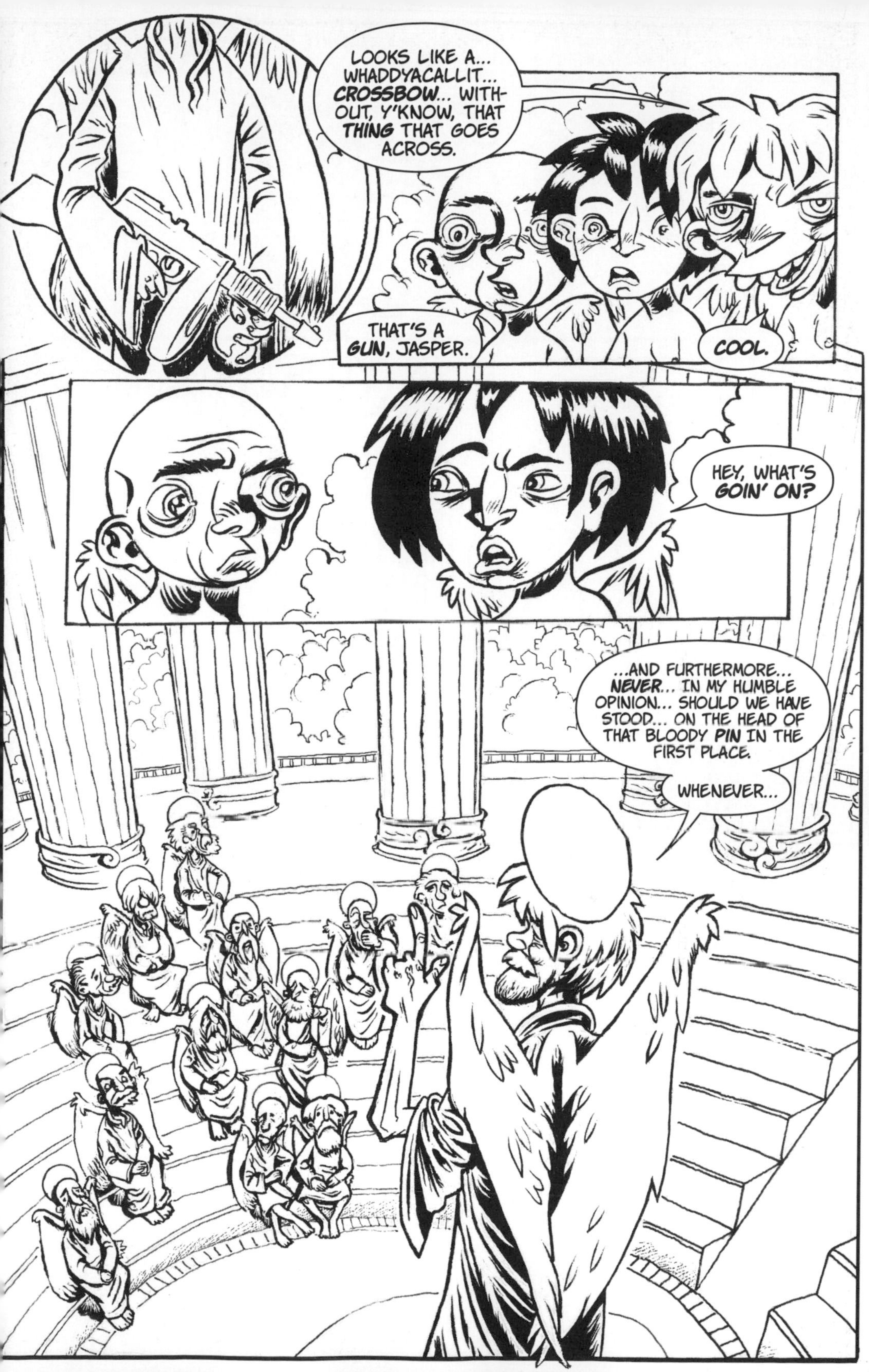

LOOKS LIKE A... WHADDYACALLIT... CROSSBOW... WITH-OUT, Y'KNOW, THAT THING THAT GOES ACROSS.
THAT'S A GUN, JASPER.
COOL.
HEY, WHAT'S GOIN' ON?
...AND FURTHERMORE... NEVER... IN MY HUMBLE OPINION... SHOULD WE HAVE STOOD... ON THE HEAD OF THAT BLOODY PIN IN THE FIRST PLACE.
WHENEVER...

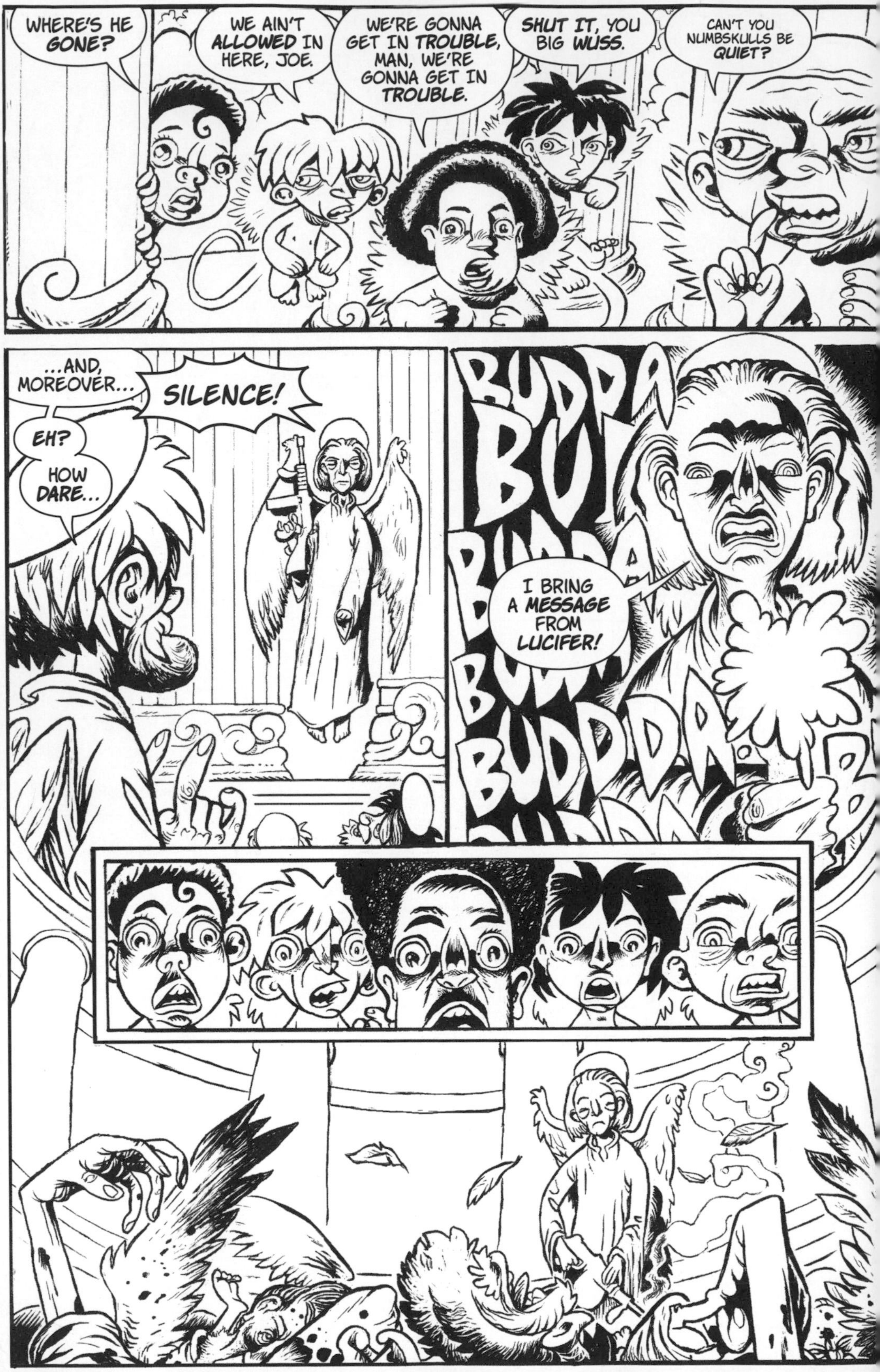
WHERE'S HE GONE?
WE AIN'T ALLOWED IN HERE, JOE.
WE'RE GONNA GET IN TROUBLE, MAN, WE'RE GONNA GET IN TROUBLE.
SHUT IT, YOU BIG WUSS.
CAN'T YOU NUMBSKULLS BE QUIET?
...AND, MOREOVER...
SILENCE!
EH?
HOW DARE...
BUDDA BUDDA BUDDA BUDDA BUDDA
I BRING A MESSAGE FROM LUCIFER!

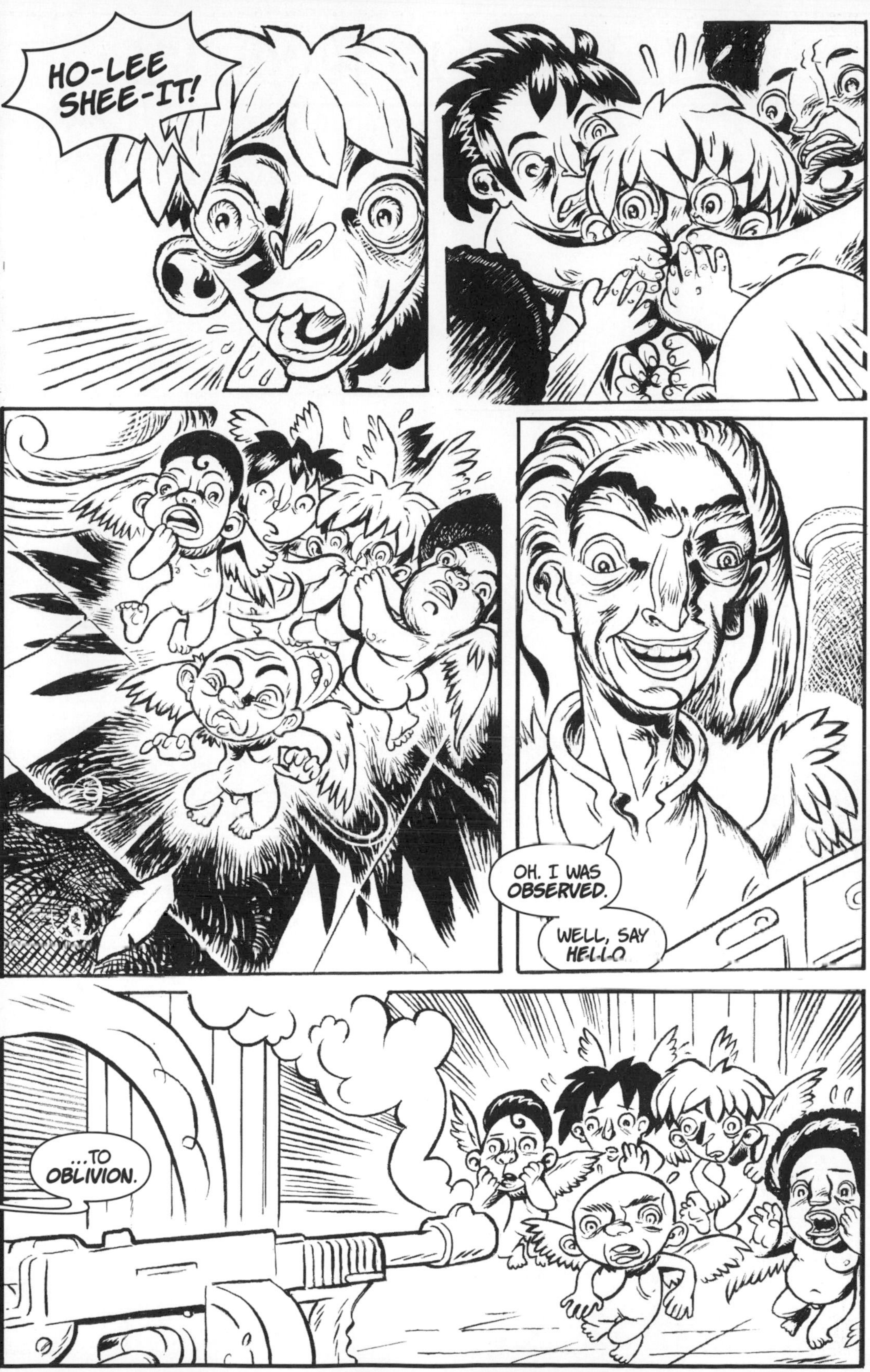
HO-LEE SHEE-IT!
OH. I WAS OBSERVED.
WELL, SAY HELLO
...TO OBLIVION.

CANTO II

ESCAPE FROM PARADISE

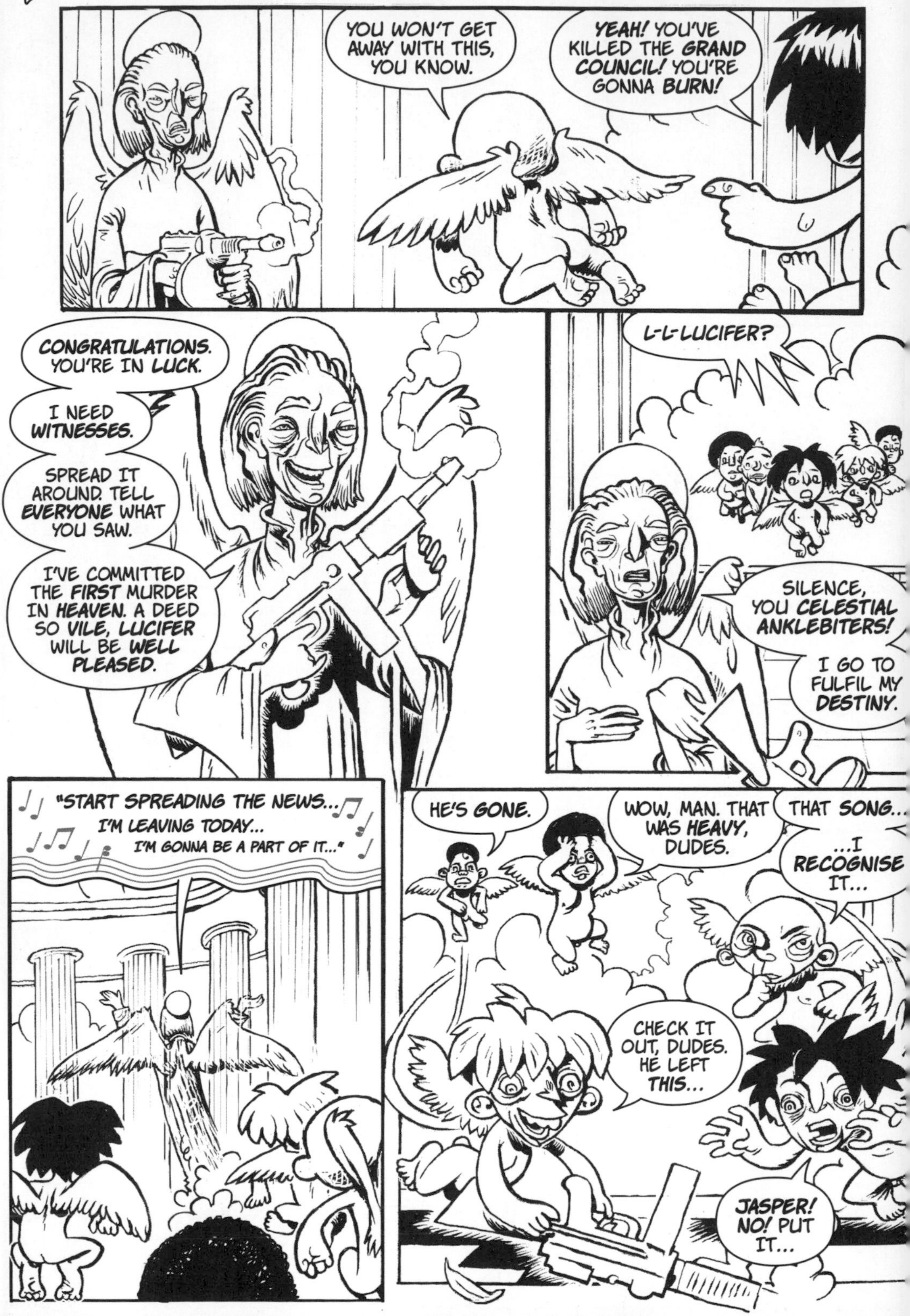

YOU WON'T GET AWAY WITH THIS, YOU KNOW.
YEAH! YOU'VE KILLED THE GRAND COUNCIL! YOU'RE GONNA BURN!
CONGRATULATIONS. YOU'RE IN LUCK.
I NEED WITNESSES.
SPREAD IT AROUND. TELL EVERYONE WHAT YOU SAW.
I'VE COMMITTED THE FIRST MURDER IN HEAVEN. A DEED SO VILE, LUCIFER WILL BE WELL PLEASED.
L-L-LUCIFER?
SILENCE, YOU CELESTIAL ANKLEBITERS!
I GO TO FULFIL MY DESTINY.
"START SPREADING THE NEWS...
I'M LEAVING TODAY...
I'M GONNA BE A PART OF IT..."
HE'S GONE.
WOW, MAN. THAT WAS HEAVY, DUDES.
THAT SONG...
...I RECOGNISE IT...
CHECK IT OUT, DUDES. HE LEFT THIS...
JASPER! NO! PUT IT...

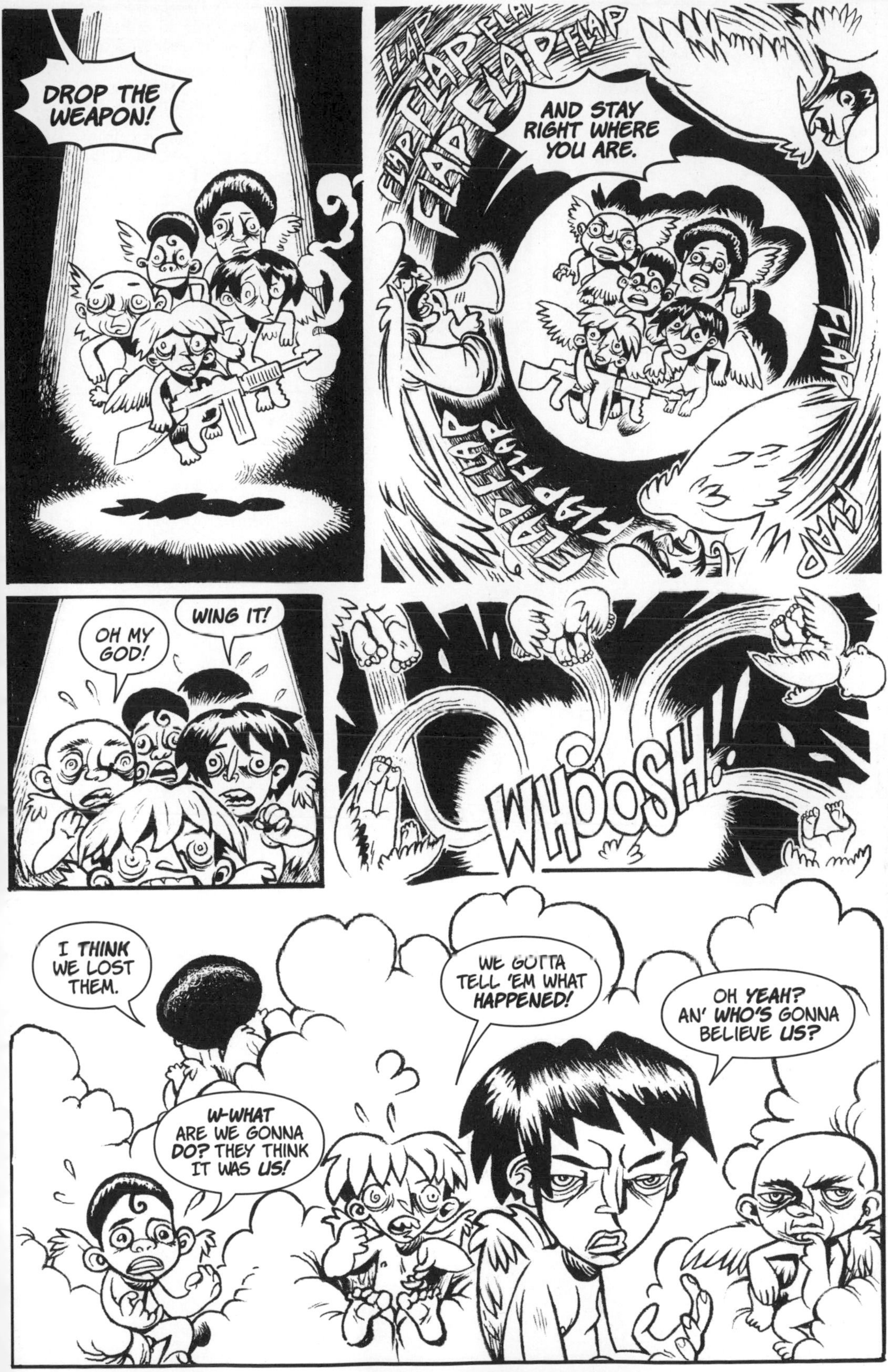

DROP THE WEAPON!
FLAP FLAP FLAP FLAP FLAP
AND STAY RIGHT WHERE YOU ARE.
FLAP
FLAP
FLAP FLAP
FLAP
OH MY GOD!
WING IT!
WHOOSH!!
I THINK WE LOST THEM.
W-WHAT ARE WE GONNA DO? THEY THINK IT WAS US!
WE GOTTA TELL 'EM WHAT HAPPENED!
OH YEAH? AN' WHO'S GONNA BELIEVE US?

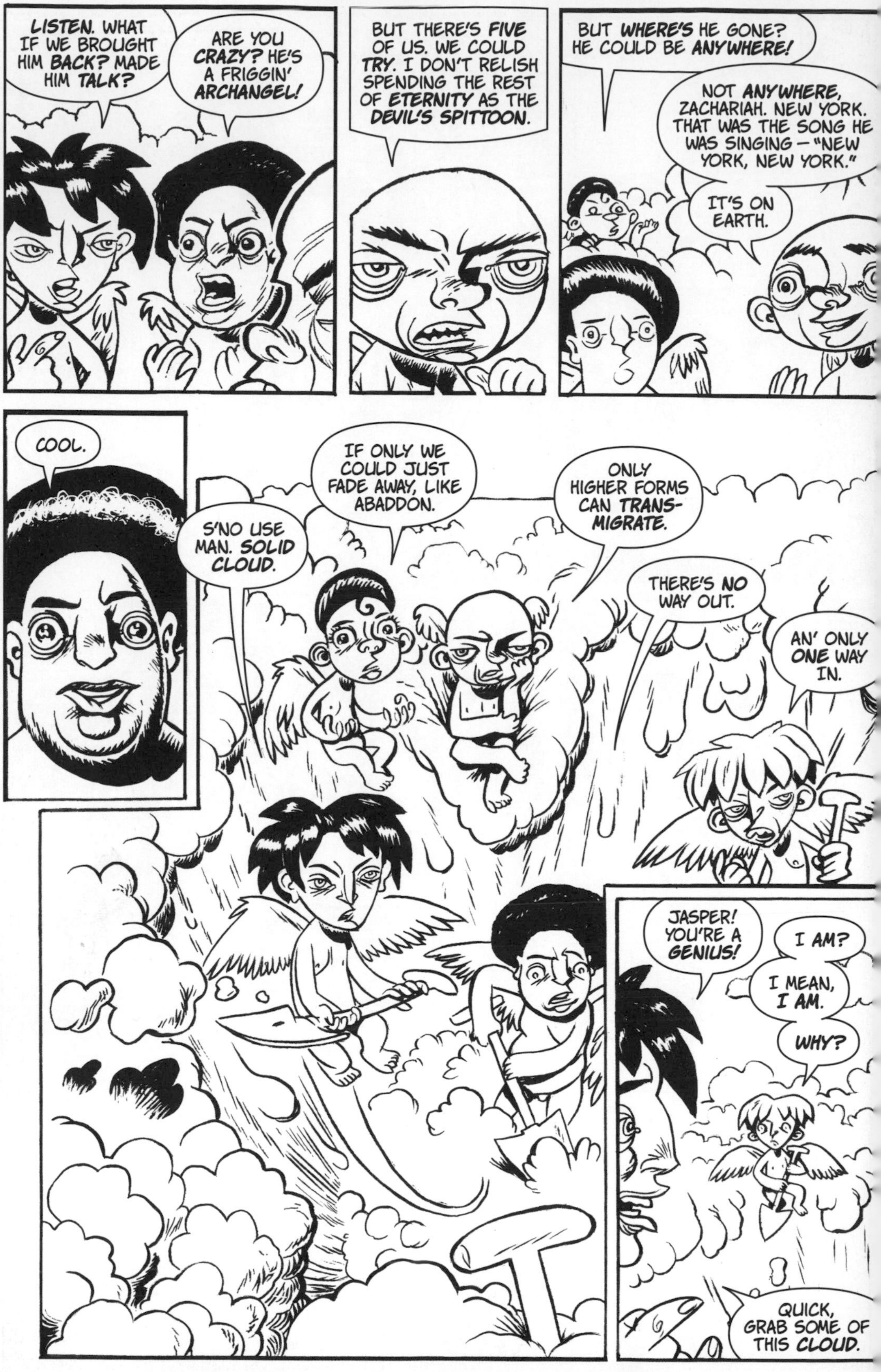

LISTEN. WHAT IF WE BROUGHT HIM BACK? MADE HIM TALK?
ARE YOU CRAZY? HE'S A FRIGGIN' ARCHANGEL!
BUT THERE'S FIVE OF US. WE COULD TRY. I DON'T RELISH SPENDING THE REST OF ETERNITY AS THE DEVIL'S SPITTOON.
BUT WHERE'S HE GONE? HE COULD BE ANYWHERE!
NOT ANYWHERE, ZACHARIAH. NEW YORK. THAT WAS THE SONG HE WAS SINGING — "NEW YORK, NEW YORK."
IT'S ON EARTH.
COOL.
S'NO USE MAN. SOLID CLOUD.
IF ONLY WE COULD JUST FADE AWAY, LIKE ABADDON.
ONLY HIGHER FORMS CAN TRANS-MIGRATE.
THERE'S NO WAY OUT.
AN' ONLY ONE WAY IN.
JASPER! YOU'RE A GENIUS!
I AM?
I MEAN, I AM.
WHY?
QUICK, GRAB SOME OF THIS CLOUD.

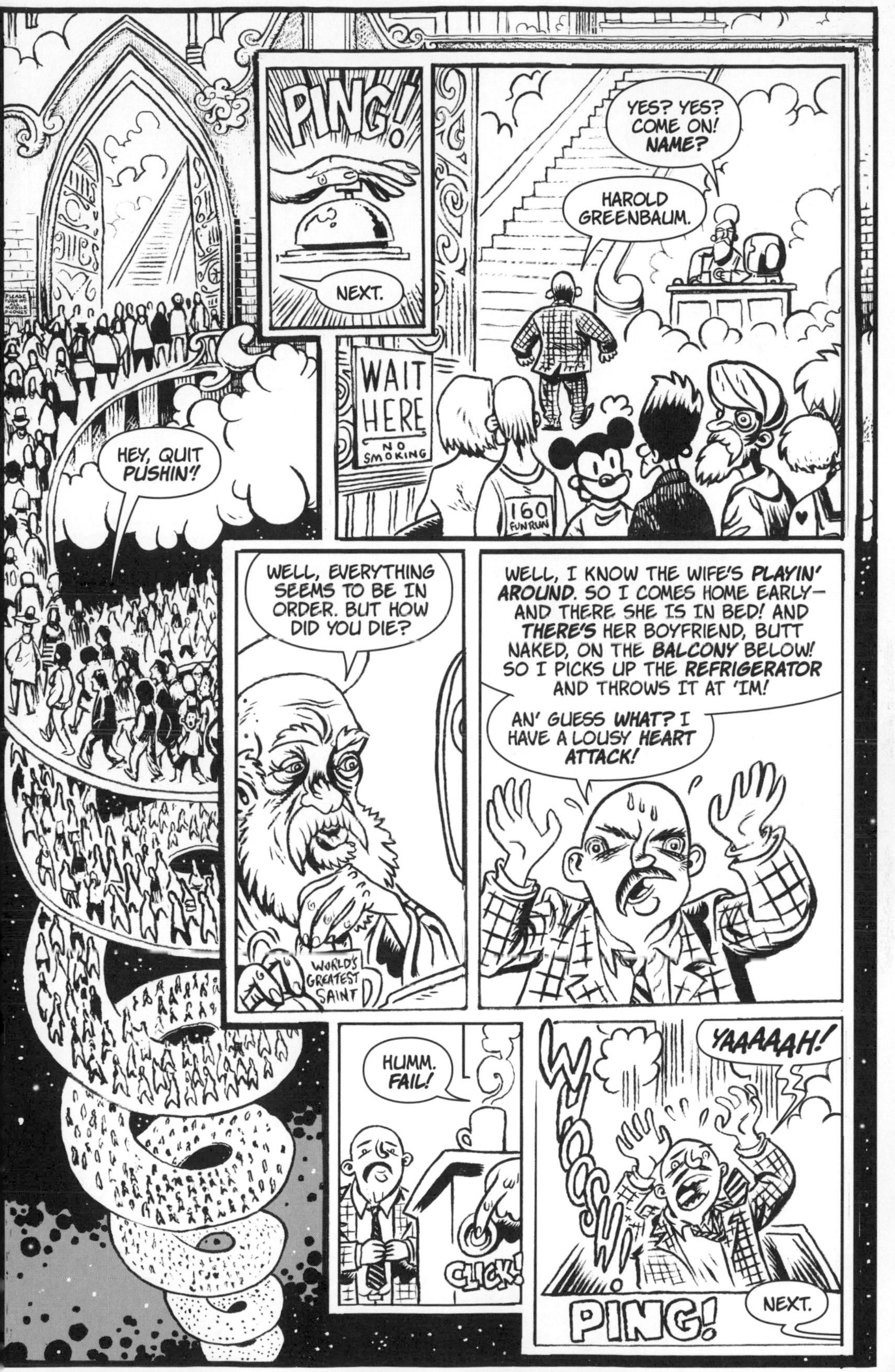
PLEASE SWITCH OFF ALL MOBILE PHONES
PING!
NEXT.
YES? YES? COME ON! NAME?
HAROLD GREENBAUM.
WAIT HERE
NO SMOKING
HEY, QUIT PUSHIN'!
160 FUN RUN
WELL, EVERYTHING SEEMS TO BE IN ORDER. BUT HOW DID YOU DIE?
WELL, I KNOW THE WIFE'S PLAYIN' AROUND. SO I COMES HOME EARLY— AND THERE SHE IS IN BED! AND THERE'S HER BOYFRIEND, BUTT NAKED, ON THE BALCONY BELOW! SO I PICKS UP THE REFRIGERATOR AND THROWS IT AT 'IM!
AN' GUESS WHAT? I HAVE A LOUSY HEART ATTACK!
WORLD'S GREATEST SAINT
HUMM. FAIL!
CLICK!
YAAAAAH!
WHOOSH!
PING!
NEXT.

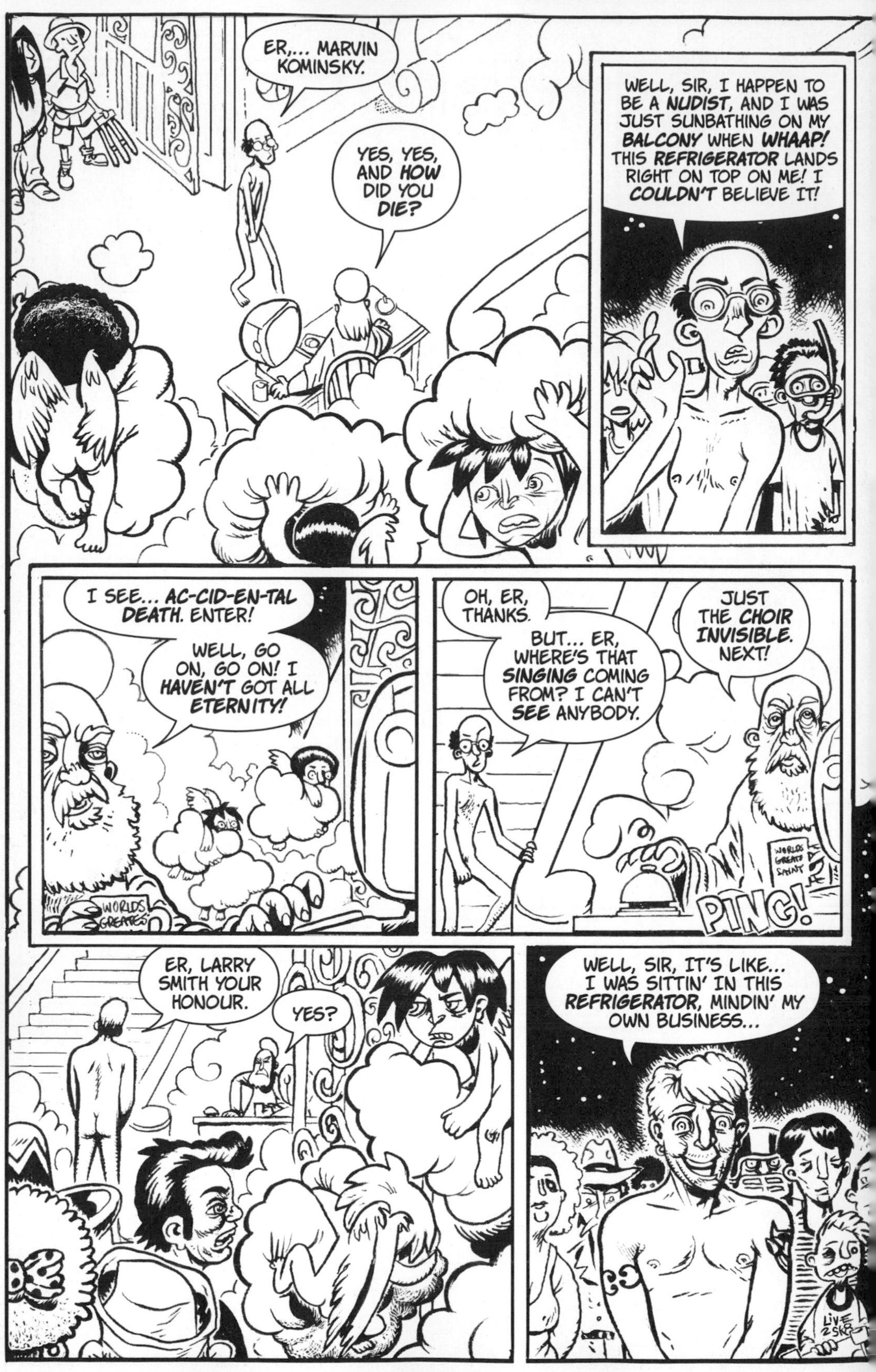
ER,... MARVIN KOMINSKY.
YES, YES, AND HOW DID YOU DIE?
WELL, SIR, I HAPPEN TO BE A NUDIST, AND I WAS JUST SUNBATHING ON MY BALCONY WHEN WHAAP! THIS REFRIGERATOR LANDS RIGHT ON TOP ON ME! I COULDN'T BELIEVE IT!
I SEE... AC-CID-EN-TAL DEATH. ENTER!
WELL, GO ON, GO ON! I HAVEN'T GOT ALL ETERNITY!
WORLDS GREATES
OH, ER, THANKS.
BUT... ER, WHERE'S THAT SINGING COMING FROM? I CAN'T SEE ANYBODY.
JUST THE CHOIR INVISIBLE. NEXT!
WORLDS GREATEST SAINT
PING!
ER, LARRY SMITH YOUR HONOUR.
YES?
WELL, SIR, IT'S LIKE... I WAS SITTIN' IN THIS REFRIGERATOR, MINDIN' MY OWN BUSINESS...

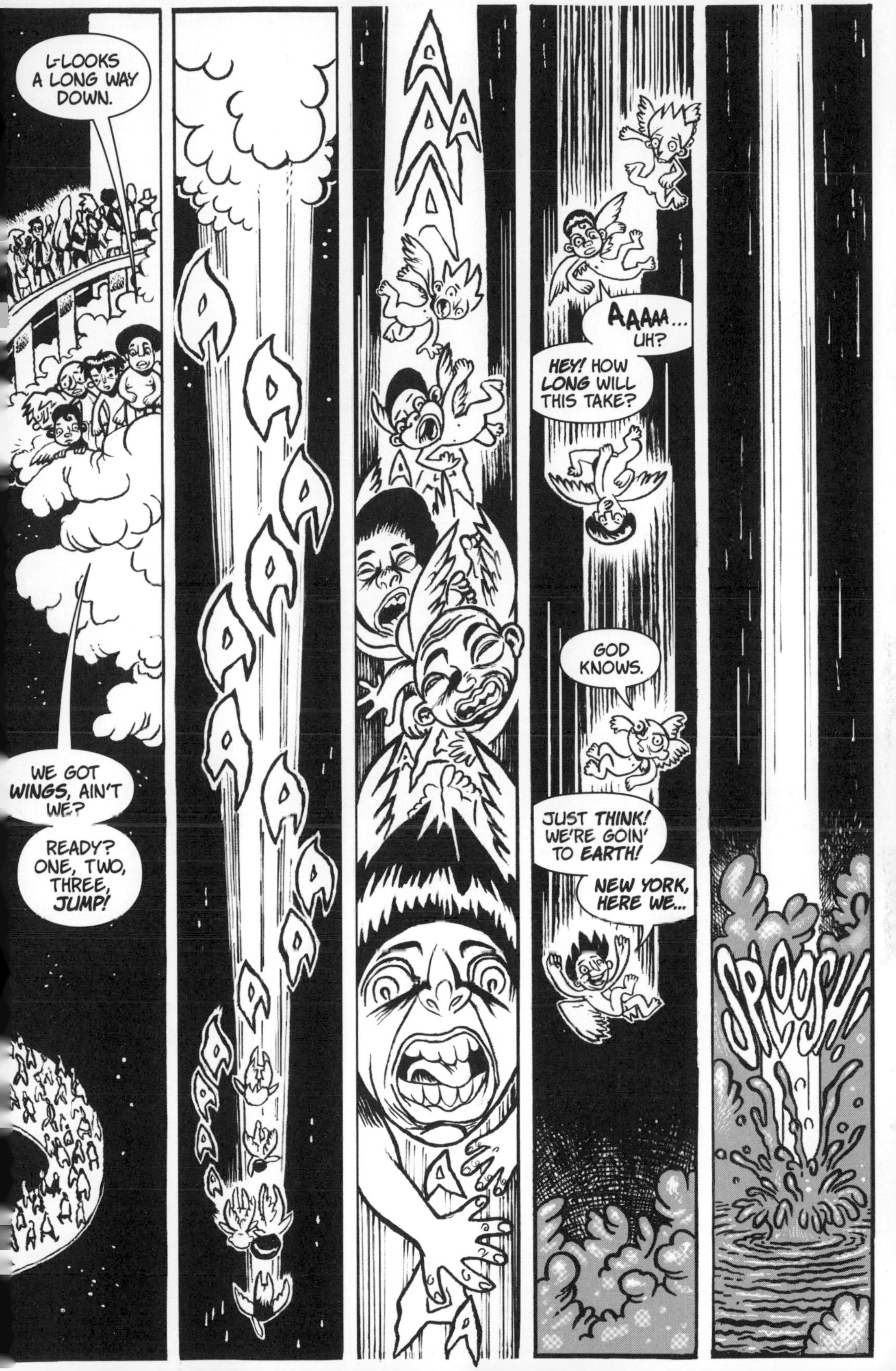
L-LOOKS A LONG WAY DOWN.
WE GOT WINGS, AIN'T WE?
READY? ONE, TWO, THREE, JUMP!
AAAAA...
AAAAA... UH?
HEY! HOW LONG WILL THIS TAKE?
GOD KNOWS.
JUST THINK! WE'RE GOIN' TO EARTH!
NEW YORK, HERE WE...
SPLOOSH!

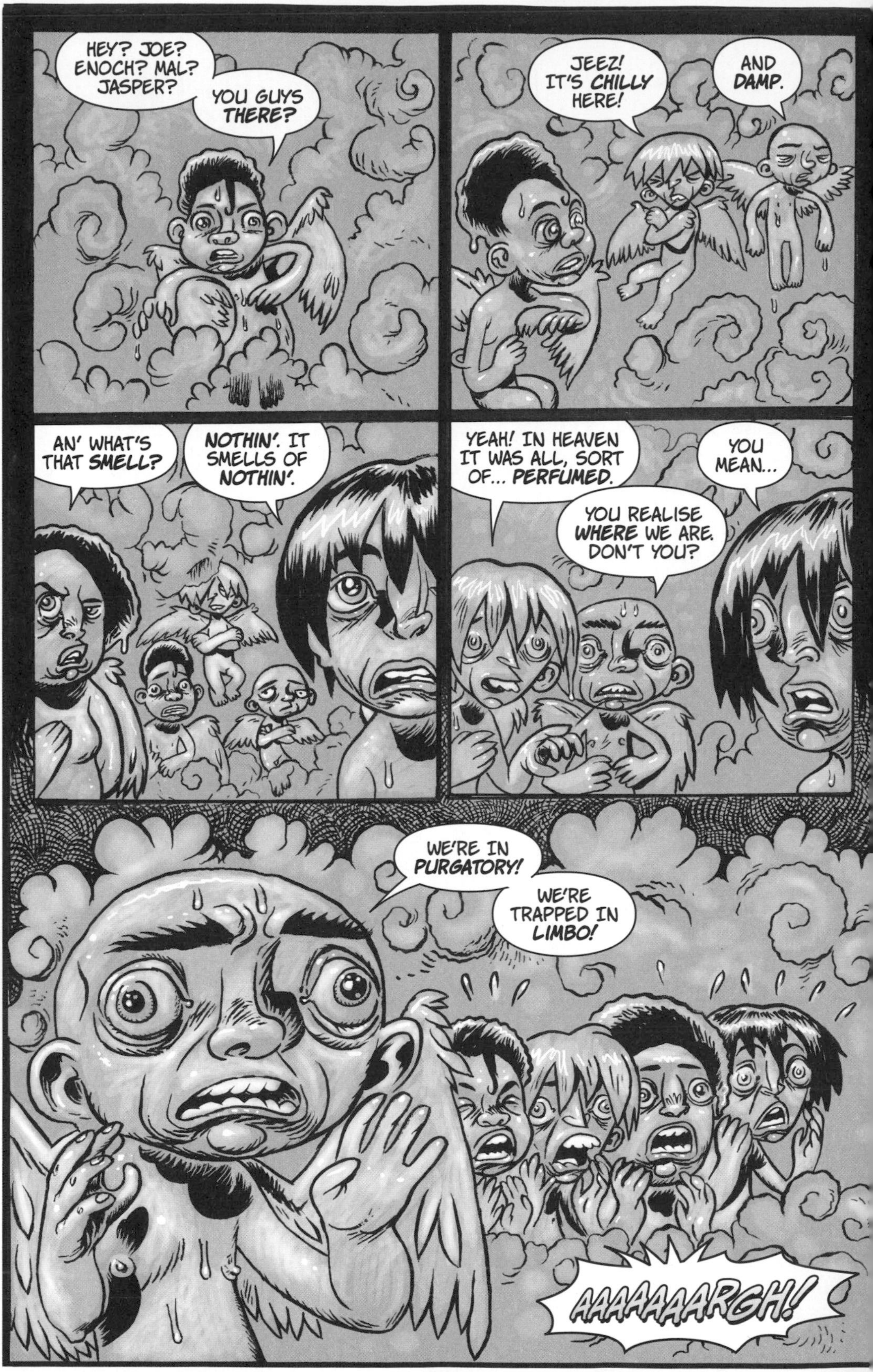
HEY? JOE? ENOCH? MAL? JASPER?
YOU GUYS THERE?
JEEZ! IT'S CHILLY HERE!
AND DAMP.
AN' WHAT'S THAT SMELL?
NOTHIN'. IT SMELLS OF NOTHIN'.
YEAH! IN HEAVEN IT WAS ALL, SORT OF... PERFUMED.
YOU MEAN...
YOU REALISE WHERE WE ARE. DON'T YOU?
WE'RE IN PURGATORY!
WE'RE TRAPPED IN LIMBO!
AAAAAAARGH!

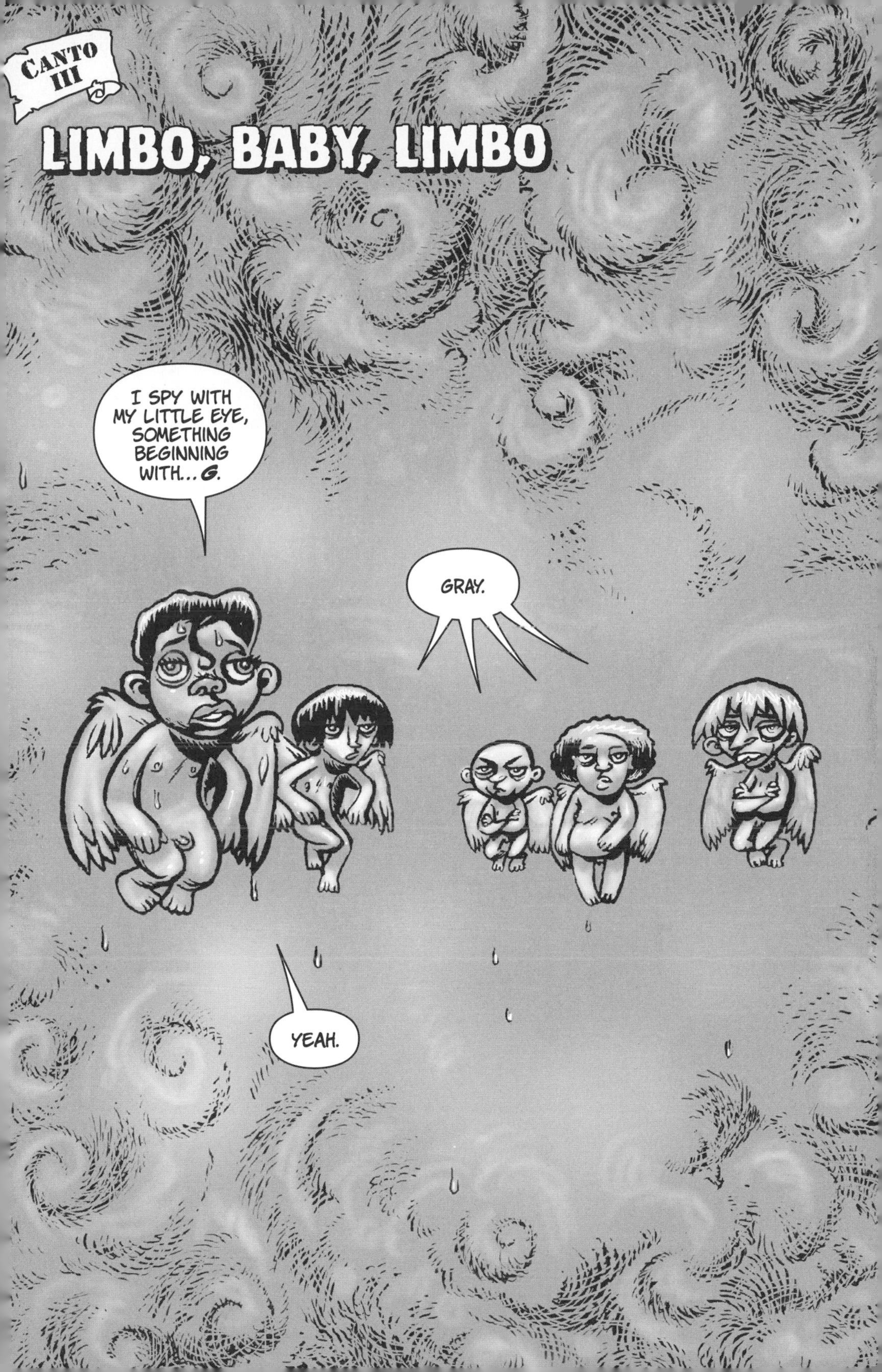
CANTO III
LIMBO, BABY, LIMBO
I SPY WITH MY LITTLE EYE, SOMETHING BEGINNING WITH... G.
GRAY.
YEAH.

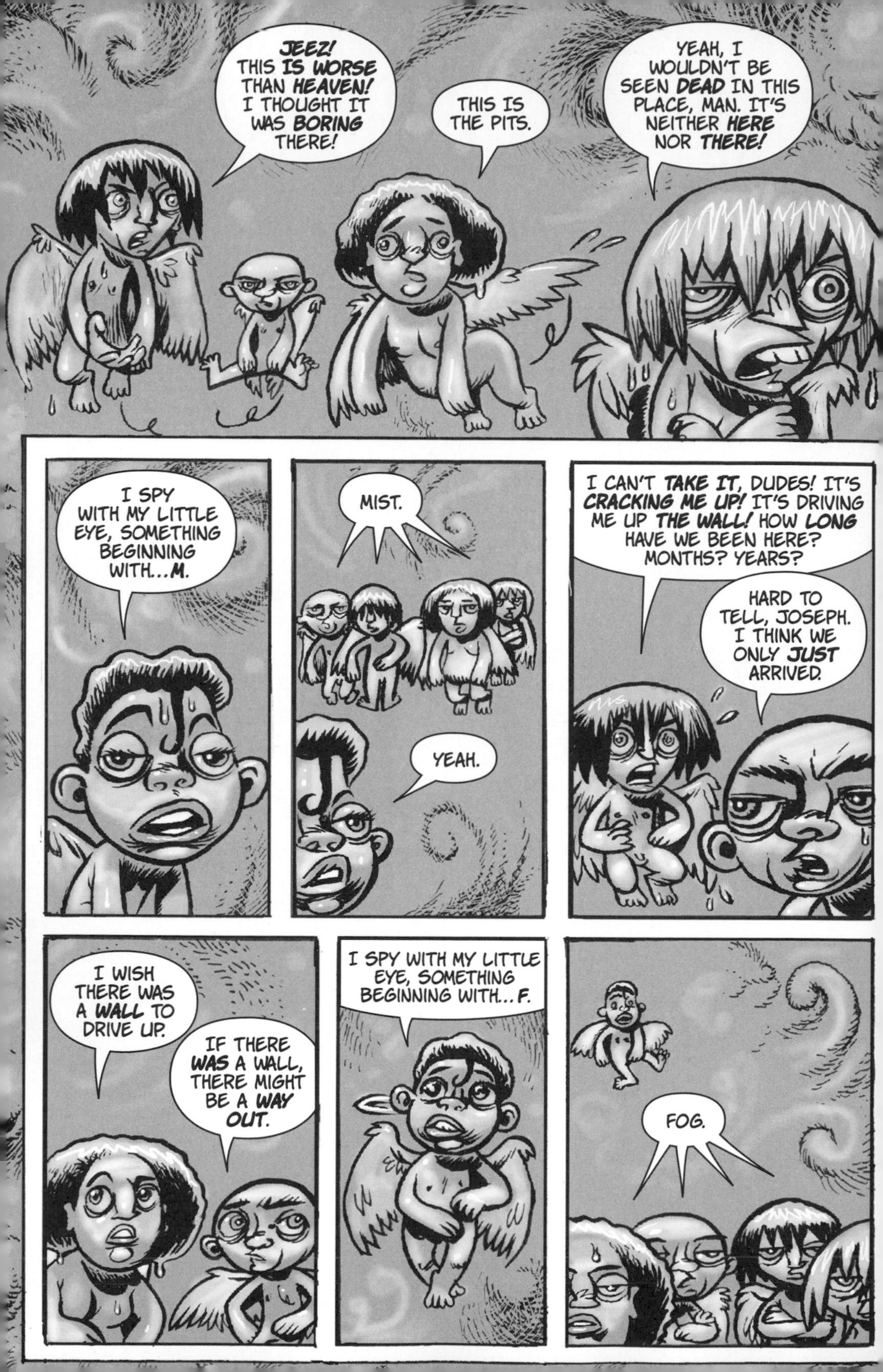
JEEZ! THIS IS WORSE THAN HEAVEN! I THOUGHT IT WAS BORING THERE!
THIS IS THE PITS.
YEAH, I WOULDN'T BE SEEN DEAD IN THIS PLACE, MAN. IT'S NEITHER HERE NOR THERE!
I SPY WITH MY LITTLE EYE, SOMETHING BEGINNING WITH... M.
MIST.
YEAH.
I CAN'T TAKE IT, DUDES! IT'S CRACKING ME UP! IT'S DRIVING ME UP THE WALL! HOW LONG HAVE WE BEEN HERE? MONTHS? YEARS?
HARD TO TELL, JOSEPH. I THINK WE ONLY JUST ARRIVED.
I WISH THERE WAS A WALL TO DRIVE UP.
IF THERE WAS A WALL, THERE MIGHT BE A WAY OUT.
I SPY WITH MY LITTLE EYE, SOMETHING BEGINNING WITH... F.
FOG.

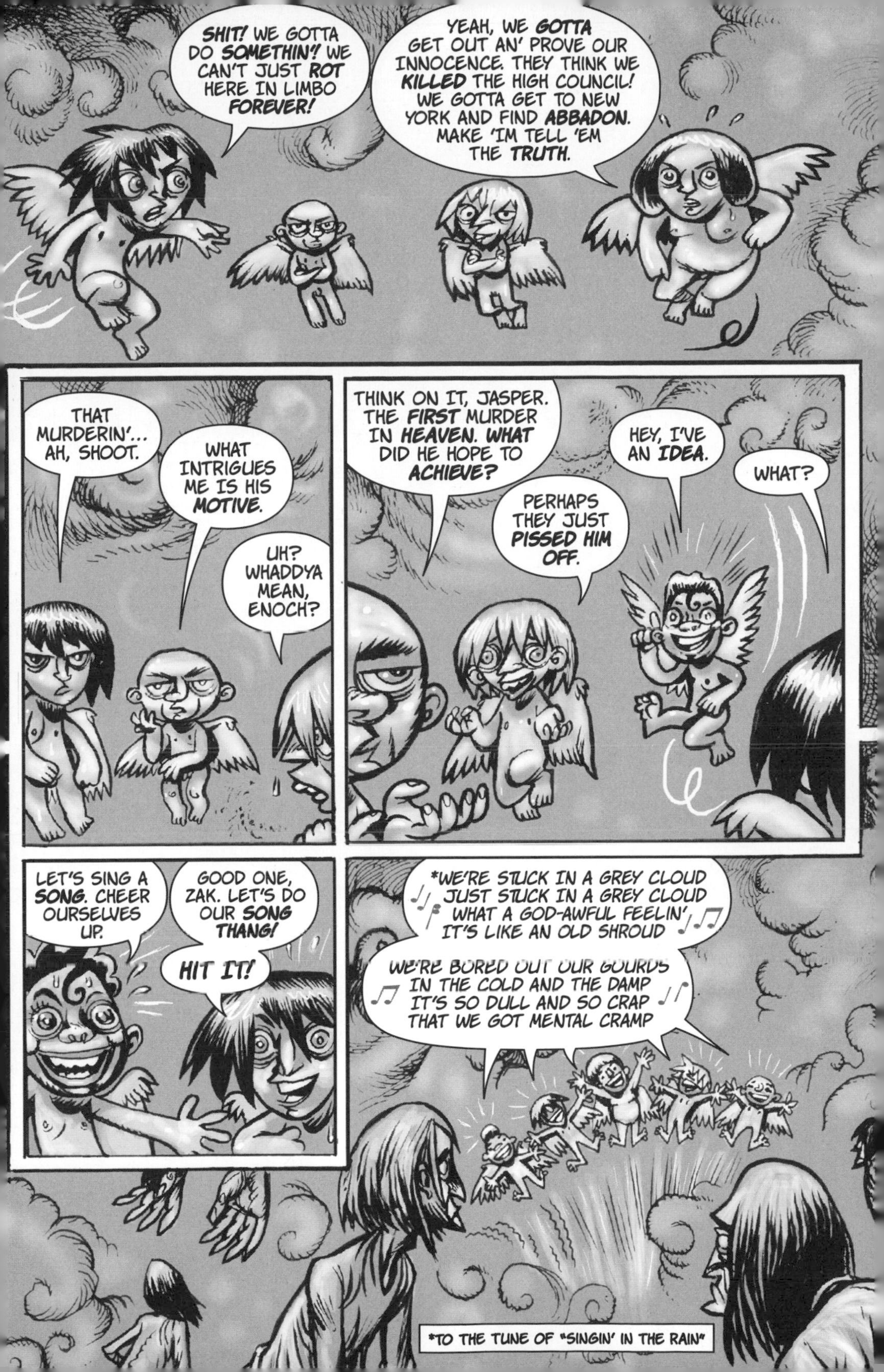
SHIT! WE GOTTA DO SOMETHIN'! WE CAN'T JUST ROT HERE IN LIMBO FOREVER!
YEAH, WE GOTTA GET OUT AN' PROVE OUR INNOCENCE. THEY THINK WE KILLED THE HIGH COUNCIL! WE GOTTA GET TO NEW YORK AND FIND ABBADON. MAKE 'IM TELL 'EM THE TRUTH.
THAT MURDERIN'... AH, SHOOT.
WHAT INTRIGUES ME IS HIS MOTIVE.
UH? WHADDYA MEAN, ENOCH?
THINK ON IT, JASPER. THE FIRST MURDER IN HEAVEN. WHAT DID HE HOPE TO ACHIEVE?
PERHAPS THEY JUST PISSED HIM OFF.
HEY, I'VE AN IDEA.
WHAT?
LET'S SING A SONG. CHEER OURSELVES UP.
GOOD ONE, ZAK. LET'S DO OUR SONG THANG!
HIT IT!
*WE'RE STUCK IN A GREY CLOUD JUST STUCK IN A GREY CLOUD WHAT A GOD-AWFUL FEELIN' IT'S LIKE AN OLD SHROUD
WE'RE BORED OUT OUR GOURDS IN THE COLD AND THE DAMP IT'S SO DULL AND SO CRAP THAT WE GOT MENTAL CRAMP
*TO THE TUNE OF "SINGIN' IN THE RAIN"

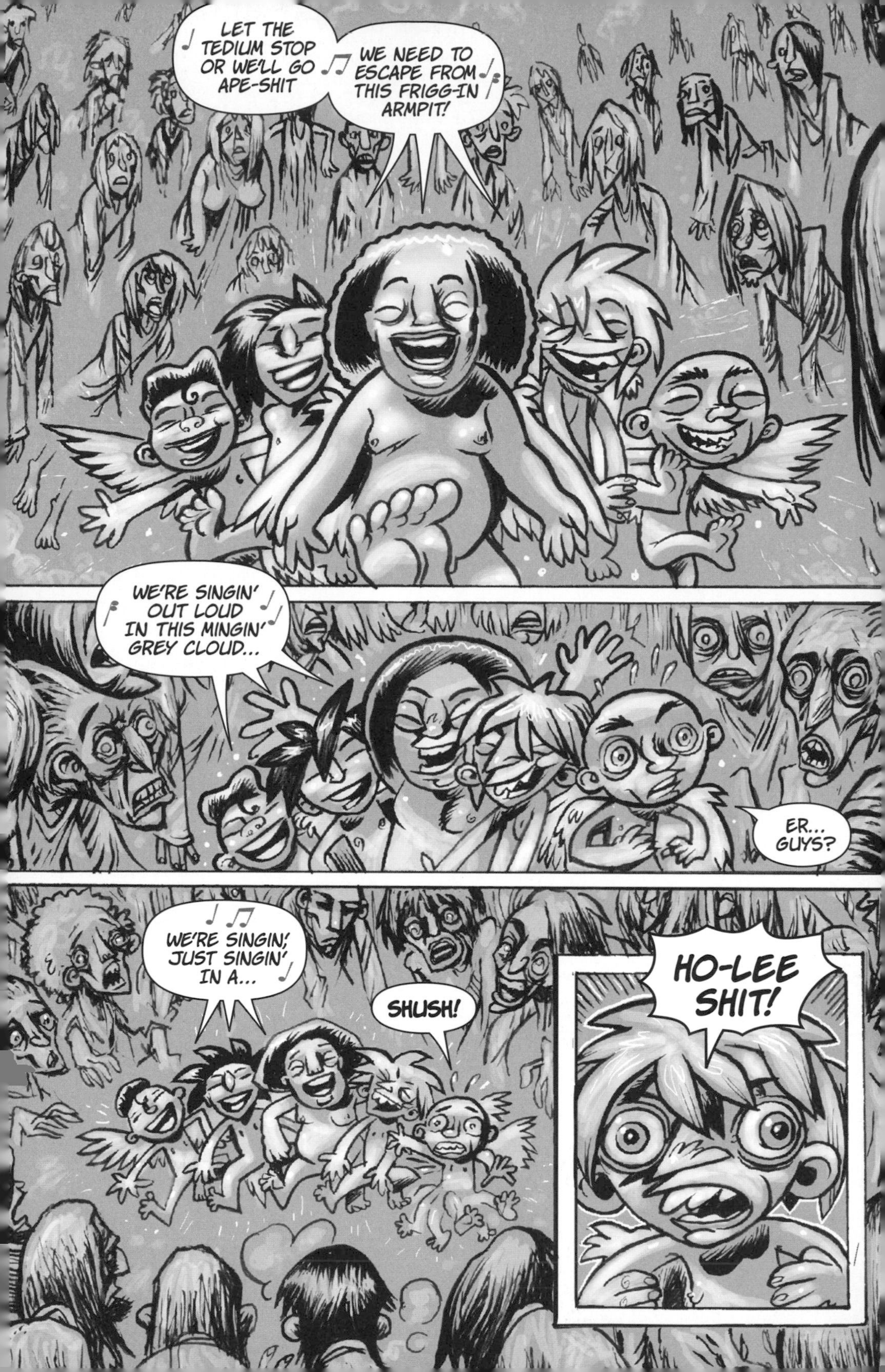
LET THE TEDIUM STOP OR WE'LL GO APE-SHIT
WE NEED TO ESCAPE FROM THIS FRIGG-IN ARMPIT!
WE'RE SINGIN' OUT LOUD IN THIS MINGIN' GREY CLOUD...
ER... GUYS?
WE'RE SINGIN', JUST SINGIN' IN A...
SHUSH!
HO-LEE SHIT!

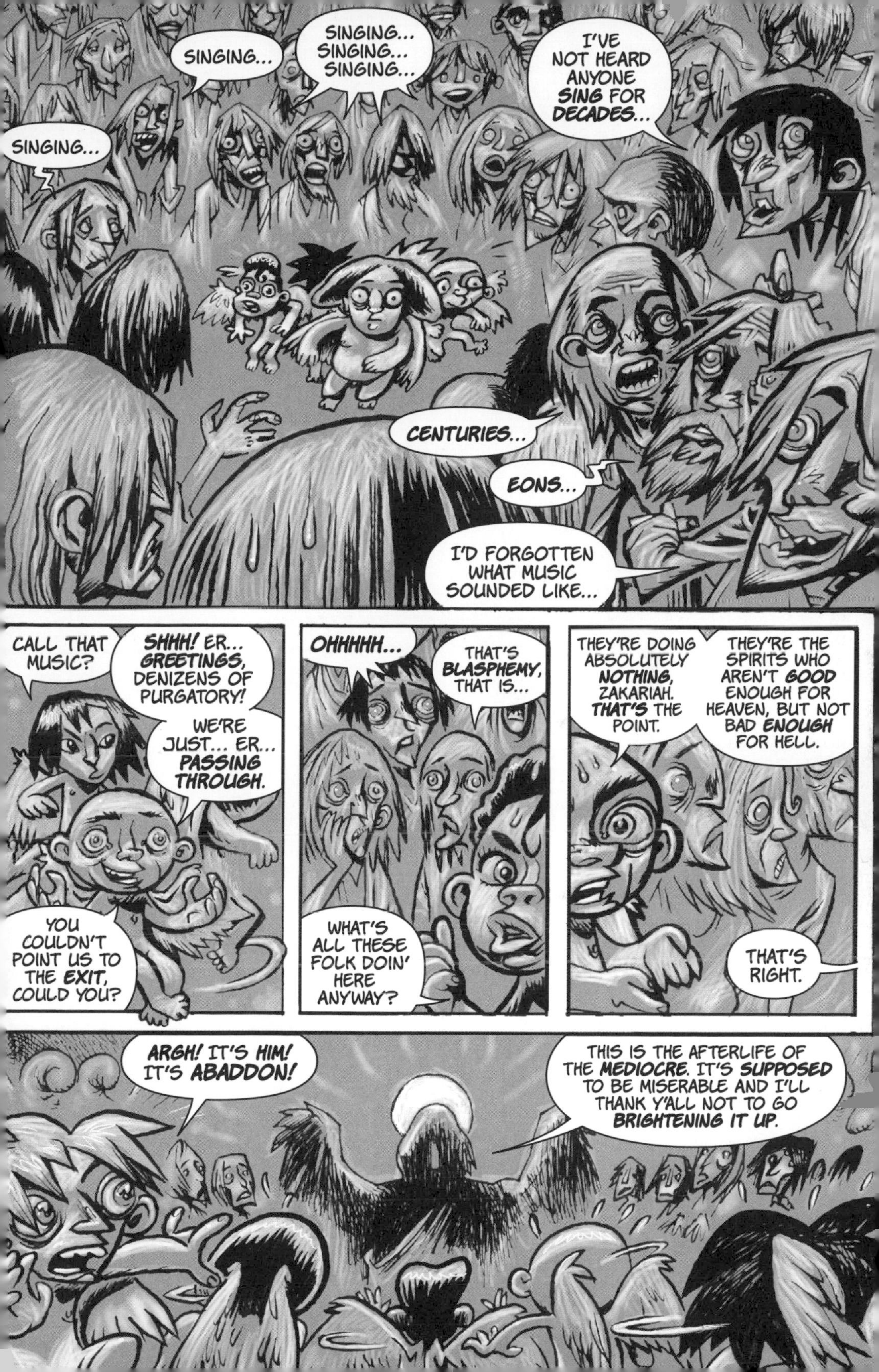
SINGING...
SINGING... SINGING... SINGING...
I'VE NOT HEARD ANYONE SING FOR DECADES...
SINGING...
CENTURIES...
EONS...
I'D FORGOTTEN WHAT MUSIC SOUNDED LIKE...
CALL THAT MUSIC?
SHHH! ER... GREETINGS, DENIZENS OF PURGATORY!
WE'RE JUST... ER... PASSING THROUGH.
YOU COULDN'T POINT US TO THE EXIT, COULD YOU?
OHHHHH...
THAT'S BLASPHEMY, THAT IS...
WHAT'S ALL THESE FOLK DOIN' HERE ANYWAY?
THEY'RE DOING ABSOLUTELY NOTHING, ZAKARIAH. THAT'S THE POINT.
THEY'RE THE SPIRITS WHO AREN'T GOOD ENOUGH FOR HEAVEN, BUT NOT BAD ENOUGH FOR HELL.
THAT'S RIGHT.
ARGH! IT'S HIM! IT'S ABADDON!
THIS IS THE AFTERLIFE OF THE MEDIOCRE. IT'S SUPPOSED TO BE MISERABLE AND I'LL THANK Y'ALL NOT TO GO BRIGHTENING IT UP.

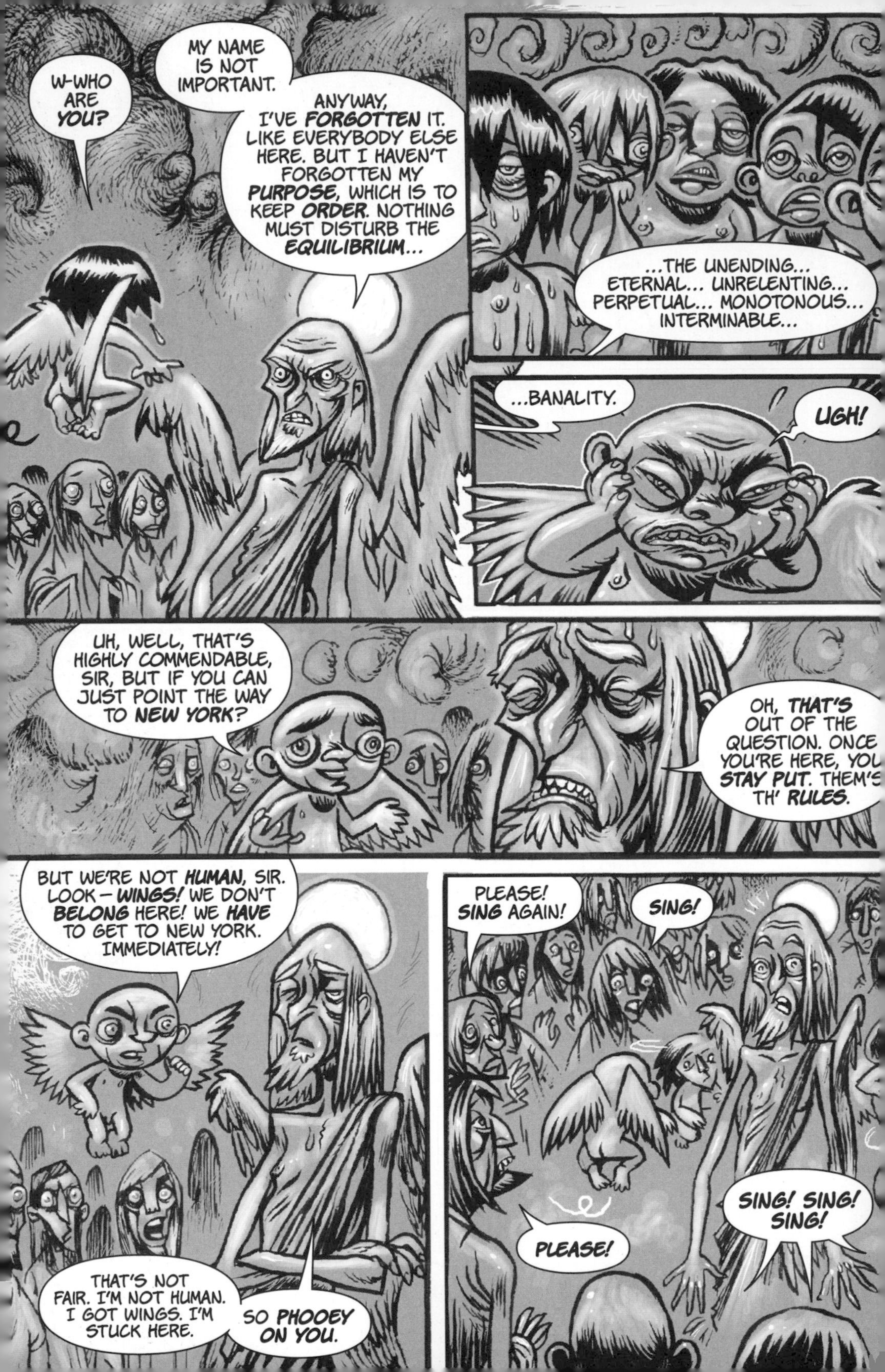
W-WHO ARE YOU?
MY NAME IS NOT IMPORTANT.
ANYWAY, I'VE FORGOTTEN IT. LIKE EVERYBODY ELSE HERE. BUT I HAVEN'T FORGOTTEN MY PURPOSE, WHICH IS TO KEEP ORDER. NOTHING MUST DISTURB THE EQUILIBRIUM...
...THE UNENDING... ETERNAL... UNRELENTING... PERPETUAL... MONOTONOUS... INTERMINABLE...
...BANALITY.
UGH!
UH, WELL, THAT'S HIGHLY COMMENDABLE, SIR, BUT IF YOU CAN JUST POINT THE WAY TO NEW YORK?
OH, THAT'S OUT OF THE QUESTION. ONCE YOU'RE HERE, YOU STAY PUT. THEM'S TH' RULES.
BUT WE'RE NOT HUMAN, SIR. LOOK—WINGS! WE DON'T BELONG HERE! WE HAVE TO GET TO NEW YORK. IMMEDIATELY!
THAT'S NOT FAIR. I'M NOT HUMAN. I GOT WINGS. I'M STUCK HERE.
SO PHOOEY ON YOU.
PLEASE! SING AGAIN!
SING!
PLEASE!
SING! SING! SING!

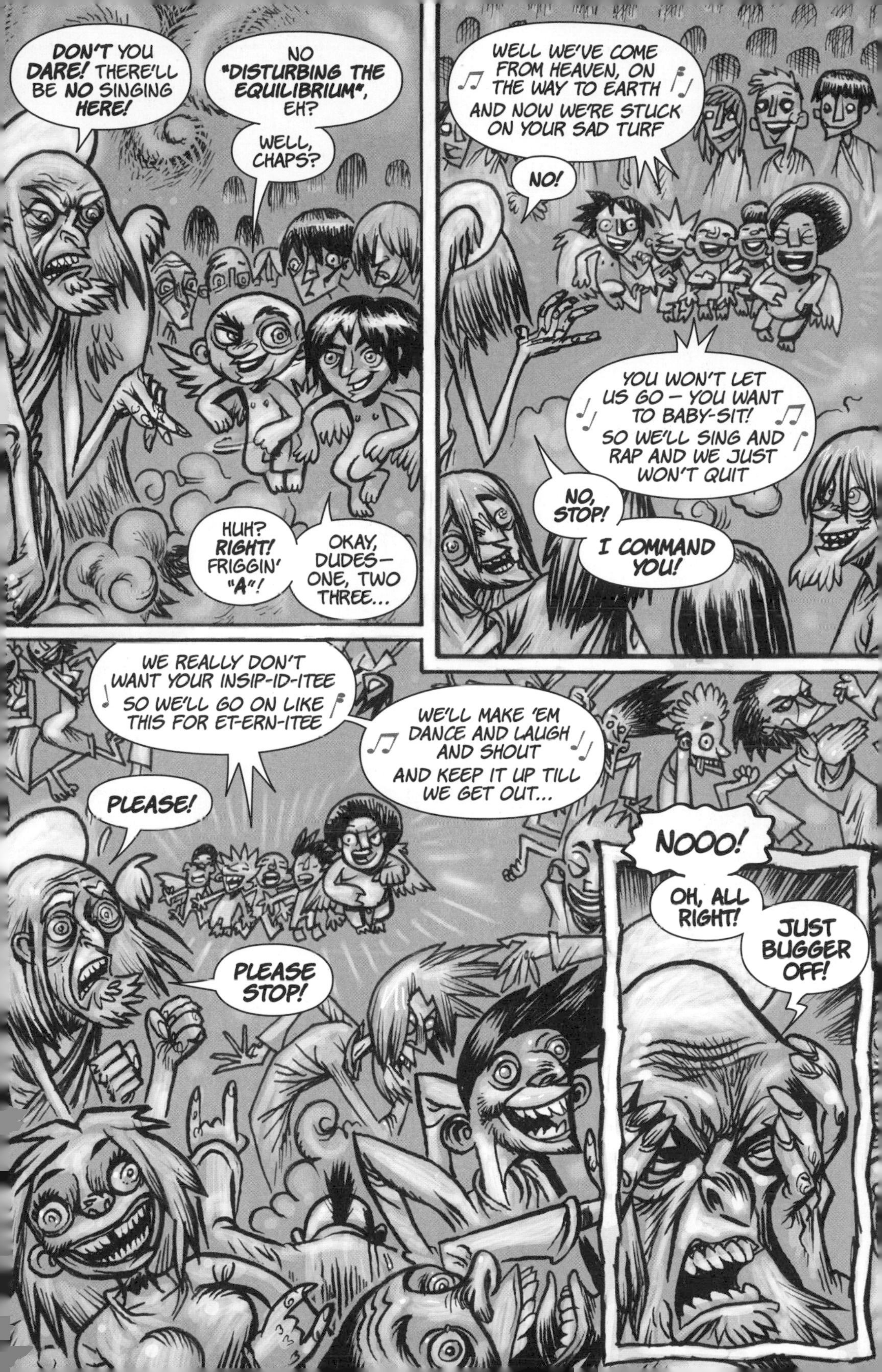

DON'T YOU DARE! THERE'LL BE NO SINGING HERE!
NO "DISTURBING THE EQUILIBRIUM", EH?
WELL, CHAPS?
HUH? RIGHT! FRIGGIN' "A"!
OKAY, DUDES— ONE, TWO THREE...
WELL WE'VE COME FROM HEAVEN, ON THE WAY TO EARTH AND NOW WE'RE STUCK ON YOUR SAD TURF
NO!
YOU WON'T LET US GO – YOU WANT TO BABY-SIT! SO WE'LL SING AND RAP AND WE JUST WON'T QUIT
NO, STOP!
I COMMAND YOU!
WE REALLY DON'T WANT YOUR INSIP-ID-ITEE SO WE'LL GO ON LIKE THIS FOR ET-ERN-ITEE
PLEASE!
WE'LL MAKE 'EM DANCE AND LAUGH AND SHOUT AND KEEP IT UP TILL WE GET OUT...
PLEASE STOP!
NOOO!
OH, ALL RIGHT!
JUST BUGGER OFF!

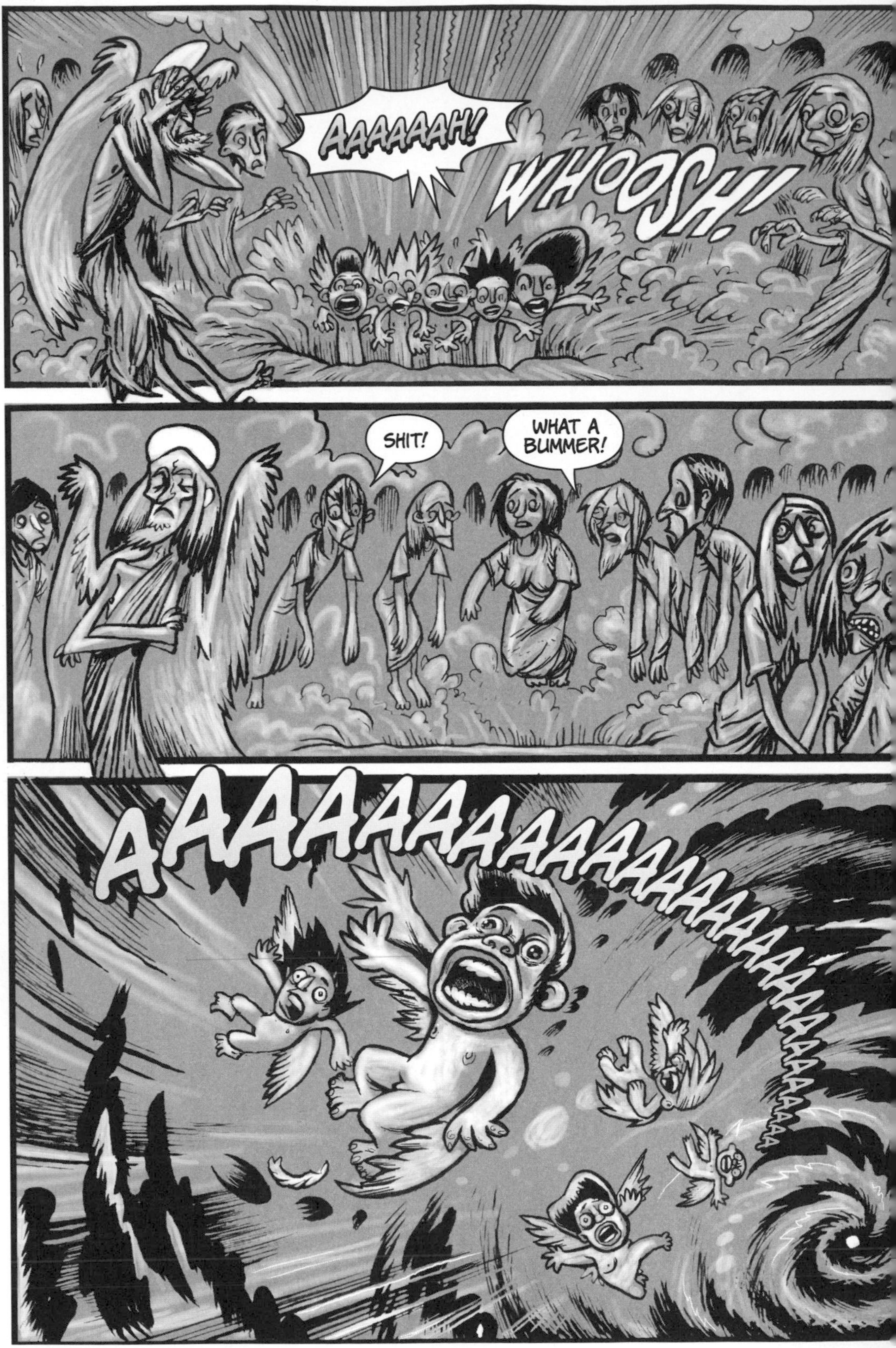
AAAAAAH!
WHOOSH!
SHIT!
WHAT A BUMMER!
AAAAAAAAAAAAAAAAAAAAAAAAAAAAAA

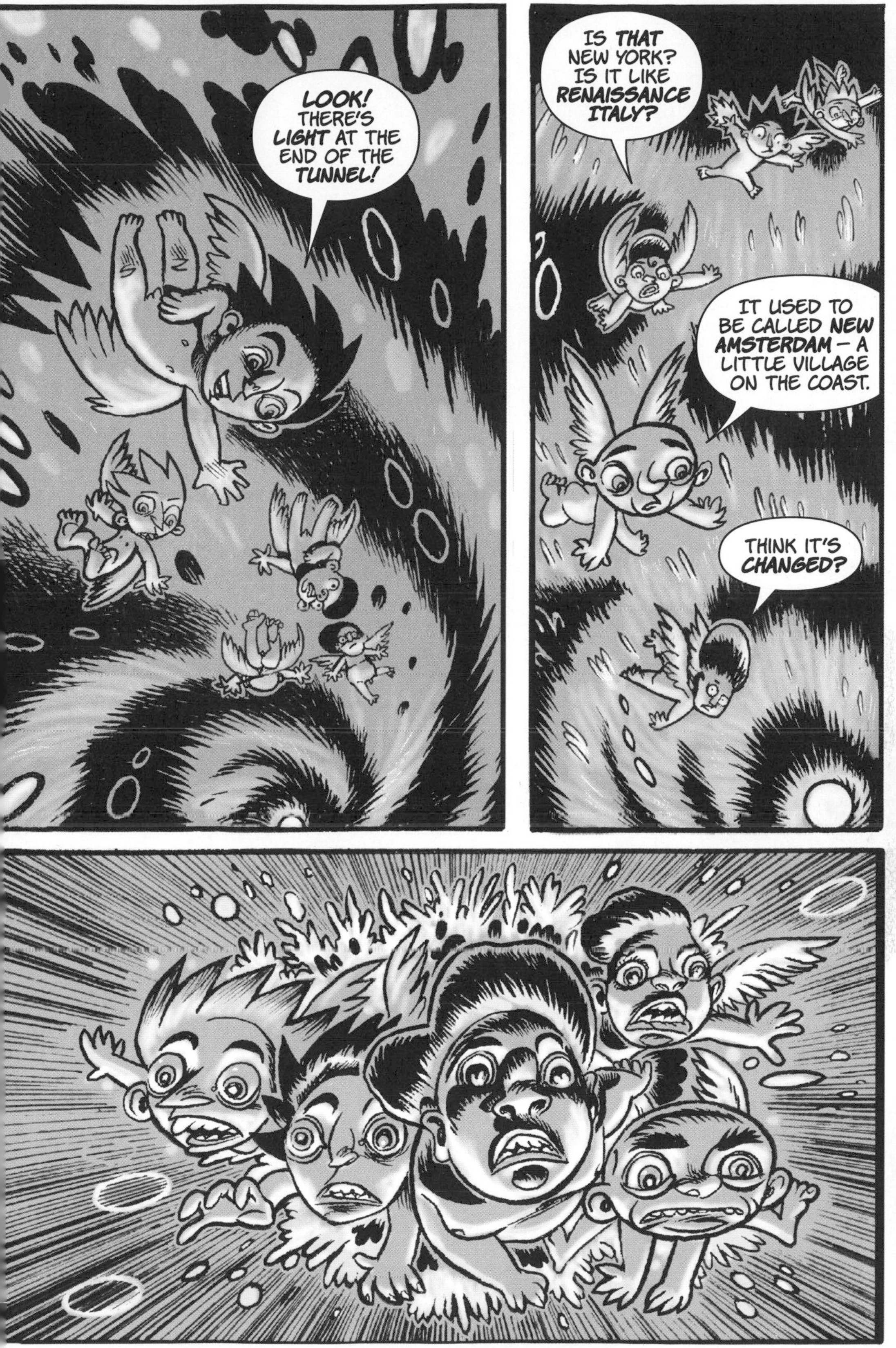
LOOK! THERE'S LIGHT AT THE END OF THE TUNNEL!
IS THAT NEW YORK? IS IT LIKE RENAISSANCE ITALY?
IT USED TO BE CALLED NEW AMSTERDAM — A LITTLE VILLAGE ON THE COAST.
THINK IT'S CHANGED?

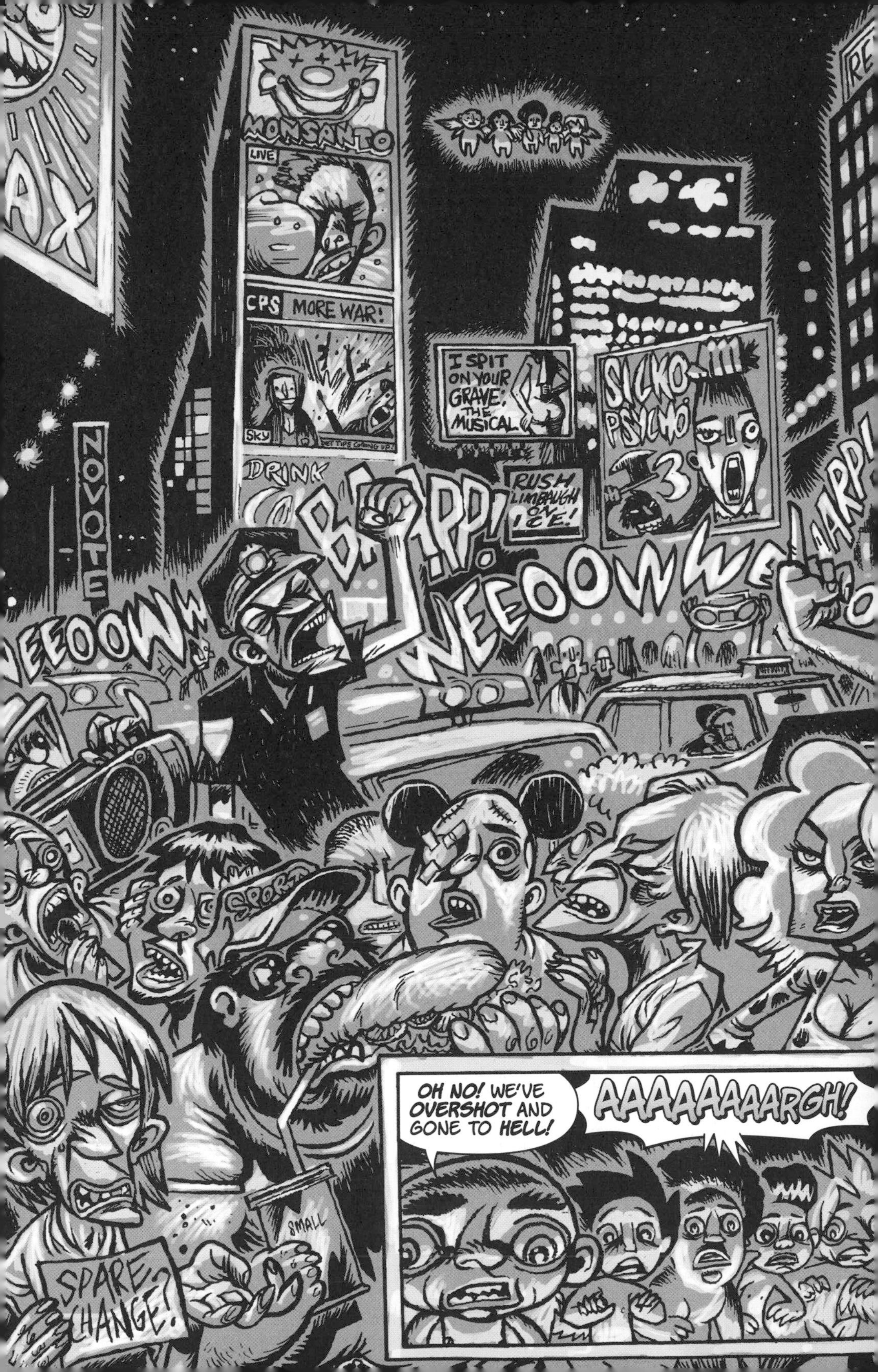
MONSANTO
LIVE
CPS
MORE WAR!
SKY
I SPIT ON YOUR GRAVE: THE MUSICAL
SICKO PSYCHO 3
NOVOTE
DRINK
RUSH LIMBAUGH ON ICE!
BRAPP!
WEEOOWW
WEEOOWWE
HARP!
SPORT
SMALL
SPARE CHANGE?
OH NO! WE'VE OVERSHOT AND GONE TO HELL!
AAAAAAAARGH!

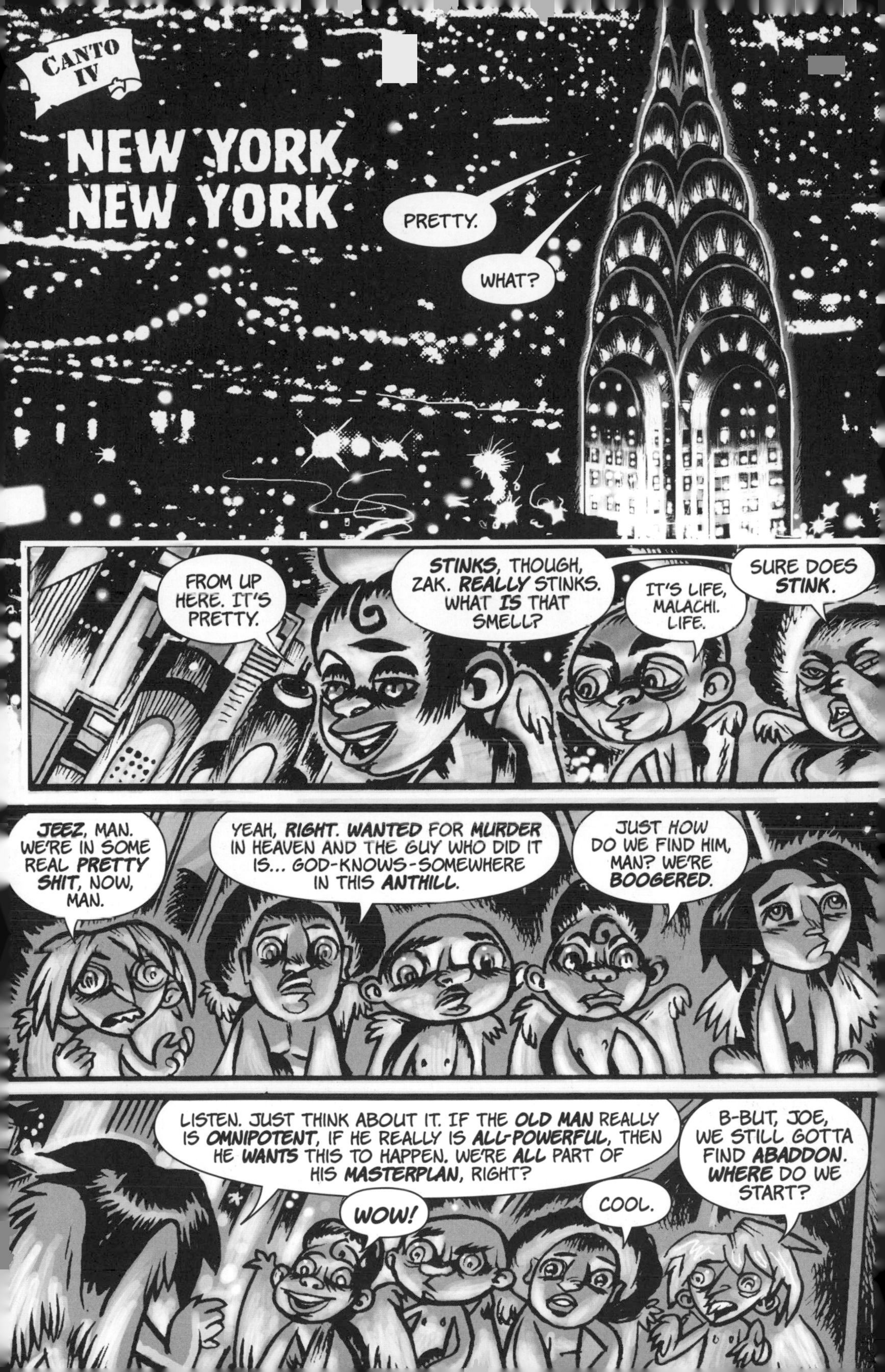
CANTO IV
NEW YORK, NEW YORK
PRETTY.
WHAT?
FROM UP HERE. IT'S PRETTY.
STINKS, THOUGH, ZAK. REALLY STINKS. WHAT IS THAT SMELL?
IT'S LIFE, MALACHI. LIFE.
SURE DOES STINK.
JEEZ, MAN. WE'RE IN SOME REAL PRETTY SHIT, NOW, MAN.
YEAH, RIGHT. WANTED FOR MURDER IN HEAVEN AND THE GUY WHO DID IT IS... GOD-KNOWS-SOMEWHERE IN THIS ANTHILL.
JUST HOW DO WE FIND HIM, MAN? WE'RE BOOGERED.
LISTEN. JUST THINK ABOUT IT. IF THE OLD MAN REALLY IS OMNIPOTENT, IF HE REALLY IS ALL-POWERFUL, THEN HE WANTS THIS TO HAPPEN. WE'RE ALL PART OF HIS MASTERPLAN, RIGHT?
WOW!
COOL.
B-BUT, JOE, WE STILL GOTTA FIND ABADDON. WHERE DO WE START?

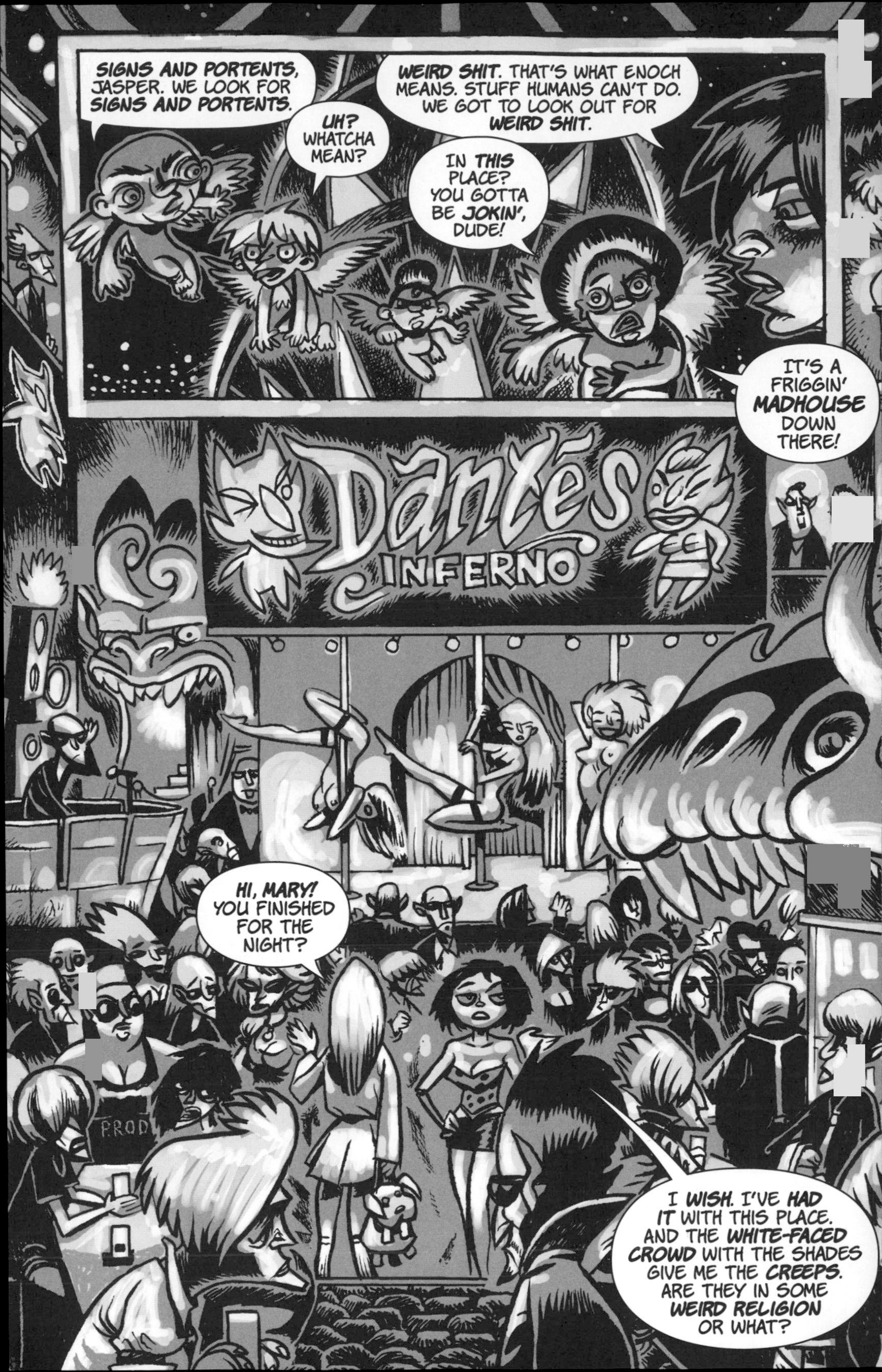
SIGNS AND PORTENTS, JASPER. WE LOOK FOR SIGNS AND PORTENTS.
UH? WHATCHA MEAN?
WEIRD SHIT. THAT'S WHAT ENOCH MEANS. STUFF HUMANS CAN'T DO. WE GOT TO LOOK OUT FOR WEIRD SHIT.
IN THIS PLACE? YOU GOTTA BE JOKIN', DUDE!
IT'S A FRIGGIN' MADHOUSE DOWN THERE!
DANTE'S INFERNO
HI, MARY! YOU FINISHED FOR THE NIGHT?
PROD
I WISH. I'VE HAD IT WITH THIS PLACE. AND THE WHITE-FACED CROWD WITH THE SHADES GIVE ME THE CREEPS. ARE THEY IN SOME WEIRD RELIGION OR WHAT?

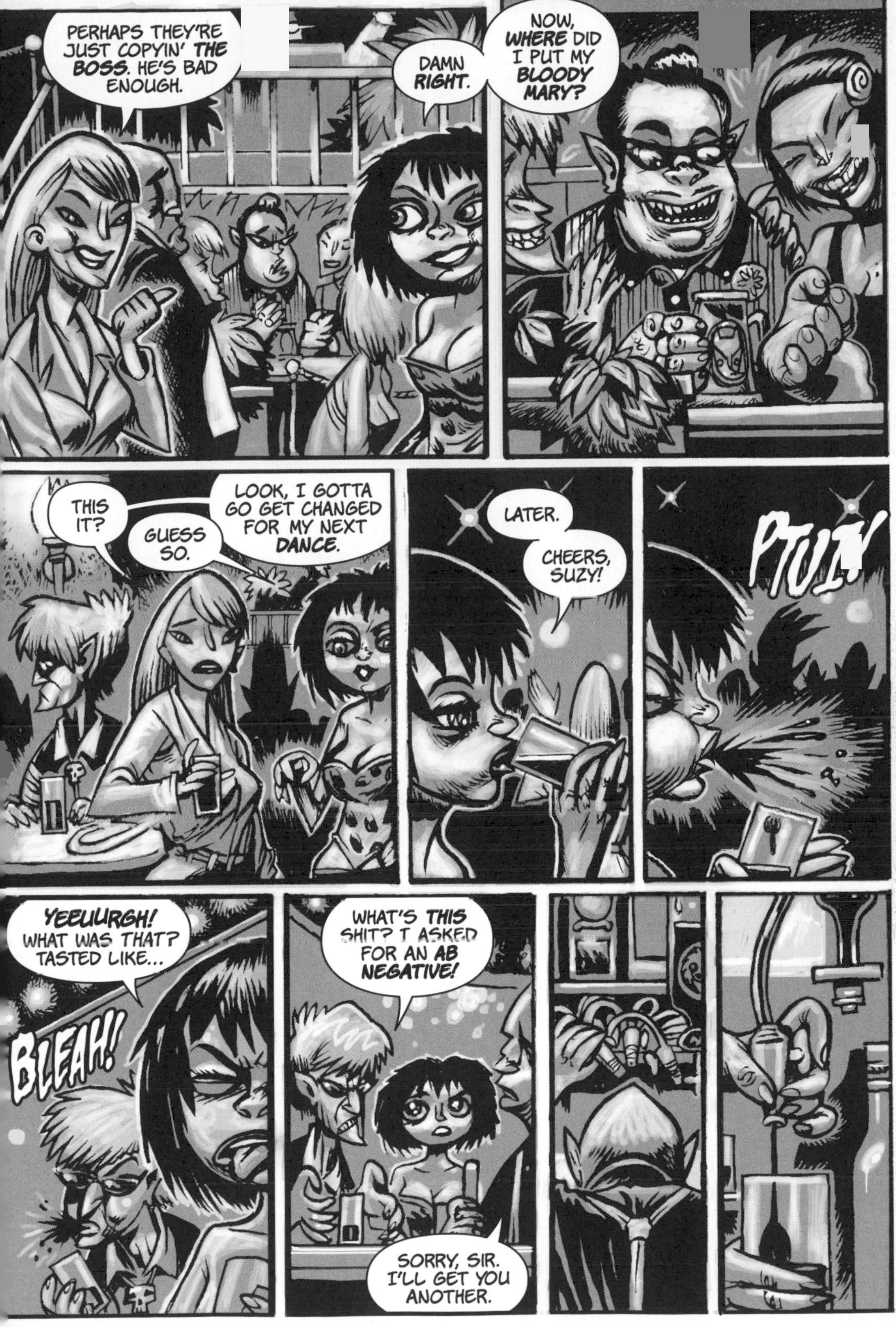
PERHAPS THEY'RE JUST COPYIN' **THE BOSS**. HE'S BAD ENOUGH.
DAMN **RIGHT**.
NOW, **WHERE** DID I PUT MY **BLOODY MARY?**
THIS IT?
GUESS SO.
LOOK, I GOTTA GO GET CHANGED FOR MY NEXT **DANCE**.
LATER.
CHEERS, SUZY!
PTUI
YEEUURGH! WHAT WAS THAT? TASTED LIKE...
BLEAH!
WHAT'S **THIS** SHIT? I ASKED FOR AN **AB NEGATIVE!**
SORRY, SIR. I'LL GET YOU ANOTHER.

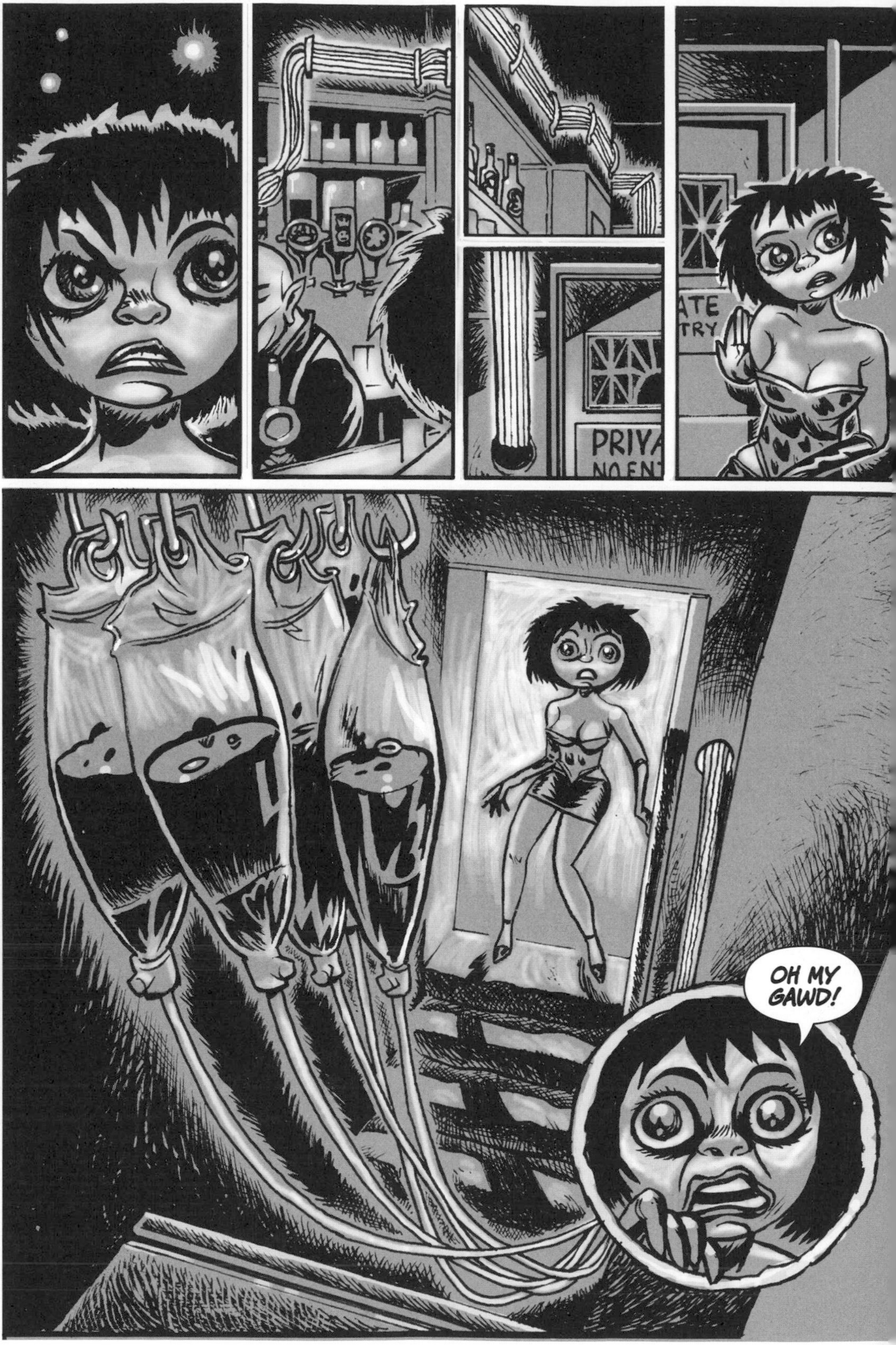
ATE
TRY
PRIVA
NO ENT
OH MY GAWD!

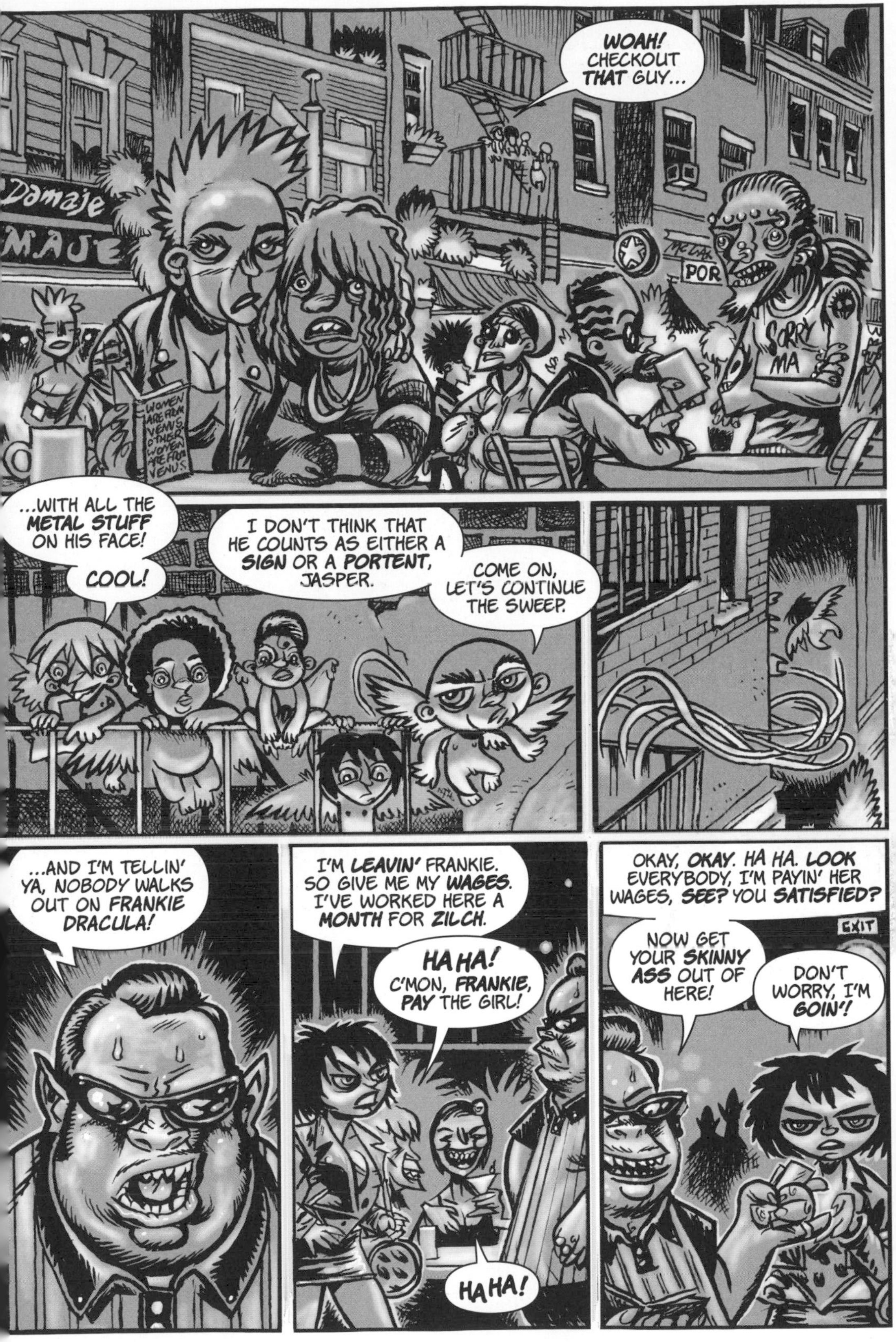

WOAH! CHECKOUT THAT GUY...
Damaje
POR
SORRY MA
WOMEN ARE FROM VENUS, OTHER WOMEN ARE FROM VENUS
...WITH ALL THE METAL STUFF ON HIS FACE!
COOL!
I DON'T THINK THAT HE COUNTS AS EITHER A SIGN OR A PORTENT, JASPER.
COME ON, LET'S CONTINUE THE SWEEP.
...AND I'M TELLIN' YA, NOBODY WALKS OUT ON FRANKIE DRACULA!
I'M LEAVIN' FRANKIE. SO GIVE ME MY WAGES. I'VE WORKED HERE A MONTH FOR ZILCH.
HA HA! C'MON, FRANKIE, PAY THE GIRL!
HA HA!
OKAY, OKAY. HA HA. LOOK EVERYBODY, I'M PAYIN' HER WAGES, SEE? YOU SATISFIED?
EXIT
NOW GET YOUR SKINNY ASS OUT OF HERE!
DON'T WORRY, I'M GOIN'!

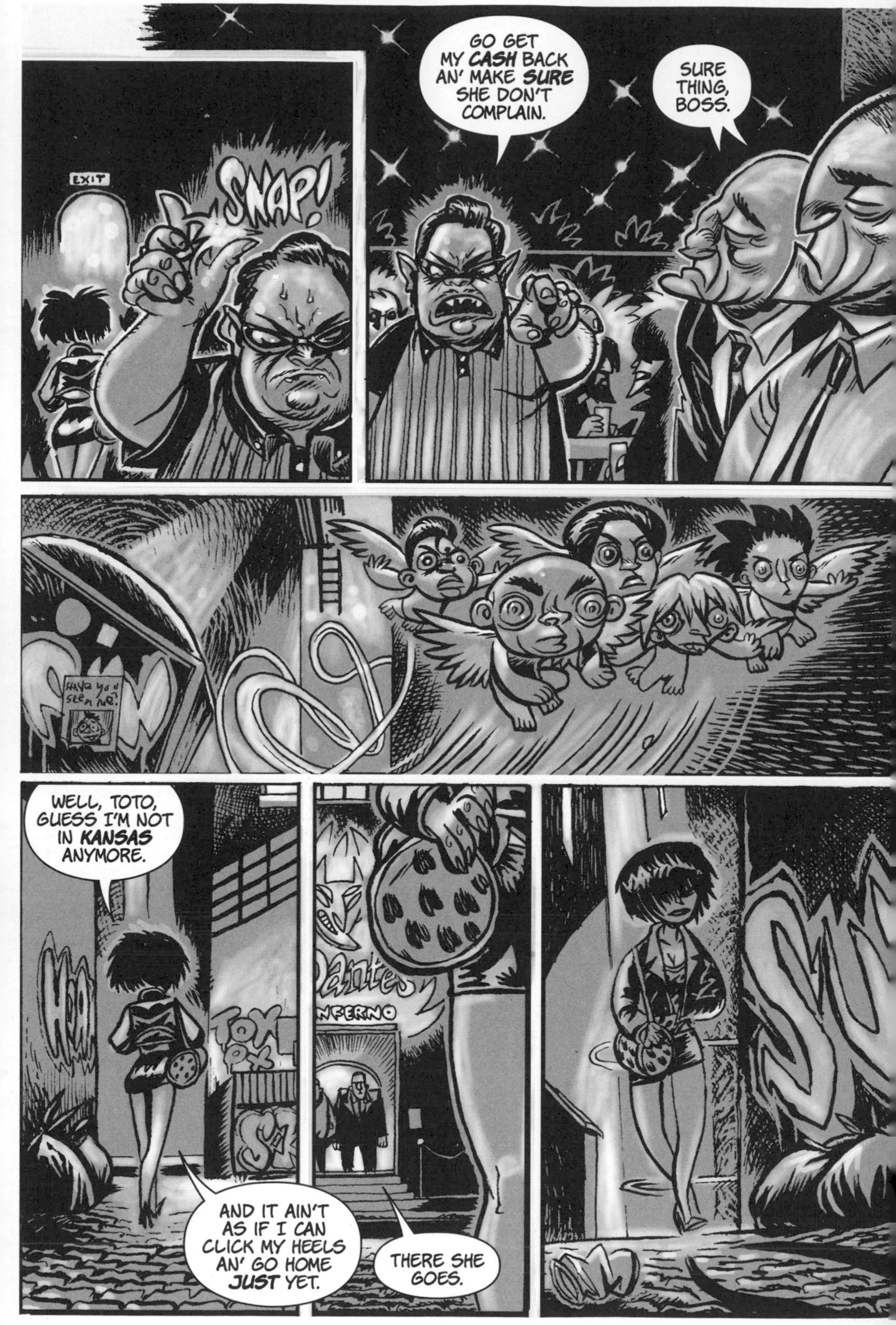
EXIT
SNAP!
GO GET MY **CASH** BACK AN' MAKE **SURE** SHE DON'T COMPLAIN.
SURE THING, BOSS.
Have you seen me?
WELL, TOTO, GUESS I'M NOT IN **KANSAS** ANYMORE.
AND IT AIN'T AS IF I CAN CLICK MY HEELS AN' GO HOME **JUST** YET.
THERE SHE GOES.

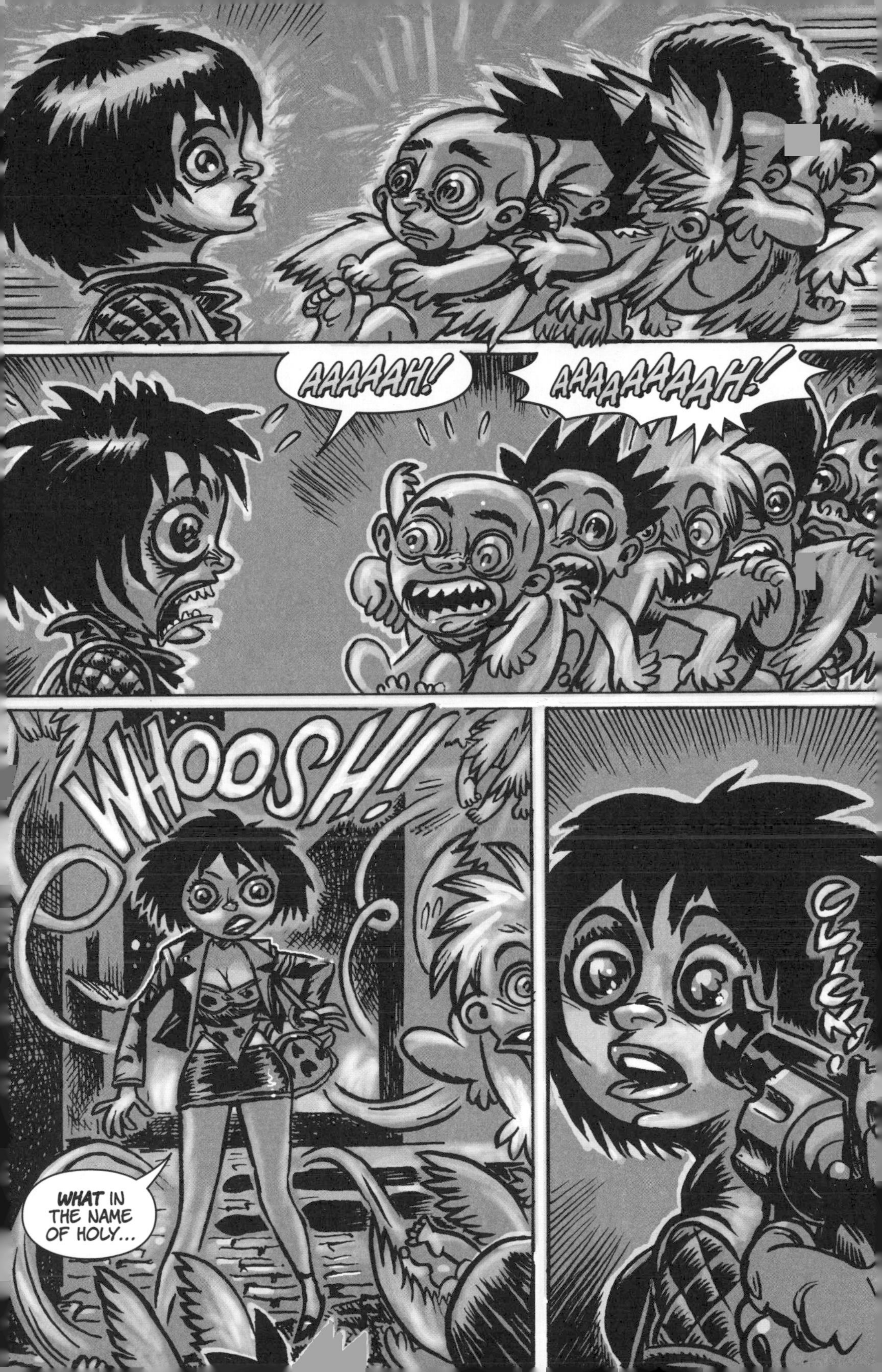
AAAAAH!
AAAAAAAAH!
WHOOSH!
WHAT IN THE NAME OF HOLY...
CLICK!

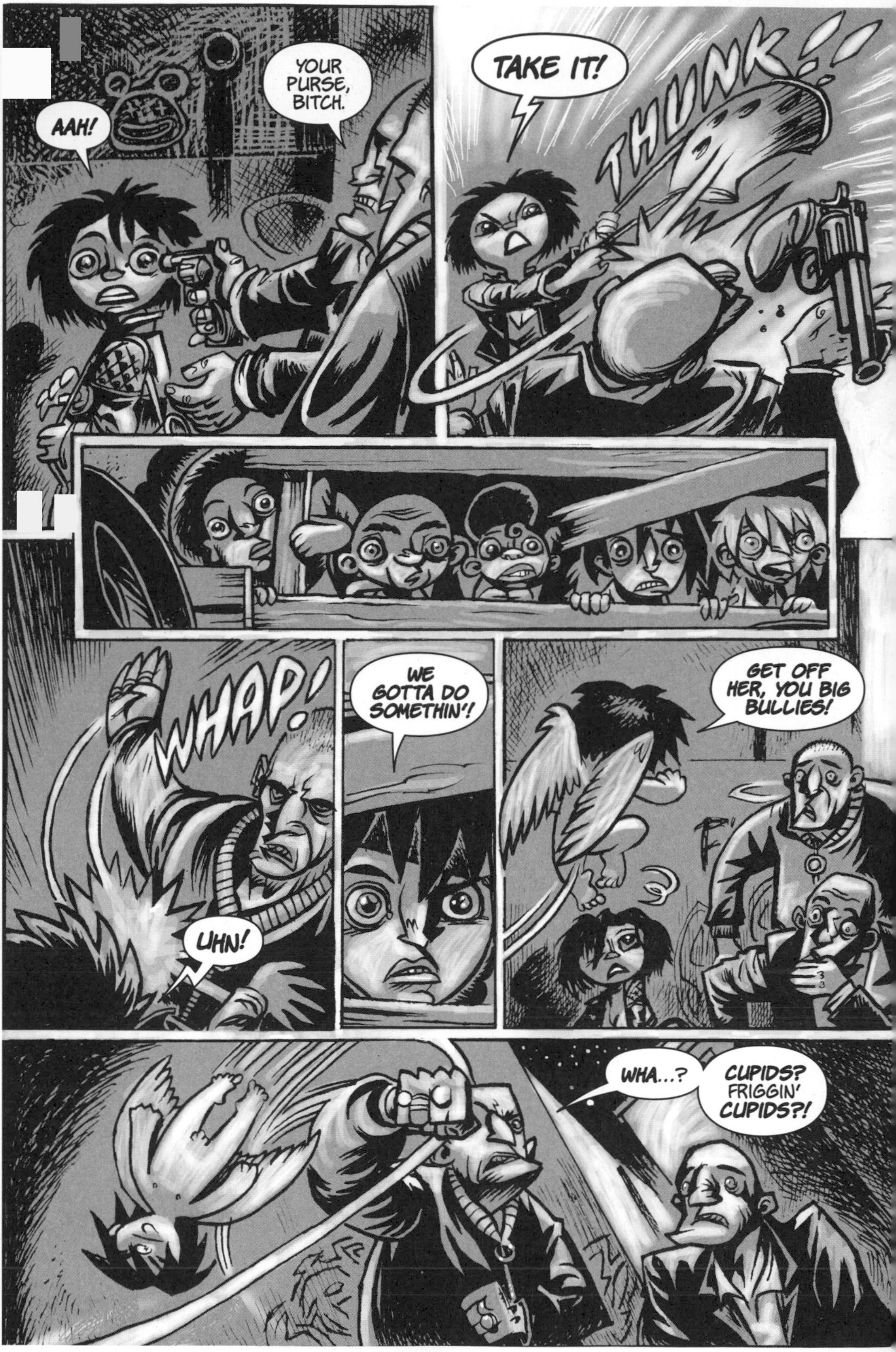
YOUR PURSE, BITCH.
AAH!
TAKE IT!
THUNK!!!
WHAP!
UHN!
WE GOTTA DO SOMETHIN'!
GET OFF HER, YOU BIG BULLIES!
WHA...?
CUPIDS? FRIGGIN' CUPIDS?!

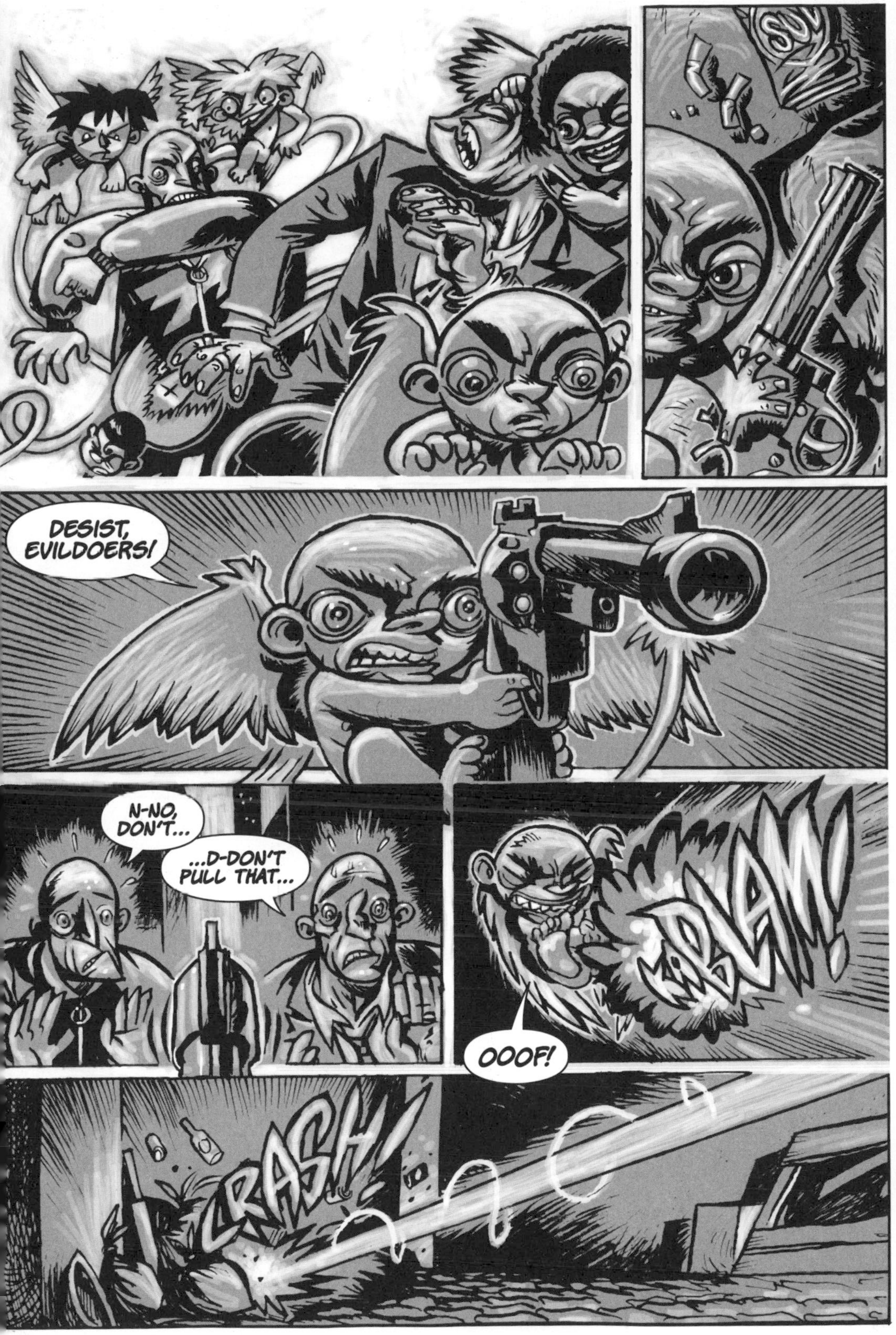

DESIST, EVILDOERS!
N-NO, DON'T...
...D-DON'T PULL THAT...
BLAM!
OOOF!
CRASH!

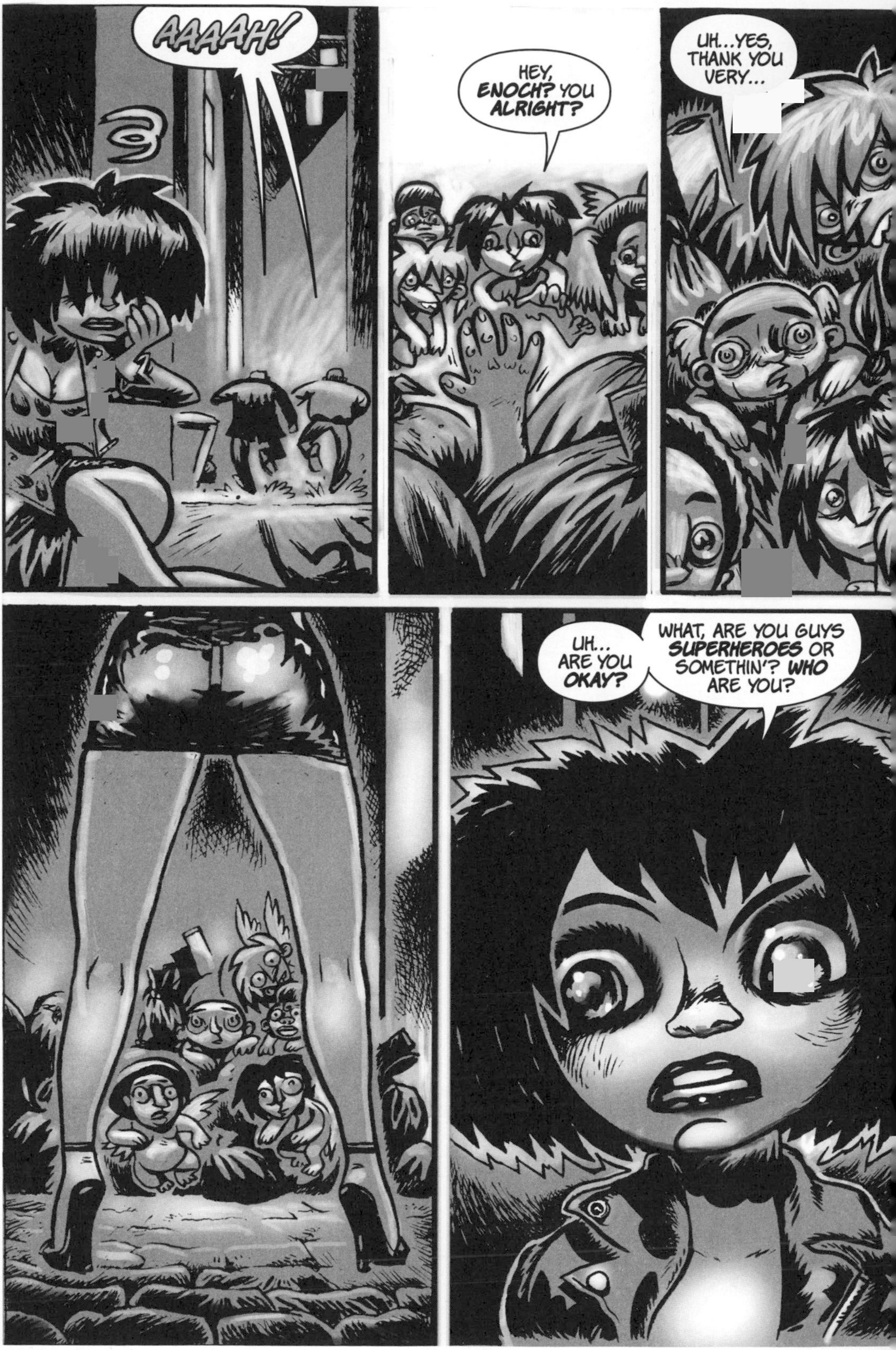
AAAAH!
HEY, ENOCH? YOU ALRIGHT?
UH...YES, THANK YOU VERY...
UH... ARE YOU OKAY?
WHAT, ARE YOU GUYS SUPERHEROES OR SOMETHIN'? WHO ARE YOU?

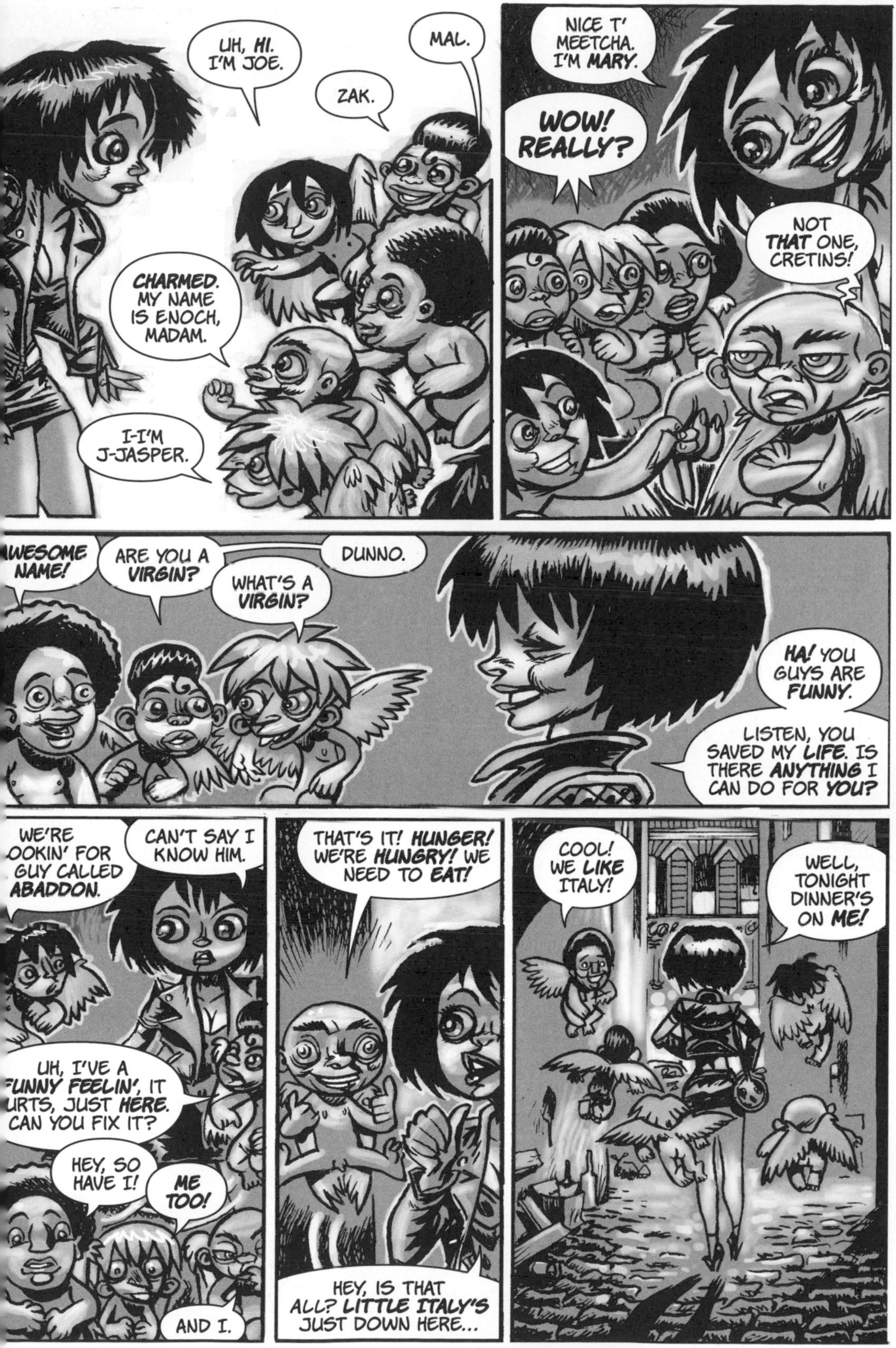

UH, HI. I'M JOE.
ZAK.
MAL.
CHARMED. MY NAME IS ENOCH, MADAM.
I-I'M J-JASPER.
NICE T' MEETCHA. I'M MARY.
WOW! REALLY?
NOT THAT ONE, CRETINS!
AWESOME NAME!
ARE YOU A VIRGIN?
DUNNO.
WHAT'S A VIRGIN?
HA! YOU GUYS ARE FUNNY.
LISTEN, YOU SAVED MY LIFE. IS THERE ANYTHING I CAN DO FOR YOU?
WE'RE LOOKIN' FOR GUY CALLED ABADDON.
CAN'T SAY I KNOW HIM.
UH, I'VE A FUNNY FEELIN', IT HURTS, JUST HERE. CAN YOU FIX IT?
HEY, SO HAVE I!
ME TOO!
AND I.
THAT'S IT! HUNGER! WE'RE HUNGRY! WE NEED TO EAT!
HEY, IS THAT ALL? LITTLE ITALY'S JUST DOWN HERE...
COOL! WE LIKE ITALY!
WELL, TONIGHT DINNER'S ON ME!

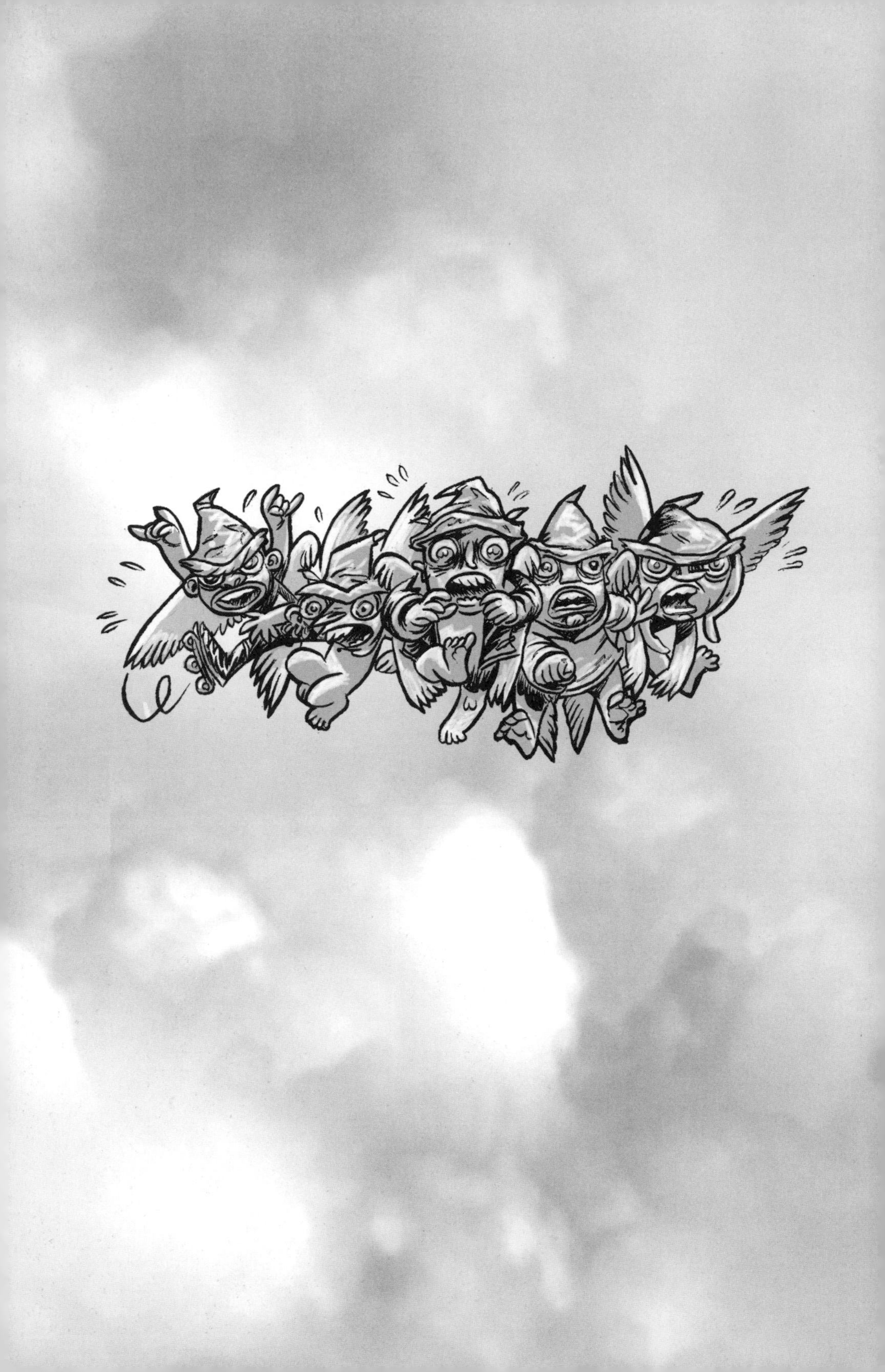

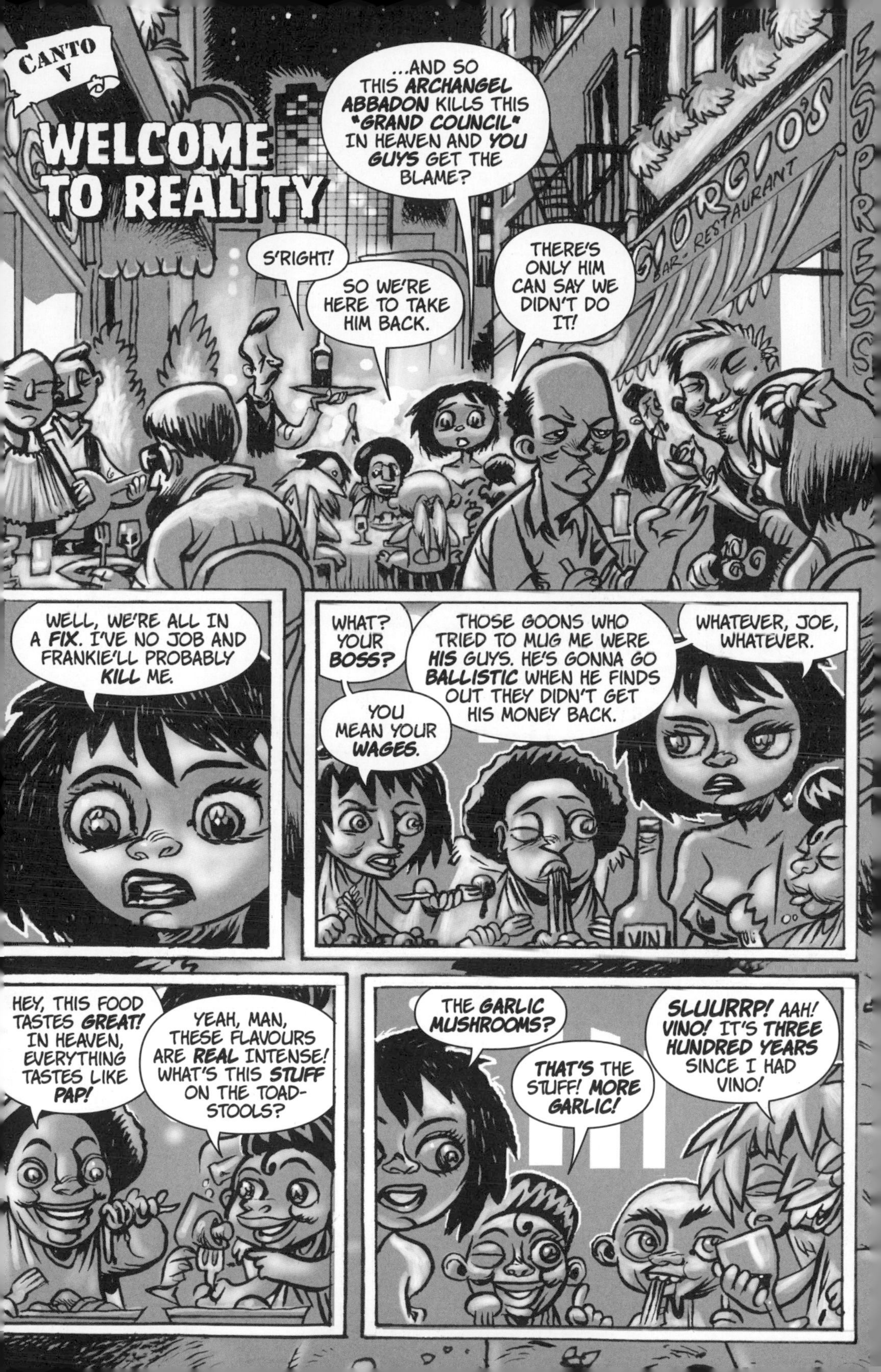

CANTO V
WELCOME TO REALITY
...AND SO THIS ARCHANGEL ABBADON KILLS THIS "GRAND COUNCIL" IN HEAVEN AND YOU GUYS GET THE BLAME?
S'RIGHT!
SO WE'RE HERE TO TAKE HIM BACK.
THERE'S ONLY HIM CAN SAY WE DIDN'T DO IT!
GIORGIO'S BAR-RESTAURANT
ESPRESSO
WELL, WE'RE ALL IN A FIX. I'VE NO JOB AND FRANKIE'LL PROBABLY KILL ME.
WHAT? YOUR BOSS?
THOSE GOONS WHO TRIED TO MUG ME WERE HIS GUYS. HE'S GONNA GO BALLISTIC WHEN HE FINDS OUT THEY DIDN'T GET HIS MONEY BACK.
WHATEVER, JOE, WHATEVER.
YOU MEAN YOUR WAGES.
VIN
HEY, THIS FOOD TASTES GREAT! IN HEAVEN, EVERYTHING TASTES LIKE PAP!
YEAH, MAN, THESE FLAVOURS ARE REAL INTENSE! WHAT'S THIS STUFF ON THE TOAD-STOOLS?
THE GARLIC MUSHROOMS?
THAT'S THE STUFF! MORE GARLIC!
SLUURRP! AAH! VINO! IT'S THREE HUNDRED YEARS SINCE I HAD VINO!

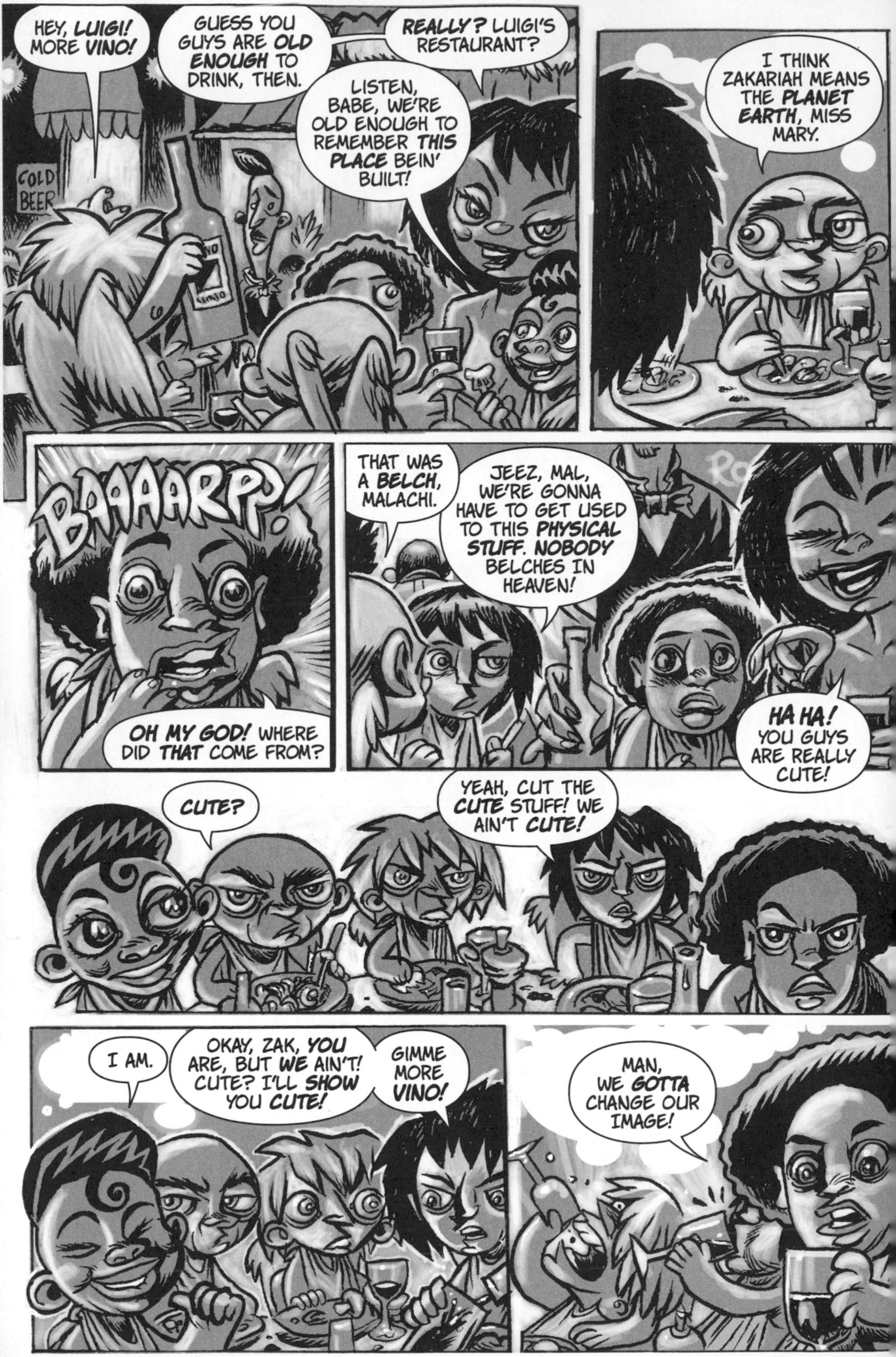
HEY, LUIGI! MORE VINO!
GUESS YOU GUYS ARE OLD ENOUGH TO DRINK, THEN.
REALLY? LUIGI'S RESTAURANT?
LISTEN, BABE, WE'RE OLD ENOUGH TO REMEMBER THIS PLACE BEIN' BUILT!
COLD BEER
I THINK ZAKARIAH MEANS THE PLANET EARTH, MISS MARY.
BAAAARP!
OH MY GOD! WHERE DID THAT COME FROM?
THAT WAS A BELCH, MALACHI.
JEEZ, MAL, WE'RE GONNA HAVE TO GET USED TO THIS PHYSICAL STUFF. NOBODY BELCHES IN HEAVEN!
HA HA! YOU GUYS ARE REALLY CUTE!
CUTE?
YEAH, CUT THE CUTE STUFF! WE AIN'T CUTE!
I AM.
OKAY, ZAK, YOU ARE, BUT WE AIN'T! CUTE? I'LL SHOW YOU CUTE!
GIMME MORE VINO!
MAN, WE GOTTA CHANGE OUR IMAGE!

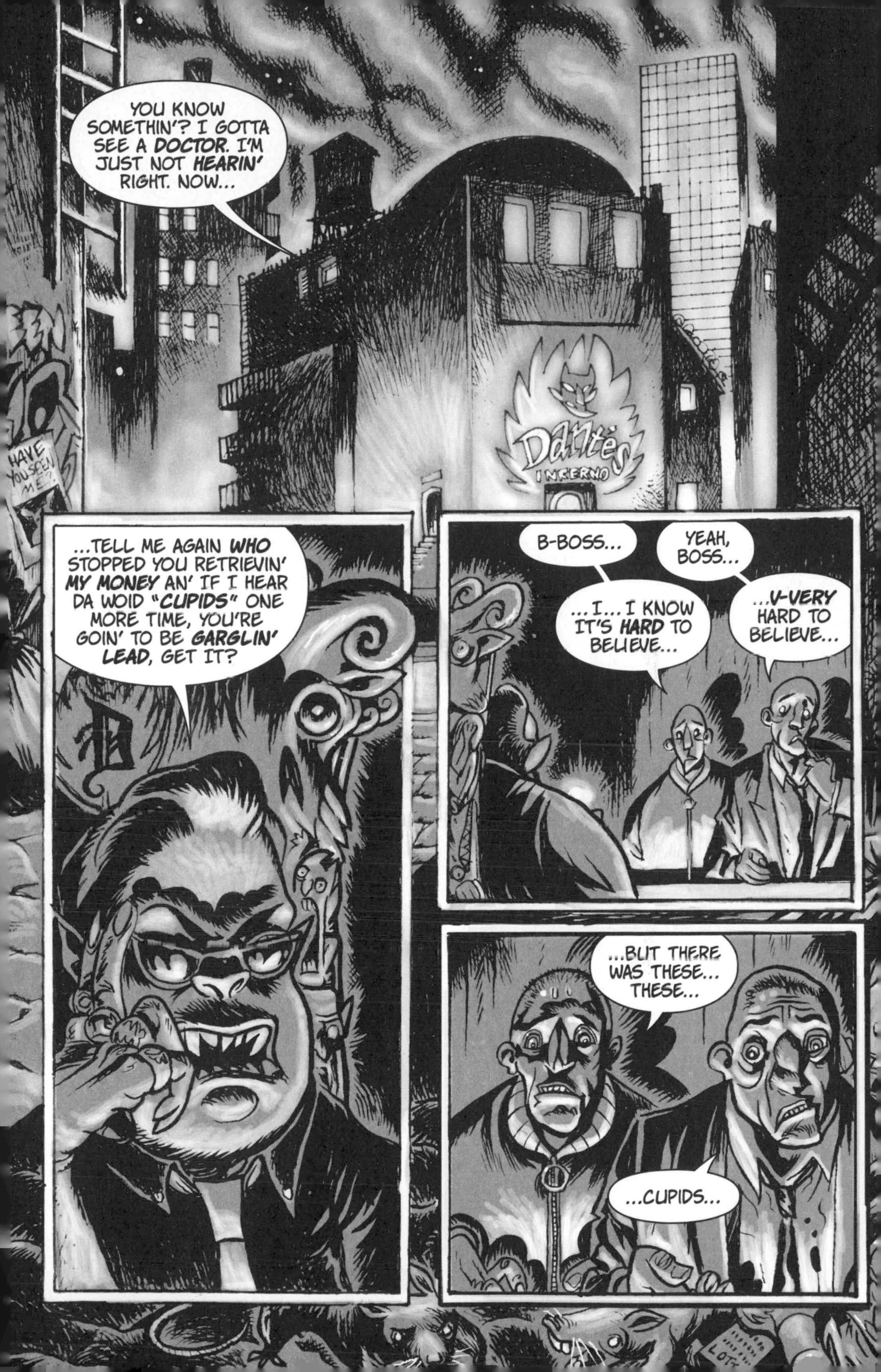

YOU KNOW SOMETHIN'? I GOTTA SEE A DOCTOR. I'M JUST NOT HEARIN' RIGHT. NOW...
HAVE YOU SEEN ME??
DANTE'S INFERNO
...TELL ME AGAIN WHO STOPPED YOU RETRIEVIN' MY MONEY AN' IF I HEAR DA WOID "CUPIDS" ONE MORE TIME, YOU'RE GOIN' TO BE GARGLIN' LEAD, GET IT?
B-BOSS...
...I... I KNOW IT'S HARD TO BELIEVE...
YEAH, BOSS...
...V-VERY HARD TO BELIEVE...
...BUT THERE WAS THESE... THESE...
...CUPIDS...

BLAM!
BLAM!

STINKIN' MORTAL TRASH.

BORIS?

BOSS?

I DON'T KNOW WHAT KINDA DEAL THIS DANCER CUT WITH THESE PUNKS, BUT *NOBODY* GETS MONEY OUT OF *FRANKIE DRACULA.*

AND DIDJA EVER HEAR ANYTHIN' AS *STUPID?* CUPIDS? CUPIDS? THERE *AIN'T* NO CUPIDS!

AT LEAST...

...NOT *ANYMORE.* NOBODY'S SEEN A CUPID SINCE THE *SEVENTEENTH CENTURY!*

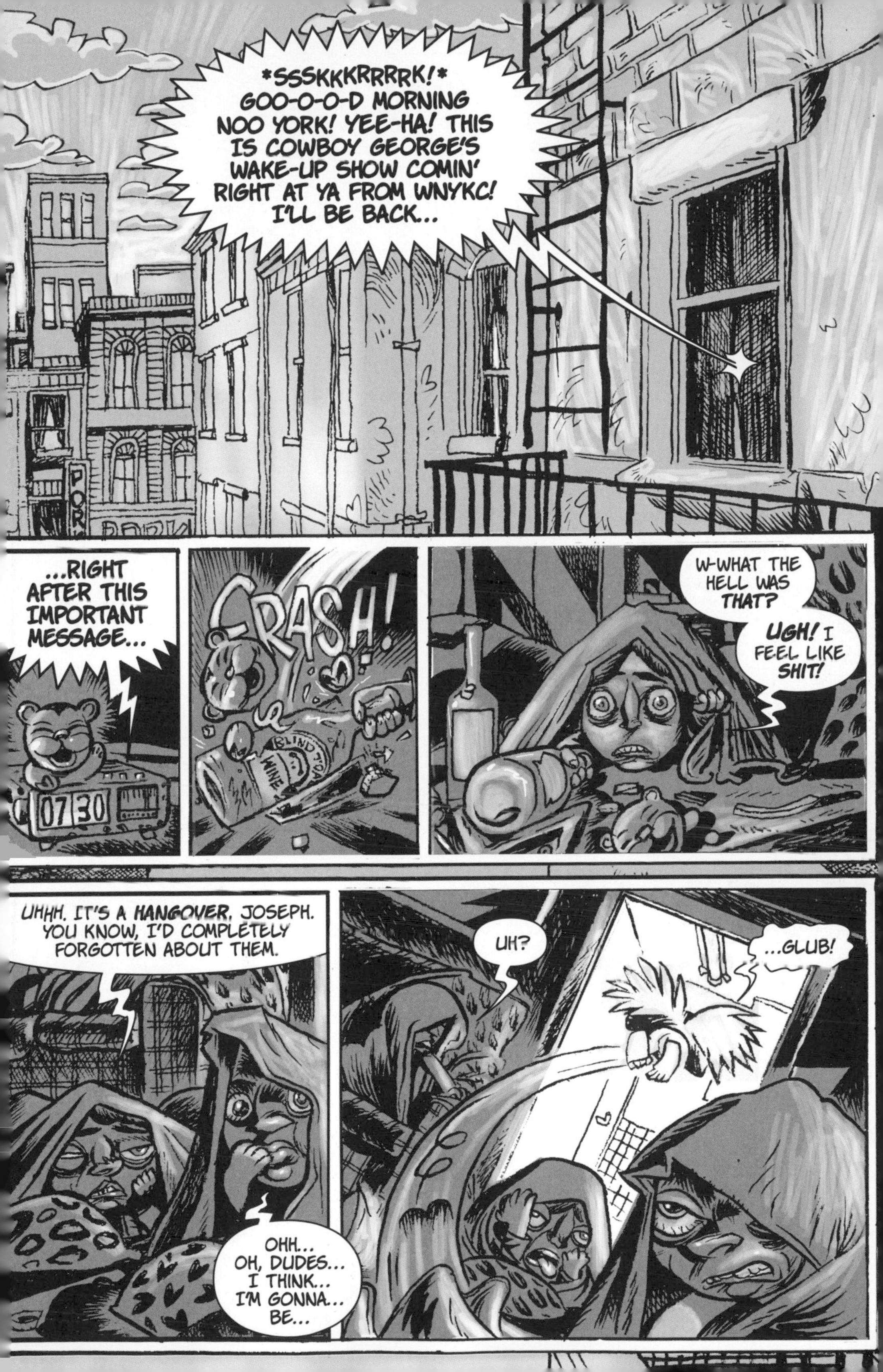
SSSKKKRRRRK! GOO-O-O-D MORNING NOO YORK! YEE-HA! THIS IS COWBOY GEORGE'S WAKE-UP SHOW COMIN' RIGHT AT YA FROM WNYKC! I'LL BE BACK...
...RIGHT AFTER THIS IMPORTANT MESSAGE...
07 30
CRASH!
BLIND TOAD WINE
W-WHAT THE HELL WAS THAT?
UGH! I FEEL LIKE SHIT!
UHHH. IT'S A HANGOVER, JOSEPH. YOU KNOW, I'D COMPLETELY FORGOTTEN ABOUT THEM.
OHH... OH, DUDES... I THINK... I'M GONNA... BE...
UH?
...GLUB!

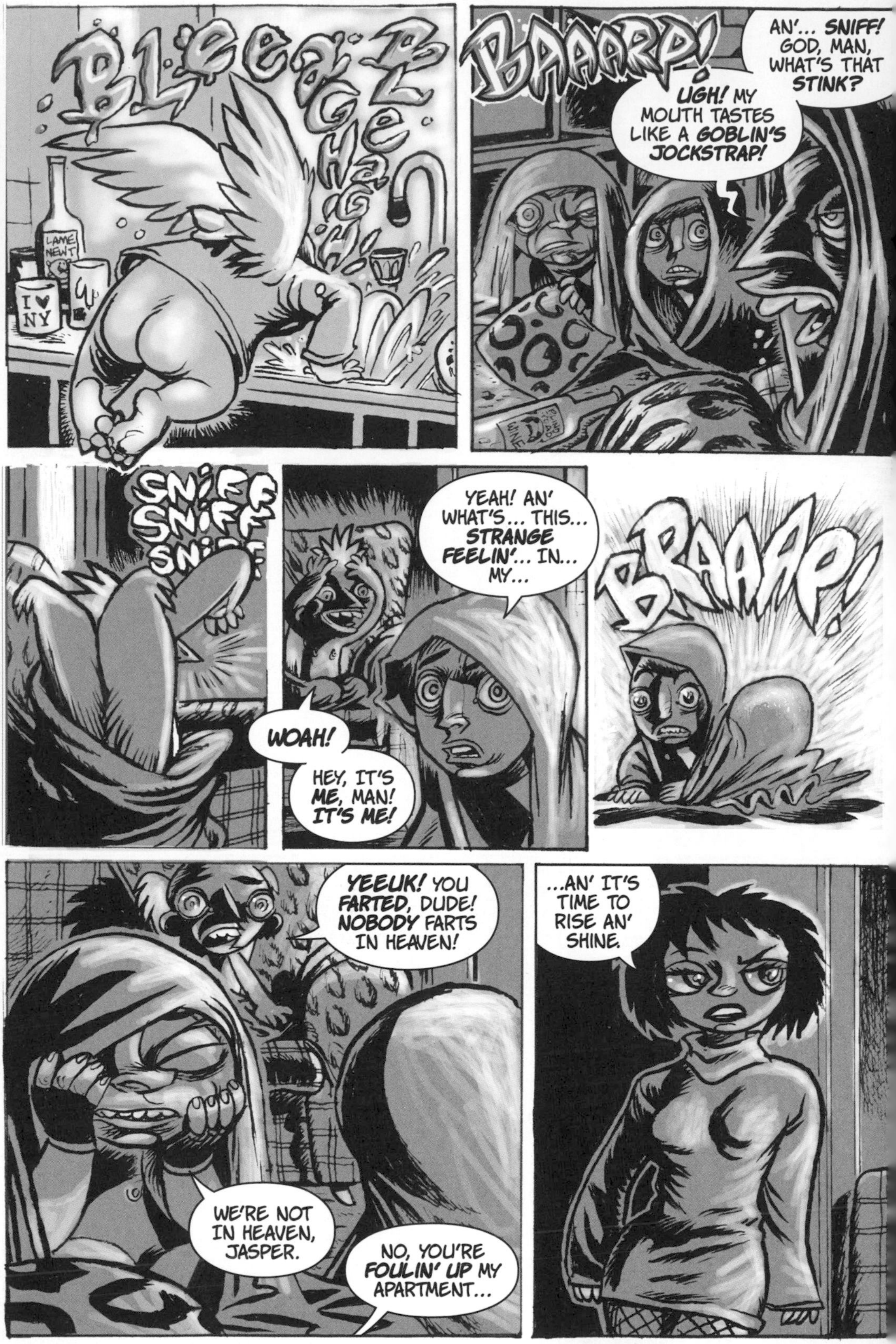
BLEEAARGGHE HAGGH!
BAAARP!
AN'... SNIFF! GOD, MAN, WHAT'S THAT STINK?
UGH! MY MOUTH TASTES LIKE A GOBLIN'S JOCKSTRAP!
LAME NEWT
I ♥ NY
SNIFF SNIFF
YEAH! AN' WHAT'S... THIS... STRANGE FEELIN'... IN... MY...
WOAH!
HEY, IT'S ME, MAN! IT'S ME!
BRAAAP!
YEEUK! YOU FARTED, DUDE! NOBODY FARTS IN HEAVEN!
WE'RE NOT IN HEAVEN, JASPER.
NO, YOU'RE FOULIN' UP MY APARTMENT...
...AN' IT'S TIME TO RISE AN' SHINE.

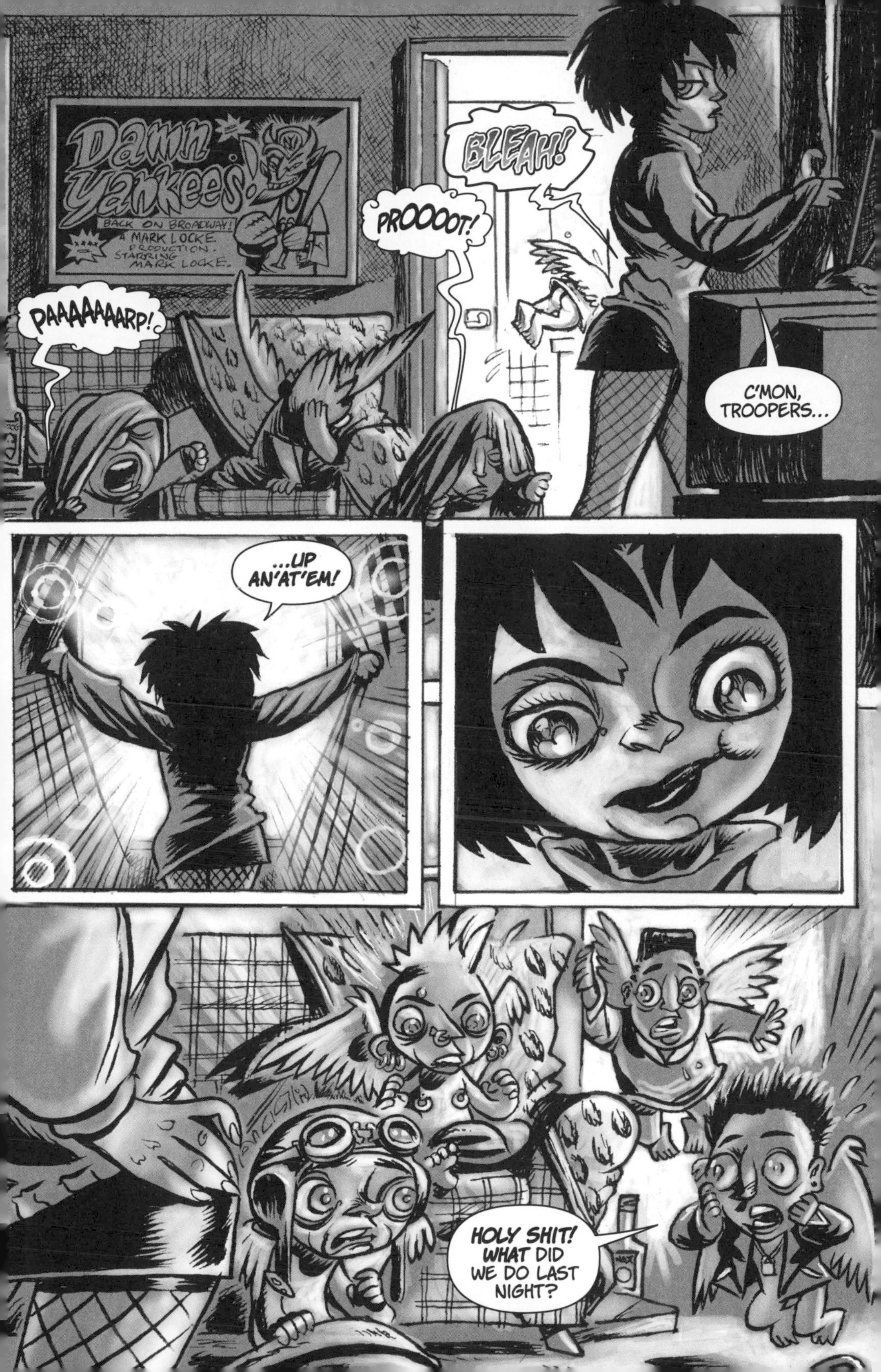
Damn Yankees!
BACK ON BROADWAY!
A MARK LOCKE PRODUCTION.
STARRING MARK LOCKE.
PAAAAAAARP!
PROOOOT!
BLEAH!
C'MON, TROOPERS...
...UP AN'AT'EM!
HOLY SHIT! WHAT DID WE DO LAST NIGHT?

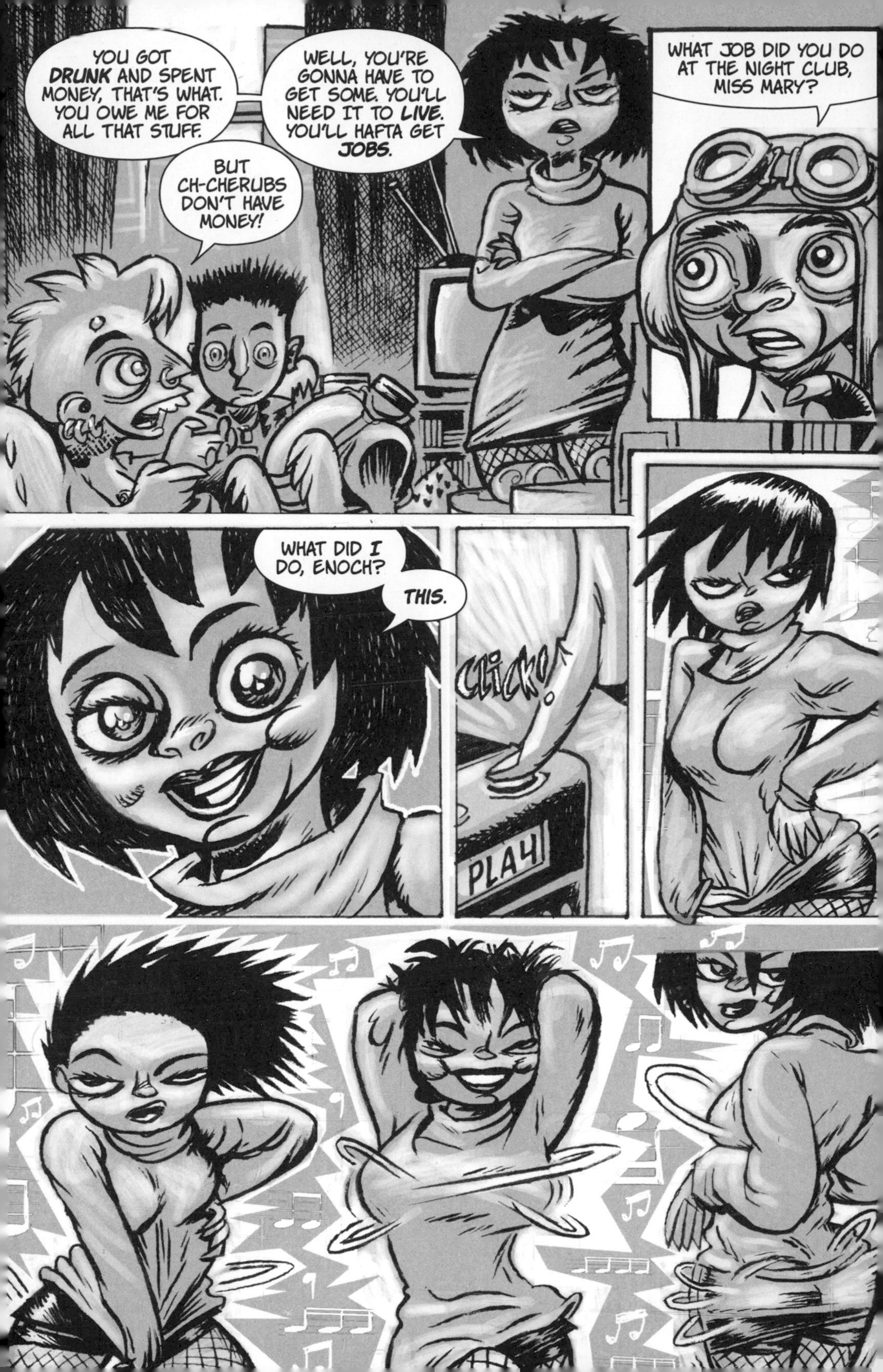
YOU GOT DRUNK AND SPENT MONEY, THAT'S WHAT. YOU OWE ME FOR ALL THAT STUFF.
BUT CH-CHERUBS DON'T HAVE MONEY!
WELL, YOU'RE GONNA HAVE TO GET SOME. YOU'LL NEED IT TO LIVE. YOU'LL HAFTA GET JOBS.
WHAT JOB DID YOU DO AT THE NIGHT CLUB, MISS MARY?
WHAT DID I DO, ENOCH?
THIS.
CLICK!
PLAY

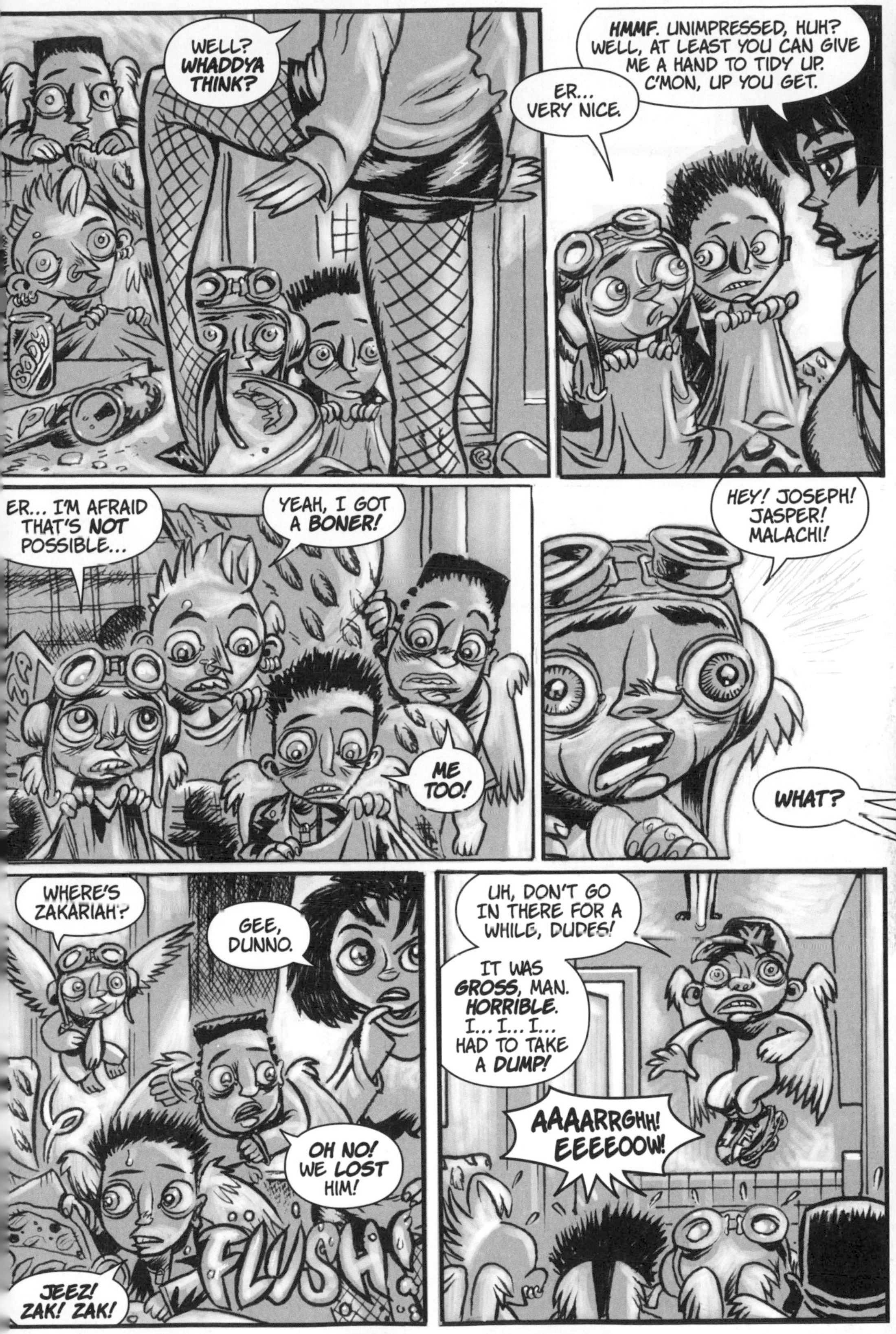
WELL? WHADDYA THINK?
ER... VERY NICE.
HMMF. UNIMPRESSED, HUH? WELL, AT LEAST YOU CAN GIVE ME A HAND TO TIDY UP. C'MON, UP YOU GET.
ER... I'M AFRAID THAT'S NOT POSSIBLE...
YEAH, I GOT A BONER!
ME TOO!
HEY! JOSEPH! JASPER! MALACHI!
WHAT?
WHERE'S ZAKARIAH?
GEE, DUNNO.
OH NO! WE LOST HIM!
FLUSH!
JEEZ! ZAK! ZAK!
UH, DON'T GO IN THERE FOR A WHILE, DUDES!
IT WAS GROSS, MAN. HORRIBLE. I... I... I... HAD TO TAKE A DUMP!
AAAARRGHH! EEEEOOW!

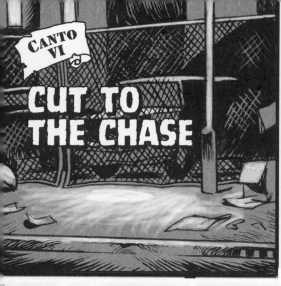

CANTO VI

CUT TO THE CHASE

WE'VE ARRIVED.

HEY, LOOK.

EXCELLENT.

MORPH.

NOW LET'S BRING THOSE *MURDERIN'* CHERUBIM TO JUSTICE!

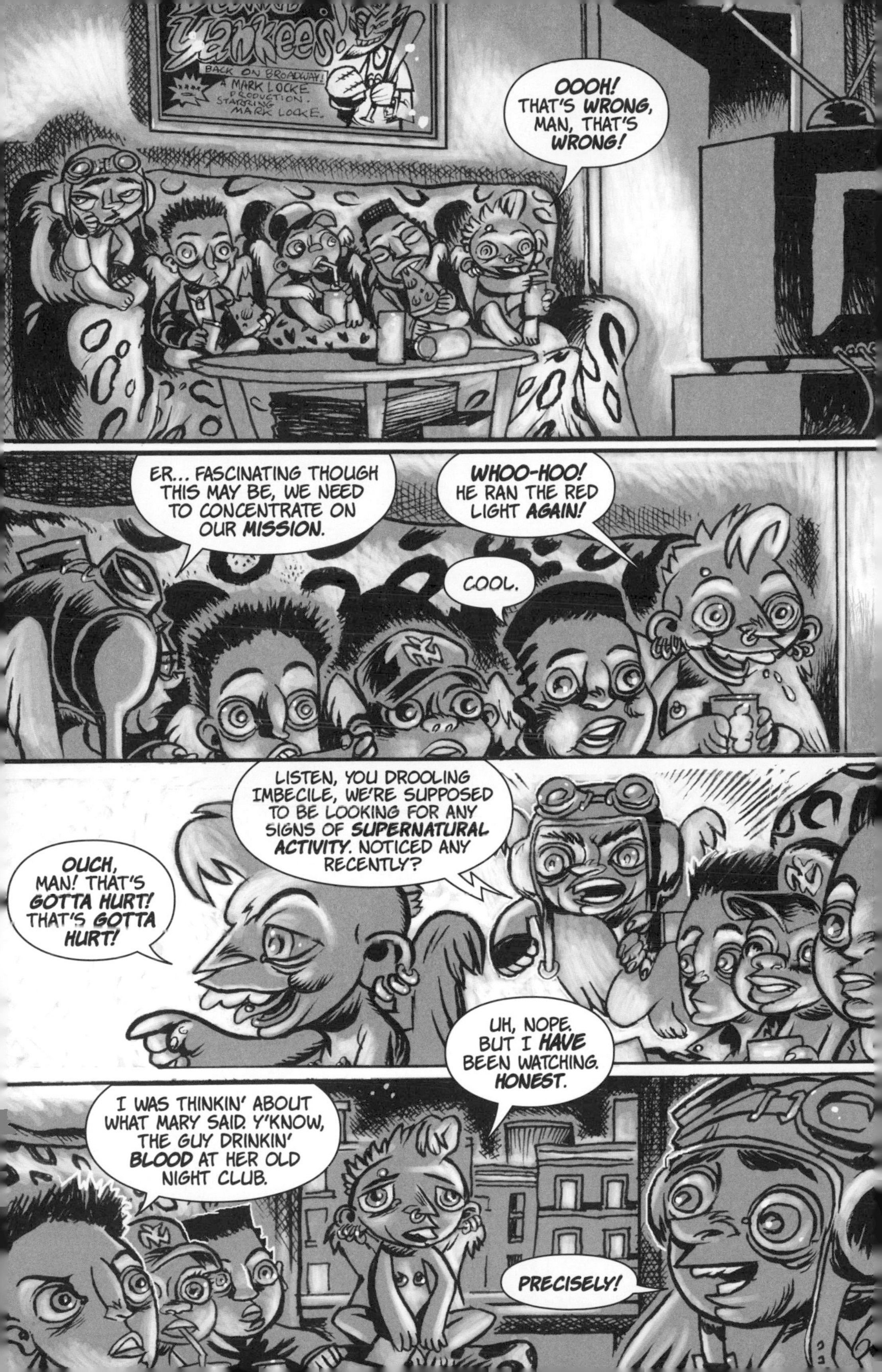
YANKEES!
BACK ON BROADWAY!
A MARK LOCKE PRODUCTION. STARRING MARK LOCKE.
OOOH! THAT'S WRONG, MAN, THAT'S WRONG!
ER... FASCINATING THOUGH THIS MAY BE, WE NEED TO CONCENTRATE ON OUR MISSION.
WHOO-HOO! HE RAN THE RED LIGHT AGAIN!
COOL.
OUCH, MAN! THAT'S GOTTA HURT! THAT'S GOTTA HURT!
LISTEN, YOU DROOLING IMBECILE, WE'RE SUPPOSED TO BE LOOKING FOR ANY SIGNS OF SUPERNATURAL ACTIVITY. NOTICED ANY RECENTLY?
UH, NOPE. BUT I HAVE BEEN WATCHING. HONEST.
I WAS THINKIN' ABOUT WHAT MARY SAID. Y'KNOW, THE GUY DRINKIN' BLOOD AT HER OLD NIGHT CLUB.
PRECISELY!

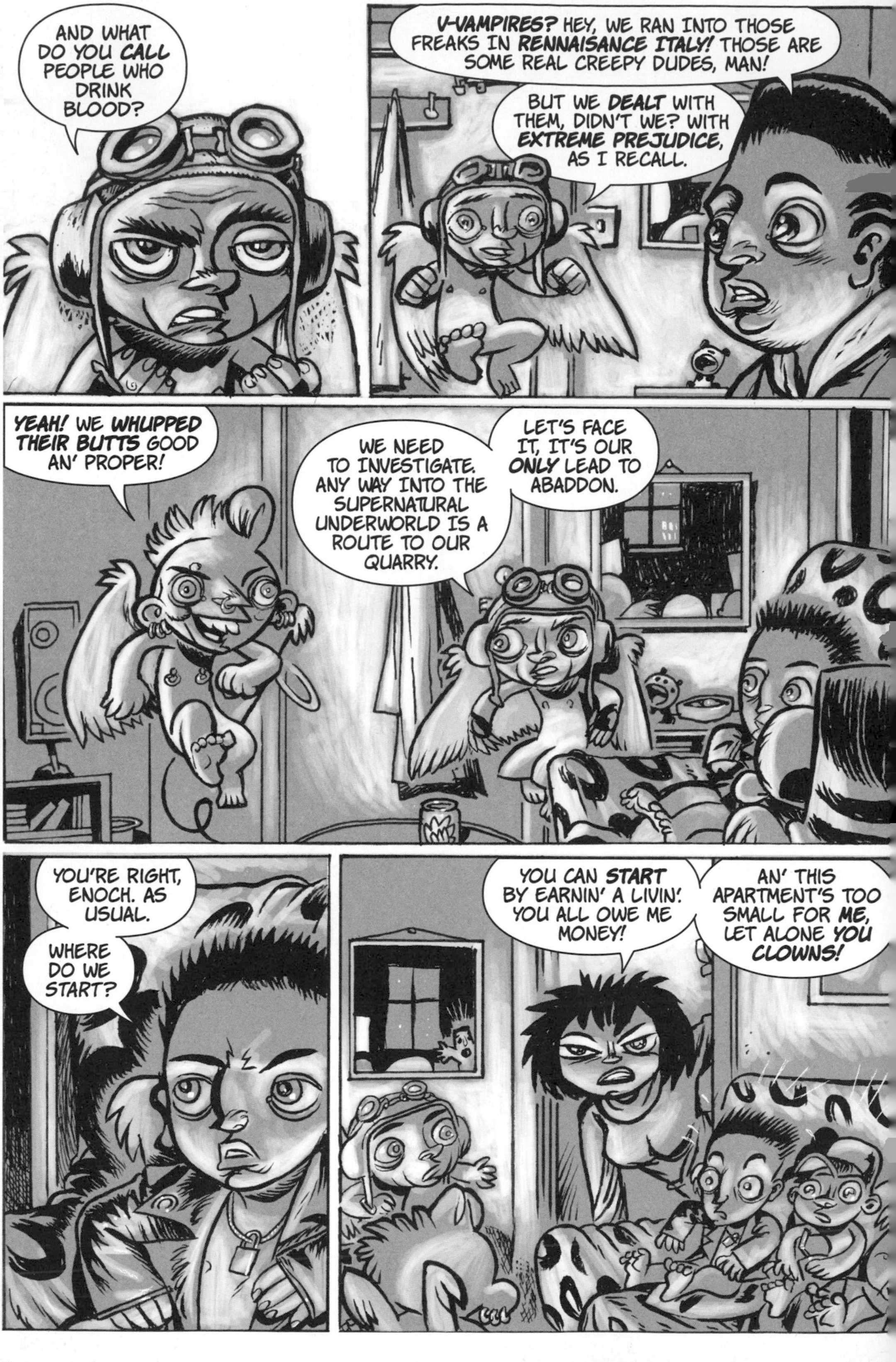
AND WHAT DO YOU CALL PEOPLE WHO DRINK BLOOD?
V-VAMPIRES? HEY, WE RAN INTO THOSE FREAKS IN RENNAISANCE ITALY! THOSE ARE SOME REAL CREEPY DUDES, MAN!
BUT WE DEALT WITH THEM, DIDN'T WE? WITH EXTREME PREJUDICE, AS I RECALL.
YEAH! WE WHUPPED THEIR BUTTS GOOD AN' PROPER!
WE NEED TO INVESTIGATE. ANY WAY INTO THE SUPERNATURAL UNDERWORLD IS A ROUTE TO OUR QUARRY.
LET'S FACE IT, IT'S OUR ONLY LEAD TO ABADDON.
YOU'RE RIGHT, ENOCH. AS USUAL.
WHERE DO WE START?
YOU CAN START BY EARNIN' A LIVIN'! YOU ALL OWE ME MONEY!
AN' THIS APARTMENT'S TOO SMALL FOR ME, LET ALONE YOU CLOWNS!

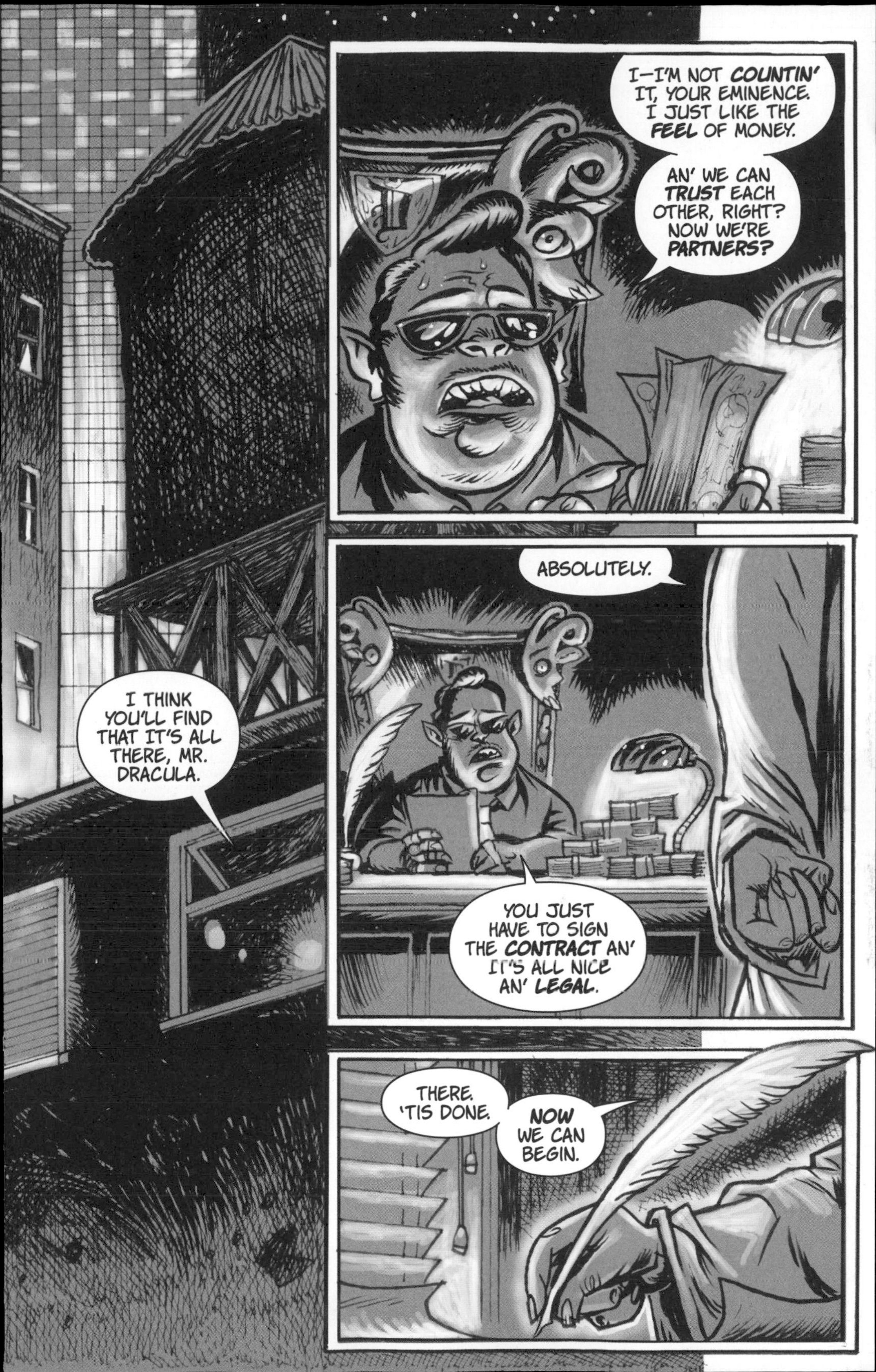
I—I'M NOT COUNTIN' IT, YOUR EMINENCE. I JUST LIKE THE FEEL OF MONEY.
AN' WE CAN TRUST EACH OTHER, RIGHT? NOW WE'RE PARTNERS?
I THINK YOU'LL FIND THAT IT'S ALL THERE, MR. DRACULA.
ABSOLUTELY.
YOU JUST HAVE TO SIGN THE CONTRACT AN' IT'S ALL NICE AN' LEGAL.
THERE. 'TIS DONE.
NOW WE CAN BEGIN.

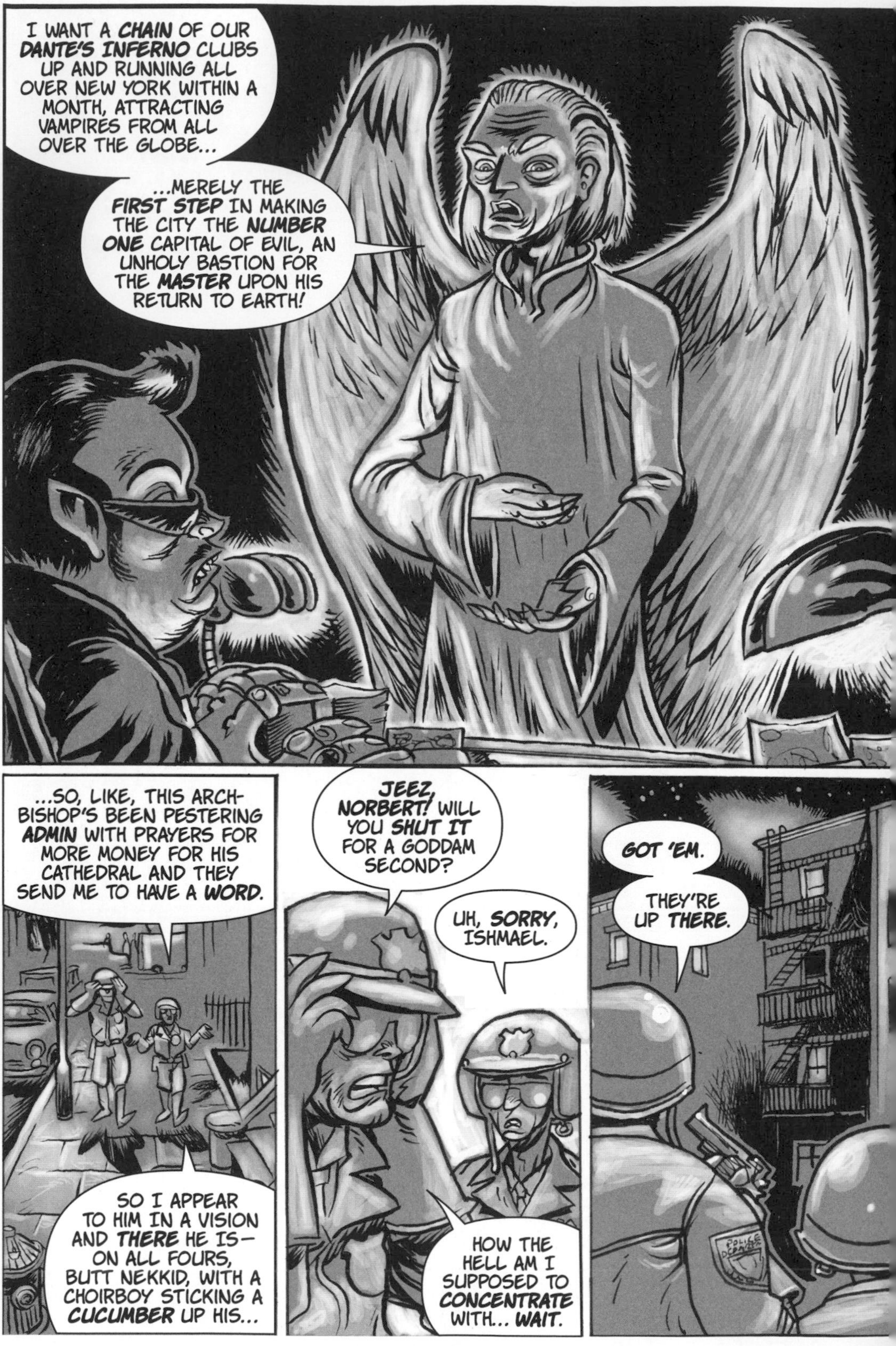
I WANT A CHAIN OF OUR DANTE'S INFERNO CLUBS UP AND RUNNING ALL OVER NEW YORK WITHIN A MONTH, ATTRACTING VAMPIRES FROM ALL OVER THE GLOBE...
...MERELY THE FIRST STEP IN MAKING THE CITY THE NUMBER ONE CAPITAL OF EVIL, AN UNHOLY BASTION FOR THE MASTER UPON HIS RETURN TO EARTH!
...SO, LIKE, THIS ARCH-BISHOP'S BEEN PESTERING ADMIN WITH PRAYERS FOR MORE MONEY FOR HIS CATHEDRAL AND THEY SEND ME TO HAVE A WORD.
SO I APPEAR TO HIM IN A VISION AND THERE HE IS— ON ALL FOURS, BUTT NEKKID, WITH A CHOIRBOY STICKING A CUCUMBER UP HIS...
JEEZ, NORBERT! WILL YOU SHUT IT FOR A GODDAM SECOND?
UH, SORRY, ISHMAEL.
HOW THE HELL AM I SUPPOSED TO CONCENTRATE WITH... WAIT.
GOT 'EM.
THEY'RE UP THERE.

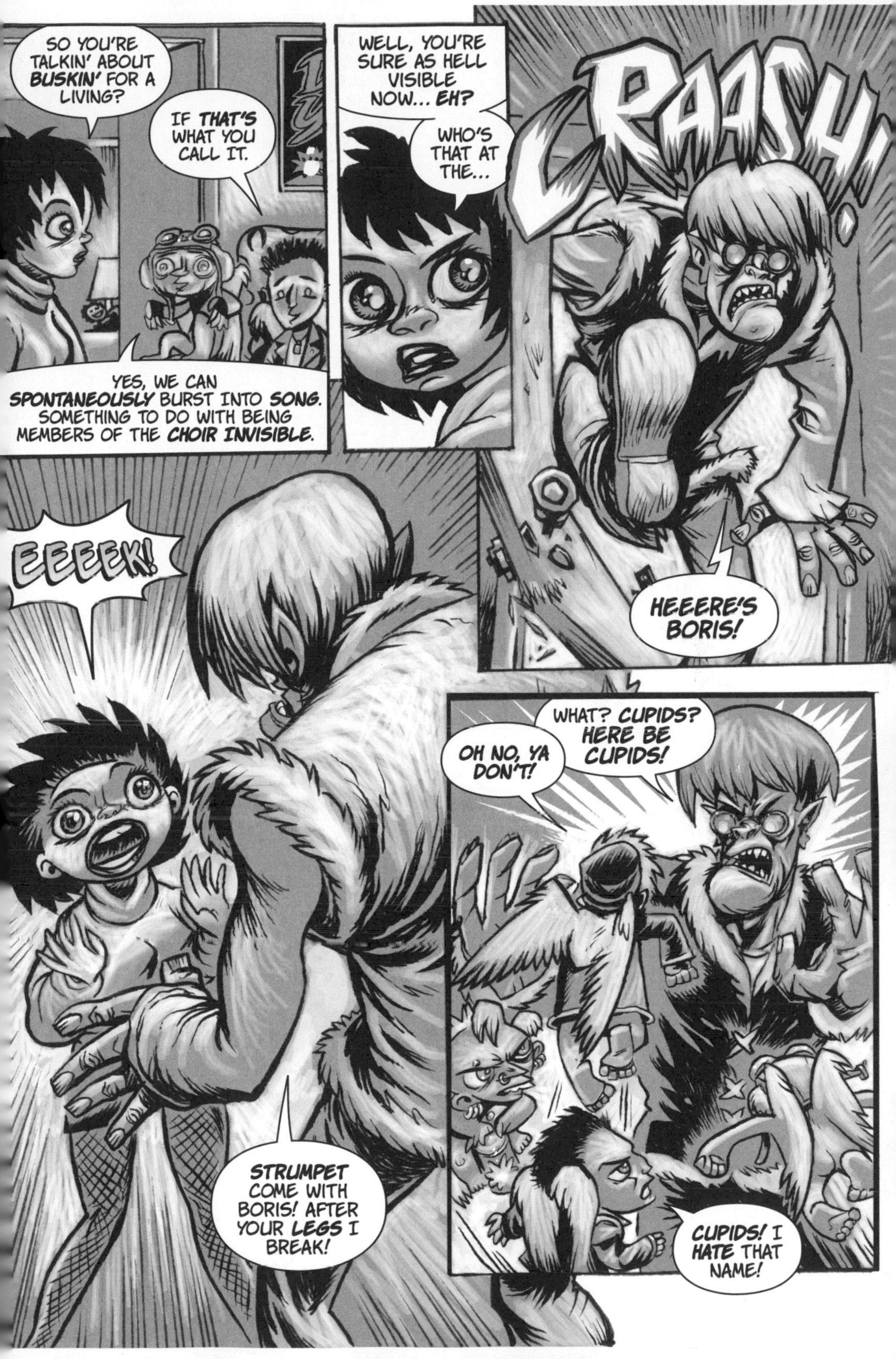
SO YOU'RE TALKIN' ABOUT BUSKIN' FOR A LIVING?
IF THAT'S WHAT YOU CALL IT.
YES, WE CAN SPONTANEOUSLY BURST INTO SONG. SOMETHING TO DO WITH BEING MEMBERS OF THE CHOIR INVISIBLE.
WELL, YOU'RE SURE AS HELL VISIBLE NOW... EH?
WHO'S THAT AT THE...
CRAASH!
HEEEERE'S BORIS!
EEEEEK!
STRUMPET COME WITH BORIS! AFTER YOUR LEGS I BREAK!
WHAT? CUPIDS? HERE BE CUPIDS!
OH NO, YA DON'T!
CUPIDS! I HATE THAT NAME!

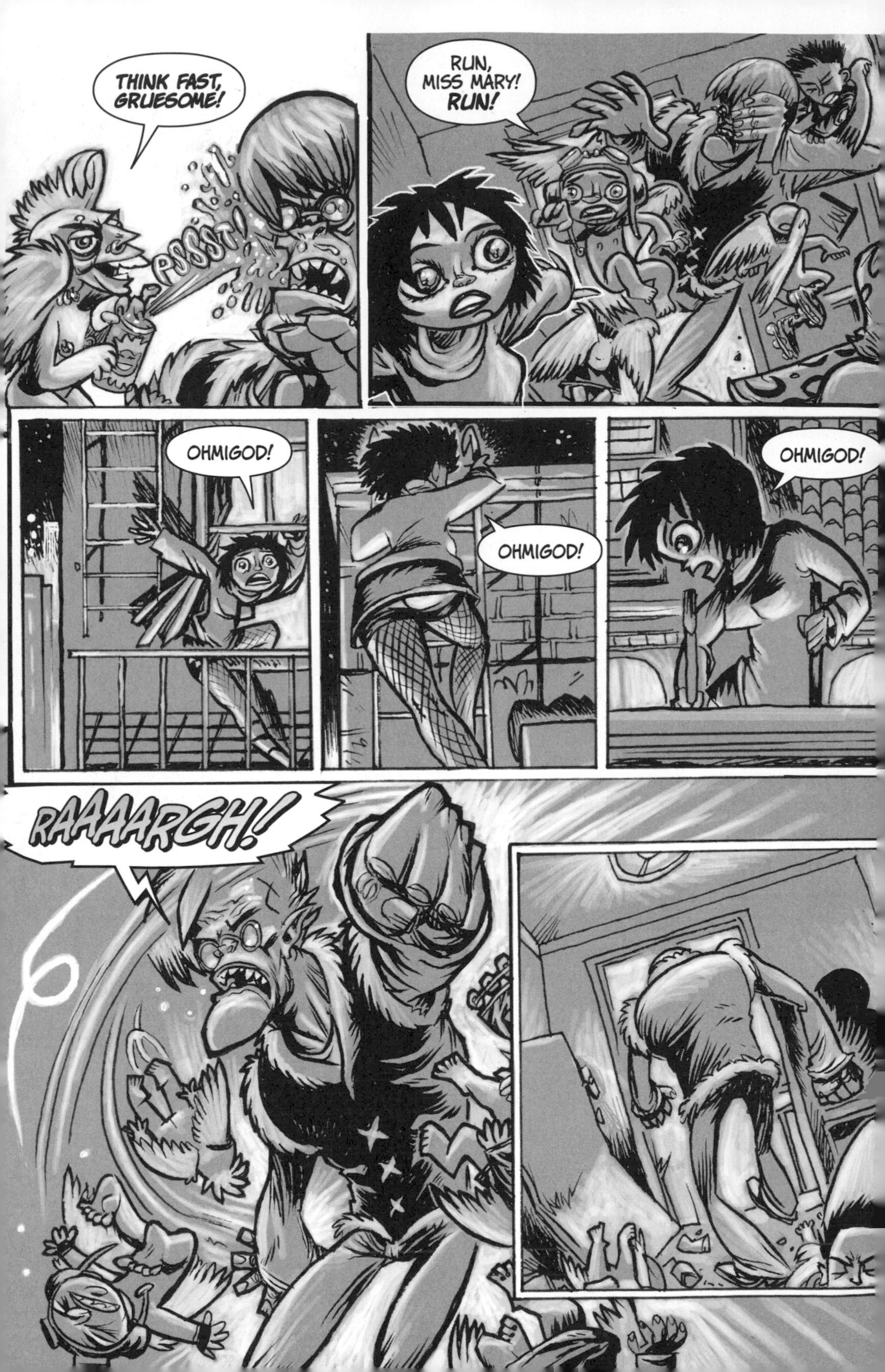
THINK FAST, GRUESOME!
PSSSST!
RUN, MISS MARY! RUN!
OHMIGOD!
OHMIGOD!
OHMIGOD!
RAAAARGH!

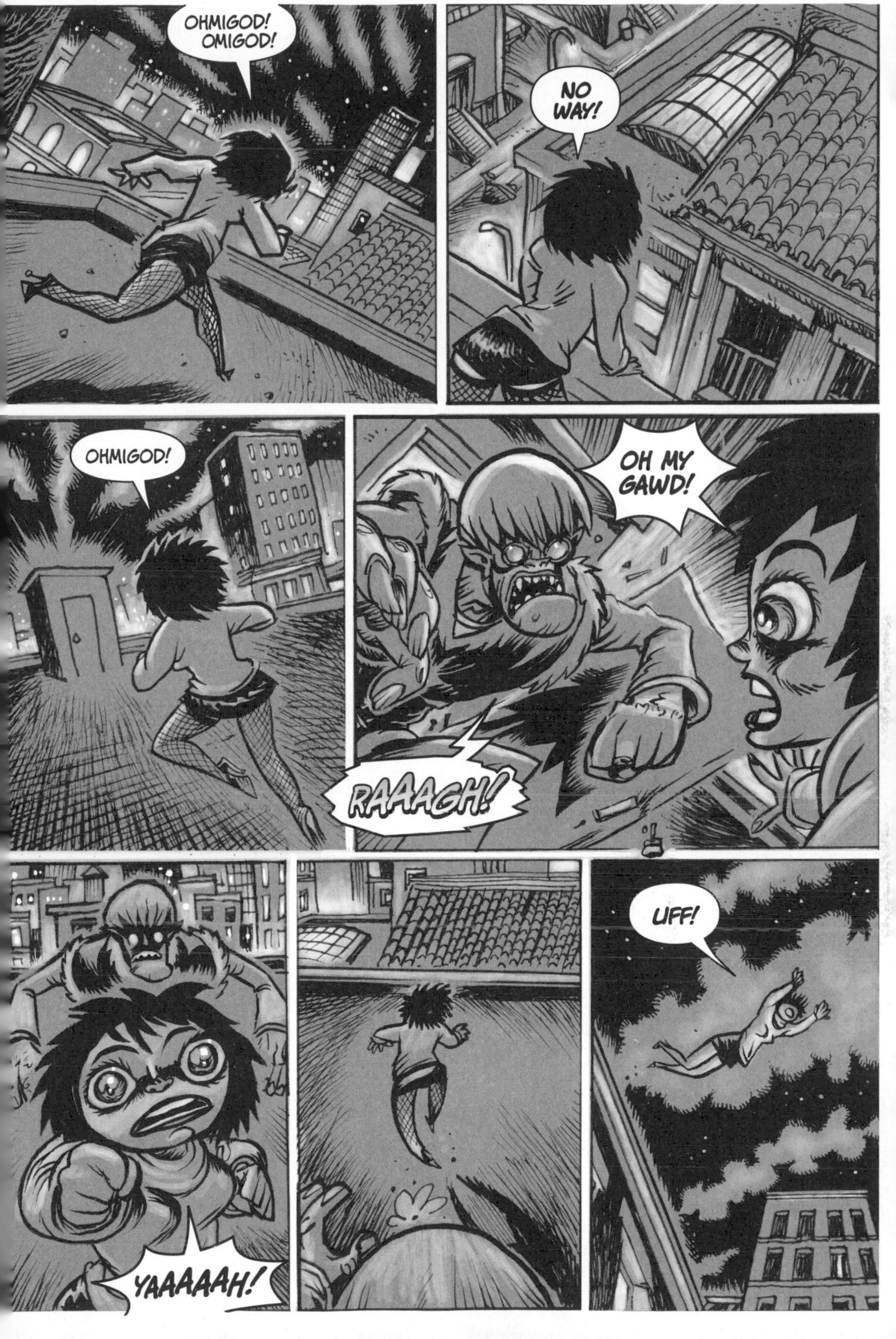
OHMIGOD! OMIGOD!
NO WAY!
OHMIGOD!
OH MY GAWD!
RAAAGH!
YAAAAAH!
UFF!

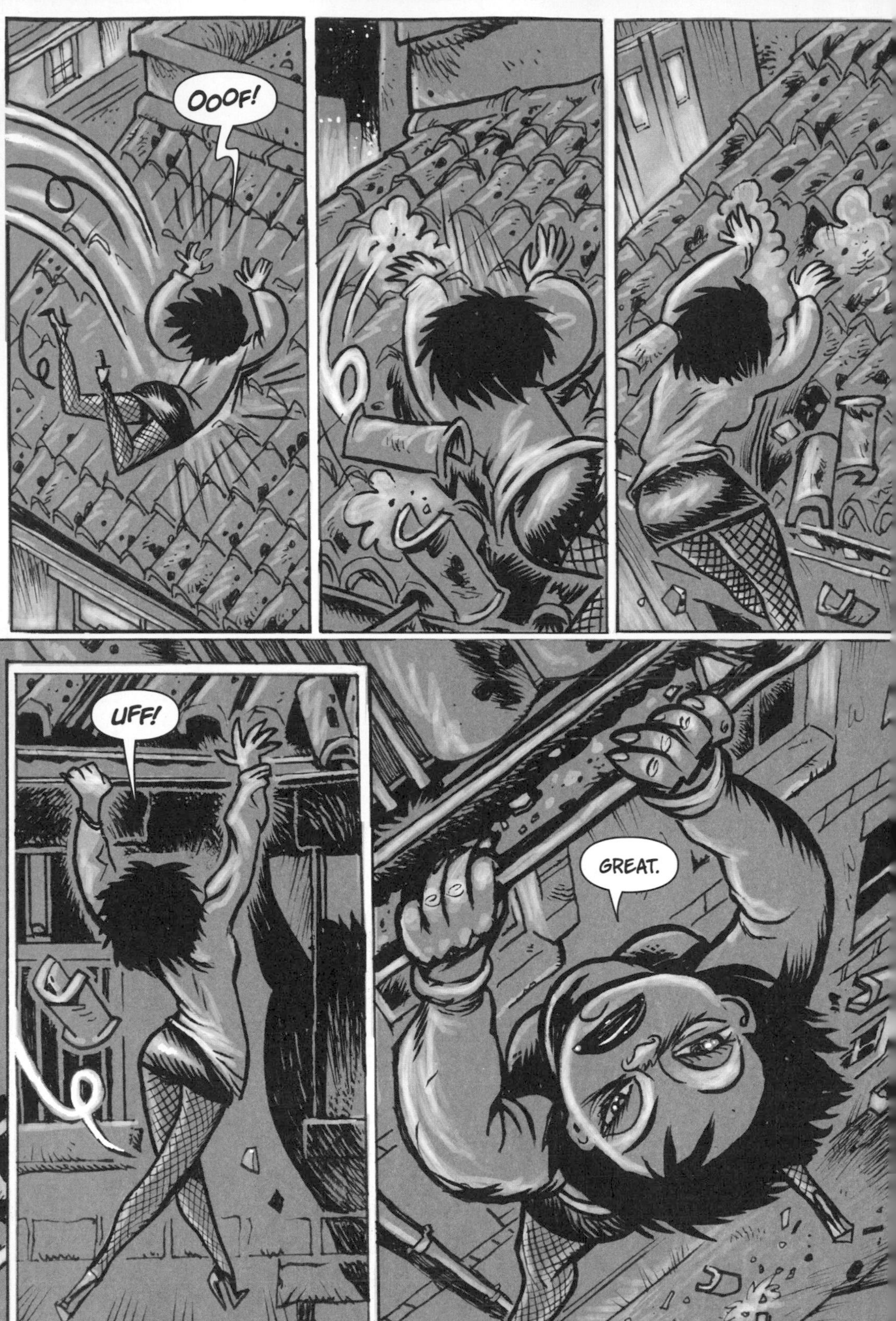
OOOF!
UFF!
GREAT.

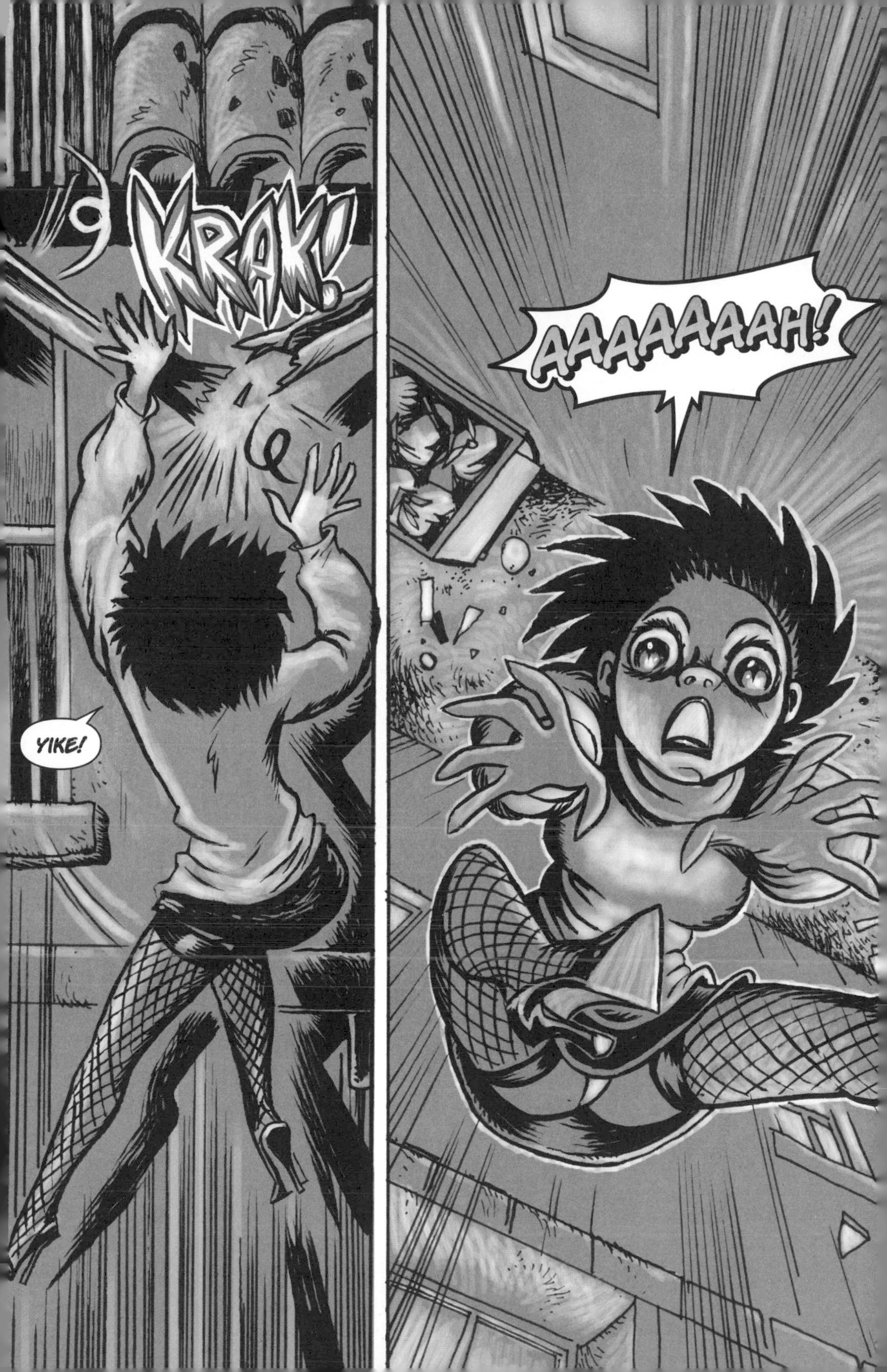
KRAK!
YIKE!
AAAAAAAH!

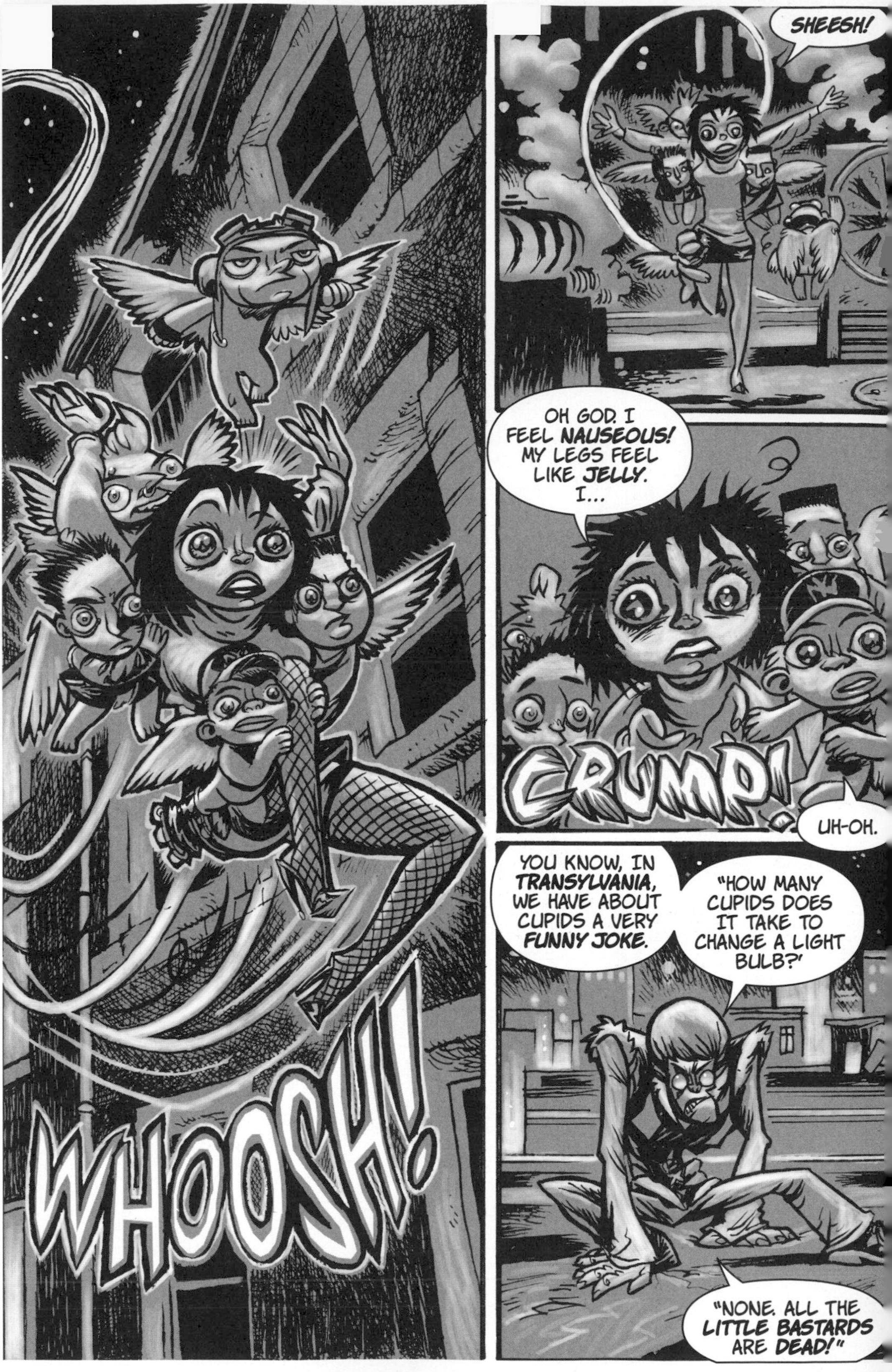
WHOOSH!
SHEESH!
OH GOD. I FEEL NAUSEOUS! MY LEGS FEEL LIKE JELLY. I...
CRUMP!
UH-OH.
YOU KNOW, IN TRANSYLVANIA, WE HAVE ABOUT CUPIDS A VERY FUNNY JOKE.
"HOW MANY CUPIDS DOES IT TAKE TO CHANGE A LIGHT BULB?'
"NONE. ALL THE LITTLE BASTARDS ARE DEAD!"

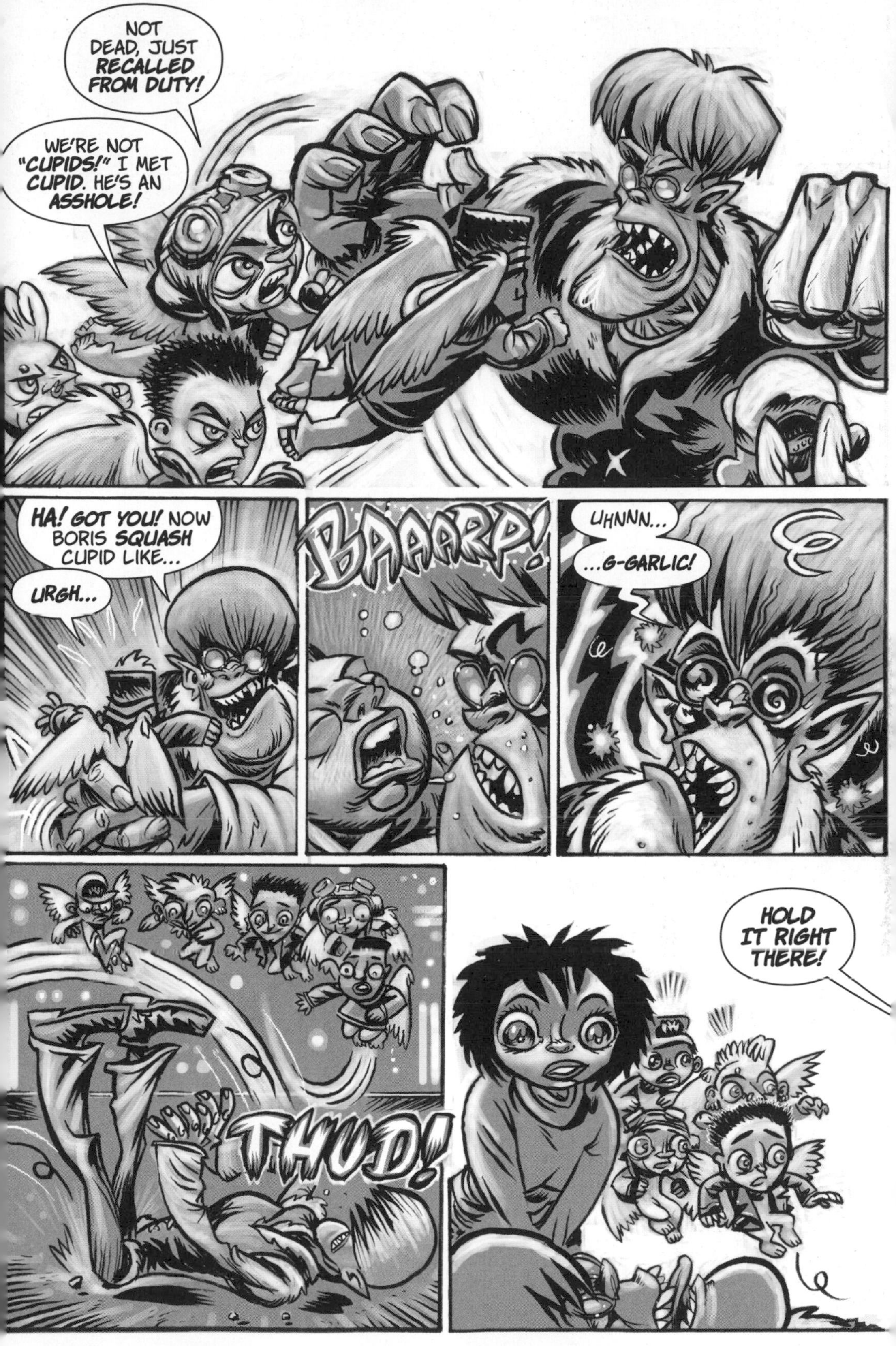

NOT DEAD, JUST RECALLED FROM DUTY!
WE'RE NOT "CUPIDS!" I MET CUPID. HE'S AN ASSHOLE!
HA! GOT YOU! NOW BORIS SQUASH CUPID LIKE...
URGH...
BAAARP!
UHNNN...
...G-GARLIC!
THUD!
HOLD IT RIGHT THERE!

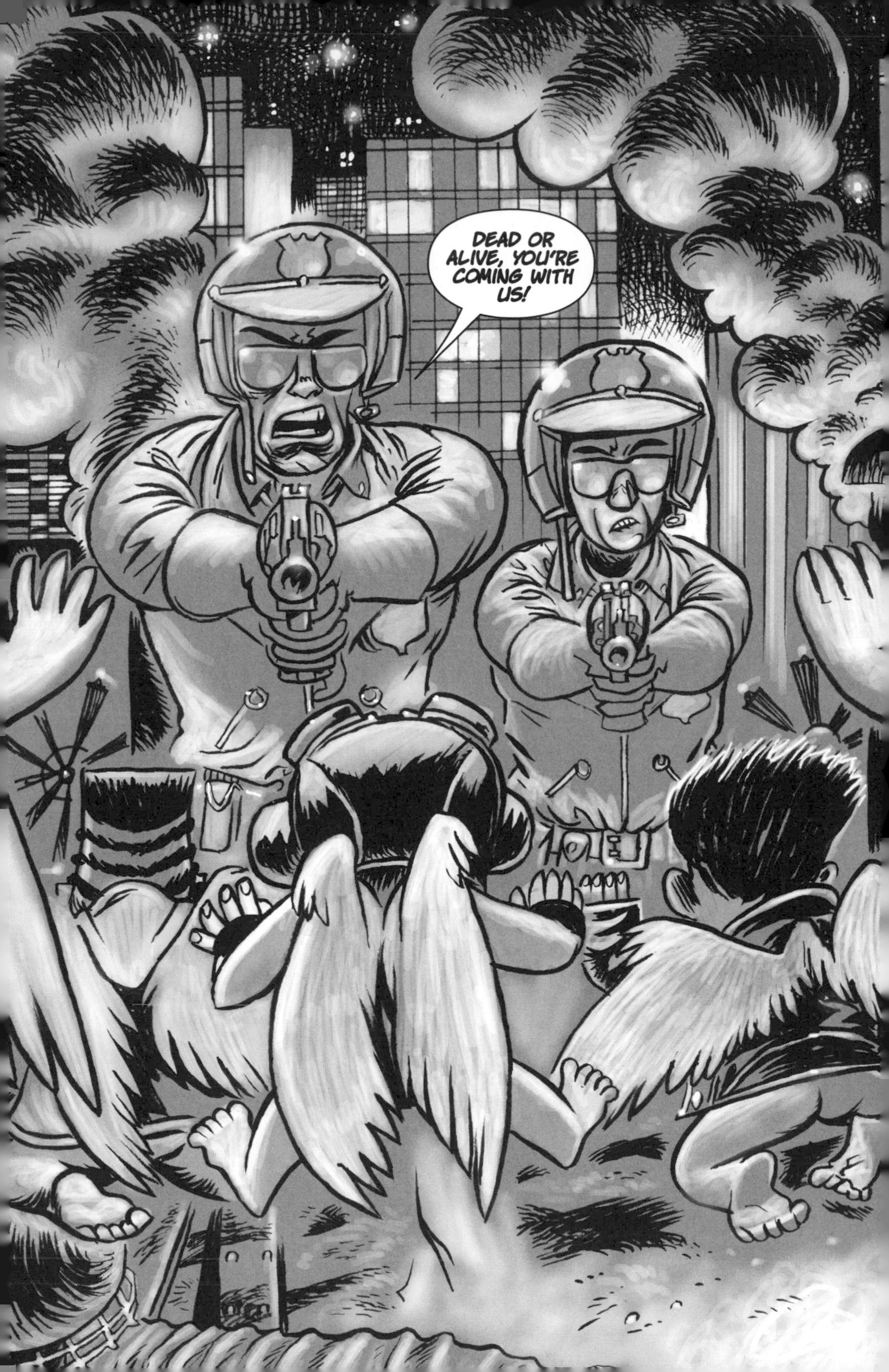
DEAD OR ALIVE, YOU'RE COMING WITH US!

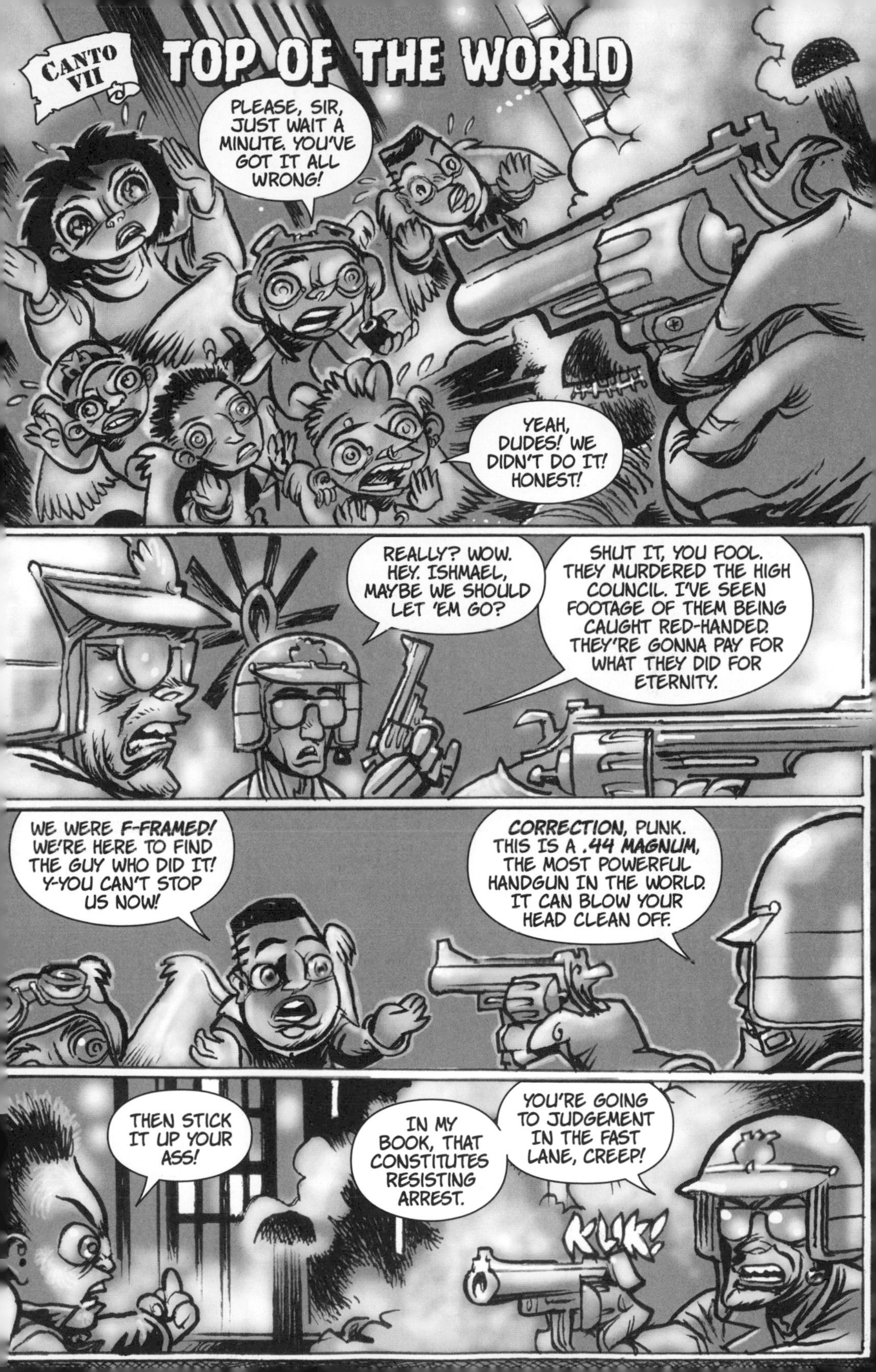
CANTO VII
TOP OF THE WORLD
PLEASE, SIR, JUST WAIT A MINUTE. YOU'VE GOT IT ALL WRONG!
YEAH, DUDES! WE DIDN'T DO IT! HONEST!
REALLY? WOW. HEY. ISHMAEL, MAYBE WE SHOULD LET 'EM GO?
SHUT IT, YOU FOOL. THEY MURDERED THE HIGH COUNCIL. I'VE SEEN FOOTAGE OF THEM BEING CAUGHT RED-HANDED. THEY'RE GONNA PAY FOR WHAT THEY DID FOR ETERNITY.
WE WERE F-FRAMED! WE'RE HERE TO FIND THE GUY WHO DID IT! Y-YOU CAN'T STOP US NOW!
CORRECTION, PUNK. THIS IS A .44 MAGNUM, THE MOST POWERFUL HANDGUN IN THE WORLD. IT CAN BLOW YOUR HEAD CLEAN OFF.
THEN STICK IT UP YOUR ASS!
IN MY BOOK, THAT CONSTITUTES RESISTING ARREST.
YOU'RE GOING TO JUDGEMENT IN THE FAST LANE, CREEP!
KLIK!

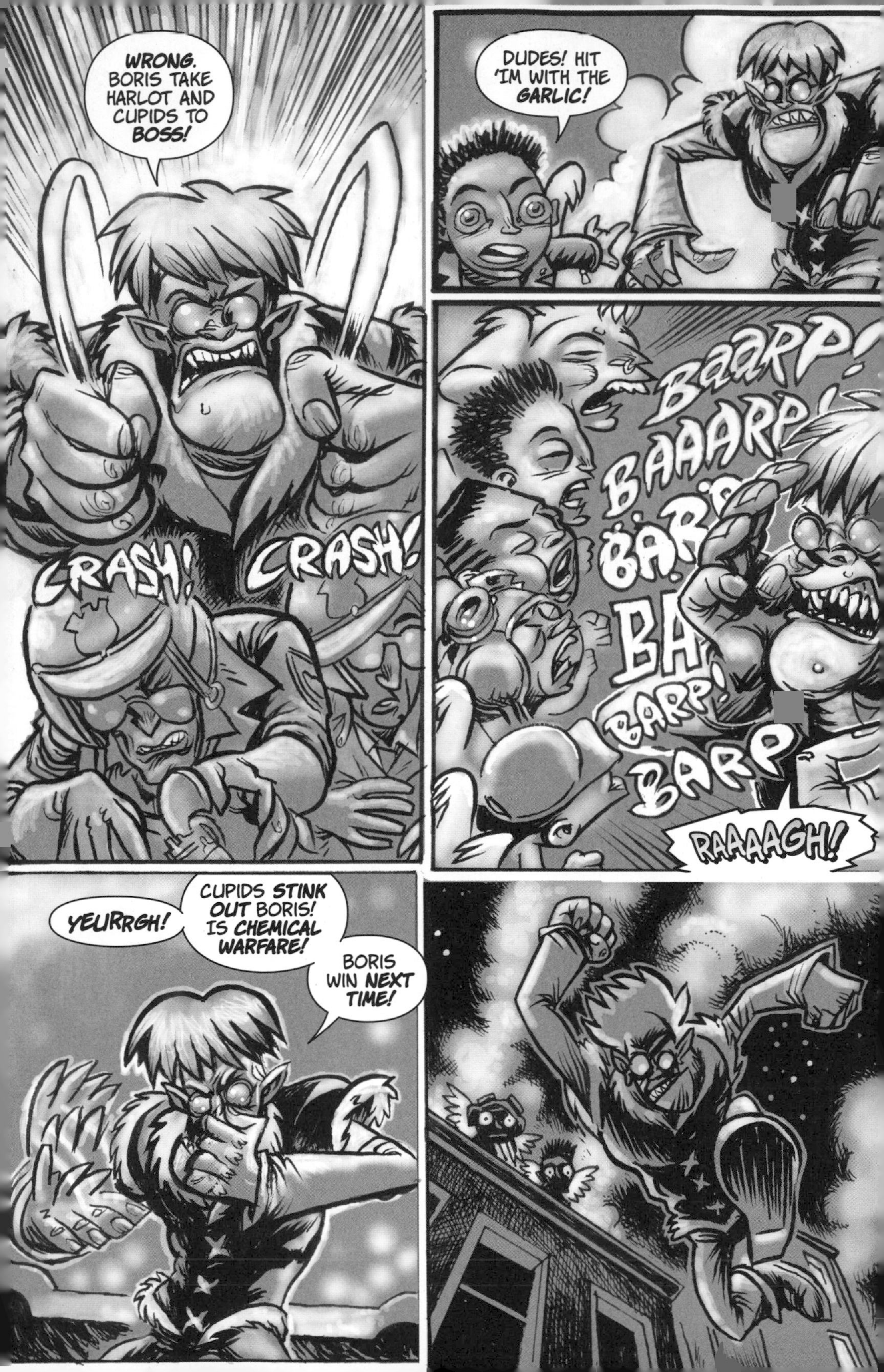
WRONG. BORIS TAKE HARLOT AND CUPIDS TO BOSS!
CRASH!
CRASH!
DUDES! HIT 'IM WITH THE GARLIC!
BAARP!
BAAARP
BAARP
BA
BA
BARP!
BARP
RAAAAGH!
YEURRGH!
CUPIDS STINK OUT BORIS! IS CHEMICAL WARFARE!
BORIS WIN NEXT TIME!

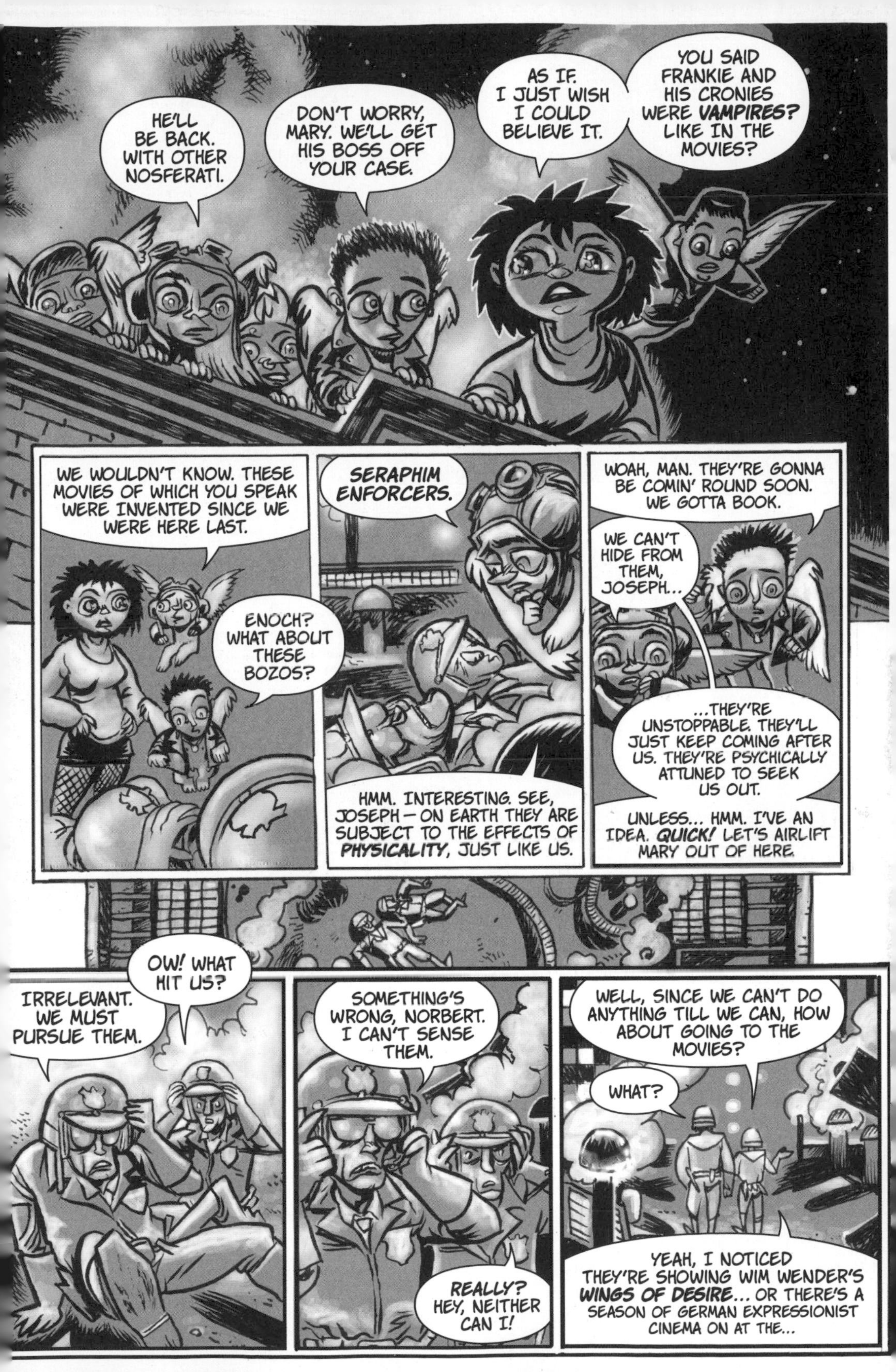

HE'LL BE BACK. WITH OTHER NOSFERATI.
DON'T WORRY, MARY. WE'LL GET HIS BOSS OFF YOUR CASE.
AS IF. I JUST WISH I COULD BELIEVE IT.
YOU SAID FRANKIE AND HIS CRONIES WERE **VAMPIRES?** LIKE IN THE MOVIES?
WE WOULDN'T KNOW. THESE MOVIES OF WHICH YOU SPEAK WERE INVENTED SINCE WE WERE HERE LAST.
ENOCH? WHAT ABOUT THESE BOZOS?
SERAPHIM ENFORCERS.
HMM. INTERESTING. SEE, JOSEPH—ON EARTH THEY ARE SUBJECT TO THE EFFECTS OF ***PHYSICALITY***, JUST LIKE US.
WOAH, MAN. THEY'RE GONNA BE COMIN' ROUND SOON. WE GOTTA BOOK.
WE CAN'T HIDE FROM THEM, JOSEPH...
...THEY'RE UNSTOPPABLE. THEY'LL JUST KEEP COMING AFTER US. THEY'RE PSYCHICALLY ATTUNED TO SEEK US OUT.
UNLESS... HMM. I'VE AN IDEA. ***QUICK!*** LET'S AIRLIFT MARY OUT OF HERE.
OW! WHAT HIT US?
IRRELEVANT. WE MUST PURSUE THEM.
SOMETHING'S WRONG, NORBERT. I CAN'T SENSE THEM.
REALLY? HEY, NEITHER CAN I!
WELL, SINCE WE CAN'T DO ANYTHING TILL WE CAN, HOW ABOUT GOING TO THE MOVIES?
WHAT?
YEAH, I NOTICED THEY'RE SHOWING WIM WENDER'S ***WINGS OF DESIRE***... OR THERE'S A SEASON OF GERMAN EXPRESSIONIST CINEMA ON AT THE...

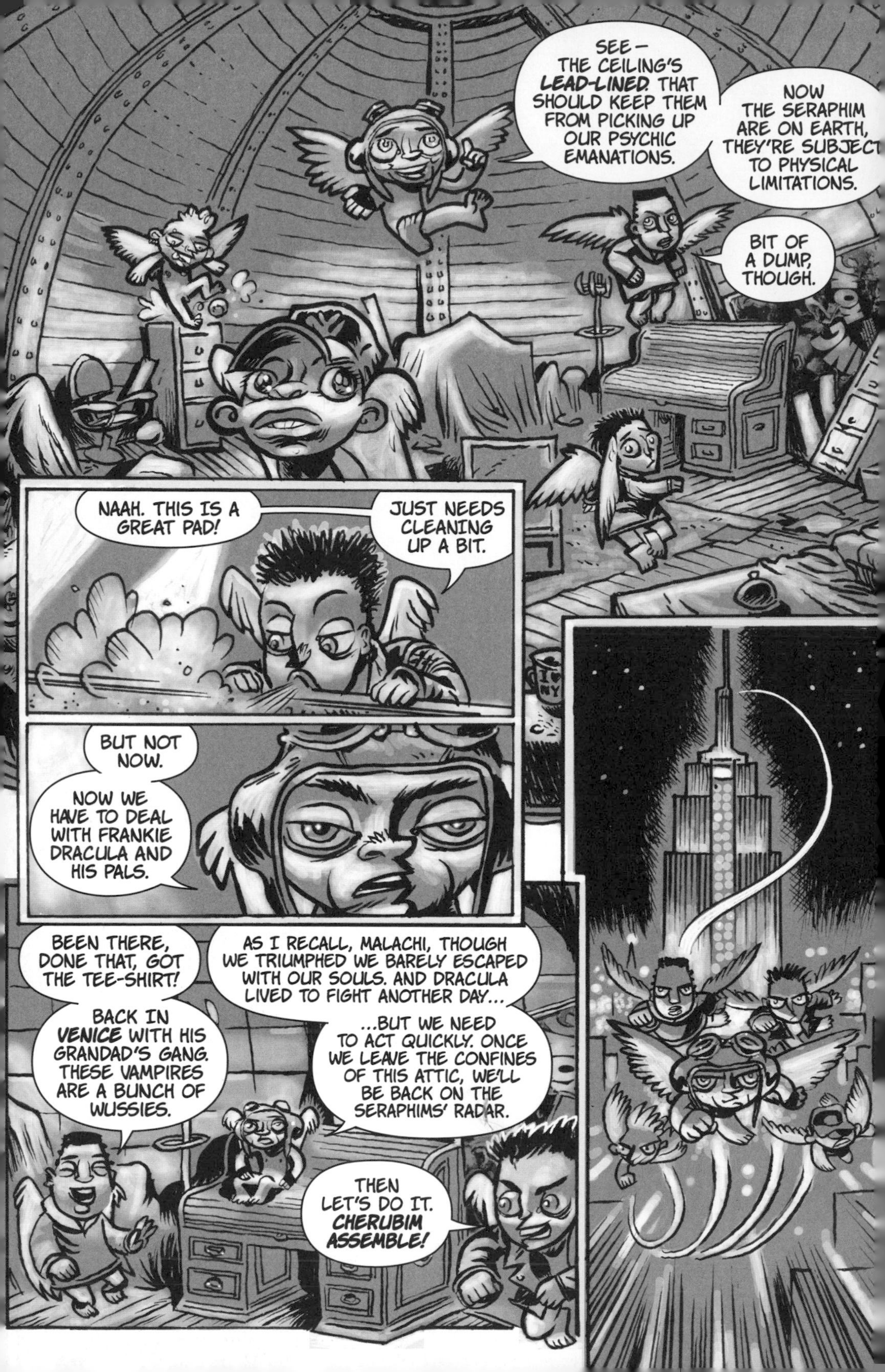
SEE— THE CEILING'S LEAD-LINED. THAT SHOULD KEEP THEM FROM PICKING UP OUR PSYCHIC EMANATIONS.
NOW THE SERAPHIM ARE ON EARTH, THEY'RE SUBJECT TO PHYSICAL LIMITATIONS.
BIT OF A DUMP, THOUGH.
NAAH. THIS IS A GREAT PAD!
JUST NEEDS CLEANING UP A BIT.
I ♥ NY
BUT NOT NOW.
NOW WE HAVE TO DEAL WITH FRANKIE DRACULA AND HIS PALS.
BEEN THERE, DONE THAT, GOT THE TEE-SHIRT!
BACK IN VENICE WITH HIS GRANDAD'S GANG. THESE VAMPIRES ARE A BUNCH OF WUSSIES.
AS I RECALL, MALACHI, THOUGH WE TRIUMPHED WE BARELY ESCAPED WITH OUR SOULS. AND DRACULA LIVED TO FIGHT ANOTHER DAY...
...BUT WE NEED TO ACT QUICKLY. ONCE WE LEAVE THE CONFINES OF THIS ATTIC, WE'LL BE BACK ON THE SERAPHIMS' RADAR.
THEN LET'S DO IT. CHERUBIM ASSEMBLE!

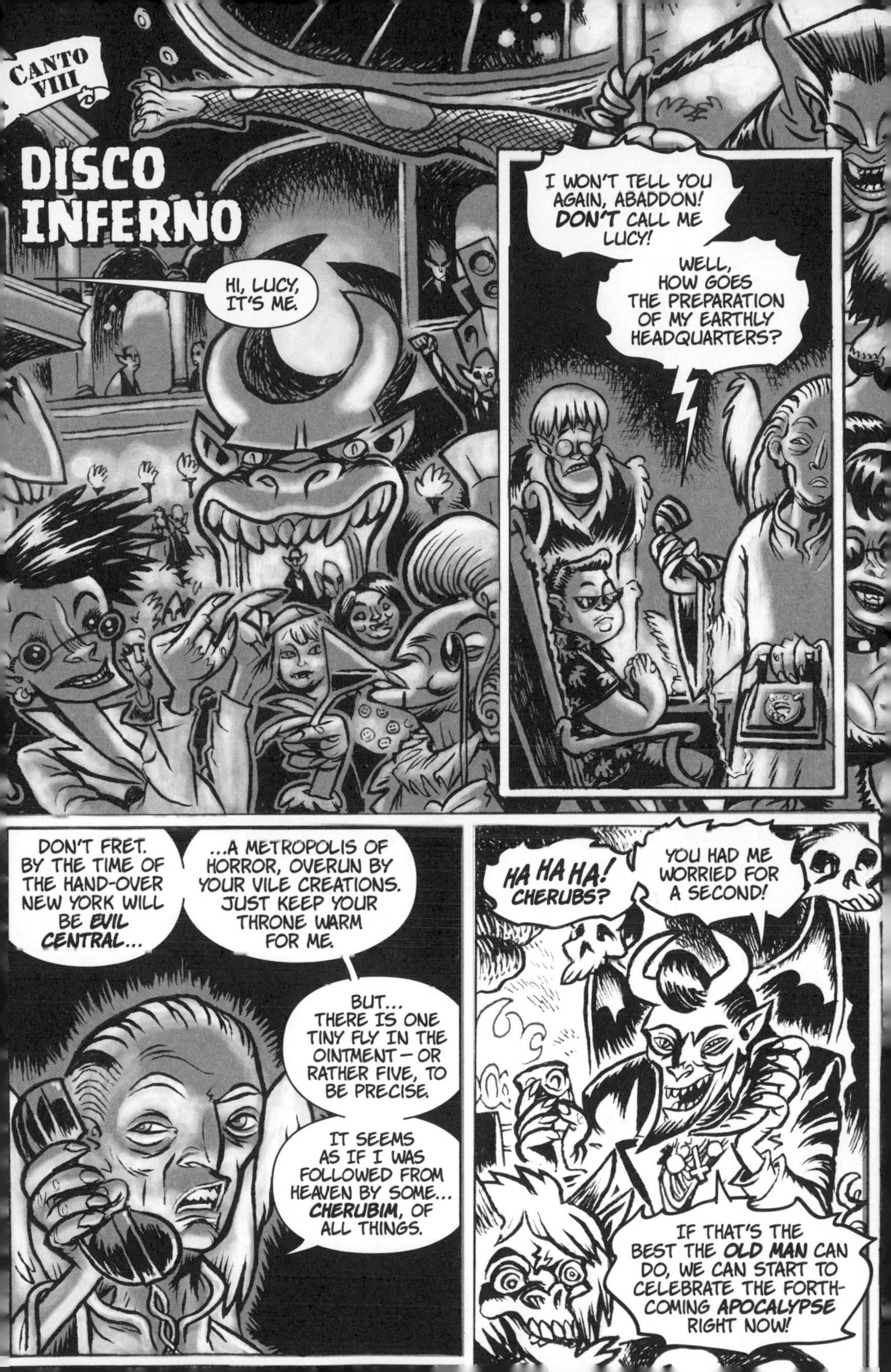
CANTO VIII
DISCO INFERNO
HI, LUCY, IT'S ME.
I WON'T TELL YOU AGAIN, ABADDON! DON'T CALL ME LUCY!
WELL, HOW GOES THE PREPARATION OF MY EARTHLY HEADQUARTERS?
DON'T FRET. BY THE TIME OF THE HAND-OVER NEW YORK WILL BE EVIL CENTRAL...
...A METROPOLIS OF HORROR, OVERRUN BY YOUR VILE CREATIONS. JUST KEEP YOUR THRONE WARM FOR ME.
BUT... THERE IS ONE TINY FLY IN THE OINTMENT — OR RATHER FIVE, TO BE PRECISE.
IT SEEMS AS IF I WAS FOLLOWED FROM HEAVEN BY SOME... CHERUBIM, OF ALL THINGS.
HA HA HA! CHERUBS?
YOU HAD ME WORRIED FOR A SECOND!
IF THAT'S THE BEST THE OLD MAN CAN DO, WE CAN START TO CELEBRATE THE FORTH-COMING APOCALYPSE RIGHT NOW!

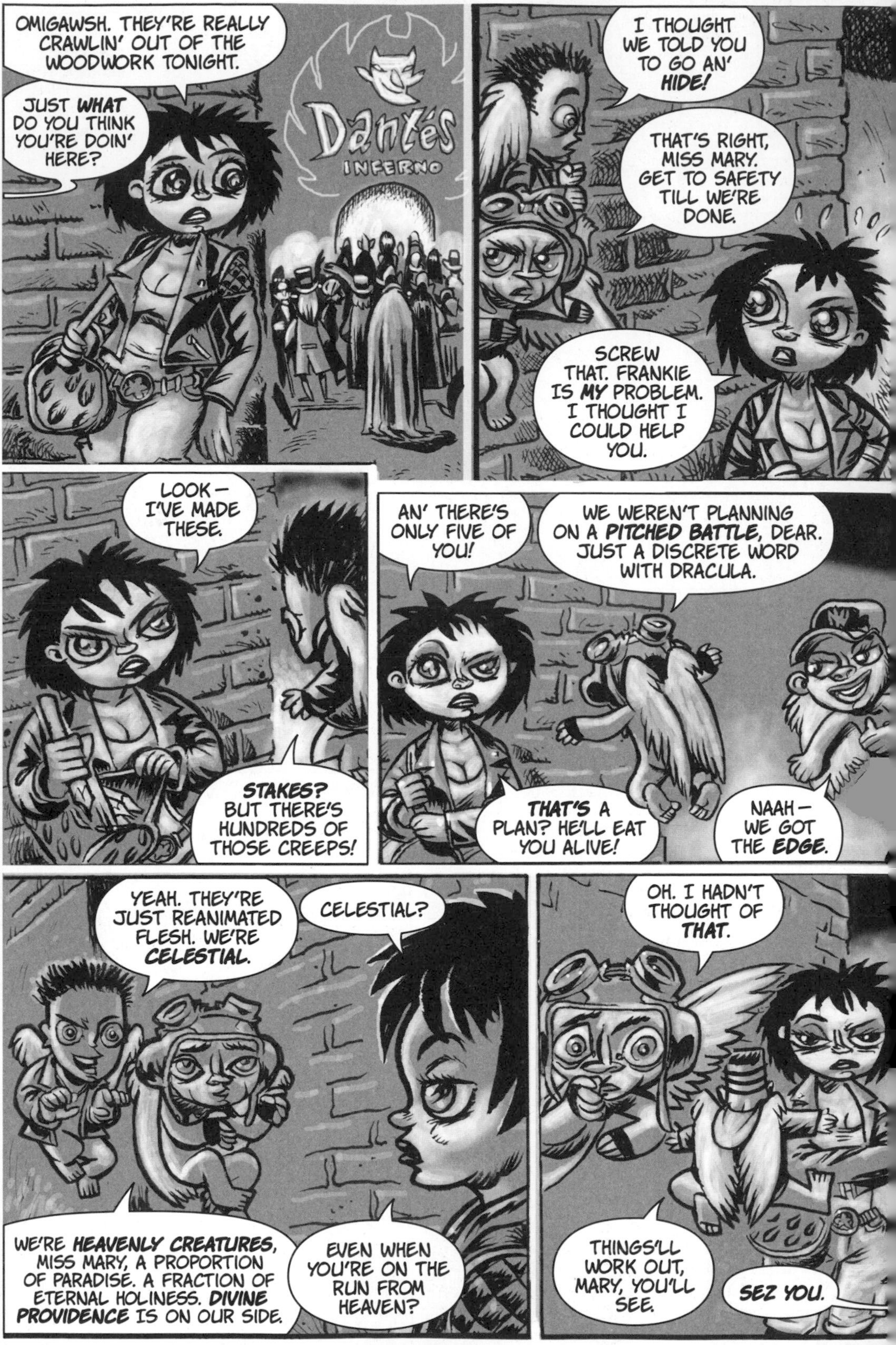
OMIGAWSH. THEY'RE REALLY CRAWLIN' OUT OF THE WOODWORK TONIGHT.
JUST **WHAT** DO YOU THINK YOU'RE DOIN' HERE?
Dante's
INFERNO
I THOUGHT WE TOLD YOU TO GO AN' **HIDE!**
THAT'S RIGHT, MISS MARY. GET TO SAFETY TILL WE'RE DONE.
SCREW THAT. FRANKIE IS **MY** PROBLEM. I THOUGHT I COULD HELP YOU.
LOOK— I'VE MADE THESE.
STAKES? BUT THERE'S HUNDREDS OF THOSE CREEPS!
AN' THERE'S ONLY FIVE OF YOU!
WE WEREN'T PLANNING ON A **PITCHED BATTLE**, DEAR. JUST A DISCRETE WORD WITH DRACULA.
THAT'S A PLAN? HE'LL EAT YOU ALIVE!
NAAH— WE GOT THE **EDGE**.
YEAH. THEY'RE JUST REANIMATED FLESH. WE'RE **CELESTIAL**.
CELESTIAL?
WE'RE **HEAVENLY CREATURES**, MISS MARY, A PROPORTION OF PARADISE. A FRACTION OF ETERNAL HOLINESS. **DIVINE PROVIDENCE** IS ON OUR SIDE.
EVEN WHEN YOU'RE ON THE RUN FROM HEAVEN?
OH. I HADN'T THOUGHT OF **THAT**.
THINGS'LL WORK OUT, MARY, YOU'LL SEE.
SEZ YOU.

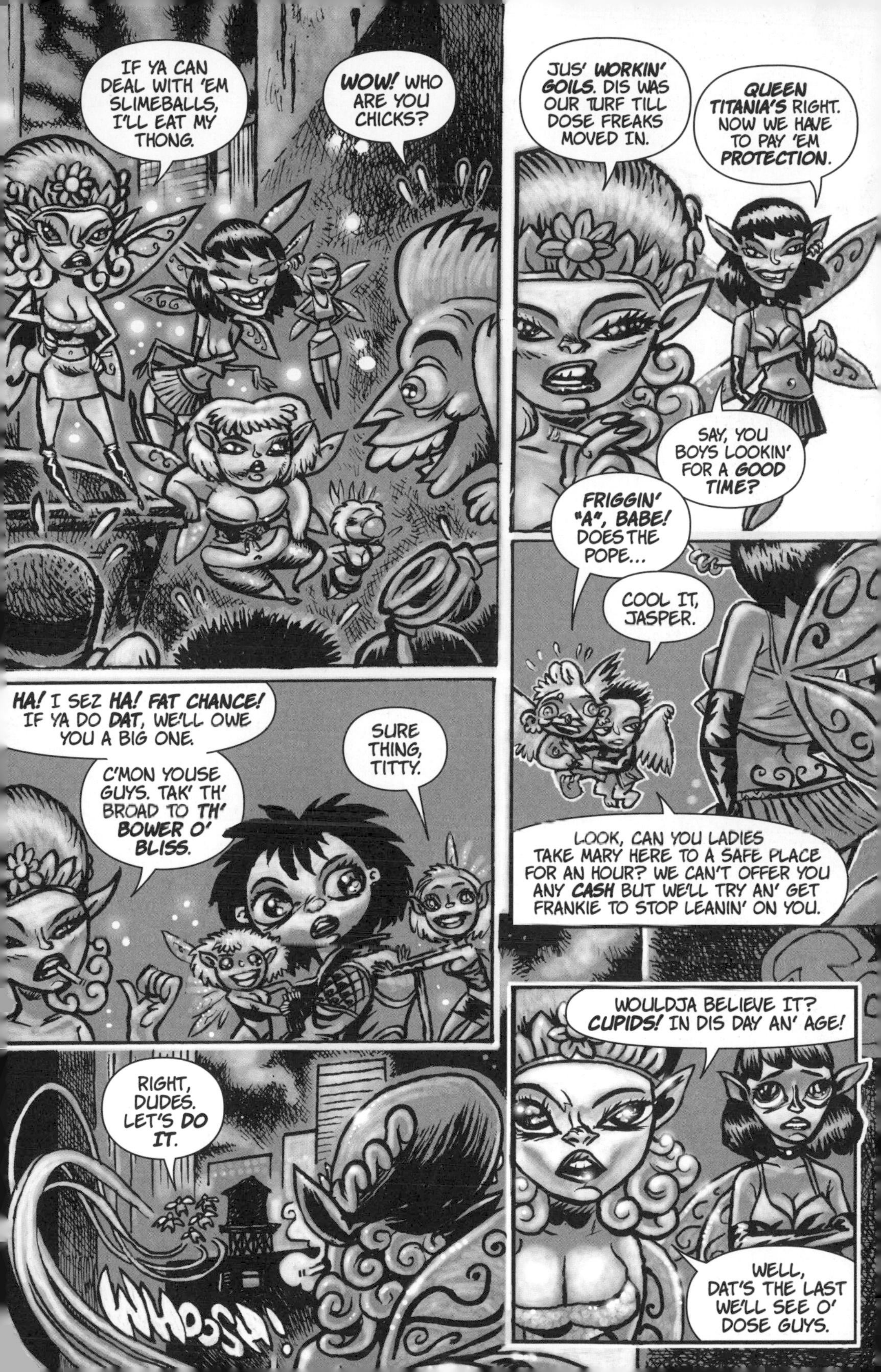
IF YA CAN DEAL WITH 'EM SLIMEBALLS, I'LL EAT MY THONG.
WOW! WHO ARE YOU CHICKS?
JUS' WORKIN' GOILS. DIS WAS OUR TURF TILL DOSE FREAKS MOVED IN.
QUEEN TITANIA'S RIGHT. NOW WE HAVE TO PAY 'EM PROTECTION.
SAY, YOU BOYS LOOKIN' FOR A GOOD TIME?
FRIGGIN' "A", BABE! DOES THE POPE...
COOL IT, JASPER.
LOOK, CAN YOU LADIES TAKE MARY HERE TO A SAFE PLACE FOR AN HOUR? WE CAN'T OFFER YOU ANY CASH BUT WE'LL TRY AN' GET FRANKIE TO STOP LEANIN' ON YOU.
HA! I SEZ HA! FAT CHANCE! IF YA DO DAT, WE'LL OWE YOU A BIG ONE.
C'MON YOUSE GUYS. TAK' TH' BROAD TO TH' BOWER O' BLISS.
SURE THING, TITTY.
RIGHT, DUDES. LET'S DO IT.
WHOOSH!
WOULDJA BELIEVE IT? CUPIDS! IN DIS DAY AN' AGE!
WELL, DAT'S THE LAST WE'LL SEE O' DOSE GUYS.

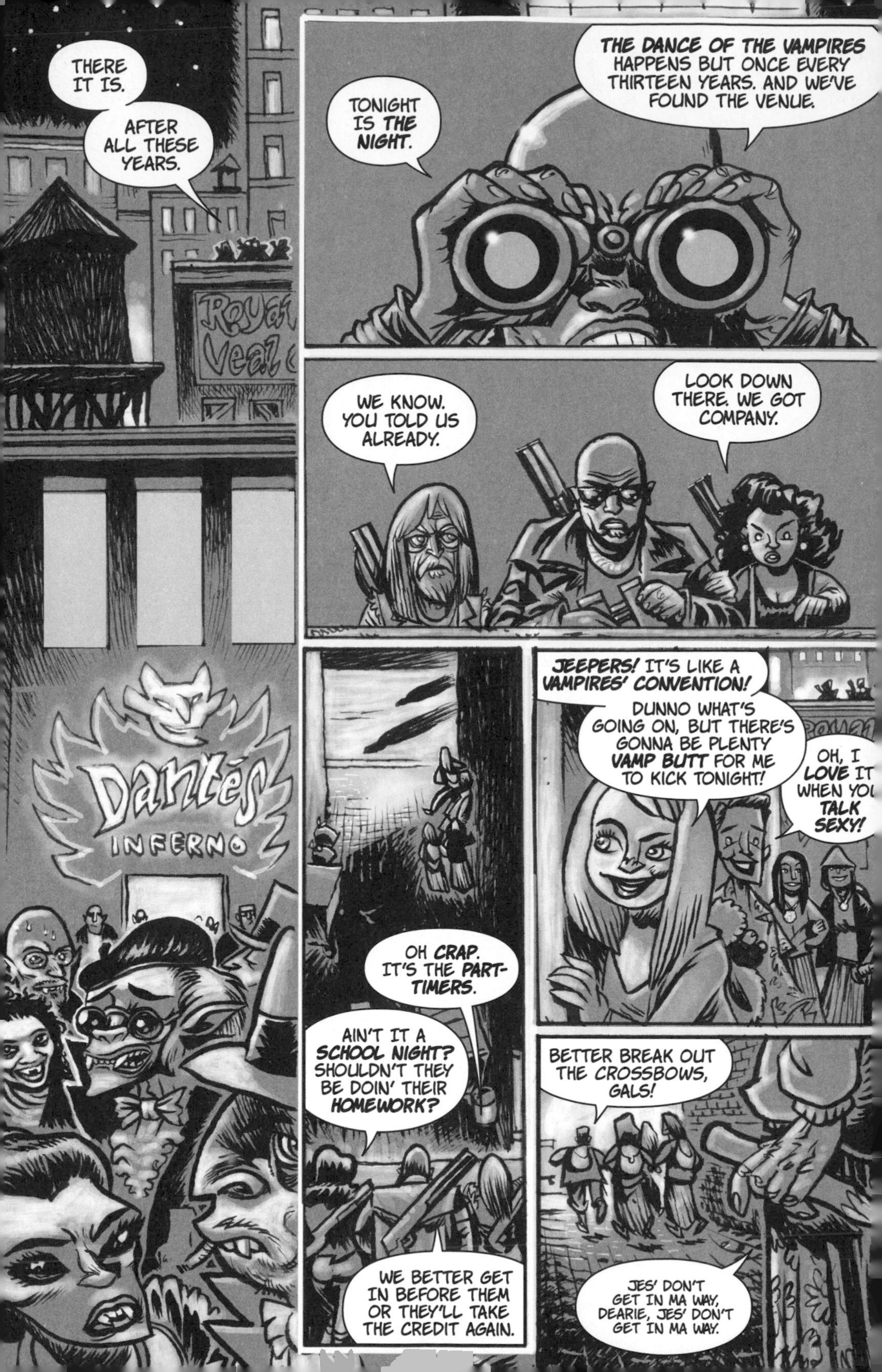
THERE IT IS.
AFTER ALL THESE YEARS.
TONIGHT IS THE NIGHT.
THE DANCE OF THE VAMPIRES HAPPENS BUT ONCE EVERY THIRTEEN YEARS. AND WE'VE FOUND THE VENUE.
WE KNOW. YOU TOLD US ALREADY.
LOOK DOWN THERE. WE GOT COMPANY.
Dantés INFERNO
JEEPERS! IT'S LIKE A VAMPIRES' CONVENTION!
DUNNO WHAT'S GOING ON, BUT THERE'S GONNA BE PLENTY VAMP BUTT FOR ME TO KICK TONIGHT!
OH, I LOVE IT WHEN YOU TALK SEXY!
OH CRAP. IT'S THE PART-TIMERS.
AIN'T IT A SCHOOL NIGHT? SHOULDN'T THEY BE DOIN' THEIR HOMEWORK?
WE BETTER GET IN BEFORE THEM OR THEY'LL TAKE THE CREDIT AGAIN.
BETTER BREAK OUT THE CROSSBOWS, GALS!
JES' DON'T GET IN MA WAY, DEARIE, JES' DON'T GET IN MA WAY.

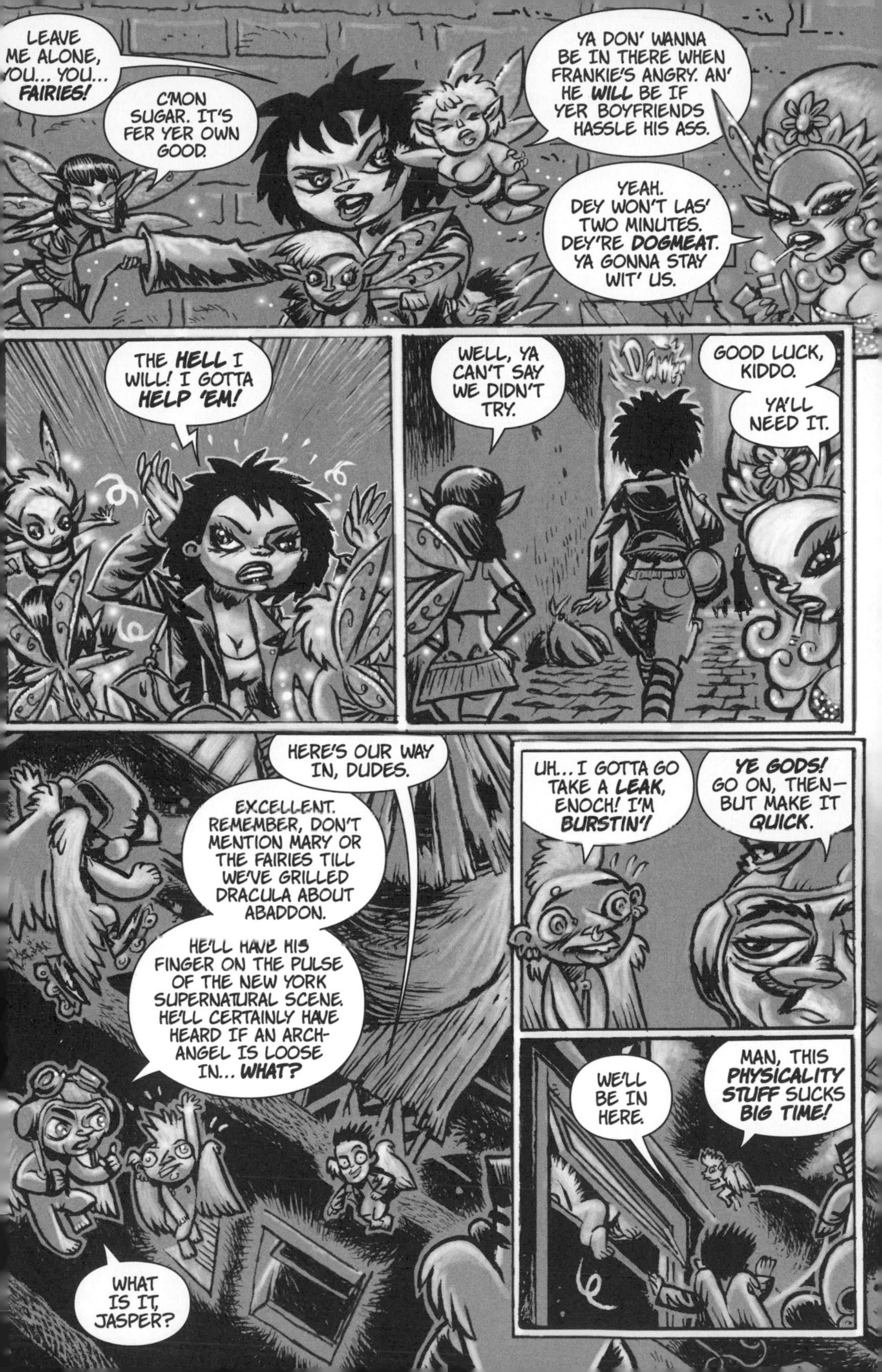
LEAVE ME ALONE, YOU... YOU... FAIRIES!
C'MON SUGAR. IT'S FER YER OWN GOOD.
YA DON' WANNA BE IN THERE WHEN FRANKIE'S ANGRY. AN' HE WILL BE IF YER BOYFRIENDS HASSLE HIS ASS.
YEAH. DEY WON'T LAS' TWO MINUTES. DEY'RE DOGMEAT. YA GONNA STAY WIT' US.
THE HELL I WILL! I GOTTA HELP 'EM!
WELL, YA CAN'T SAY WE DIDN'T TRY.
GOOD LUCK, KIDDO.
YA'LL NEED IT.
HERE'S OUR WAY IN, DUDES.
EXCELLENT. REMEMBER, DON'T MENTION MARY OR THE FAIRIES TILL WE'VE GRILLED DRACULA ABOUT ABADDON.
HE'LL HAVE HIS FINGER ON THE PULSE OF THE NEW YORK SUPERNATURAL SCENE. HE'LL CERTAINLY HAVE HEARD IF AN ARCH-ANGEL IS LOOSE IN... WHAT?
WHAT IS IT, JASPER?
UH... I GOTTA GO TAKE A LEAK, ENOCH! I'M BURSTIN'!
YE GODS! GO ON, THEN— BUT MAKE IT QUICK.
WE'LL BE IN HERE.
MAN, THIS PHYSICALITY STUFF SUCKS BIG TIME!

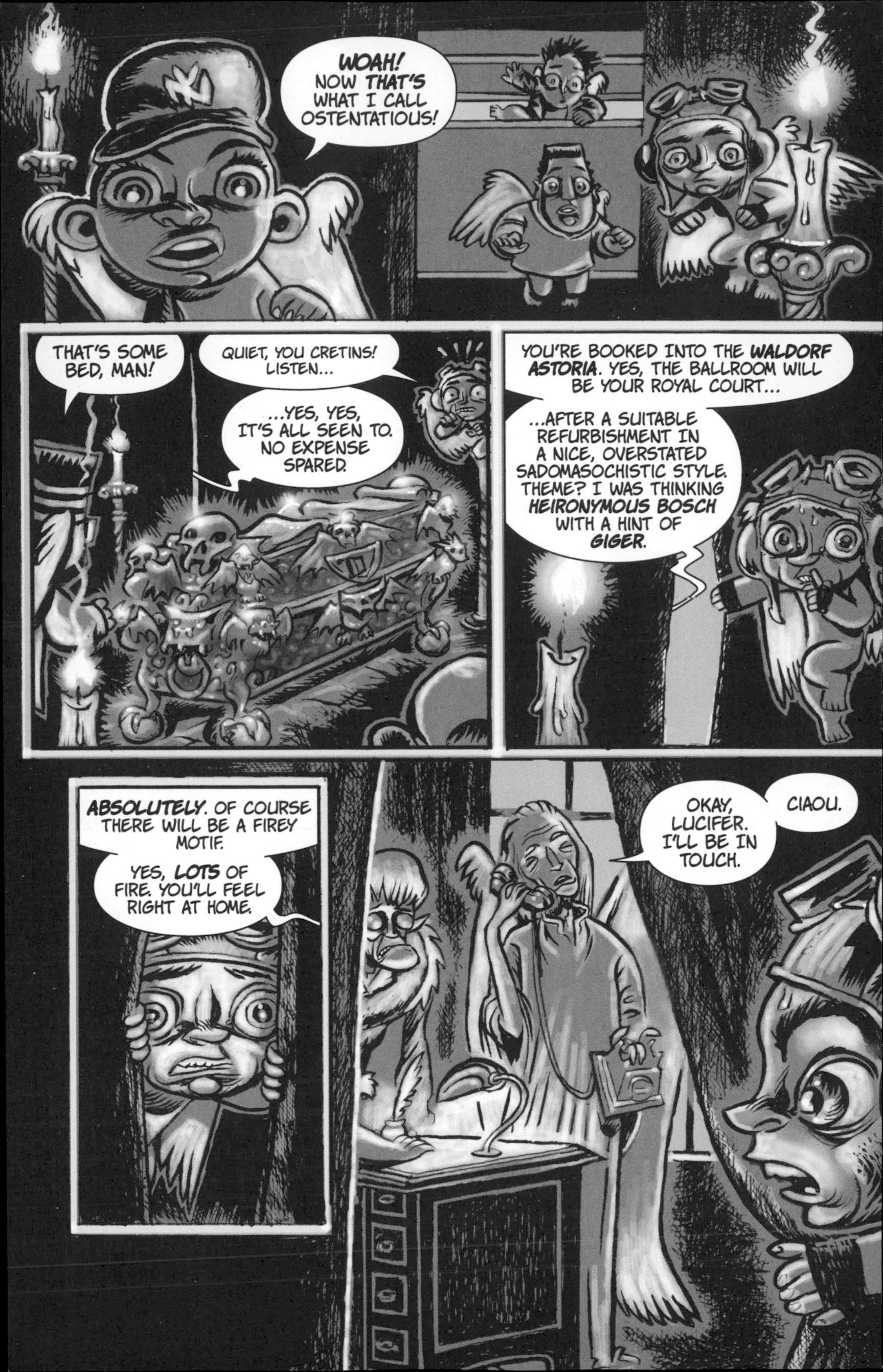
WOAH! NOW THAT'S WHAT I CALL OSTENTATIOUS!
THAT'S SOME BED, MAN!
QUIET, YOU CRETINS! LISTEN...
...YES, YES, IT'S ALL SEEN TO. NO EXPENSE SPARED.
YOU'RE BOOKED INTO THE WALDORF ASTORIA. YES, THE BALLROOM WILL BE YOUR ROYAL COURT...
...AFTER A SUITABLE REFURBISHMENT IN A NICE, OVERSTATED SADOMASOCHISTIC STYLE. THEME? I WAS THINKING HEIRONYMOUS BOSCH WITH A HINT OF GIGER.
ABSOLUTELY. OF COURSE THERE WILL BE A FIREY MOTIF.
YES, LOTS OF FIRE. YOU'LL FEEL RIGHT AT HOME.
OKAY, LUCIFER. I'LL BE IN TOUCH.
CIAOU.

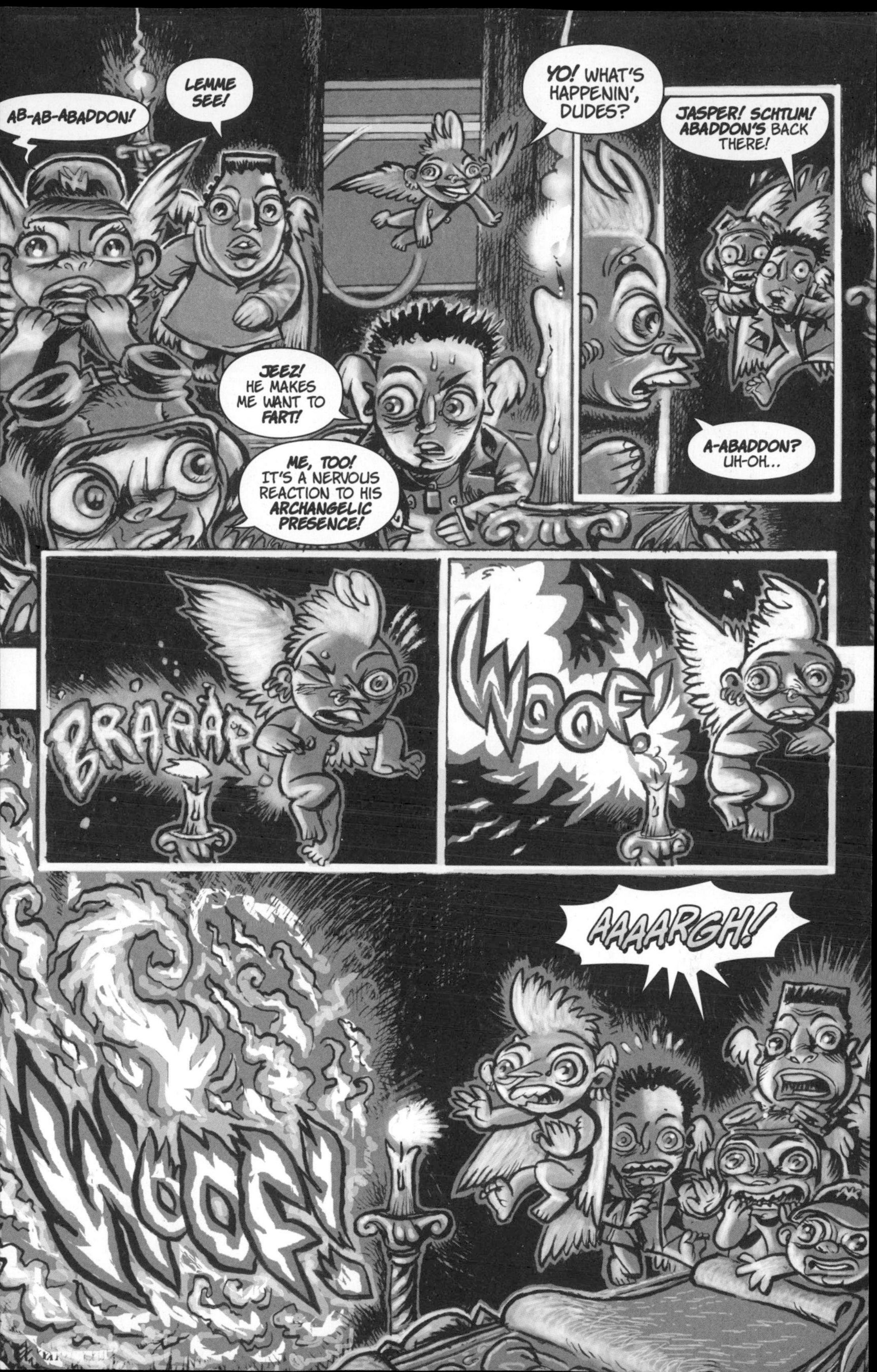
AB-AB-ABADDON!
LEMME SEE!
YO! WHAT'S HAPPENIN', DUDES?
JASPER! SCHTUM! ABADDON'S BACK THERE!
JEEZ! HE MAKES ME WANT TO FART!
ME, TOO! IT'S A NERVOUS REACTION TO HIS ARCHANGELIC PRESENCE!
A-ABADDON? UH-OH...
BRAAAP
WOOF!
AAAARGH!
WOOF!

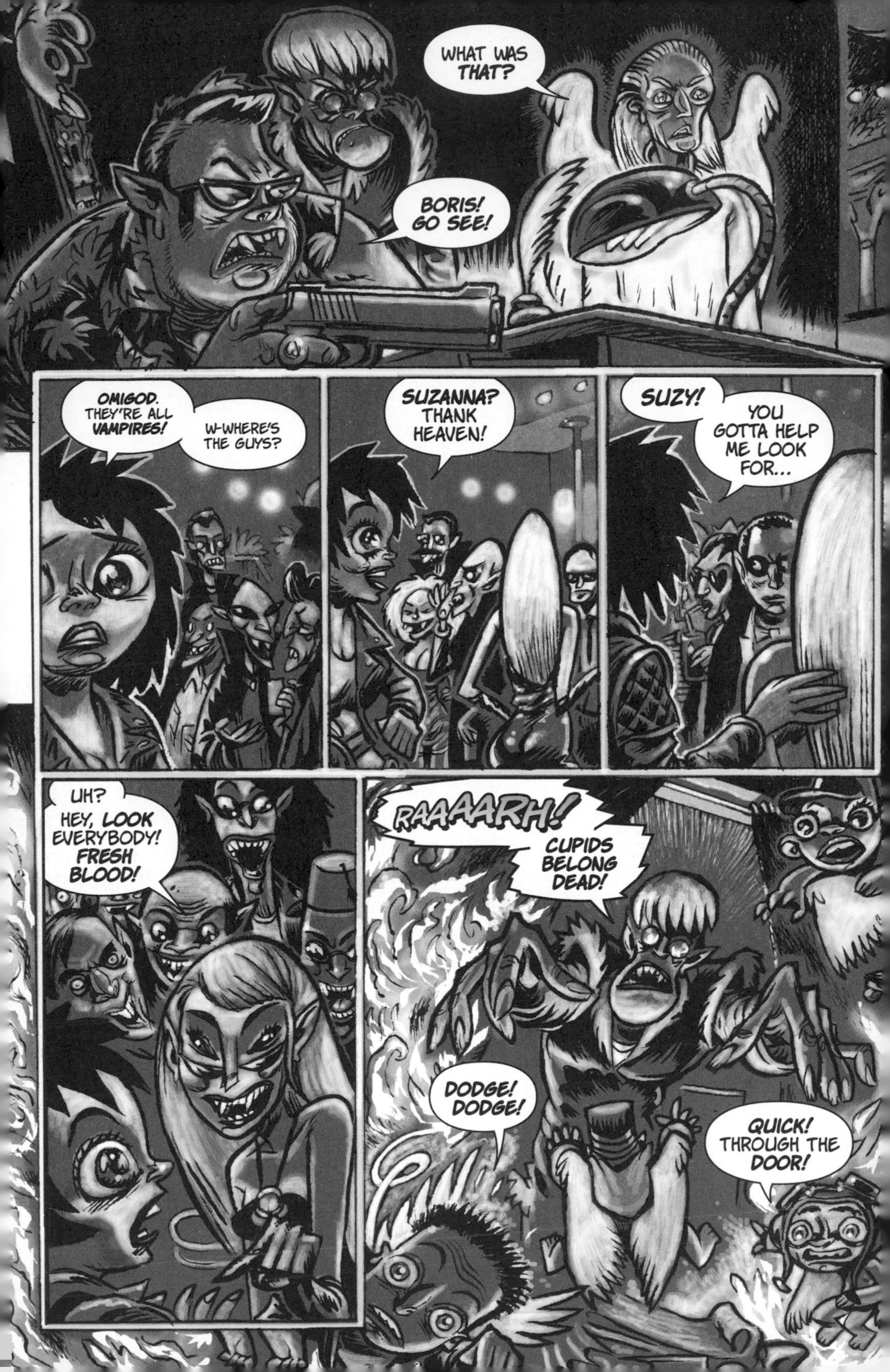
WHAT WAS THAT?
BORIS! GO SEE!
OMIGOD. THEY'RE ALL VAMPIRES!
W-WHERE'S THE GUYS?
SUZANNA? THANK HEAVEN!
SUZY!
YOU GOTTA HELP ME LOOK FOR...
UH?
HEY, LOOK EVERYBODY! FRESH BLOOD!
RAAAARH!
CUPIDS BELONG DEAD!
DODGE! DODGE!
QUICK! THROUGH THE DOOR!

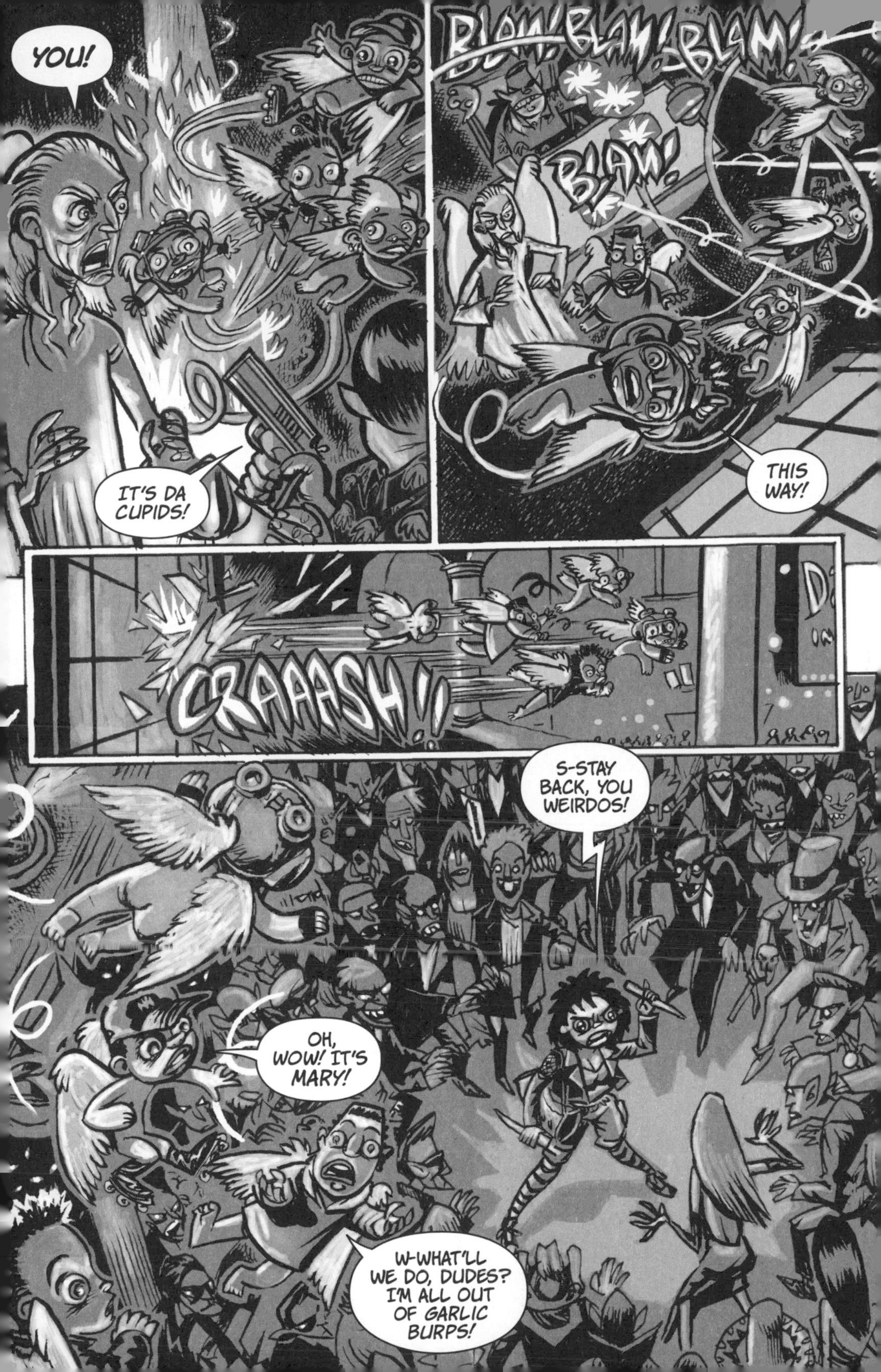
YOU!
IT'S DA CUPIDS!
BLAM! BLAM! BLAM!
BLAM!
THIS WAY!
CRAAASH!!
S-STAY BACK, YOU WEIRDOS!
OH, WOW! IT'S MARY!
W-WHAT'LL WE DO, DUDES? I'M ALL OUT OF GARLIC BURPS!

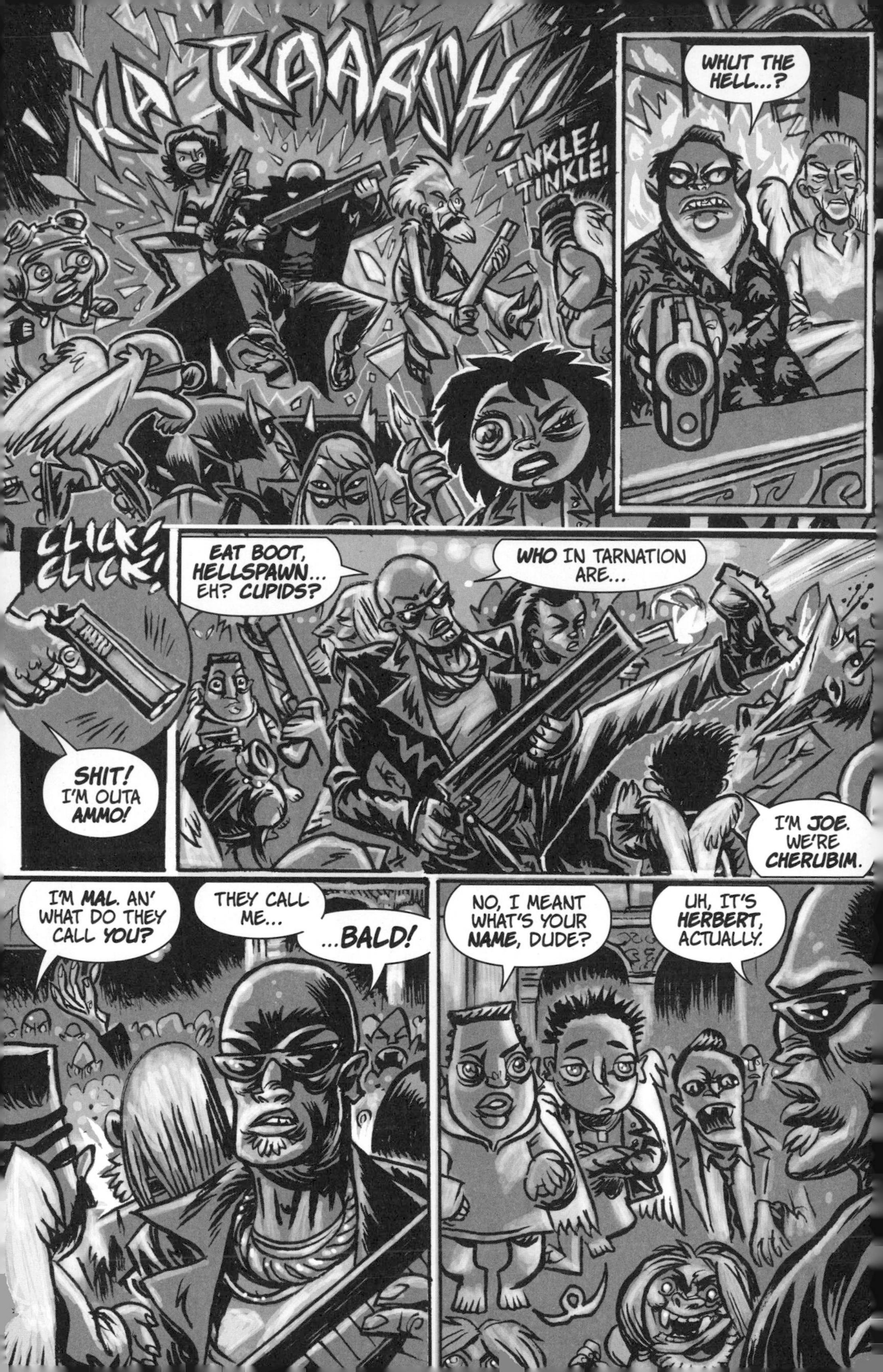
KA-RAASH!
TINKLE! TINKLE!
WHUT THE HELL...?
CLICK! CLICK!
SHIT! I'M OUTA AMMO!
EAT BOOT, HELLSPAWN... EH? CUPIDS?
WHO IN TARNATION ARE...
I'M JOE. WE'RE CHERUBIM.
I'M MAL. AN' WHAT DO THEY CALL YOU?
THEY CALL ME...
...BALD!
NO, I MEANT WHAT'S YOUR NAME, DUDE?
UH, IT'S HERBERT, ACTUALLY.

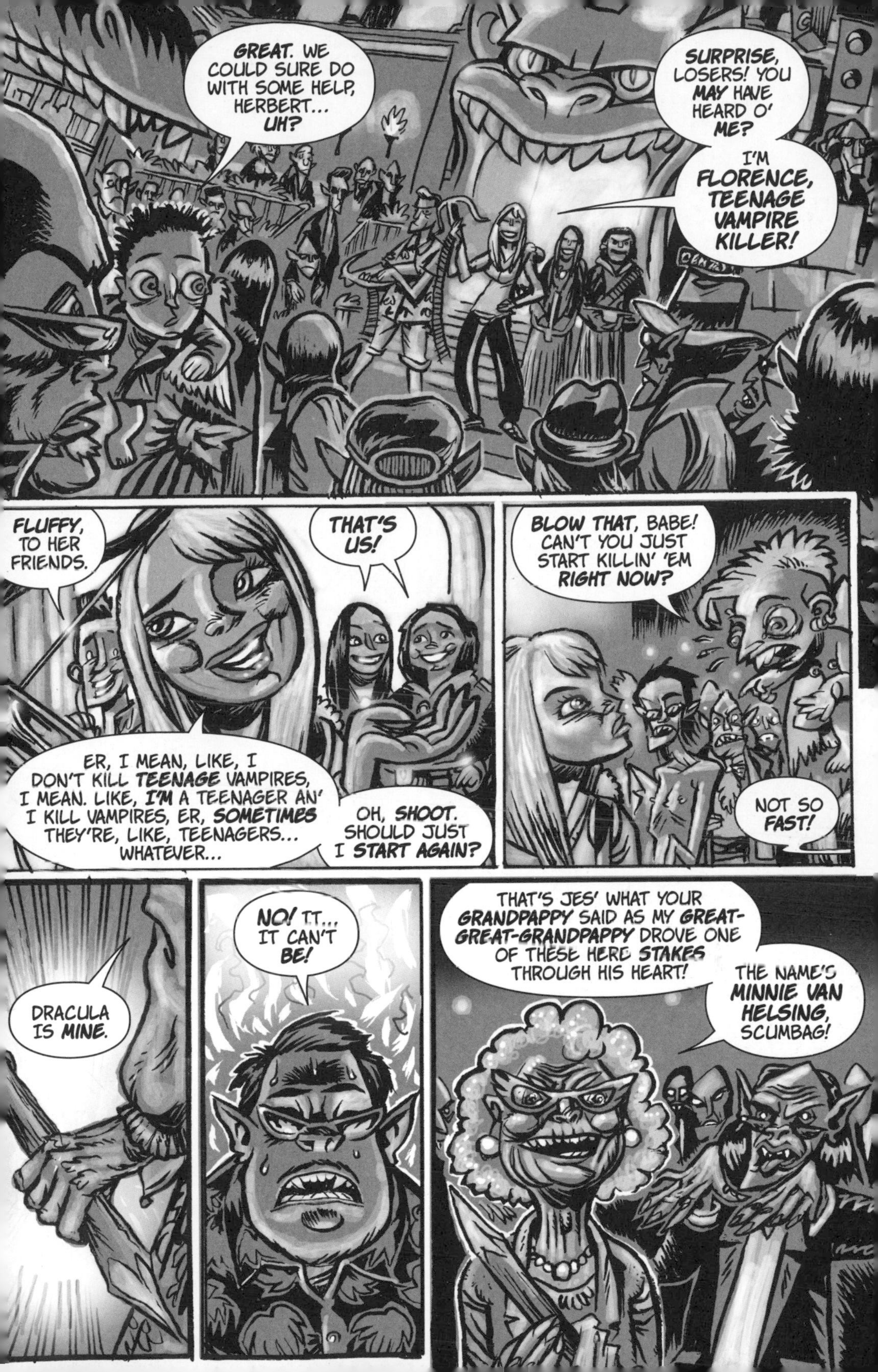
GREAT. WE COULD SURE DO WITH SOME HELP, HERBERT... UH?
SURPRISE, LOSERS! YOU MAY HAVE HEARD O' ME?
I'M FLORENCE, TEENAGE VAMPIRE KILLER!
FLUFFY, TO HER FRIENDS.
THAT'S US!
ER, I MEAN, LIKE, I DON'T KILL TEENAGE VAMPIRES, I MEAN. LIKE, I'M A TEENAGER AN' I KILL VAMPIRES, ER, SOMETIMES THEY'RE, LIKE, TEENAGERS... WHATEVER...
OH, SHOOT. SHOULD JUST I START AGAIN?
BLOW THAT, BABE! CAN'T YOU JUST START KILLIN' 'EM RIGHT NOW?
NOT SO FAST!
DRACULA IS MINE.
NO! IT... IT CAN'T BE!
THAT'S JES' WHAT YOUR GRANDPAPPY SAID AS MY GREAT-GREAT-GRANDPAPPY DROVE ONE OF THESE HERE STAKES THROUGH HIS HEART!
THE NAME'S MINNIE VAN HELSING, SCUMBAG!

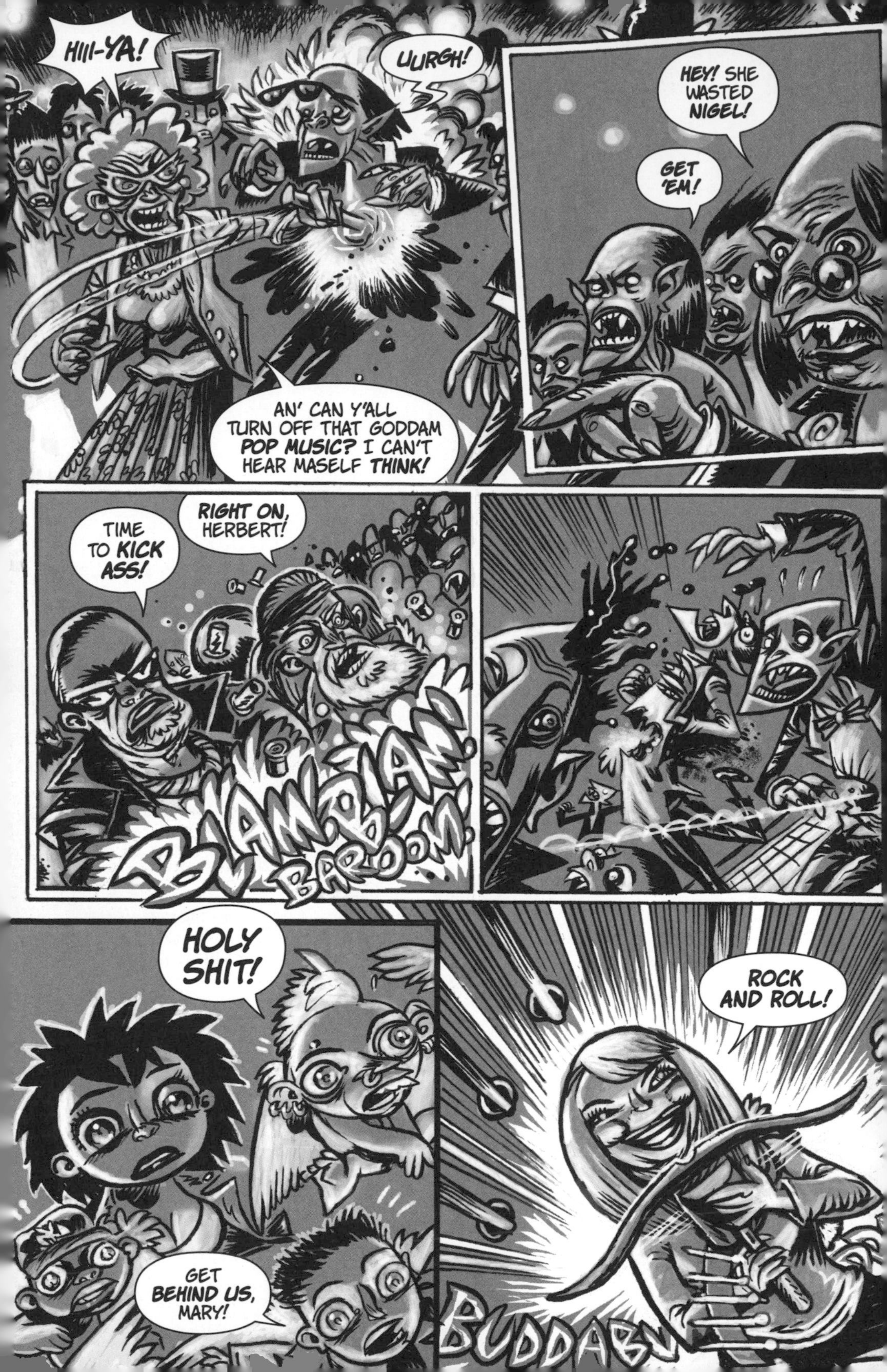
HIII-YA!
UURGH!
HEY! SHE WASTED NIGEL!
GET 'EM!
AN' CAN Y'ALL TURN OFF THAT GODDAM POP MUSIC? I CAN'T HEAR MASELF THINK!
TIME TO KICK ASS!
RIGHT ON, HERBERT!
BLAM BLAM!
BAROOM!
HOLY SHIT!
GET BEHIND US, MARY!
ROCK AND ROLL!
BUDDABL

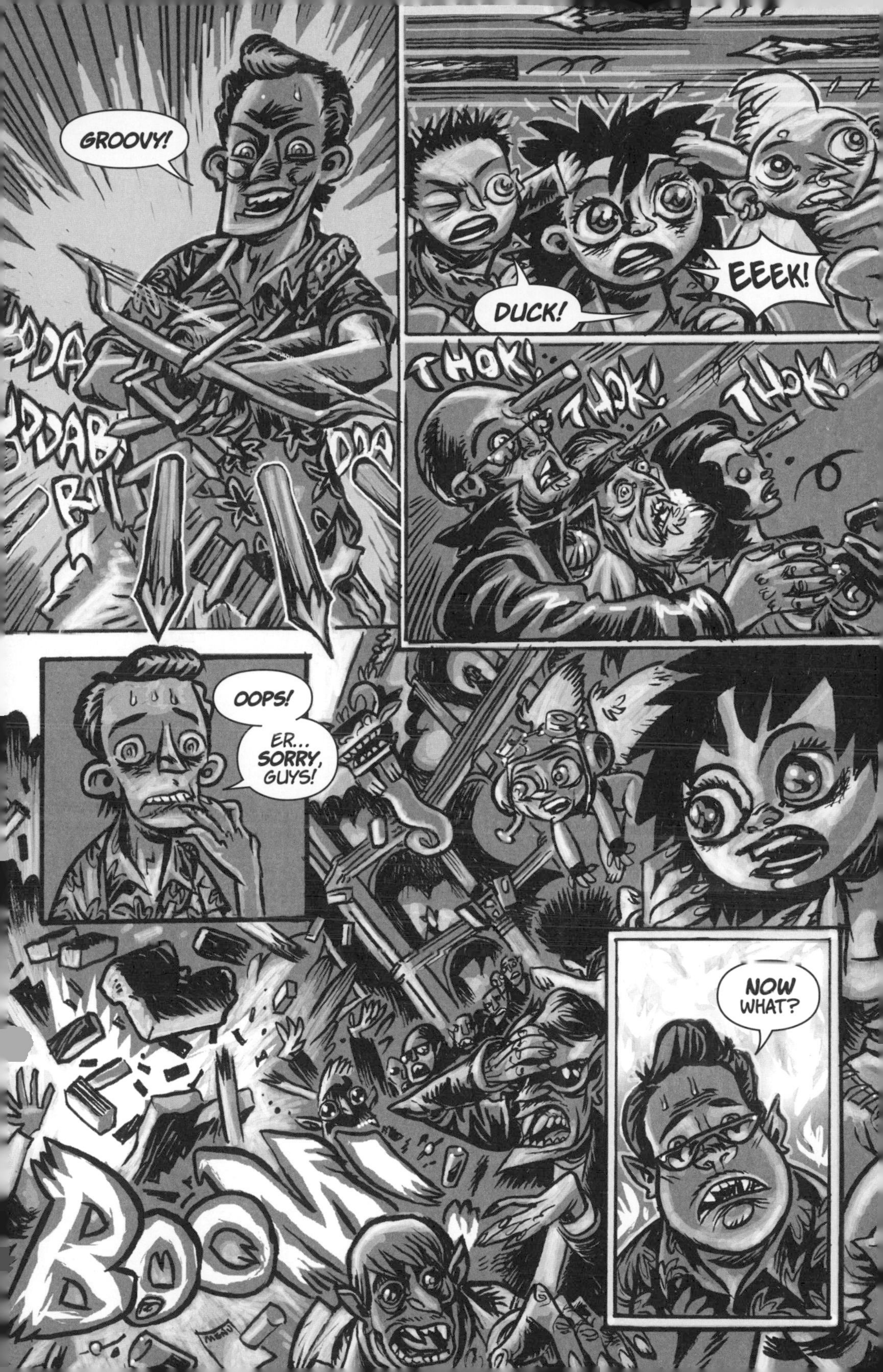
GROOVY!
DUCK!
EEEK!
THOK!
THOK!
THOK!
OOPS!
ER... SORRY, GUYS!
NOW WHAT?

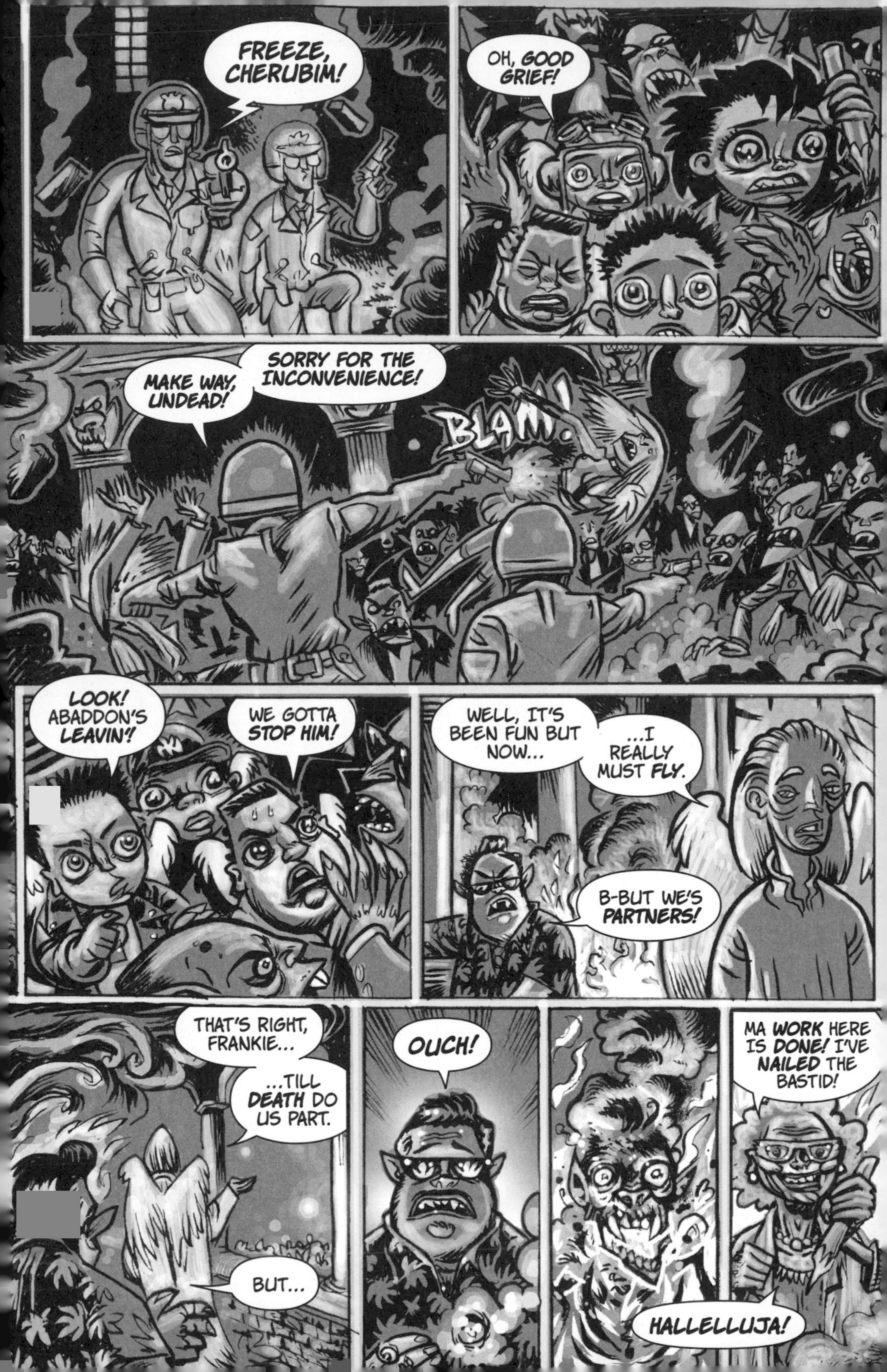
FREEZE, CHERUBIM!
OH, GOOD GRIEF!
MAKE WAY, UNDEAD!
SORRY FOR THE INCONVENIENCE!
BLAM!
LOOK! ABADDON'S LEAVIN'!
WE GOTTA STOP HIM!
WELL, IT'S BEEN FUN BUT NOW...
...I REALLY MUST FLY.
B-BUT WE'S PARTNERS!
THAT'S RIGHT, FRANKIE...
...TILL DEATH DO US PART.
BUT...
OUCH!
MA WORK HERE IS DONE! I'VE NAILED THE BASTID!
HALLELLUJA!

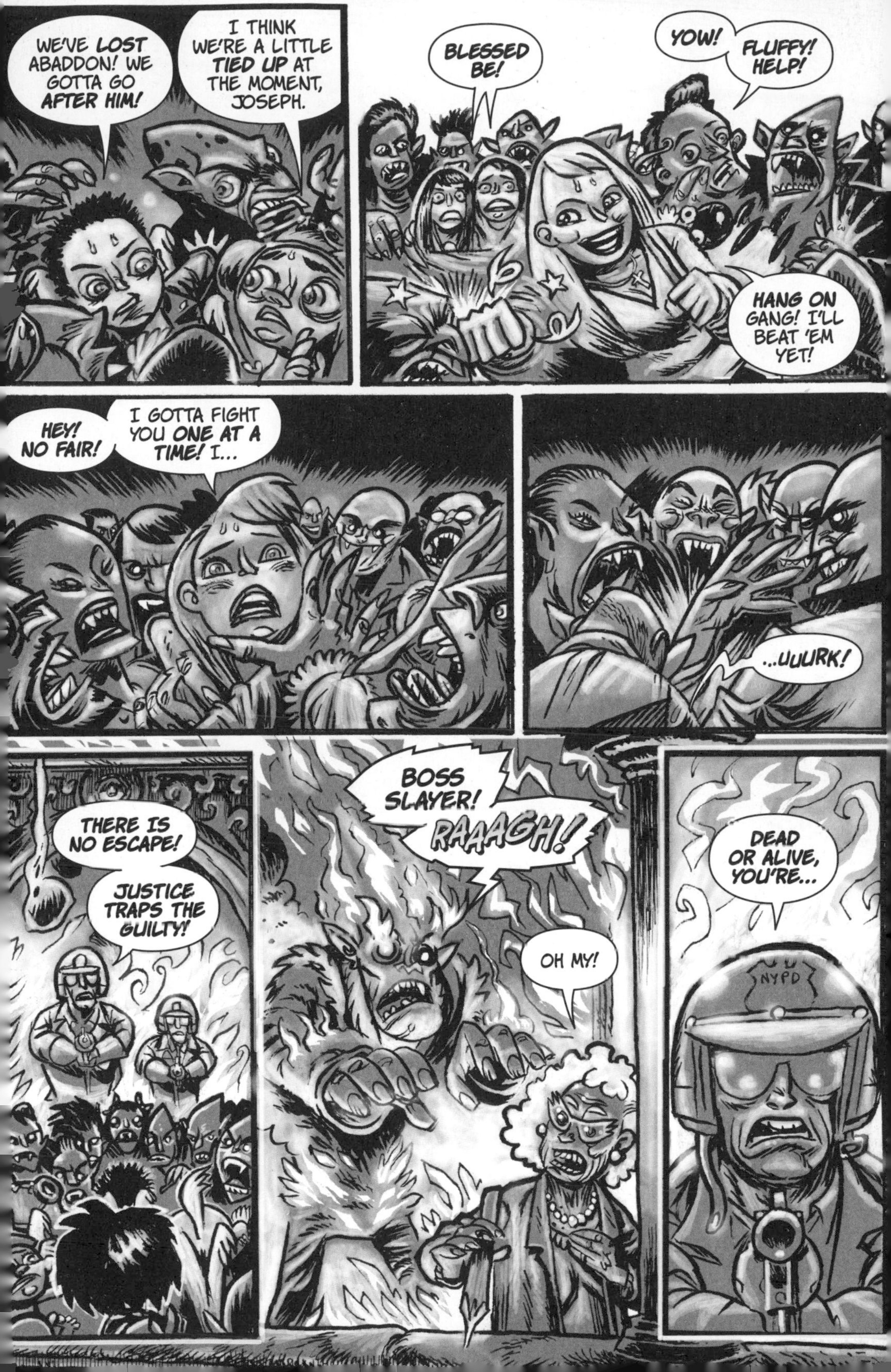
WE'VE LOST ABADDON! WE GOTTA GO AFTER HIM!
I THINK WE'RE A LITTLE TIED UP AT THE MOMENT, JOSEPH.
BLESSED BE!
YOW!
FLUFFY! HELP!
HANG ON GANG! I'LL BEAT 'EM YET!
HEY! NO FAIR!
I GOTTA FIGHT YOU ONE AT A TIME! I...
...UUURK!
THERE IS NO ESCAPE!
JUSTICE TRAPS THE GUILTY!
BOSS SLAYER!
RAAAGH!
OH MY!
DEAD OR ALIVE, YOU'RE...
NYPD

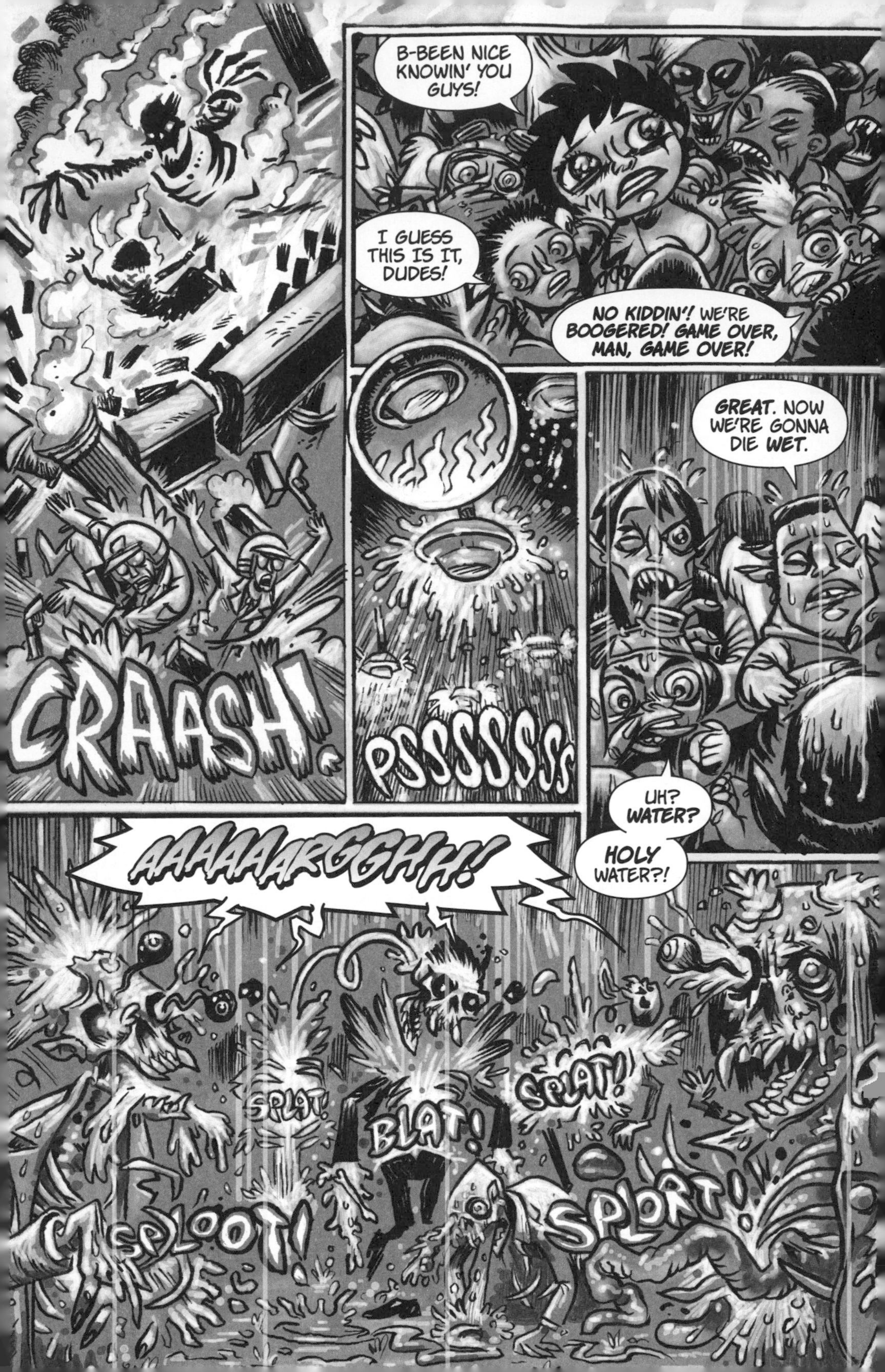
CRAASH!
B-BEEN NICE KNOWIN' YOU GUYS!
I GUESS THIS IS IT, DUDES!
NO KIDDIN'! WE'RE BOOGERED! GAME OVER, MAN, GAME OVER!
PSSSSSSS
GREAT. NOW WE'RE GONNA DIE WET.
UH? WATER?
HOLY WATER?!
AAAAAARGGHH!
SPLAT!
BLAT!
SPLAT!
SPLOOT!
SPLORT!

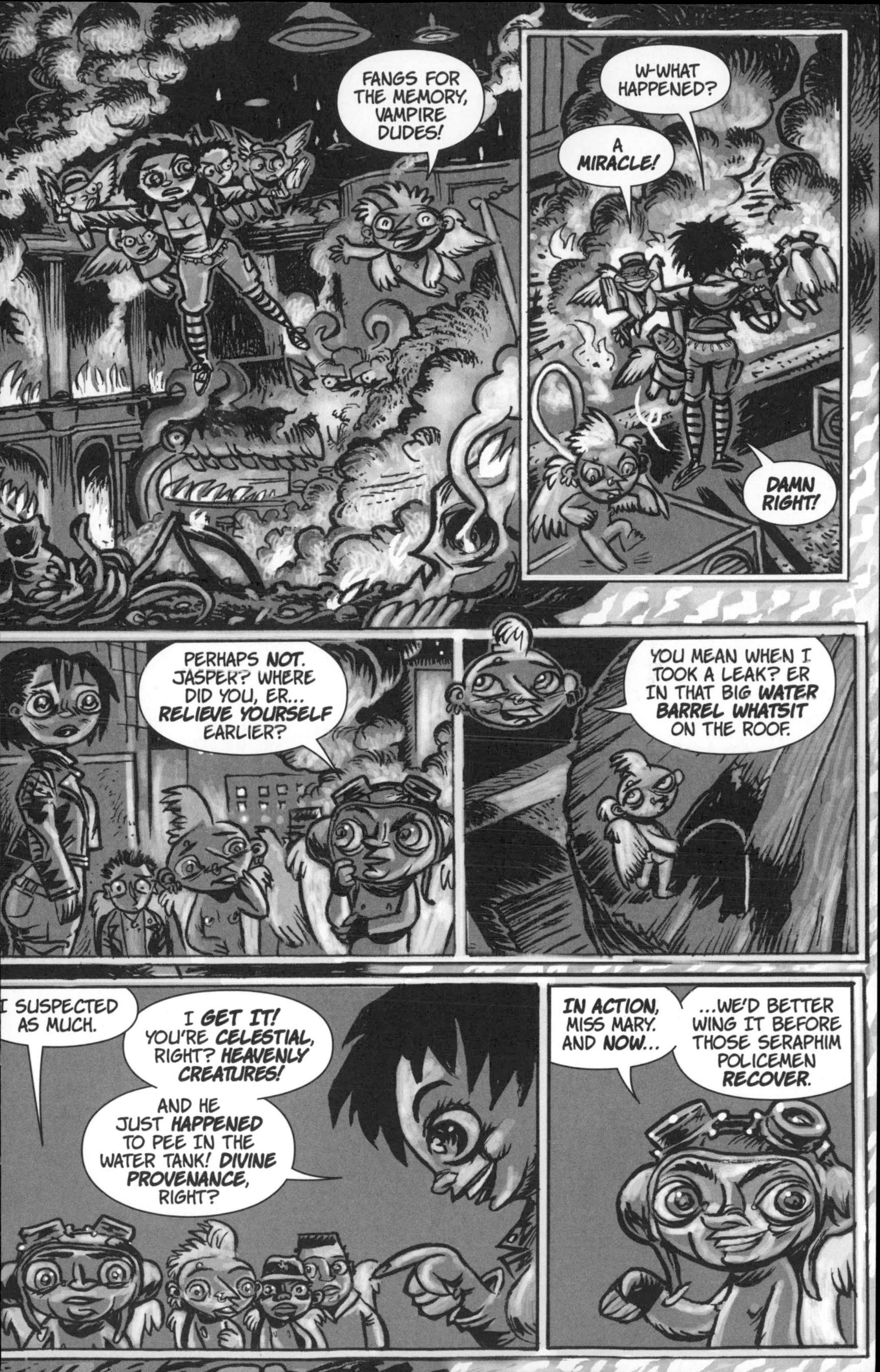
FANGS FOR THE MEMORY, VAMPIRE DUDES!
W-WHAT HAPPENED?
A MIRACLE!
DAMN RIGHT!
PERHAPS NOT. JASPER? WHERE DID YOU, ER... RELIEVE YOURSELF EARLIER?
YOU MEAN WHEN I TOOK A LEAK? ER IN THAT BIG WATER BARREL WHATSIT ON THE ROOF.
I SUSPECTED AS MUCH.
I GET IT! YOU'RE CELESTIAL, RIGHT? HEAVENLY CREATURES!
AND HE JUST HAPPENED TO PEE IN THE WATER TANK! DIVINE PROVENANCE, RIGHT?
IN ACTION, MISS MARY. AND NOW...
...WE'D BETTER WING IT BEFORE THOSE SERAPHIM POLICEMEN RECOVER.

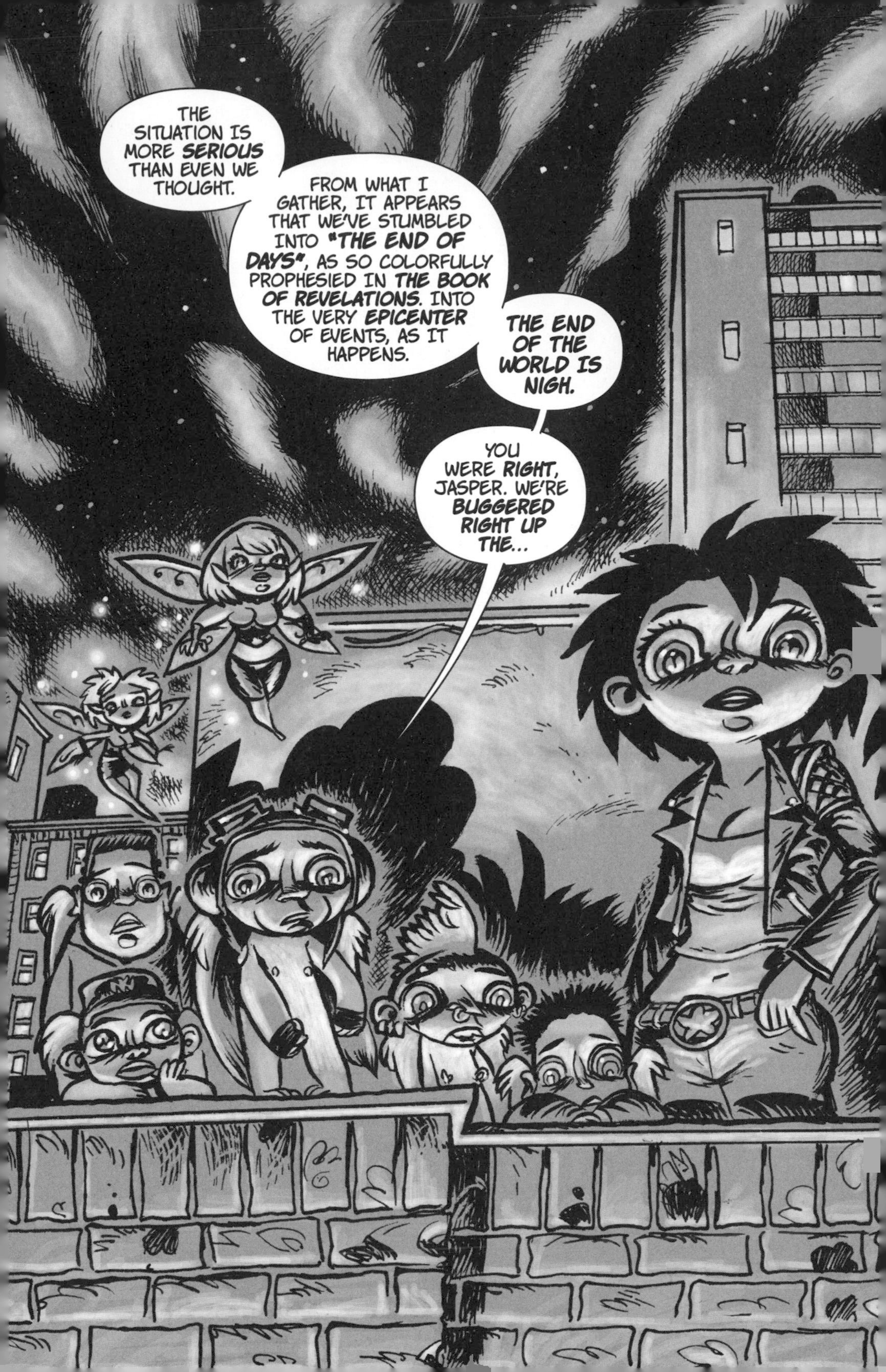
THE SITUATION IS MORE **SERIOUS** THAN EVEN WE THOUGHT.
FROM WHAT I GATHER, IT APPEARS THAT WE'VE STUMBLED INTO **"THE END OF DAYS"**, AS SO COLORFULLY PROPHESIED IN **THE BOOK OF REVELATIONS**. INTO THE VERY **EPICENTER** OF EVENTS, AS IT HAPPENS.
THE END OF THE WORLD IS NIGH.
YOU WERE **RIGHT**, JASPER. WE'RE **BUGGERED** RIGHT UP THE...

CANTICA II

HELL ON EARTH

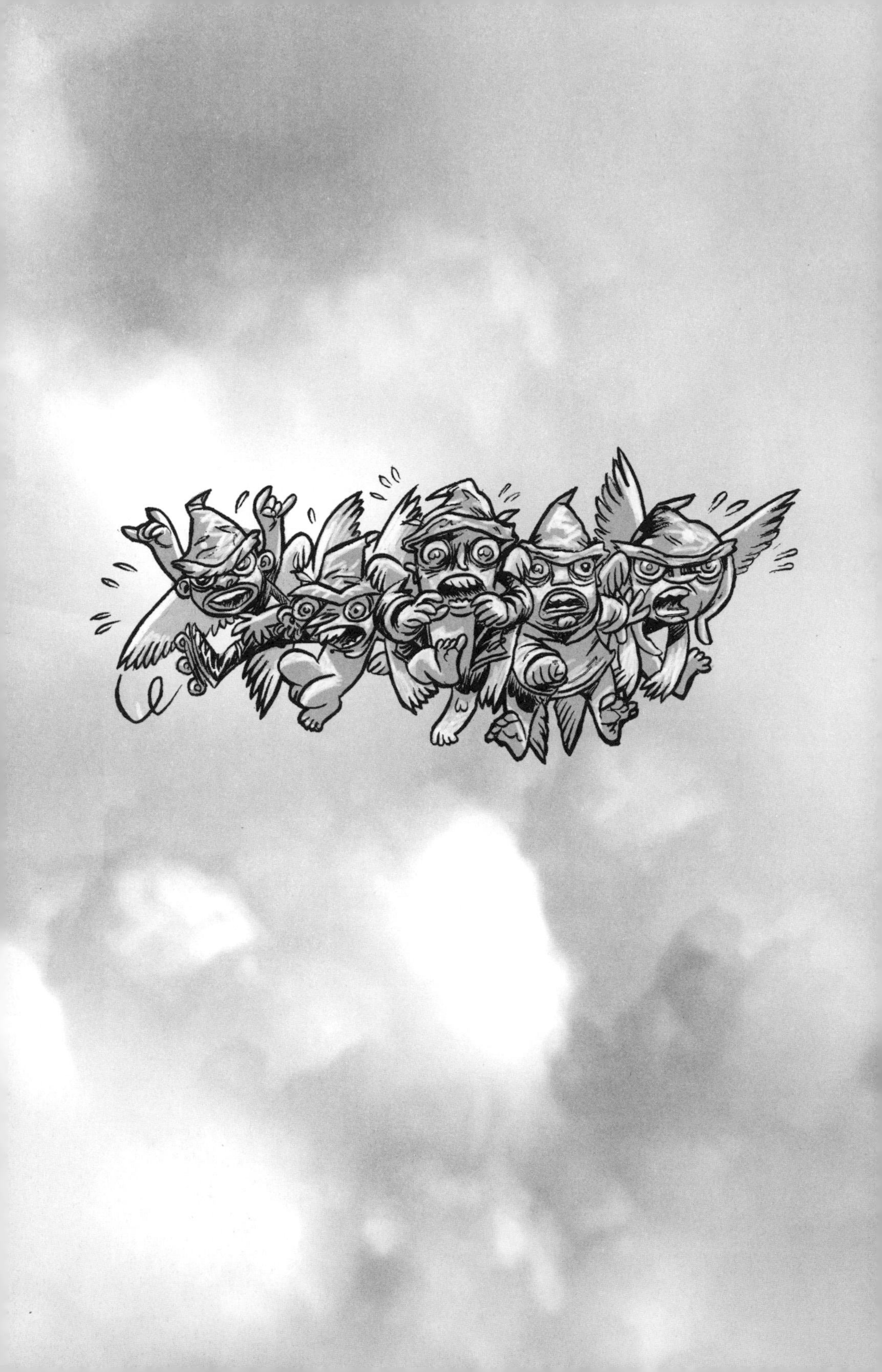

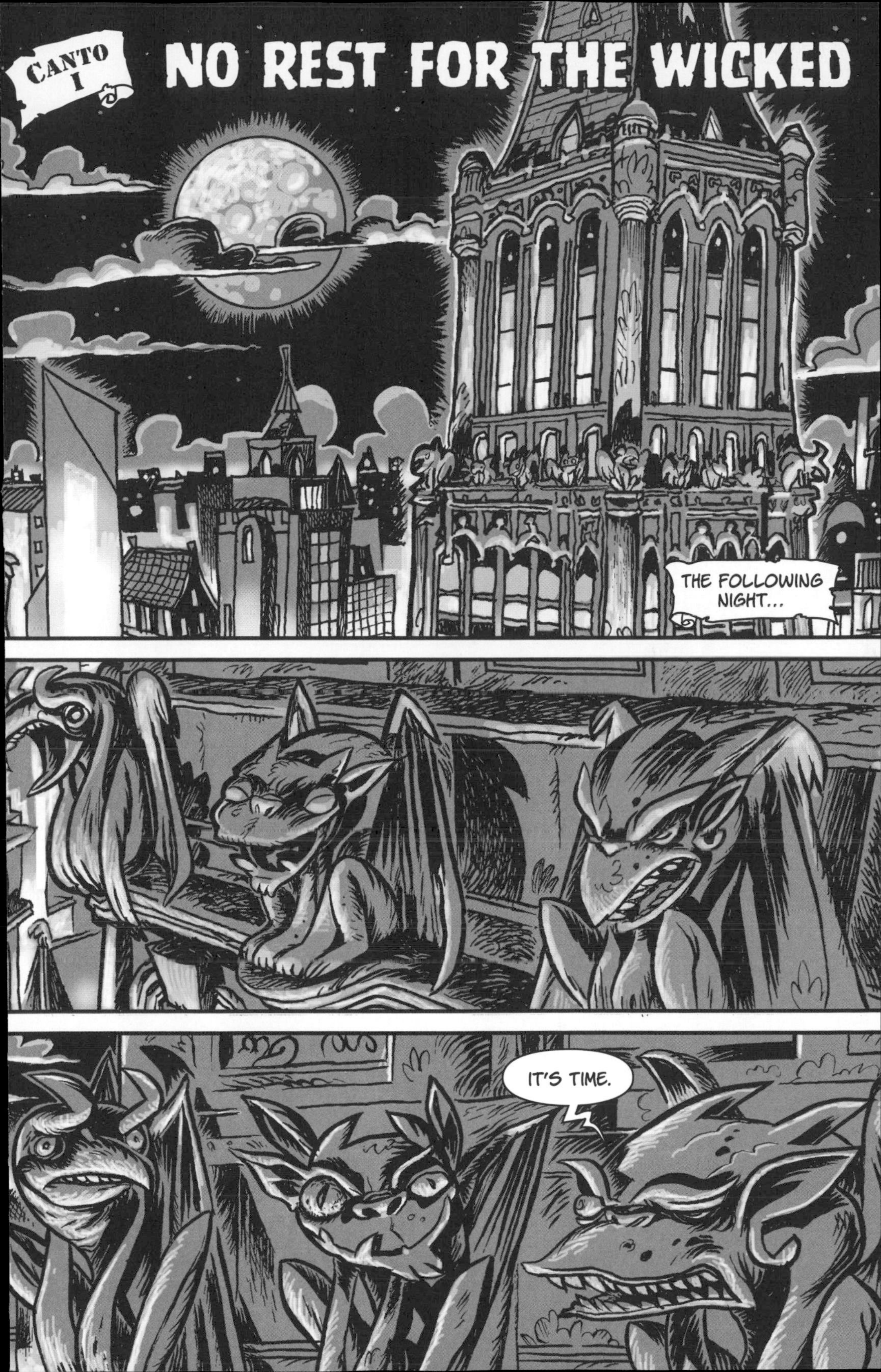
CANTO I
NO REST FOR THE WICKED
THE FOLLOWING NIGHT...
IT'S TIME.

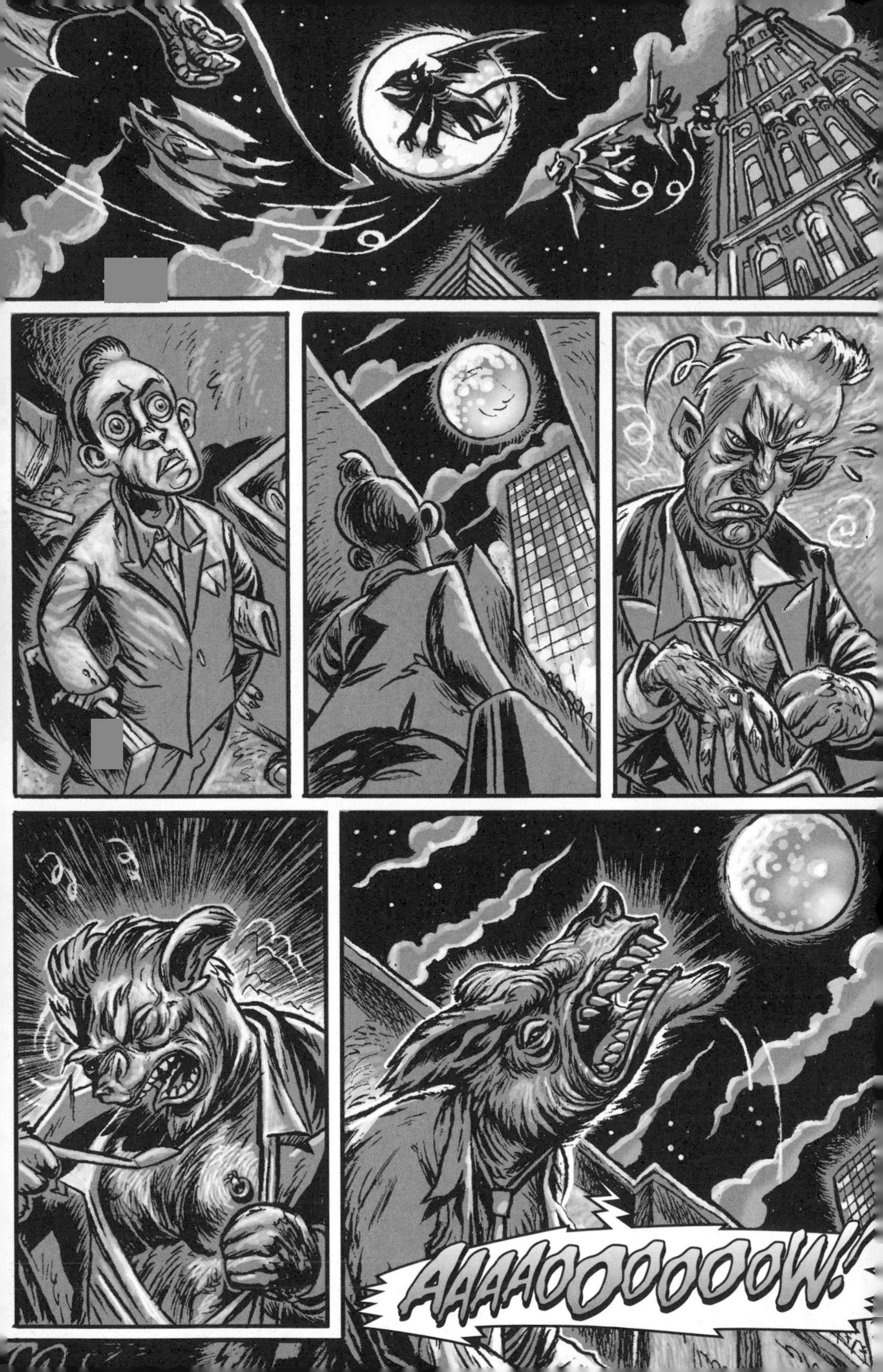
AAAOOOOOOOW!

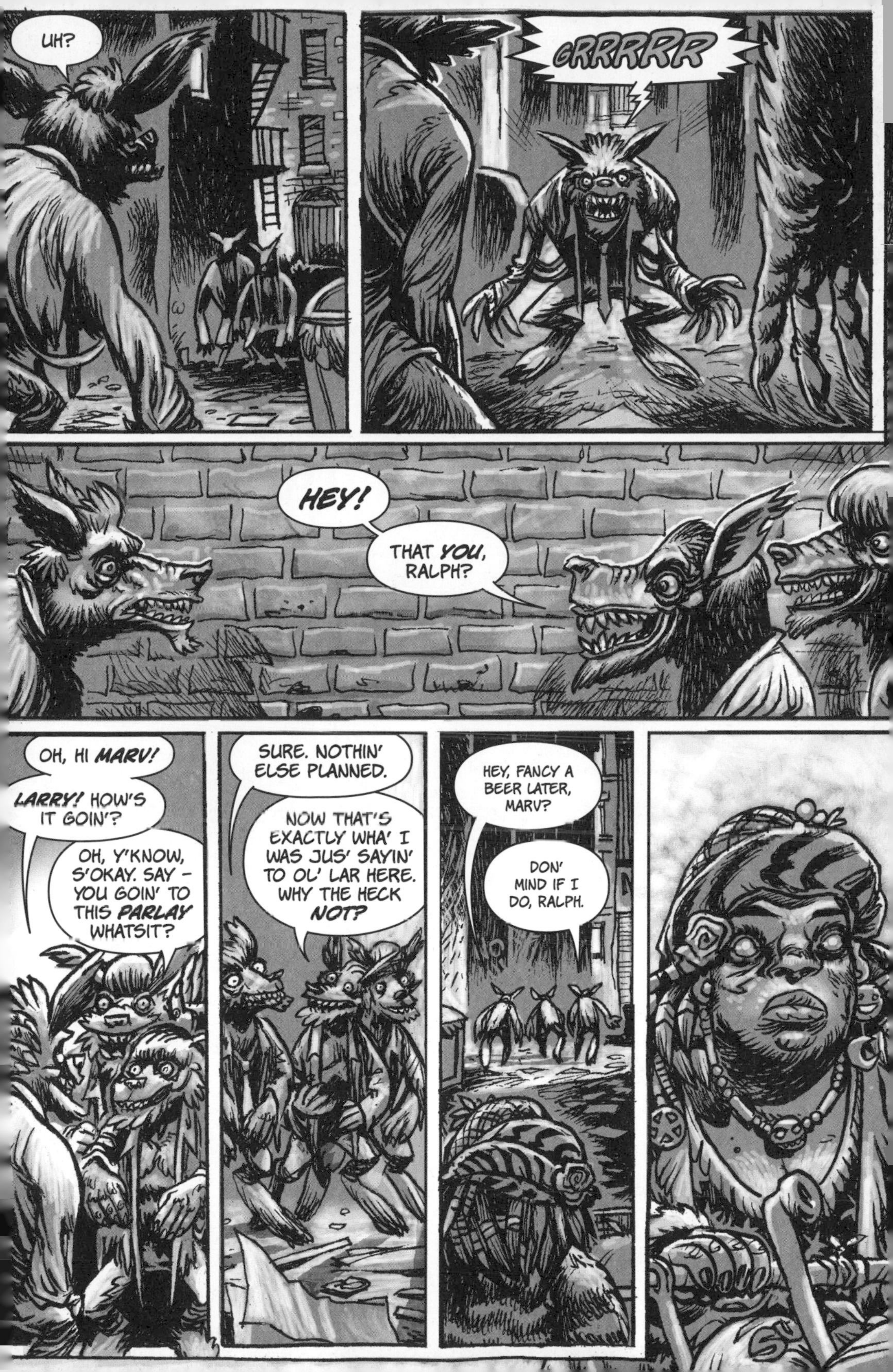

UH?
GRRRRR
HEY!
THAT YOU, RALPH?
OH, HI MARV!
LARRY! HOW'S IT GOIN'?
OH, Y'KNOW, S'OKAY. SAY - YOU GOIN' TO THIS PARLAY WHATSIT?
SURE. NOTHIN' ELSE PLANNED.
NOW THAT'S EXACTLY WHA' I WAS JUS' SAYIN' TO OL' LAR HERE. WHY THE HECK NOT?
HEY, FANCY A BEER LATER, MARV?
DON' MIND IF I DO, RALPH.

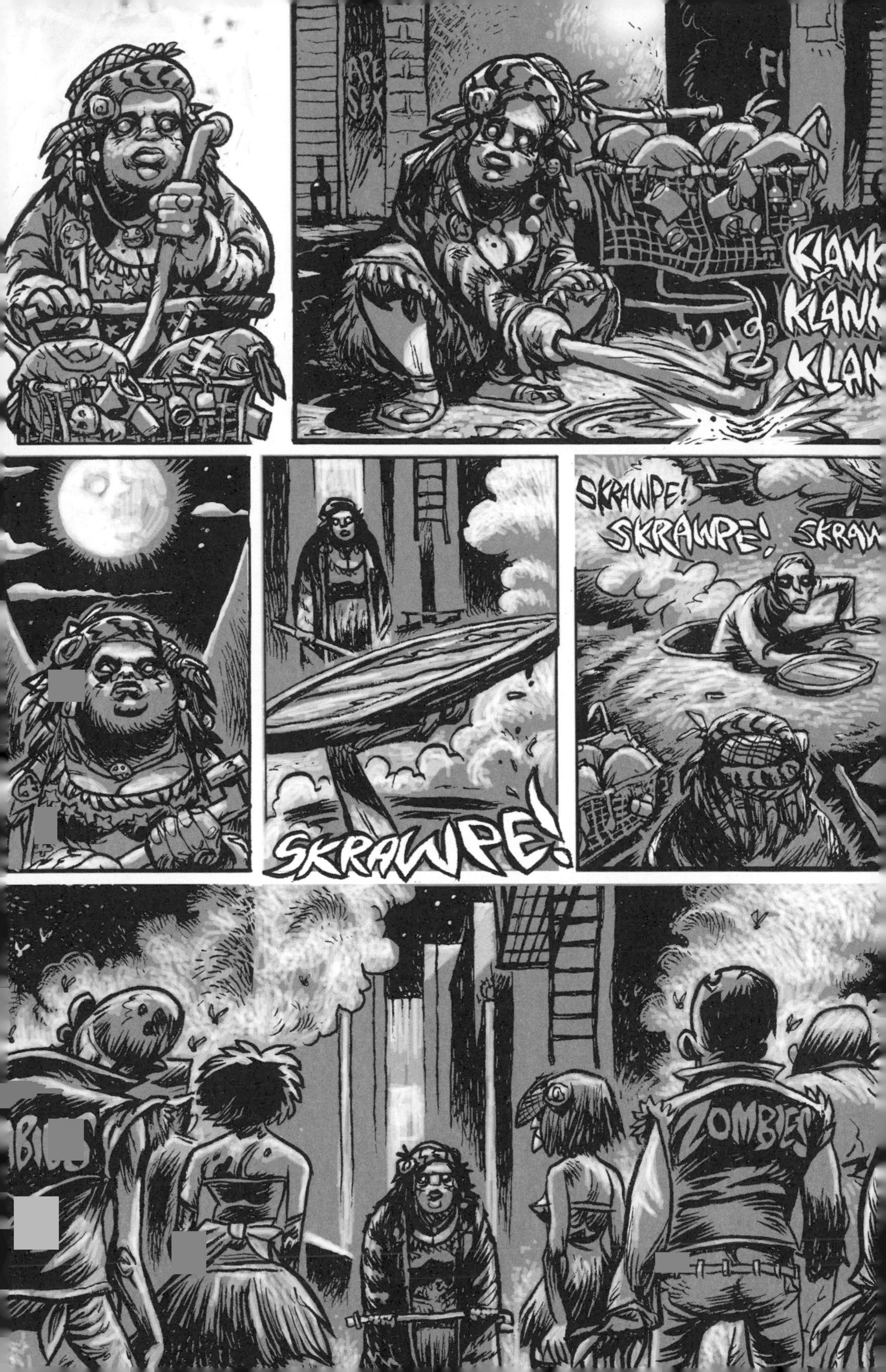

APE SEX
KLANK
KLANK
KLAN
SKRAWPE!
SKRAWPE!
SKRAWPE!
SKRAW
ZOMBIE

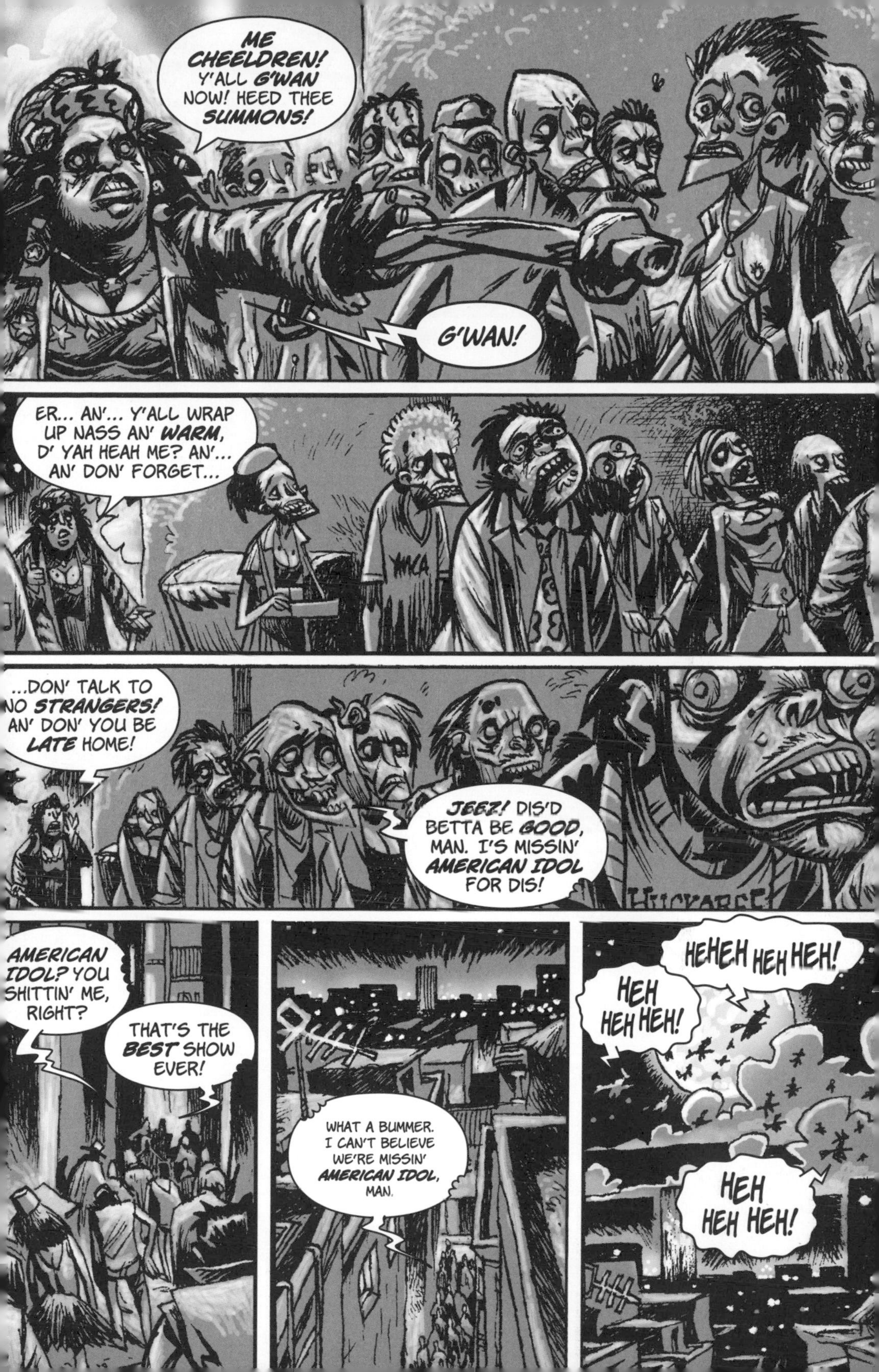
ME CHEELDREN! Y'ALL G'WAN NOW! HEED THEE SUMMONS!
G'WAN!
ER... AN'... Y'ALL WRAP UP NASS AN' WARM, D' YAH HEAH ME? AN'... AN' DON' FORGET...
...DON' TALK TO NO STRANGERS! AN' DON' YOU BE LATE HOME!
JEEZ! DIS'D BETTA BE GOOD, MAN. I'S MISSIN' AMERICAN IDOL FOR DIS!
AMERICAN IDOL? YOU SHITTIN' ME, RIGHT?
THAT'S THE BEST SHOW EVER!
WHAT A BUMMER. I CAN'T BELIEVE WE'RE MISSIN' AMERICAN IDOL, MAN.
HEHEH HEH HEH!
HEH HEH HEH!
HEH HEH HEH!

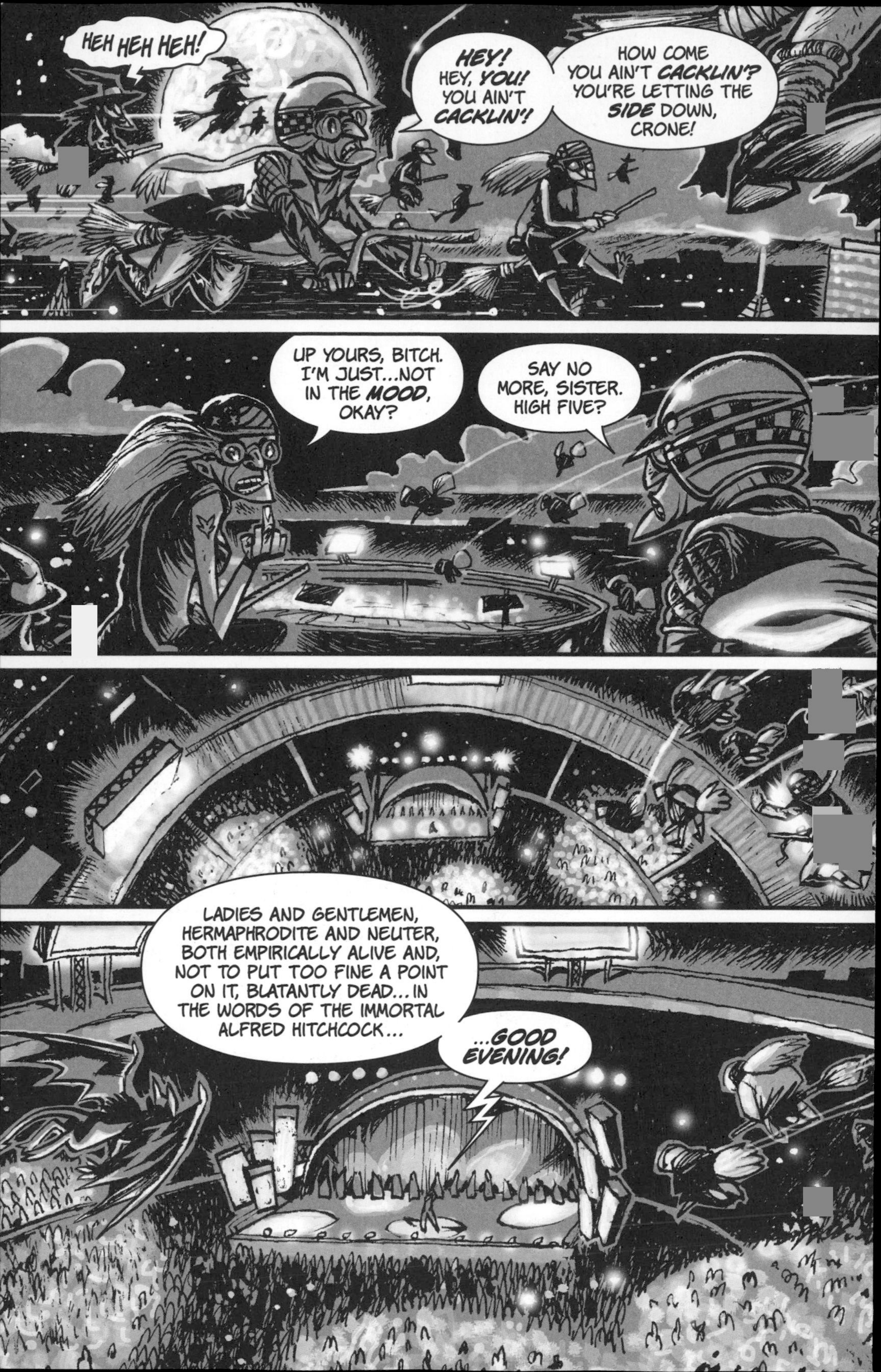
HEH HEH HEH!
HEY! HEY, YOU! YOU AIN'T CACKLIN'!
HOW COME YOU AIN'T CACKLIN'? YOU'RE LETTING THE SIDE DOWN, CRONE!
UP YOURS, BITCH. I'M JUST...NOT IN THE MOOD, OKAY?
SAY NO MORE, SISTER. HIGH FIVE?
LADIES AND GENTLEMEN, HERMAPHRODITE AND NEUTER, BOTH EMPIRICALLY ALIVE AND, NOT TO PUT TOO FINE A POINT ON IT, BLATANTLY DEAD... IN THE WORDS OF THE IMMORTAL ALFRED HITCHCOCK...
...GOOD EVENING!

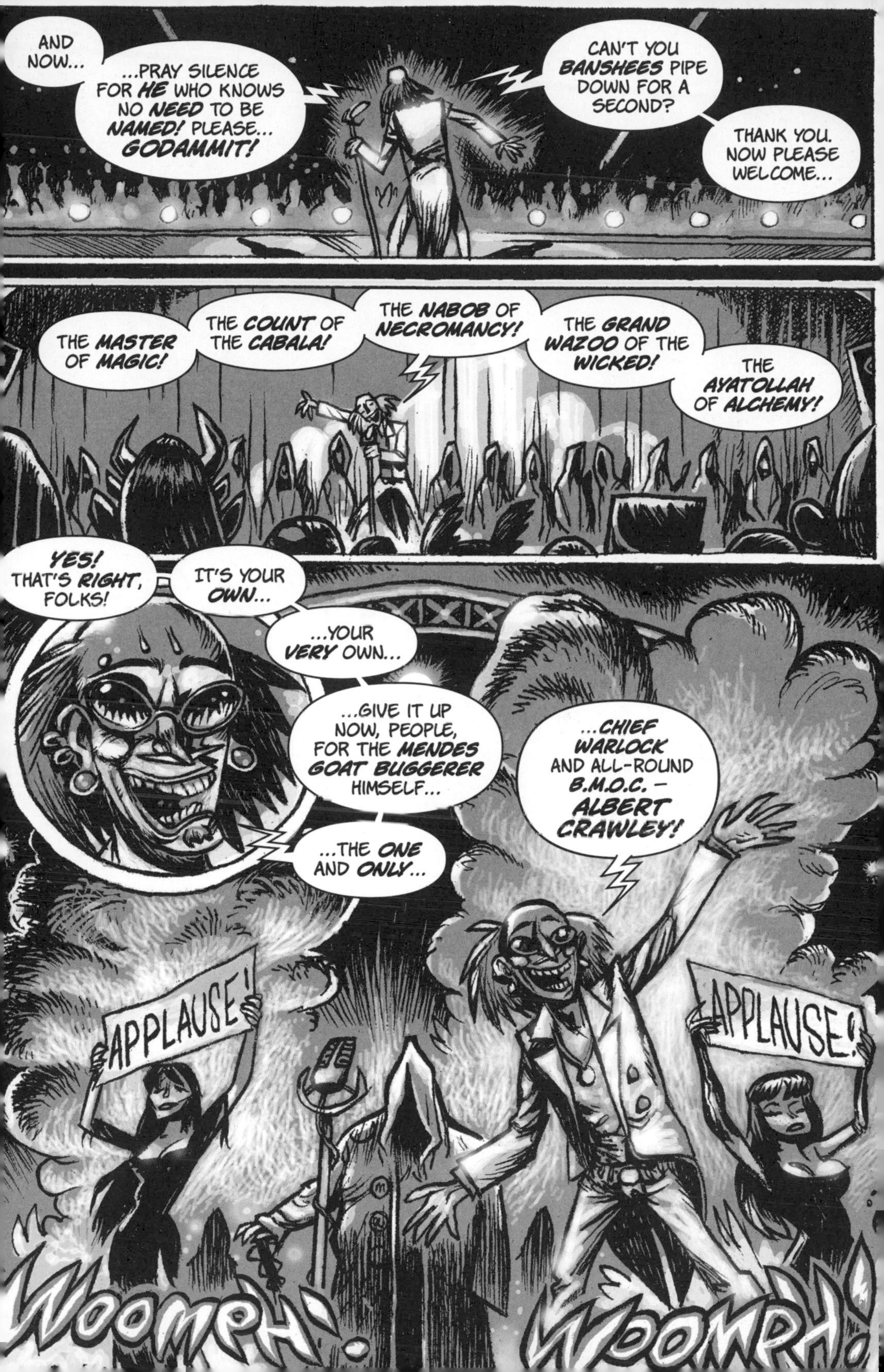
AND NOW...
...PRAY SILENCE FOR HE WHO KNOWS NO NEED TO BE NAMED! PLEASE... GODAMMIT!
CAN'T YOU BANSHEES PIPE DOWN FOR A SECOND?
THANK YOU. NOW PLEASE WELCOME...
THE MASTER OF MAGIC!
THE COUNT OF THE CABALA!
THE NABOB OF NECROMANCY!
THE GRAND WAZOO OF THE WICKED!
THE AYATOLLAH OF ALCHEMY!
YES! THAT'S RIGHT, FOLKS!
IT'S YOUR OWN...
...YOUR VERY OWN...
...GIVE IT UP NOW, PEOPLE, FOR THE MENDES GOAT BUGGERER HIMSELF...
...THE ONE AND ONLY...
...CHIEF WARLOCK AND ALL-ROUND B.M.O.C. – ALBERT CRAWLEY!
APPLAUSE!
APPLAUSE!
WOOMPH!
WOOMPH!

SHIT. IT'S OLD *FART FACE.*

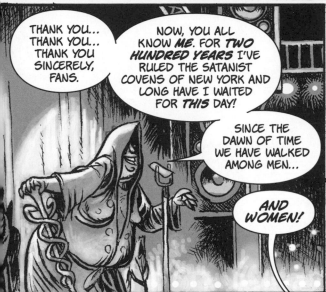

THANK YOU... THANK YOU... THANK YOU SINCERELY, FANS.

NOW, YOU ALL KNOW *ME.* FOR *TWO HUNDRED YEARS* I'VE RULED THE SATANIST COVENS OF NEW YORK AND LONG HAVE I WAITED FOR *THIS* DAY!

SINCE THE DAWN OF TIME WE HAVE WALKED AMONG MEN...

AND WOMEN!

YES, DEAR, I WAS USING THE *MALE GENERIC.* FOR, AS YOU KNOW, "MAN" *EMBRACES* "WOMAN." *HA HA! GET IT?*

SEXIST CREEP!

MAY I *FINISH?* NOW, I'VE CALLED YOU ALL HERE TO THIS... *MONUMENTAL* ASSEMBLY OF EVIL...

HEY, PIG FACE!

WHAT?

I'M NOT EVIL!

I'M A *WHITE WITCH!*

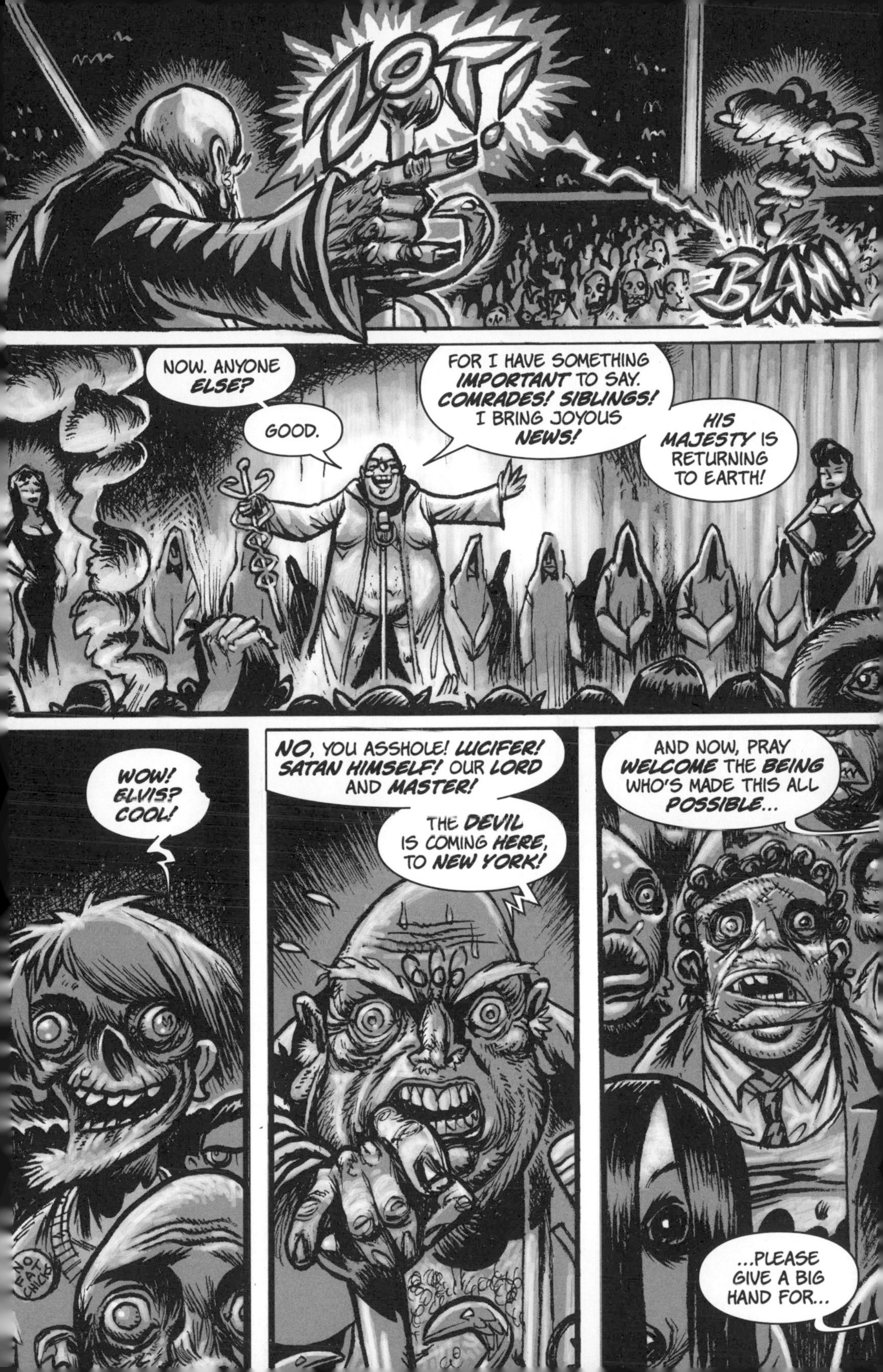
ZOT!
BLAM!
NOW. ANYONE ELSE?
GOOD.
FOR I HAVE SOMETHING IMPORTANT TO SAY. COMRADES! SIBLINGS! I BRING JOYOUS NEWS!
HIS MAJESTY IS RETURNING TO EARTH!
WOW! ELVIS? COOL!
NO FAT CHICKS
NO, YOU ASSHOLE! LUCIFER! SATAN HIMSELF! OUR LORD AND MASTER!
THE DEVIL IS COMING HERE, TO NEW YORK!
AND NOW, PRAY WELCOME THE BEING WHO'S MADE THIS ALL POSSIBLE...
...PLEASE GIVE A BIG HAND FOR...

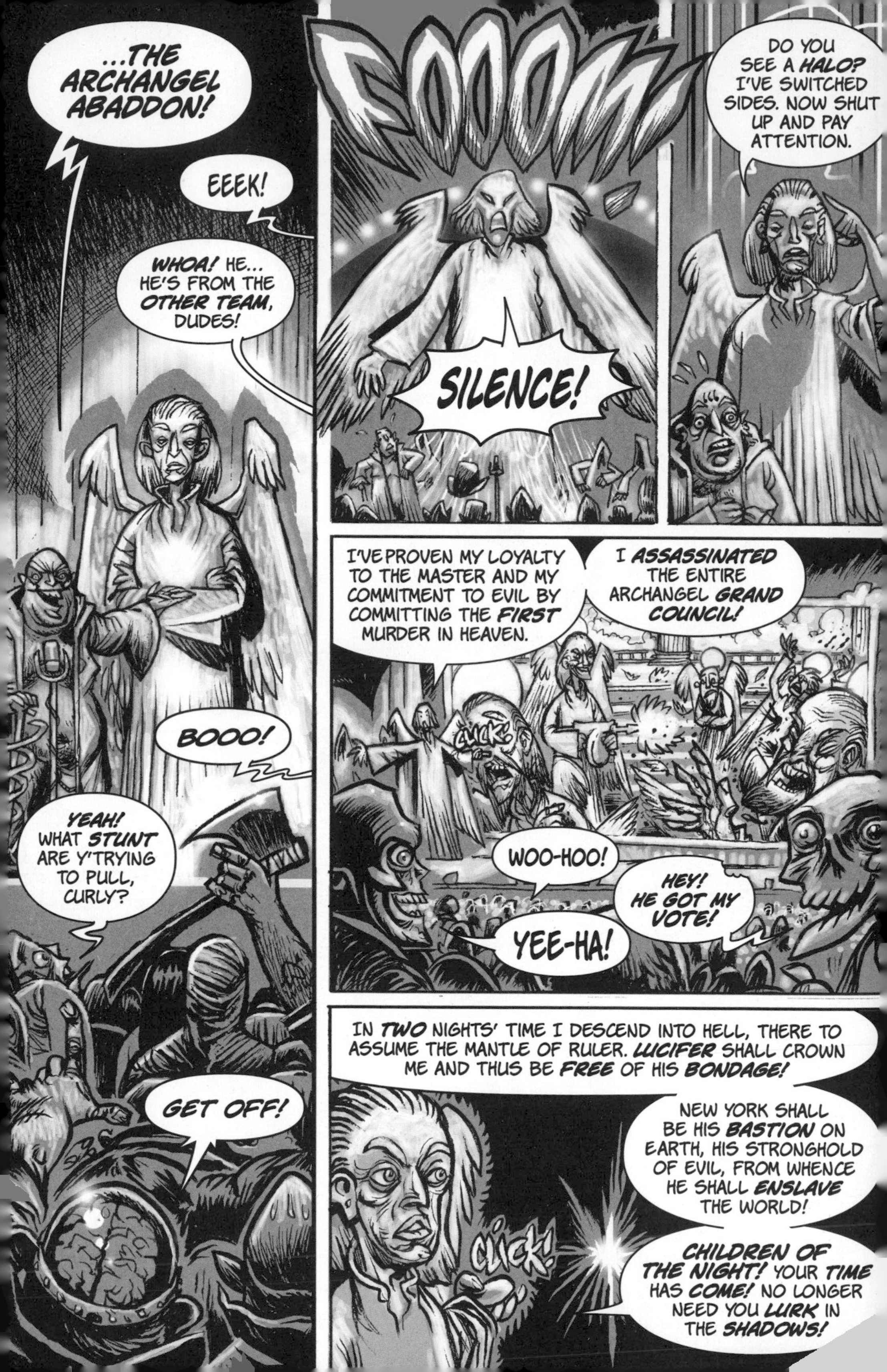
...THE ARCHANGEL ABADDON!
EEEK!
WHOA! HE... HE'S FROM THE OTHER TEAM, DUDES!
BOOO!
YEAH! WHAT STUNT ARE Y'TRYING TO PULL, CURLY?
GET OFF!
FOOOM!
SILENCE!
DO YOU SEE A HALO? I'VE SWITCHED SIDES. NOW SHUT UP AND PAY ATTENTION.
I'VE PROVEN MY LOYALTY TO THE MASTER AND MY COMMITMENT TO EVIL BY COMMITTING THE FIRST MURDER IN HEAVEN.
I ASSASSINATED THE ENTIRE ARCHANGEL GRAND COUNCIL!
CLICK!
WOO-HOO!
HEY! HE GOT MY VOTE!
YEE-HA!
IN TWO NIGHTS' TIME I DESCEND INTO HELL, THERE TO ASSUME THE MANTLE OF RULER. LUCIFER SHALL CROWN ME AND THUS BE FREE OF HIS BONDAGE!
NEW YORK SHALL BE HIS BASTION ON EARTH, HIS STRONGHOLD OF EVIL, FROM WHENCE HE SHALL ENSLAVE THE WORLD!
CLICK!
CHILDREN OF THE NIGHT! YOUR TIME HAS COME! NO LONGER NEED YOU LURK IN THE SHADOWS!

B-B-BUT I *LIKE* LURKING IN THE SHADOWS!

ER, WELL, WITH *MY* SCHEME YOU ALWAYS HAVE THE *OPTION* TO LURK SHOULD YOU BE OF A MIND TO DO SO.

NOW LISTEN CAREFULLY...

AS YOU KNOW, FRIDAY NIGHT IS *HALLOWE'EN*. THE NIGHT OF *SAMHAIN*, WHEN THE POWERS OF EVIL ARE *STRONGEST* AND THE *DOORS* BETWEEN *YOUR* WORLD AND THE WORLD OF THE MORTALS *DISSOLVE*.

STRIKE AT SUNSET! TAKE TO THE STREETS AND *RECLAIM* YOUR *INHERITANCE!* TURN THIS BURG INTO A *HOME* FITTING FOR THE *LORD OF THE FLIES!*

YEAH!

RIGHT ON!

WHEEEE!

ABSOLUTELY, OLD CHAP!

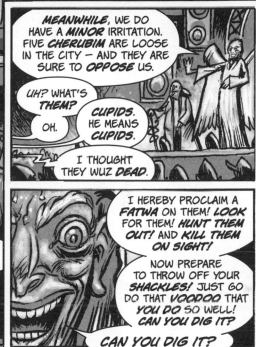

MEANWHILE, WE DO HAVE A *MINOR* IRRITATION. FIVE *CHERUBIM* ARE LOOSE IN THE CITY — AND THEY ARE SURE TO *OPPOSE* US.

UH? WHAT'S *THEM?*

OH.

CUPIDS. HE MEANS *CUPIDS.*

I THOUGHT THEY WUZ *DEAD.*

I HEREBY PROCLAIM A *FATWA* ON THEM! *LOOK* FOR THEM! *HUNT THEM OUT!* AND *KILL THEM ON SIGHT!*

NOW PREPARE TO THROW OFF YOUR *SHACKLES!* JUST GO DO THAT *VOODOO* THAT *YOU* DO SO WELL! *CAN YOU DIG IT?*

CAN YOU DIG IT?

CAAAAAAAN YOU DIG IT?

HEY, TITTY, THIS IS REALLY SOME *BAD SHIT.*

YEAH. WE GOTTA WARN THE *GUYS.*

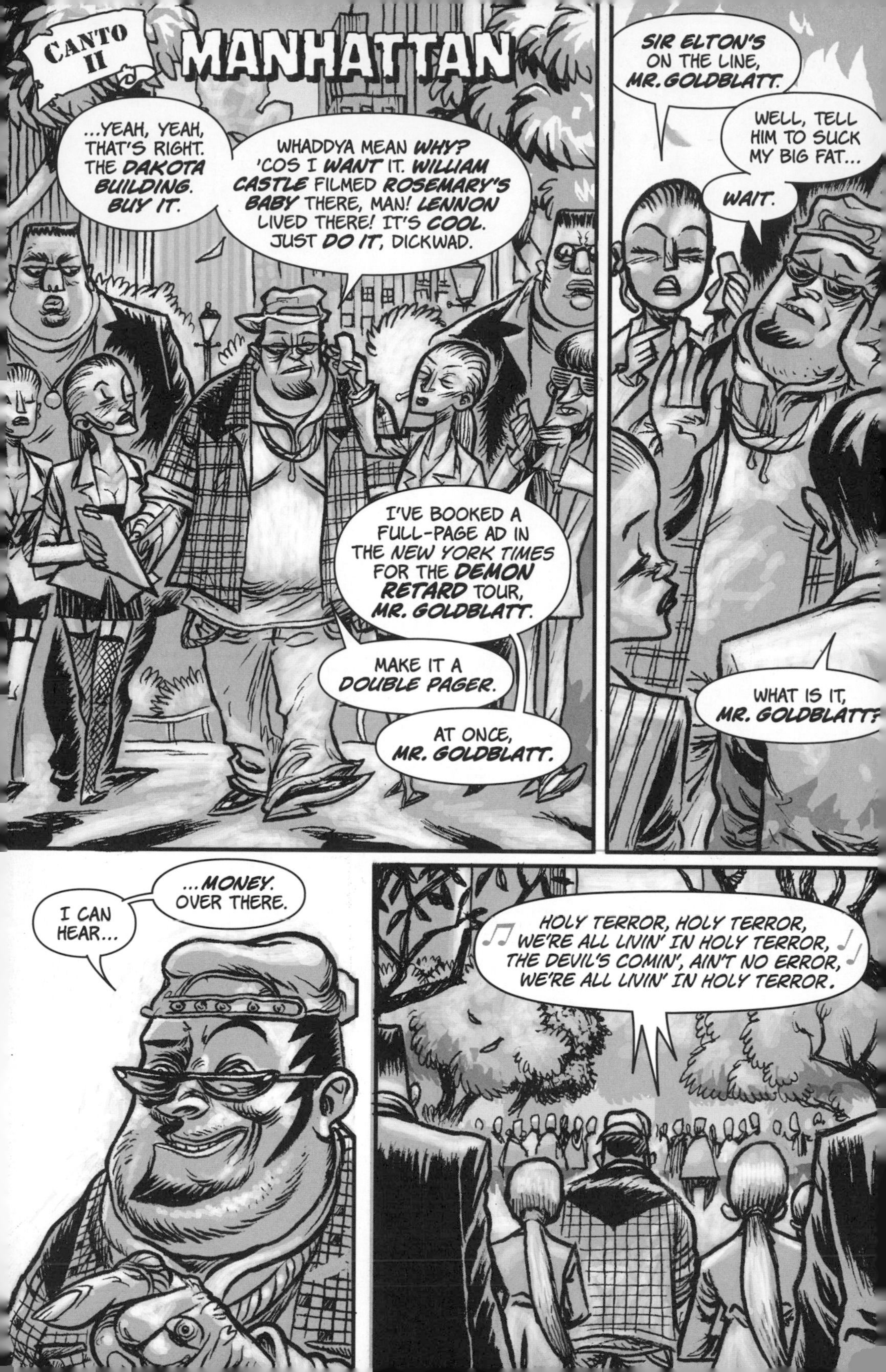
CANTO II
MANHATTAN
...YEAH, YEAH, THAT'S RIGHT. THE DAKOTA BUILDING. BUY IT.
WHADDYA MEAN WHY? 'COS I WANT IT. WILLIAM CASTLE FILMED ROSEMARY'S BABY THERE, MAN! LENNON LIVED THERE! IT'S COOL. JUST DO IT, DICKWAD.
I'VE BOOKED A FULL-PAGE AD IN THE NEW YORK TIMES FOR THE DEMON RETARD TOUR, MR. GOLDBLATT.
MAKE IT A DOUBLE PAGER.
AT ONCE, MR. GOLDBLATT.
SIR ELTON'S ON THE LINE, MR. GOLDBLATT.
WELL, TELL HIM TO SUCK MY BIG FAT...
WAIT.
WHAT IS IT, MR. GOLDBLATT?
I CAN HEAR...
...MONEY. OVER THERE.
HOLY TERROR, HOLY TERROR, WE'RE ALL LIVIN' IN HOLY TERROR, THE DEVIL'S COMIN', AIN'T NO ERROR, WE'RE ALL LIVIN' IN HOLY TERROR.

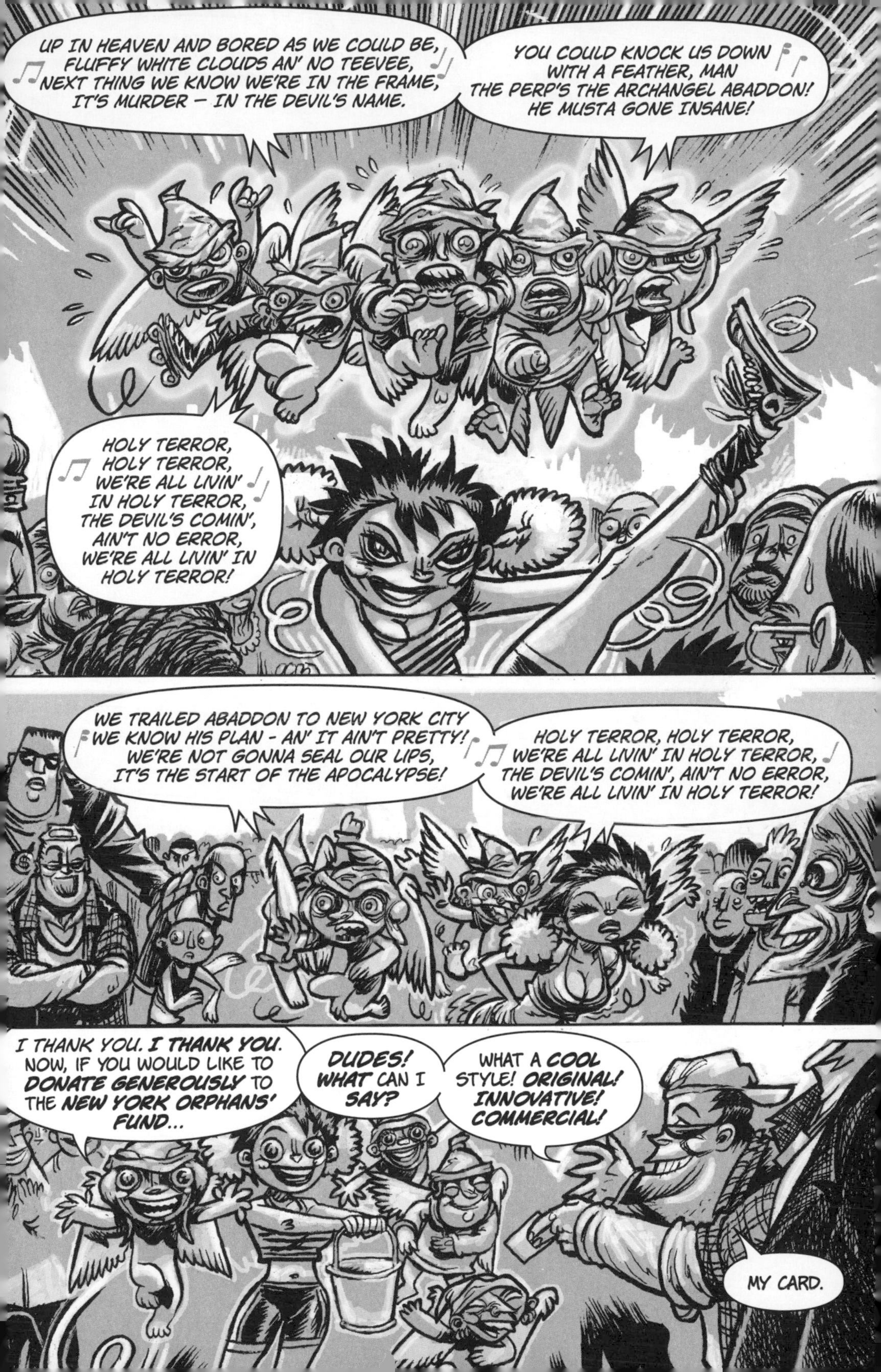
UP IN HEAVEN AND BORED AS WE COULD BE, FLUFFY WHITE CLOUDS AN' NO TEEVEE, NEXT THING WE KNOW WE'RE IN THE FRAME, IT'S MURDER — IN THE DEVIL'S NAME.
YOU COULD KNOCK US DOWN WITH A FEATHER, MAN THE PERP'S THE ARCHANGEL ABADDON! HE MUSTA GONE INSANE!
HOLY TERROR, HOLY TERROR, WE'RE ALL LIVIN' IN HOLY TERROR, THE DEVIL'S COMIN', AIN'T NO ERROR, WE'RE ALL LIVIN' IN HOLY TERROR!
WE TRAILED ABADDON TO NEW YORK CITY WE KNOW HIS PLAN - AN' IT AIN'T PRETTY! WE'RE NOT GONNA SEAL OUR LIPS, IT'S THE START OF THE APOCALYPSE!
HOLY TERROR, HOLY TERROR, WE'RE ALL LIVIN' IN HOLY TERROR, THE DEVIL'S COMIN', AIN'T NO ERROR, WE'RE ALL LIVIN' IN HOLY TERROR!
I THANK YOU. I THANK YOU. NOW, IF YOU WOULD LIKE TO DONATE GENEROUSLY TO THE NEW YORK ORPHANS' FUND...
DUDES! WHAT CAN I SAY?
WHAT A COOL STYLE! ORIGINAL! INNOVATIVE! COMMERCIAL!
MY CARD.

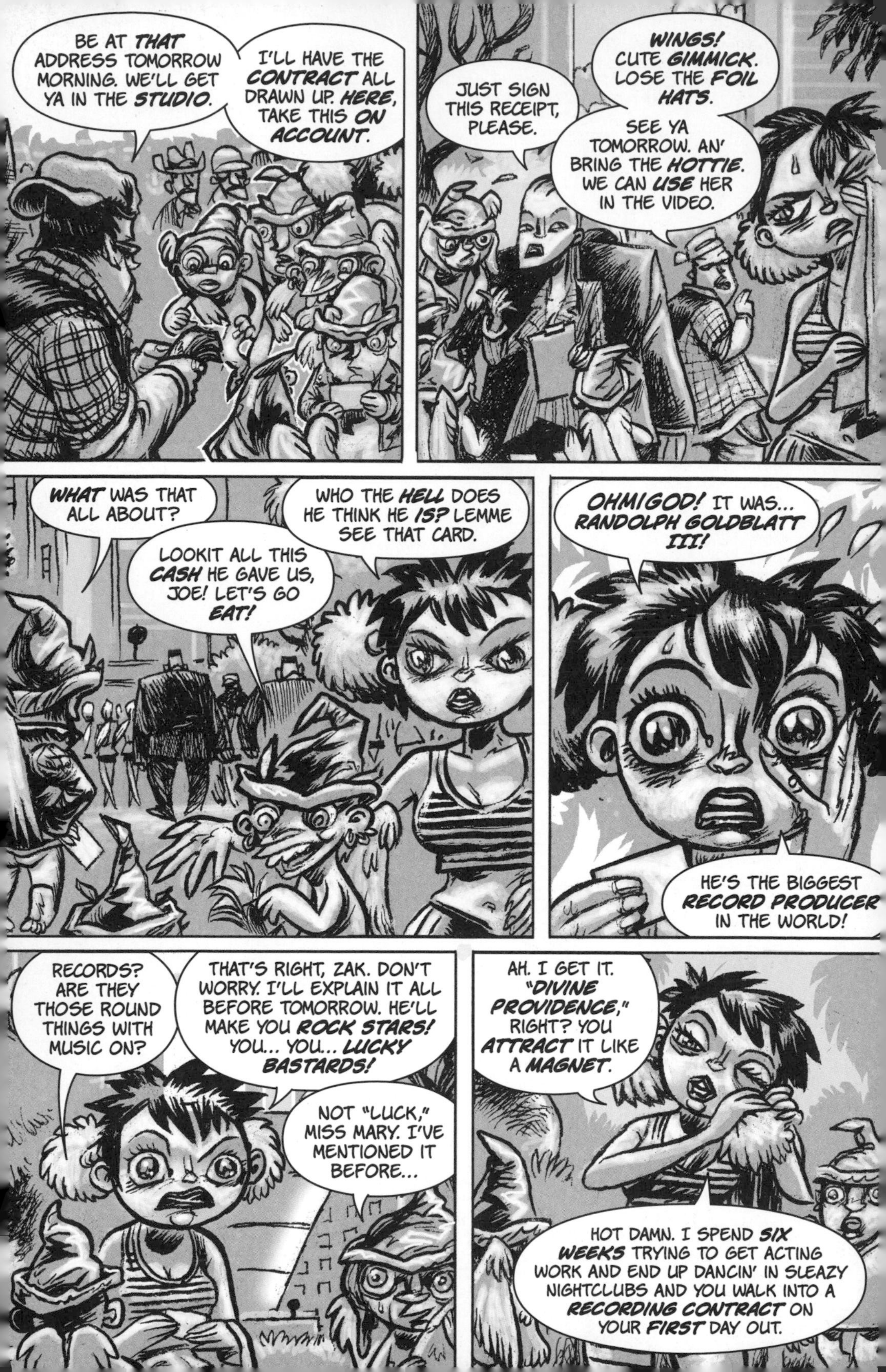
BE AT THAT ADDRESS TOMORROW MORNING. WE'LL GET YA IN THE STUDIO.
I'LL HAVE THE CONTRACT ALL DRAWN UP. HERE, TAKE THIS ON ACCOUNT.
JUST SIGN THIS RECEIPT, PLEASE.
WINGS! CUTE GIMMICK. LOSE THE FOIL HATS.
SEE YA TOMORROW. AN' BRING THE HOTTIE. WE CAN USE HER IN THE VIDEO.
WHAT WAS THAT ALL ABOUT?
WHO THE HELL DOES HE THINK HE IS? LEMME SEE THAT CARD.
LOOKIT ALL THIS CASH HE GAVE US, JOE! LET'S GO EAT!
OHMIGOD! IT WAS... RANDOLPH GOLDBLATT III!
HE'S THE BIGGEST RECORD PRODUCER IN THE WORLD!
RECORDS? ARE THEY THOSE ROUND THINGS WITH MUSIC ON?
THAT'S RIGHT, ZAK. DON'T WORRY. I'LL EXPLAIN IT ALL BEFORE TOMORROW. HE'LL MAKE YOU ROCK STARS! YOU... YOU... LUCKY BASTARDS!
NOT "LUCK," MISS MARY. I'VE MENTIONED IT BEFORE...
AH. I GET IT. "DIVINE PROVIDENCE," RIGHT? YOU ATTRACT IT LIKE A MAGNET.
HOT DAMN. I SPEND SIX WEEKS TRYING TO GET ACTING WORK AND END UP DANCIN' IN SLEAZY NIGHTCLUBS AND YOU WALK INTO A RECORDING CONTRACT ON YOUR FIRST DAY OUT.

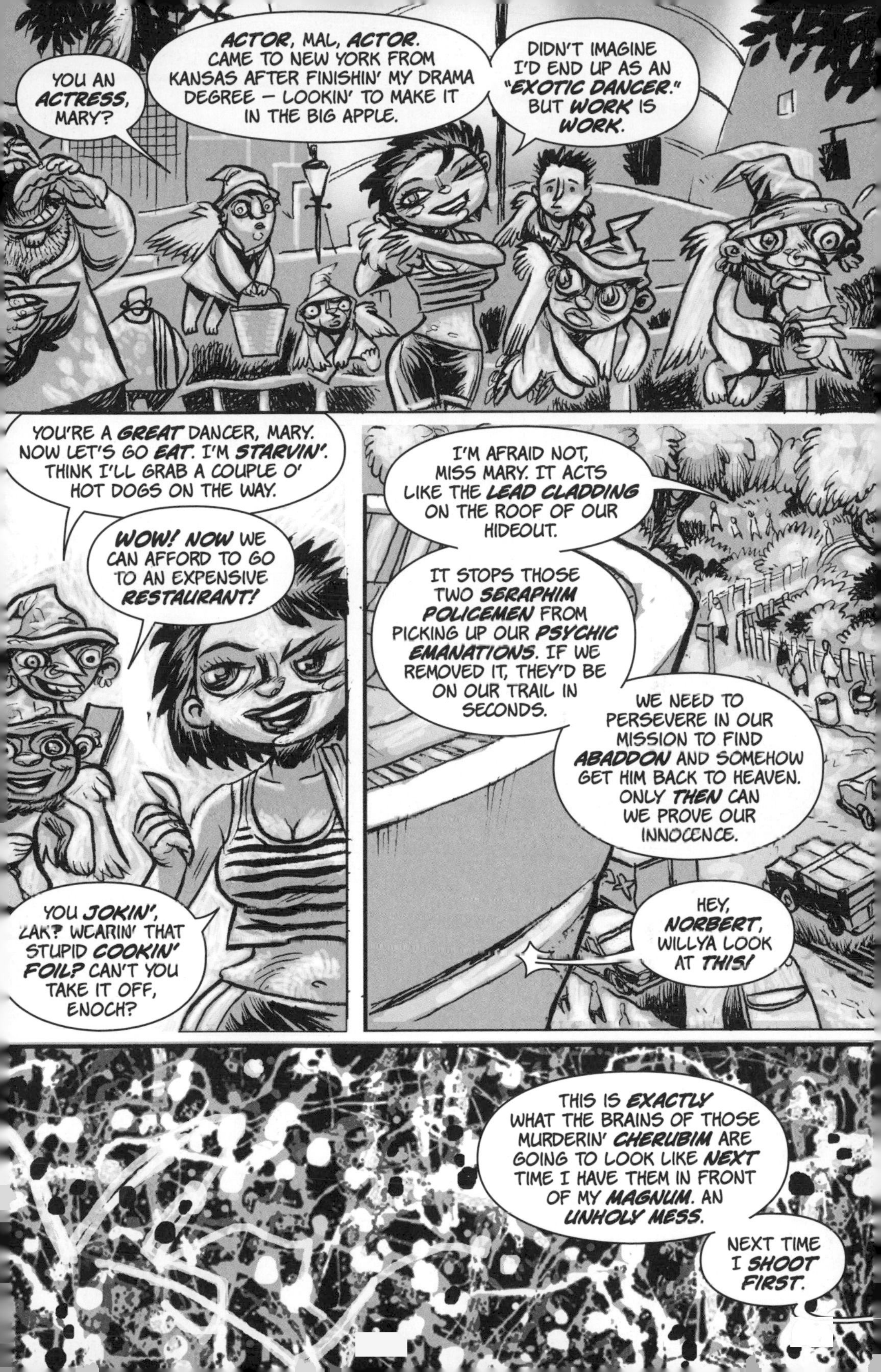
YOU AN ACTRESS, MARY?
ACTOR, MAL, ACTOR. CAME TO NEW YORK FROM KANSAS AFTER FINISHIN' MY DRAMA DEGREE — LOOKIN' TO MAKE IT IN THE BIG APPLE.
DIDN'T IMAGINE I'D END UP AS AN "EXOTIC DANCER." BUT WORK IS WORK.
YOU'RE A GREAT DANCER, MARY. NOW LET'S GO EAT. I'M STARVIN'. THINK I'LL GRAB A COUPLE O' HOT DOGS ON THE WAY.
WOW! NOW WE CAN AFFORD TO GO TO AN EXPENSIVE RESTAURANT!
YOU JOKIN', ZAK? WEARIN' THAT STUPID COOKIN' FOIL? CAN'T YOU TAKE IT OFF, ENOCH?
I'M AFRAID NOT, MISS MARY. IT ACTS LIKE THE LEAD CLADDING ON THE ROOF OF OUR HIDEOUT.
IT STOPS THOSE TWO SERAPHIM POLICEMEN FROM PICKING UP OUR PSYCHIC EMANATIONS. IF WE REMOVED IT, THEY'D BE ON OUR TRAIL IN SECONDS.
WE NEED TO PERSEVERE IN OUR MISSION TO FIND ABADDON AND SOMEHOW GET HIM BACK TO HEAVEN. ONLY THEN CAN WE PROVE OUR INNOCENCE.
HEY, NORBERT, WILLYA LOOK AT THIS!
THIS IS EXACTLY WHAT THE BRAINS OF THOSE MURDERIN' CHERUBIM ARE GOING TO LOOK LIKE NEXT TIME I HAVE THEM IN FRONT OF MY MAGNUM. AN UNHOLY MESS.
NEXT TIME I SHOOT FIRST.

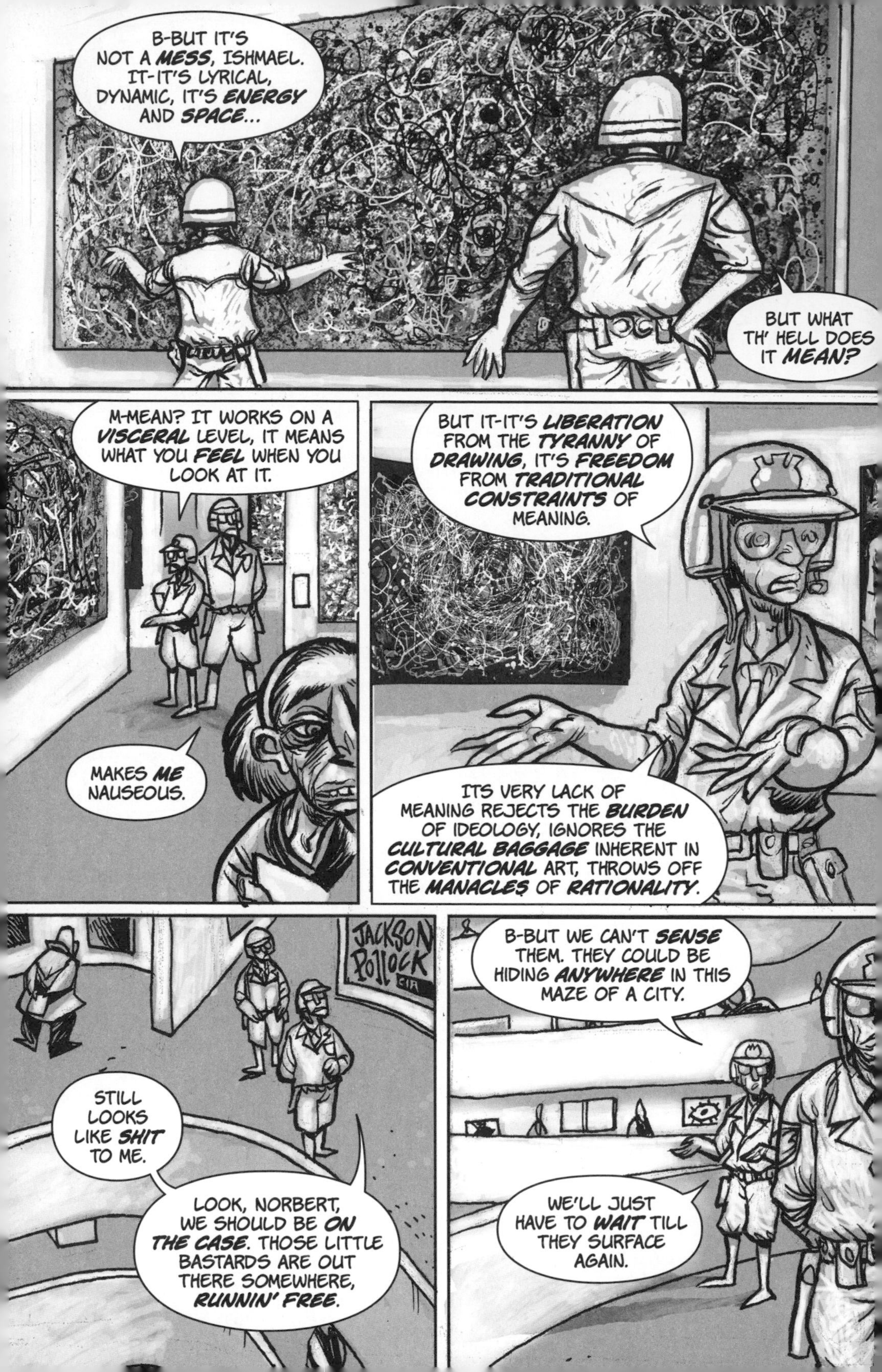
B-BUT IT'S NOT A MESS, ISHMAEL. IT-IT'S LYRICAL, DYNAMIC, IT'S ENERGY AND SPACE...
BUT WHAT TH' HELL DOES IT MEAN?
M-MEAN? IT WORKS ON A VISCERAL LEVEL, IT MEANS WHAT YOU FEEL WHEN YOU LOOK AT IT.
MAKES ME NAUSEOUS.
BUT IT-IT'S LIBERATION FROM THE TYRANNY OF DRAWING, IT'S FREEDOM FROM TRADITIONAL CONSTRAINTS OF MEANING.
ITS VERY LACK OF MEANING REJECTS THE BURDEN OF IDEOLOGY, IGNORES THE CULTURAL BAGGAGE INHERENT IN CONVENTIONAL ART, THROWS OFF THE MANACLES OF RATIONALITY.
JACKSON POLLOCK
STILL LOOKS LIKE SHIT TO ME.
LOOK, NORBERT, WE SHOULD BE ON THE CASE. THOSE LITTLE BASTARDS ARE OUT THERE SOMEWHERE, RUNNIN' FREE.
B-BUT WE CAN'T SENSE THEM. THEY COULD BE HIDING ANYWHERE IN THIS MAZE OF A CITY.
WE'LL JUST HAVE TO WAIT TILL THEY SURFACE AGAIN.

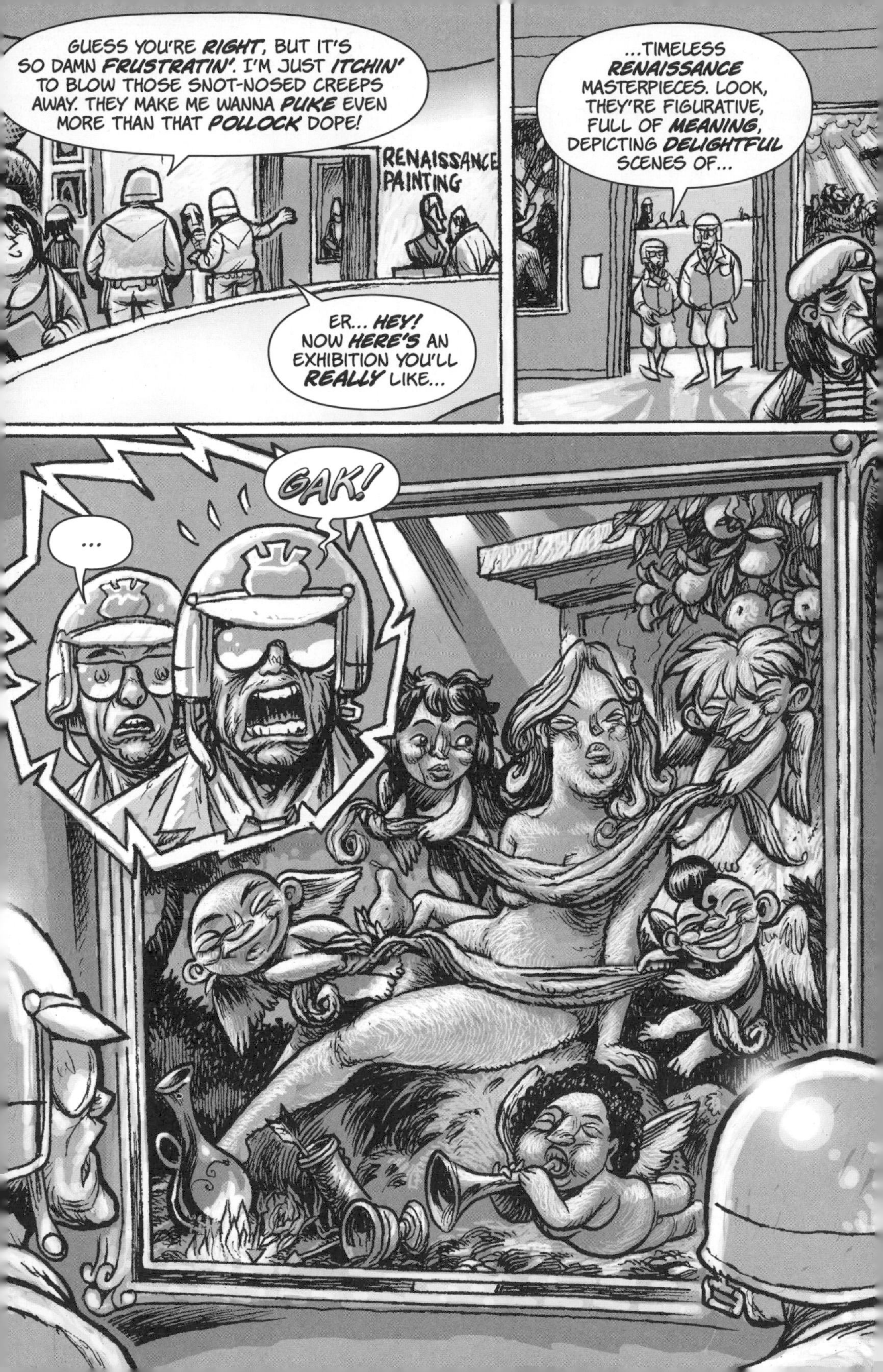
GUESS YOU'RE RIGHT, BUT IT'S SO DAMN FRUSTRATIN'. I'M JUST ITCHIN' TO BLOW THOSE SNOT-NOSED CREEPS AWAY. THEY MAKE ME WANNA PUKE EVEN MORE THAN THAT POLLOCK DOPE!
RENAISSANCE PAINTING
ER... HEY! NOW HERE'S AN EXHIBITION YOU'LL REALLY LIKE...
...TIMELESS RENAISSANCE MASTERPIECES. LOOK, THEY'RE FIGURATIVE, FULL OF MEANING, DEPICTING DELIGHTFUL SCENES OF...
...
GAK!

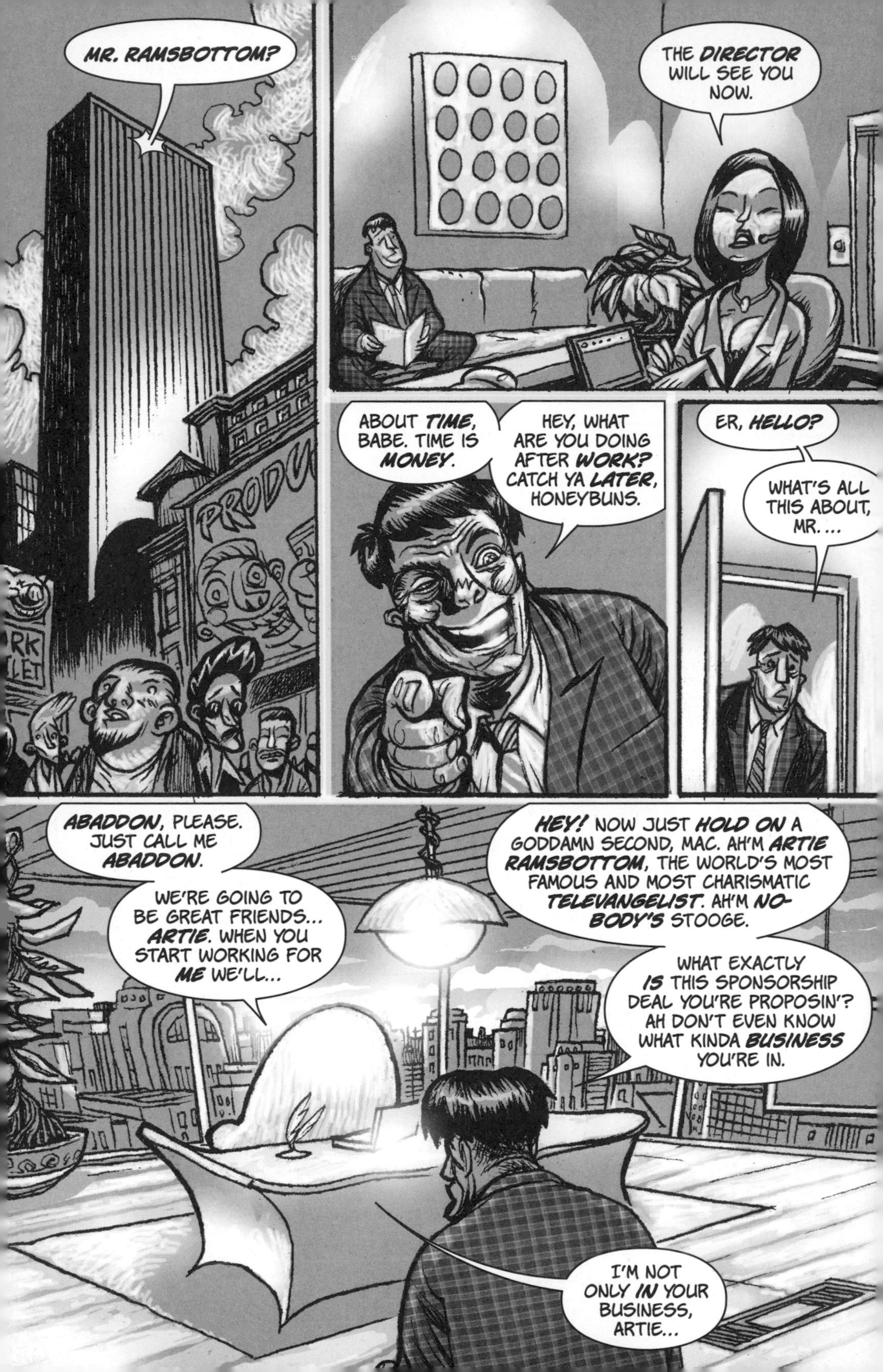
MR. RAMSBOTTOM?
THE DIRECTOR WILL SEE YOU NOW.
ABOUT TIME, BABE. TIME IS MONEY.
HEY, WHAT ARE YOU DOING AFTER WORK? CATCH YA LATER, HONEYBUNS.
ER, HELLO?
WHAT'S ALL THIS ABOUT, MR. ...
ABADDON, PLEASE. JUST CALL ME ABADDON.
WE'RE GOING TO BE GREAT FRIENDS... ARTIE. WHEN YOU START WORKING FOR ME WE'LL...
HEY! NOW JUST HOLD ON A GODDAMN SECOND, MAC. AH'M ARTIE RAMSBOTTOM, THE WORLD'S MOST FAMOUS AND MOST CHARISMATIC TELEVANGELIST. AH'M NOBODY'S STOOGE.
WHAT EXACTLY IS THIS SPONSORSHIP DEAL YOU'RE PROPOSIN'? AH DON'T EVEN KNOW WHAT KINDA BUSINESS YOU'RE IN.
I'M NOT ONLY IN YOUR BUSINESS, ARTIE...

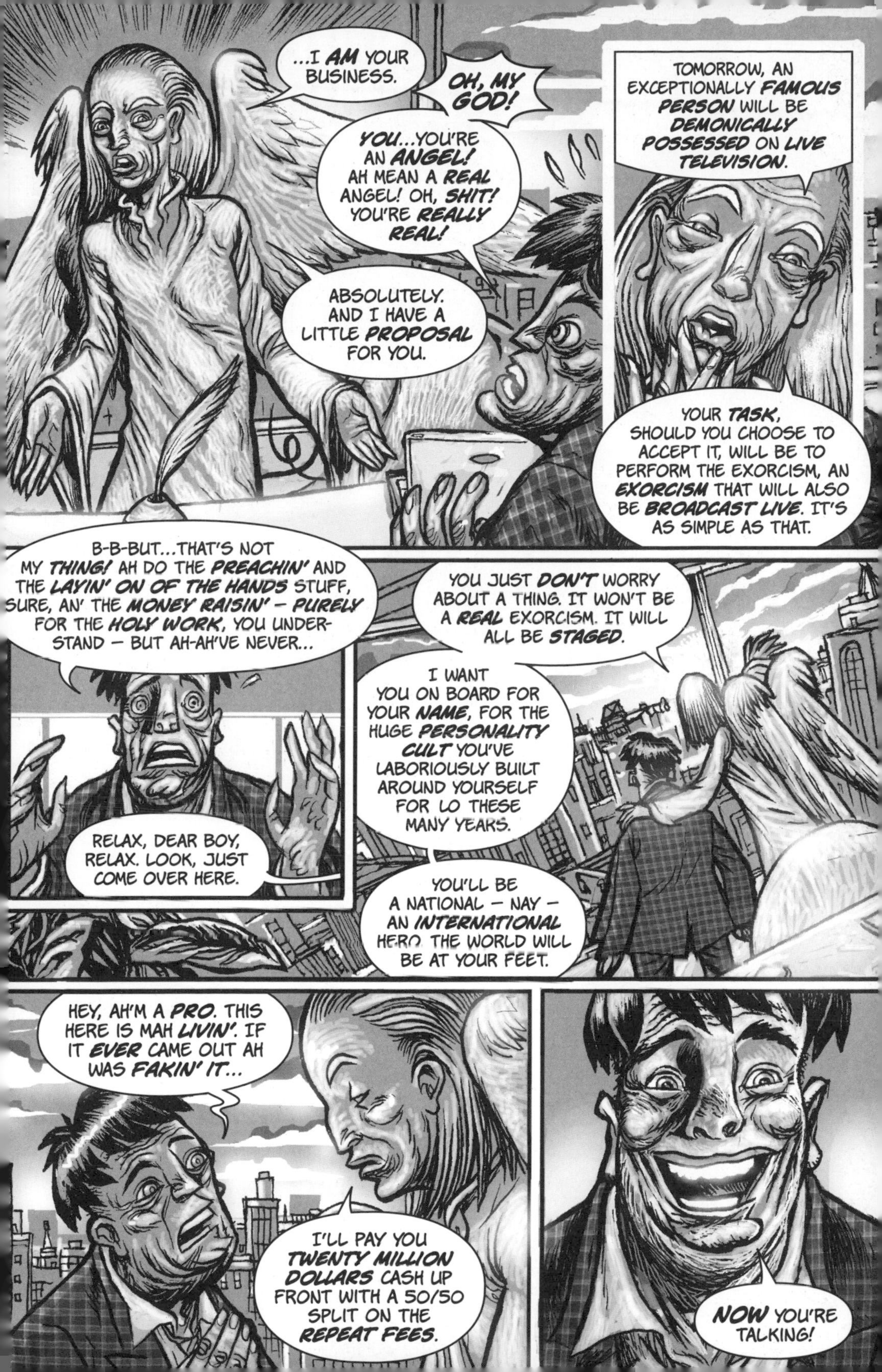

...I AM YOUR BUSINESS.
OH, MY GOD!
YOU...YOU'RE AN ANGEL! AH MEAN A REAL ANGEL! OH, SHIT! YOU'RE REALLY REAL!
ABSOLUTELY. AND I HAVE A LITTLE PROPOSAL FOR YOU.
TOMORROW, AN EXCEPTIONALLY FAMOUS PERSON WILL BE DEMONICALLY POSSESSED ON LIVE TELEVISION.
YOUR TASK, SHOULD YOU CHOOSE TO ACCEPT IT, WILL BE TO PERFORM THE EXORCISM, AN EXORCISM THAT WILL ALSO BE BROADCAST LIVE. IT'S AS SIMPLE AS THAT.
B-B-BUT...THAT'S NOT MY THING! AH DO THE PREACHIN' AND THE LAYIN' ON OF THE HANDS STUFF, SURE, AN' THE MONEY RAISIN' – PURELY FOR THE HOLY WORK, YOU UNDER-STAND – BUT AH-AH'VE NEVER...
RELAX, DEAR BOY, RELAX. LOOK, JUST COME OVER HERE.
YOU JUST DON'T WORRY ABOUT A THING. IT WON'T BE A REAL EXORCISM. IT WILL ALL BE STAGED.
I WANT YOU ON BOARD FOR YOUR NAME, FOR THE HUGE PERSONALITY CULT YOU'VE LABORIOUSLY BUILT AROUND YOURSELF FOR LO THESE MANY YEARS.
YOU'LL BE A NATIONAL – NAY – AN INTERNATIONAL HERO. THE WORLD WILL BE AT YOUR FEET.
HEY, AH'M A PRO. THIS HERE IS MAH LIVIN'. IF IT EVER CAME OUT AH WAS FAKIN' IT...
I'LL PAY YOU TWENTY MILLION DOLLARS CASH UP FRONT WITH A 50/50 SPLIT ON THE REPEAT FEES.
NOW YOU'RE TALKING!

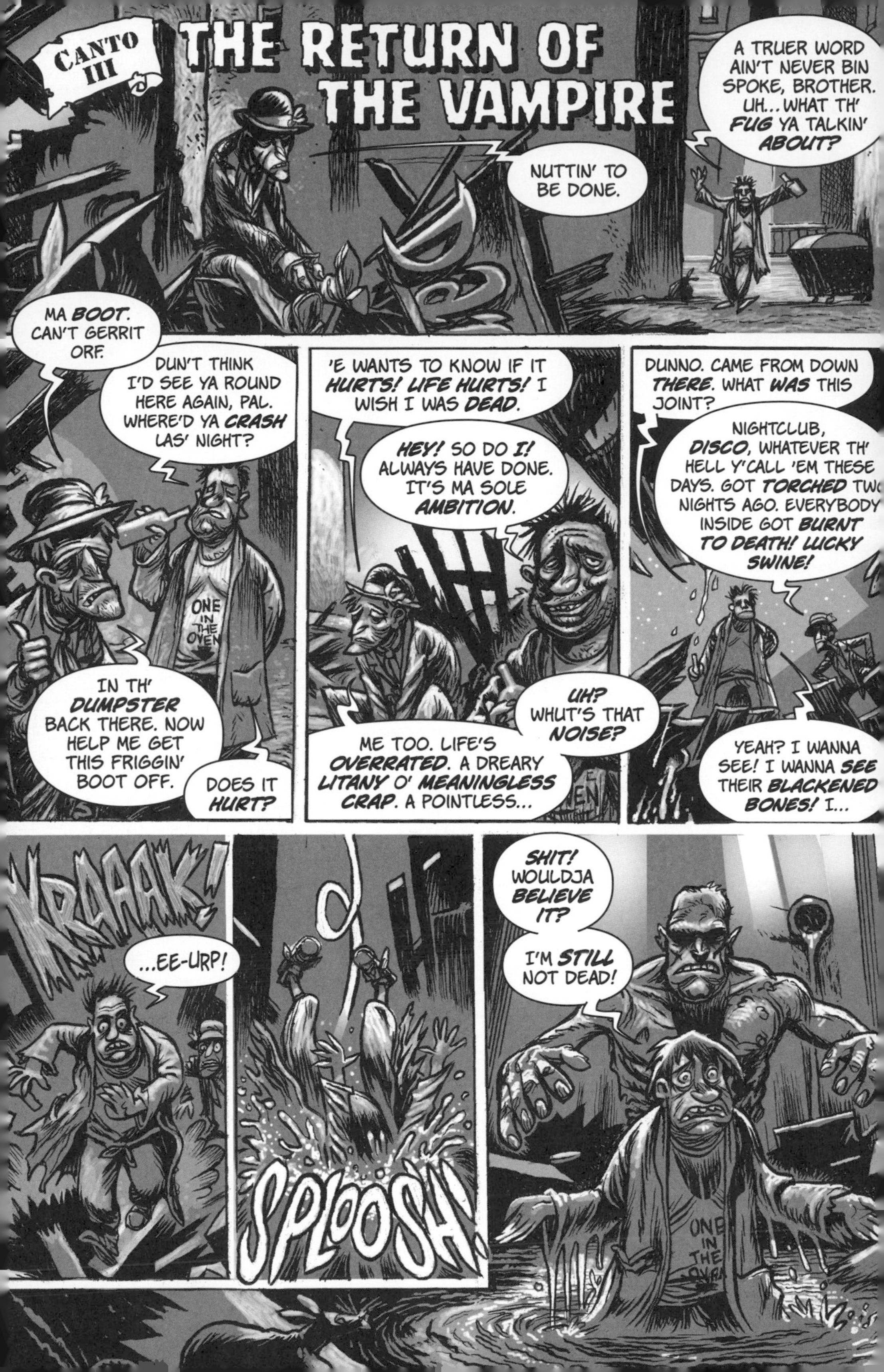
CANTO III
THE RETURN OF THE VAMPIRE
NUTTIN' TO BE DONE.
A TRUER WORD AIN'T NEVER BIN SPOKE, BROTHER. UH... WHAT TH' FUG YA TALKIN' ABOUT?
MA BOOT. CAN'T GERRIT ORF.
DUN'T THINK I'D SEE YA ROUND HERE AGAIN, PAL. WHERE'D YA CRASH LAS' NIGHT?
ONE IN THE OVEN
IN TH' DUMPSTER BACK THERE. NOW HELP ME GET THIS FRIGGIN' BOOT OFF.
DOES IT HURT?
'E WANTS TO KNOW IF IT HURTS! LIFE HURTS! I WISH I WAS DEAD.
HEY! SO DO I! ALWAYS HAVE DONE. IT'S MA SOLE AMBITION.
UH? WHUT'S THAT NOISE?
ME TOO. LIFE'S OVERRATED. A DREARY LITANY O' MEANINGLESS CRAP. A POINTLESS...
DUNNO. CAME FROM DOWN THERE. WHAT WAS THIS JOINT?
NIGHTCLUB, DISCO, WHATEVER TH' HELL Y'CALL 'EM THESE DAYS. GOT TORCHED TWO NIGHTS AGO. EVERYBODY INSIDE GOT BURNT TO DEATH! LUCKY SWINE!
YEAH? I WANNA SEE! I WANNA SEE THEIR BLACKENED BONES! I...
KRAAAK!
...EE-URP!
SPLOOSH!
SHIT! WOULDJA BELIEVE IT?
I'M STILL NOT DEAD!
ONE IN THE OVEN

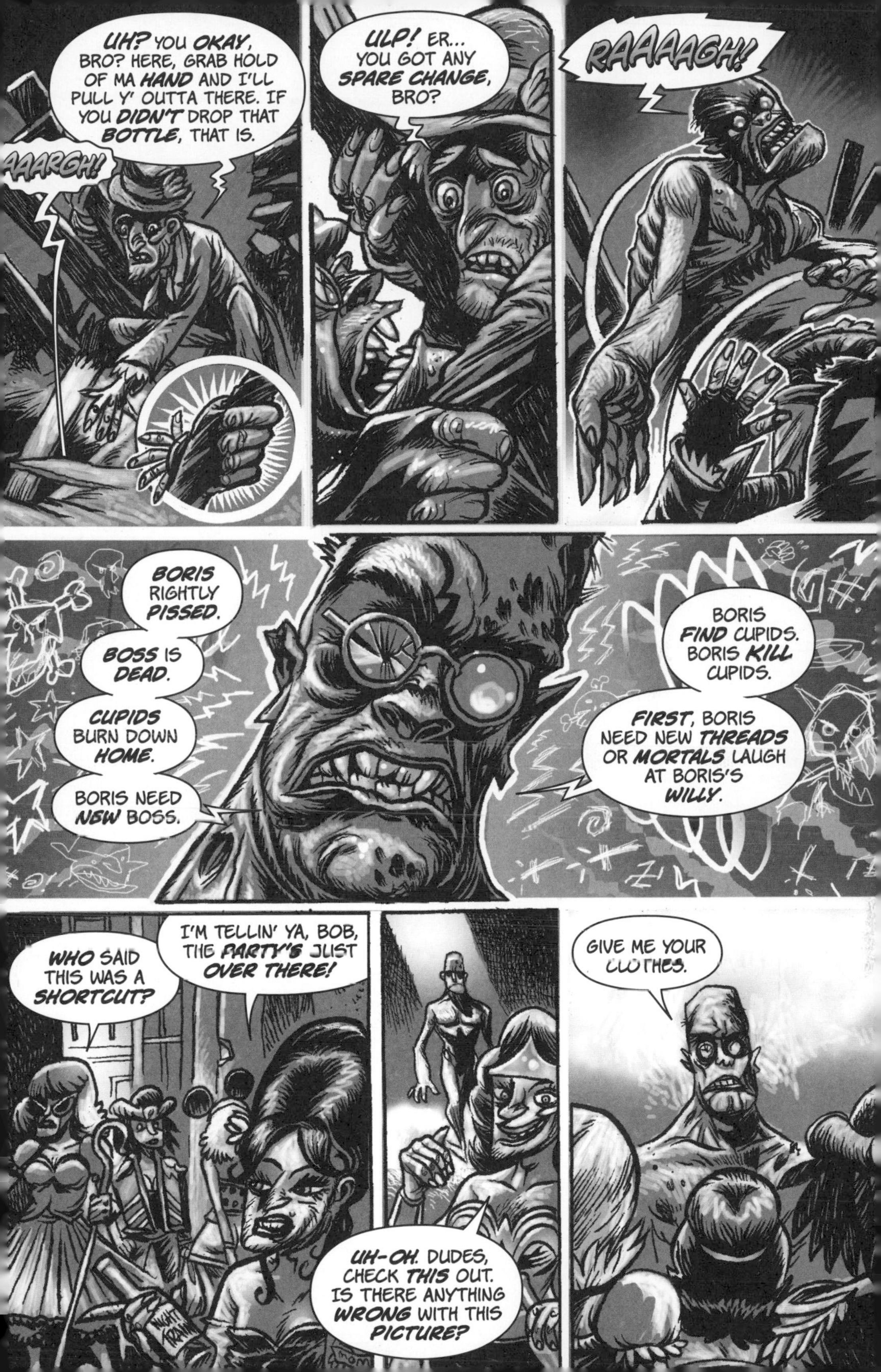
UH? YOU OKAY, BRO? HERE, GRAB HOLD OF MA HAND AND I'LL PULL Y' OUTTA THERE. IF YOU DIDN'T DROP THAT BOTTLE, THAT IS.
AAARGH!
ULP! ER... YOU GOT ANY SPARE CHANGE, BRO?
RAAAAAGH!
BORIS RIGHTLY PISSED.
BOSS IS DEAD.
CUPIDS BURN DOWN HOME.
BORIS NEED NEW BOSS.
BORIS FIND CUPIDS. BORIS KILL CUPIDS.
FIRST, BORIS NEED NEW THREADS OR MORTALS LAUGH AT BORIS'S WILLY.
WHO SAID THIS WAS A SHORTCUT?
I'M TELLIN' YA, BOB, THE PARTY'S JUST OVER THERE!
UH-OH. DUDES, CHECK THIS OUT. IS THERE ANYTHING WRONG WITH THIS PICTURE?
GIVE ME YOUR CLOTHES.

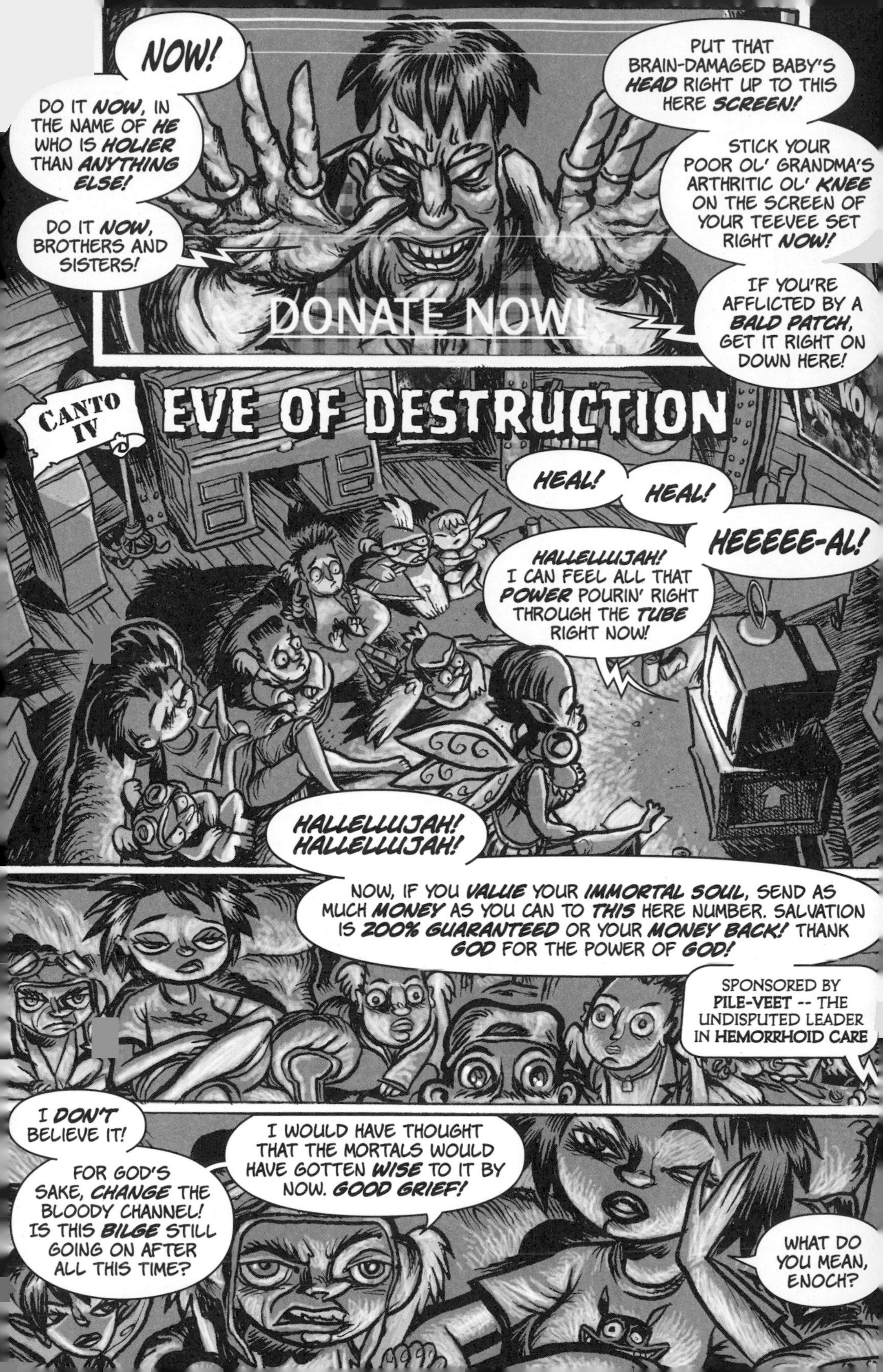
NOW!
DO IT NOW, IN THE NAME OF HE WHO IS HOLIER THAN ANYTHING ELSE!
DO IT NOW, BROTHERS AND SISTERS!
PUT THAT BRAIN-DAMAGED BABY'S HEAD RIGHT UP TO THIS HERE SCREEN!
STICK YOUR POOR OL' GRANDMA'S ARTHRITIC OL' KNEE ON THE SCREEN OF YOUR TEEVEE SET RIGHT NOW!
DONATE NOW!
IF YOU'RE AFFLICTED BY A BALD PATCH, GET IT RIGHT ON DOWN HERE!
CANTO IV
EVE OF DESTRUCTION
HEAL!
HEAL!
HEEEEE-AL!
HALLELLUJAH! I CAN FEEL ALL THAT POWER POURIN' RIGHT THROUGH THE TUBE RIGHT NOW!
HALLELLUJAH! HALLELLUJAH!
NOW, IF YOU VALUE YOUR IMMORTAL SOUL, SEND AS MUCH MONEY AS YOU CAN TO THIS HERE NUMBER. SALVATION IS 200% GUARANTEED OR YOUR MONEY BACK! THANK GOD FOR THE POWER OF GOD!
SPONSORED BY PILE-VEET -- THE UNDISPUTED LEADER IN HEMORRHOID CARE
I DON'T BELIEVE IT!
FOR GOD'S SAKE, CHANGE THE BLOODY CHANNEL! IS THIS BILGE STILL GOING ON AFTER ALL THIS TIME?
I WOULD HAVE THOUGHT THAT THE MORTALS WOULD HAVE GOTTEN WISE TO IT BY NOW. GOOD GRIEF!
WHAT DO YOU MEAN, ENOCH?

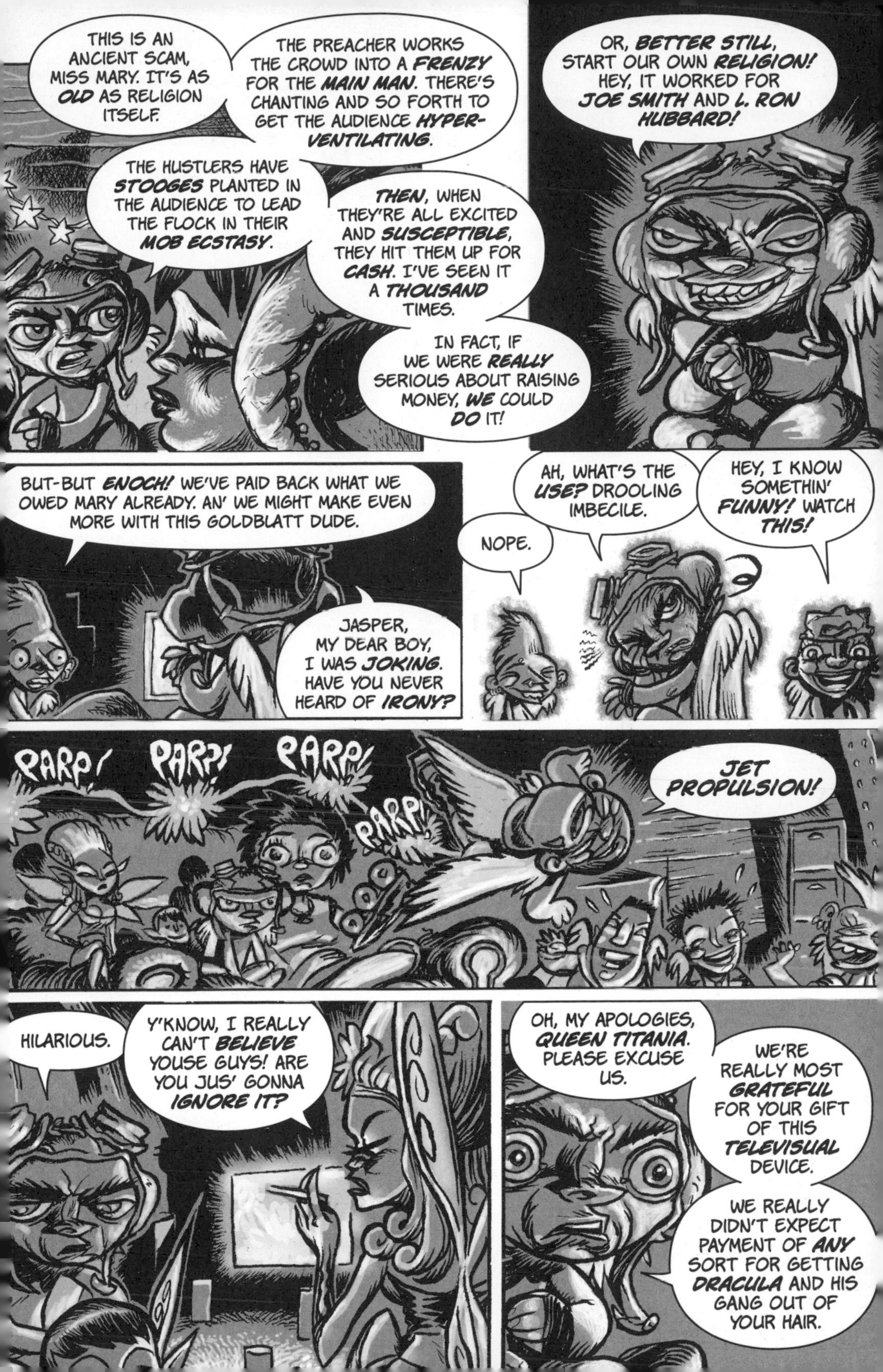

THIS IS AN ANCIENT SCAM, MISS MARY. IT'S AS OLD AS RELIGION ITSELF.
THE PREACHER WORKS THE CROWD INTO A FRENZY FOR THE MAIN MAN. THERE'S CHANTING AND SO FORTH TO GET THE AUDIENCE HYPER-VENTILATING.
THE HUSTLERS HAVE STOOGES PLANTED IN THE AUDIENCE TO LEAD THE FLOCK IN THEIR MOB ECSTASY.
THEN, WHEN THEY'RE ALL EXCITED AND SUSCEPTIBLE, THEY HIT THEM UP FOR CASH. I'VE SEEN IT A THOUSAND TIMES.
IN FACT, IF WE WERE REALLY SERIOUS ABOUT RAISING MONEY, WE COULD DO IT!
OR, BETTER STILL, START OUR OWN RELIGION! HEY, IT WORKED FOR JOE SMITH AND L. RON HUBBARD!
BUT-BUT ENOCH! WE'VE PAID BACK WHAT WE OWED MARY ALREADY. AN' WE MIGHT MAKE EVEN MORE WITH THIS GOLDBLATT DUDE.
JASPER, MY DEAR BOY, I WAS JOKING. HAVE YOU NEVER HEARD OF IRONY?
NOPE.
AH, WHAT'S THE USE? DROOLING IMBECILE.
HEY, I KNOW SOMETHIN' FUNNY! WATCH THIS!
PARP! PARP! PARP! PARP!
JET PROPULSION!
HILARIOUS.
Y'KNOW, I REALLY CAN'T BELIEVE YOUSE GUYS! ARE YOU JUS' GONNA IGNORE IT?
OH, MY APOLOGIES, QUEEN TITANIA. PLEASE EXCUSE US.
WE'RE REALLY MOST GRATEFUL FOR YOUR GIFT OF THIS TELEVISUAL DEVICE.
WE REALLY DIDN'T EXPECT PAYMENT OF ANY SORT FOR GETTING DRACULA AND HIS GANG OUT OF YOUR HAIR.

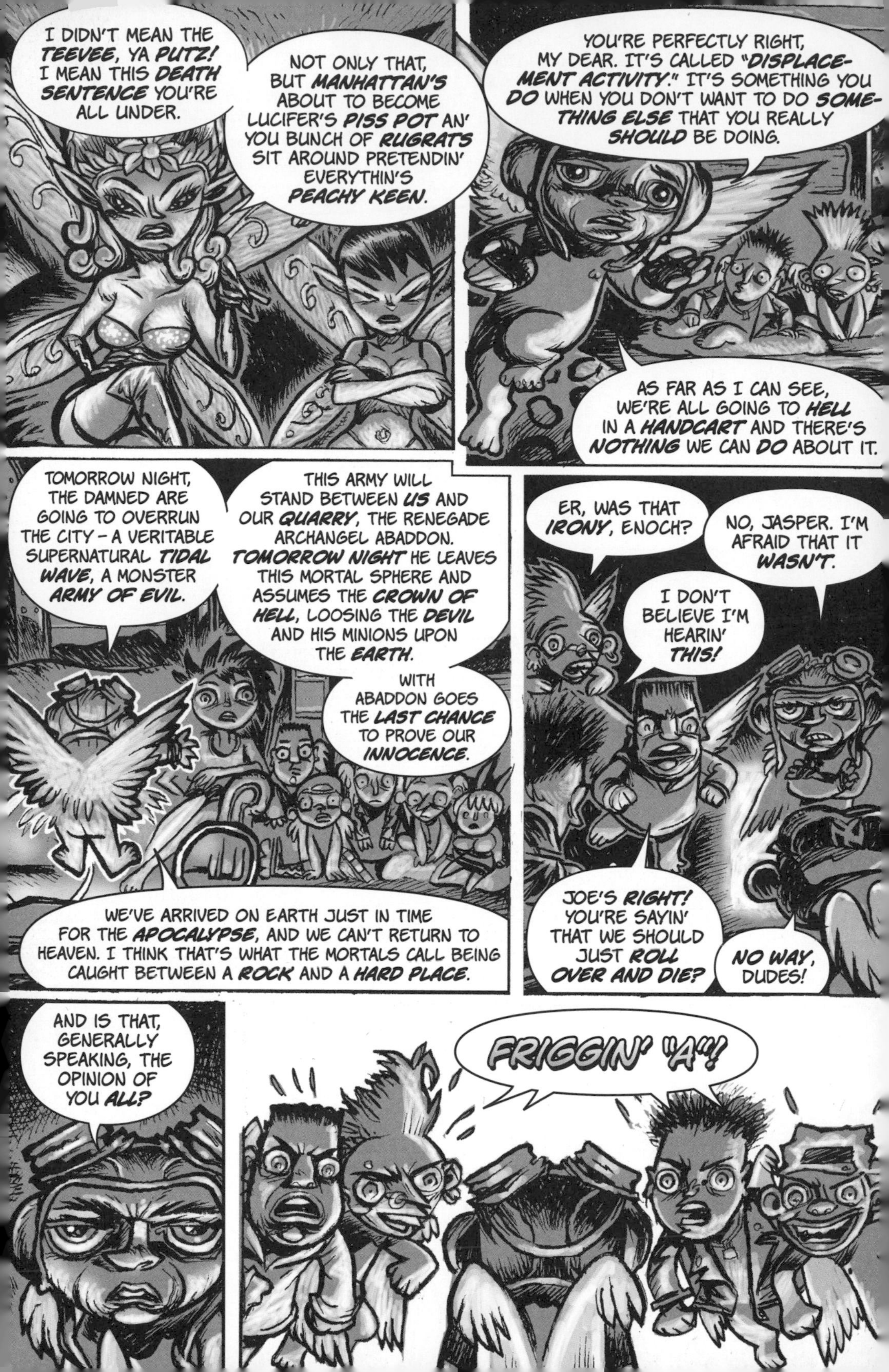
I DIDN'T MEAN THE TEEVEE, YA PUTZ! I MEAN THIS DEATH SENTENCE YOU'RE ALL UNDER.
NOT ONLY THAT, BUT MANHATTAN'S ABOUT TO BECOME LUCIFER'S PISS POT AN' YOU BUNCH OF RUGRATS SIT AROUND PRETENDIN' EVERYTHIN'S PEACHY KEEN.
YOU'RE PERFECTLY RIGHT, MY DEAR. IT'S CALLED "DISPLACEMENT ACTIVITY." IT'S SOMETHING YOU DO WHEN YOU DON'T WANT TO DO SOMETHING ELSE THAT YOU REALLY SHOULD BE DOING.
AS FAR AS I CAN SEE, WE'RE ALL GOING TO HELL IN A HANDCART AND THERE'S NOTHING WE CAN DO ABOUT IT.
TOMORROW NIGHT, THE DAMNED ARE GOING TO OVERRUN THE CITY – A VERITABLE SUPERNATURAL TIDAL WAVE, A MONSTER ARMY OF EVIL.
THIS ARMY WILL STAND BETWEEN US AND OUR QUARRY, THE RENEGADE ARCHANGEL ABADDON. TOMORROW NIGHT HE LEAVES THIS MORTAL SPHERE AND ASSUMES THE CROWN OF HELL, LOOSING THE DEVIL AND HIS MINIONS UPON THE EARTH.
WITH ABADDON GOES THE LAST CHANCE TO PROVE OUR INNOCENCE.
WE'VE ARRIVED ON EARTH JUST IN TIME FOR THE APOCALYPSE, AND WE CAN'T RETURN TO HEAVEN. I THINK THAT'S WHAT THE MORTALS CALL BEING CAUGHT BETWEEN A ROCK AND A HARD PLACE.
ER, WAS THAT IRONY, ENOCH?
NO, JASPER. I'M AFRAID THAT IT WASN'T.
I DON'T BELIEVE I'M HEARIN' THIS!
JOE'S RIGHT! YOU'RE SAYIN' THAT WE SHOULD JUST ROLL OVER AND DIE?
NO WAY, DUDES!
AND IS THAT, GENERALLY SPEAKING, THE OPINION OF YOU ALL?
FRIGGIN' "A"!

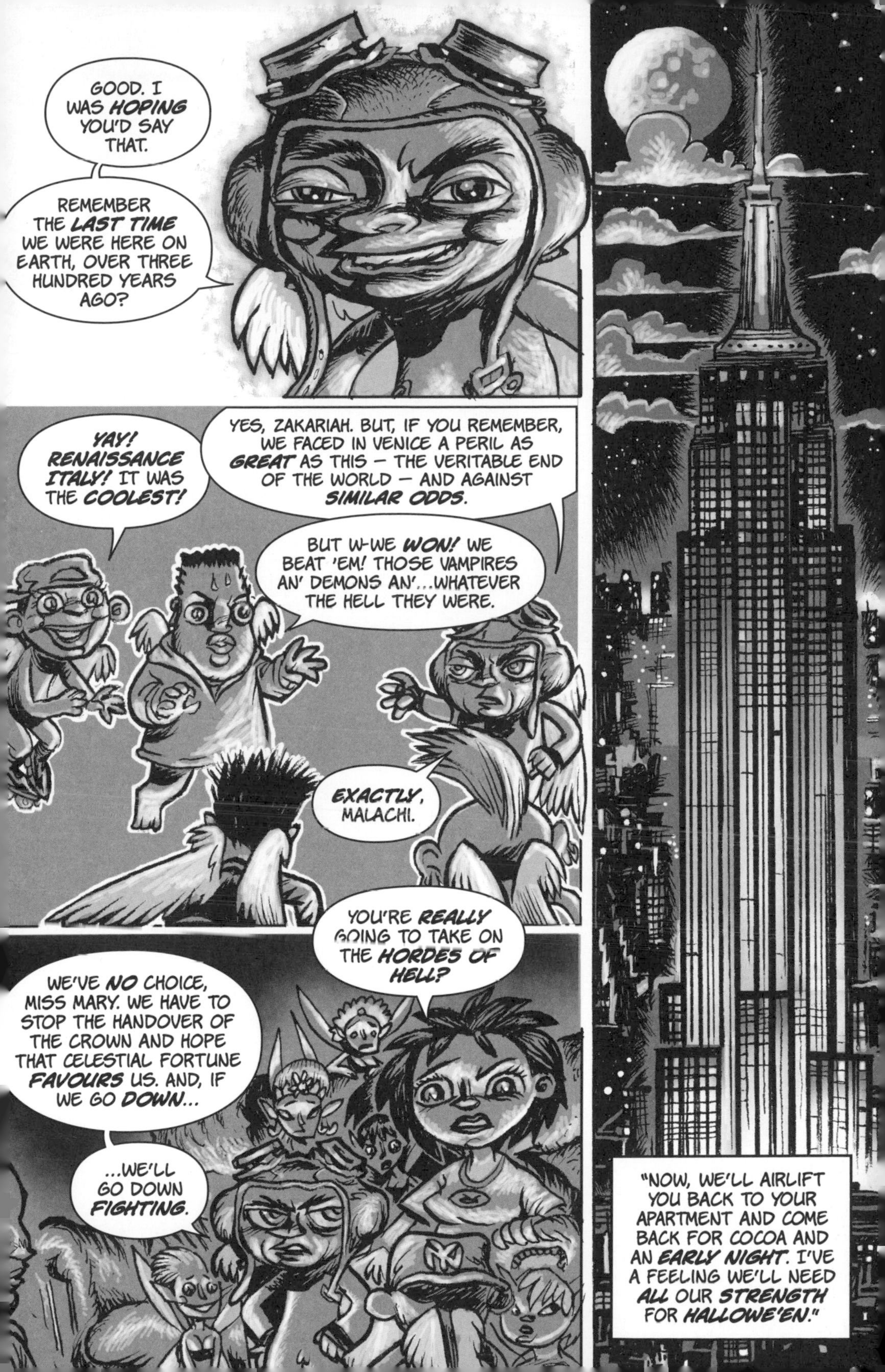
GOOD. I WAS HOPING YOU'D SAY THAT.
REMEMBER THE LAST TIME WE WERE HERE ON EARTH, OVER THREE HUNDRED YEARS AGO?
YAY! RENAISSANCE ITALY! IT WAS THE COOLEST!
YES, ZAKARIAH. BUT, IF YOU REMEMBER, WE FACED IN VENICE A PERIL AS GREAT AS THIS — THE VERITABLE END OF THE WORLD — AND AGAINST SIMILAR ODDS.
BUT W-WE WON! WE BEAT 'EM! THOSE VAMPIRES AN' DEMONS AN'...WHATEVER THE HELL THEY WERE.
EXACTLY, MALACHI.
YOU'RE REALLY GOING TO TAKE ON THE HORDES OF HELL?
WE'VE NO CHOICE, MISS MARY. WE HAVE TO STOP THE HANDOVER OF THE CROWN AND HOPE THAT CELESTIAL FORTUNE FAVOURS US. AND, IF WE GO DOWN...
...WE'LL GO DOWN FIGHTING.
"NOW, WE'LL AIRLIFT YOU BACK TO YOUR APARTMENT AND COME BACK FOR COCOA AND AN EARLY NIGHT. I'VE A FEELING WE'LL NEED ALL OUR STRENGTH FOR HALLOWE'EN."

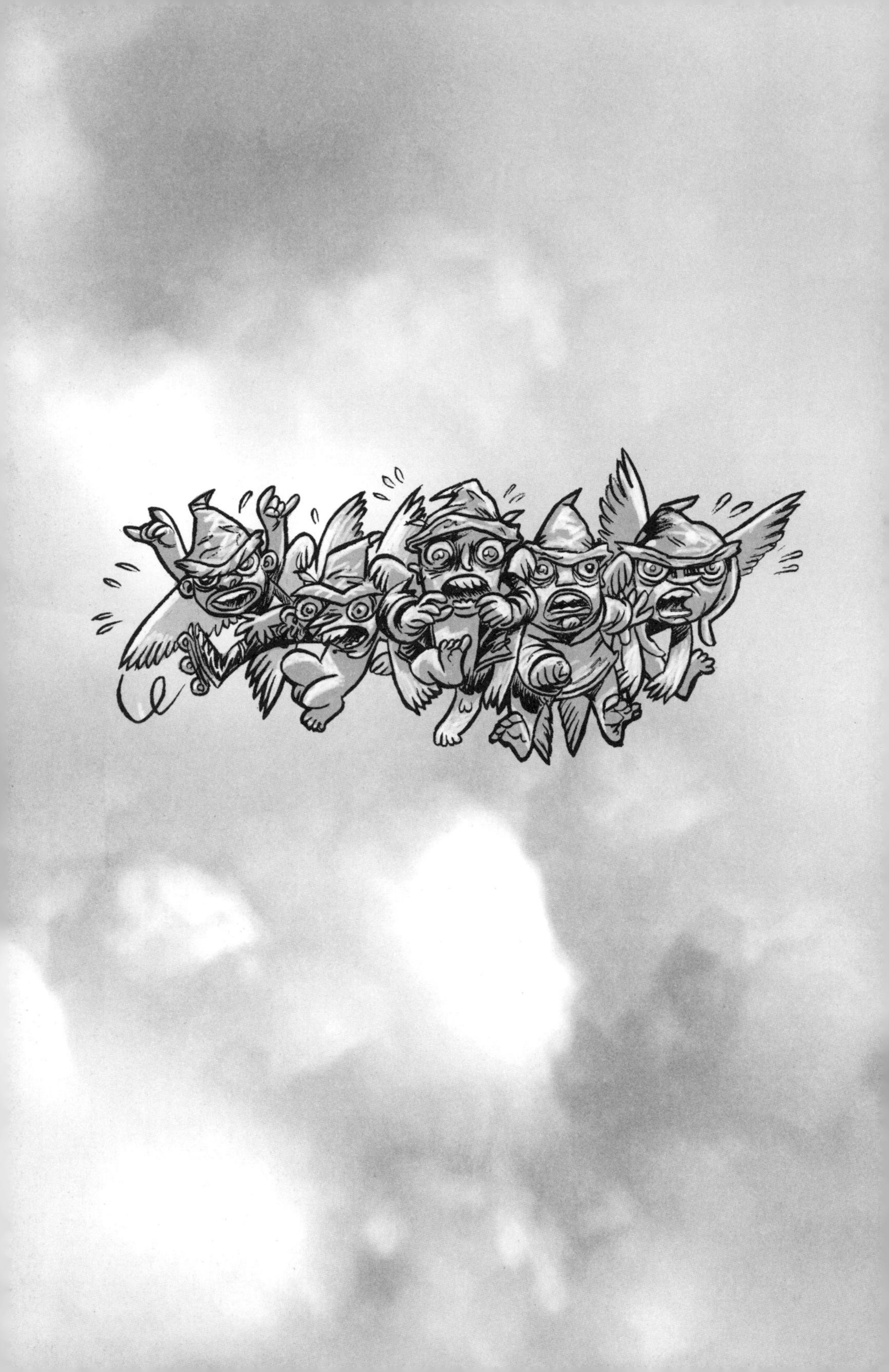

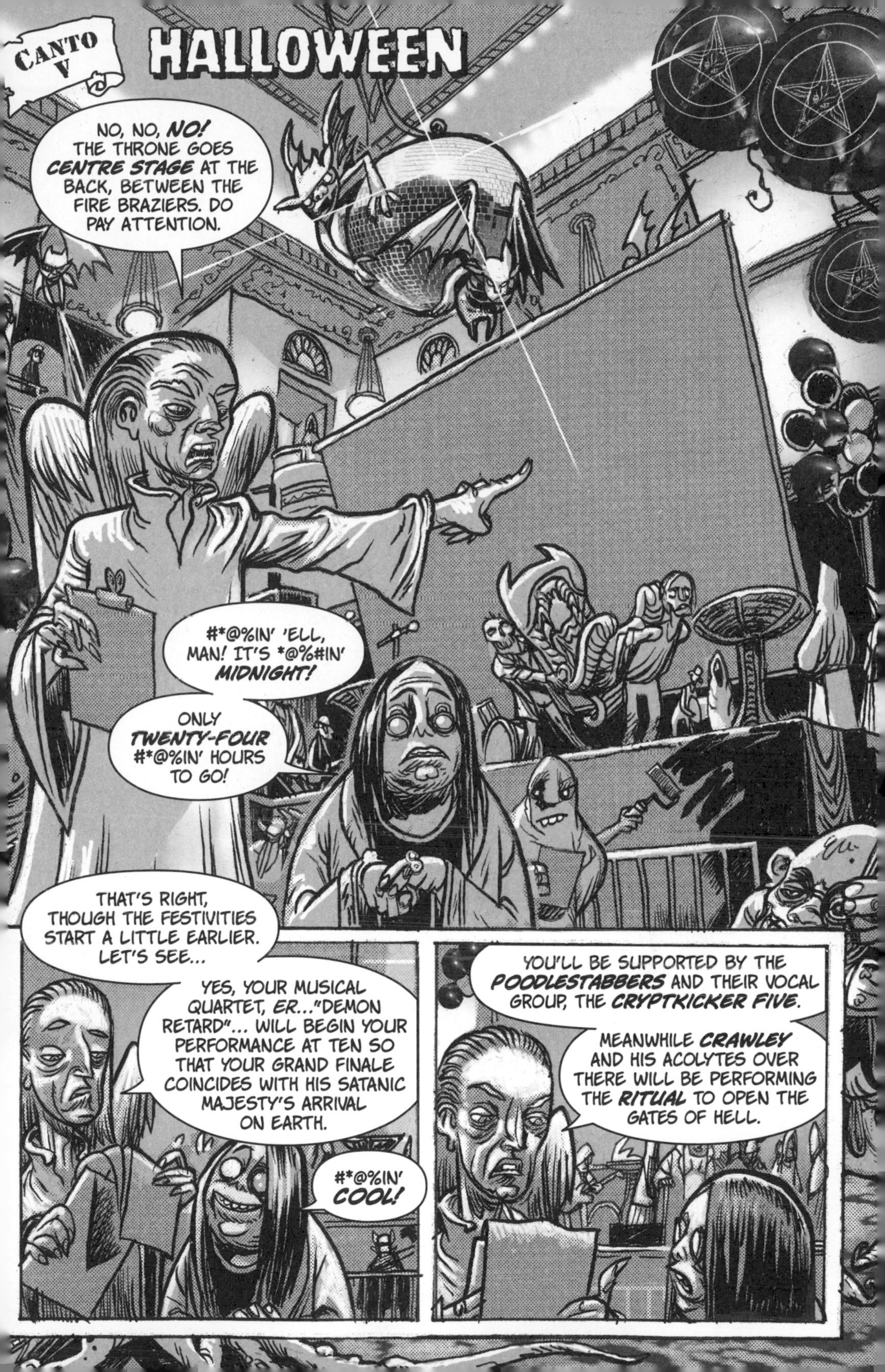
CANTO V
HALLOWEEN
NO, NO, NO! THE THRONE GOES CENTRE STAGE AT THE BACK, BETWEEN THE FIRE BRAZIERS. DO PAY ATTENTION.
#*@%IN' 'ELL, MAN! IT'S *@%#IN' MIDNIGHT!
ONLY TWENTY-FOUR #*@%IN' HOURS TO GO!
THAT'S RIGHT, THOUGH THE FESTIVITIES START A LITTLE EARLIER. LET'S SEE...
YES, YOUR MUSICAL QUARTET, ER..."DEMON RETARD"... WILL BEGIN YOUR PERFORMANCE AT TEN SO THAT YOUR GRAND FINALE COINCIDES WITH HIS SATANIC MAJESTY'S ARRIVAL ON EARTH.
#*@%IN' COOL!
YOU'LL BE SUPPORTED BY THE POODLESTABBERS AND THEIR VOCAL GROUP, THE CRYPTKICKER FIVE.
MEANWHILE CRAWLEY AND HIS ACOLYTES OVER THERE WILL BE PERFORMING THE RITUAL TO OPEN THE GATES OF HELL.

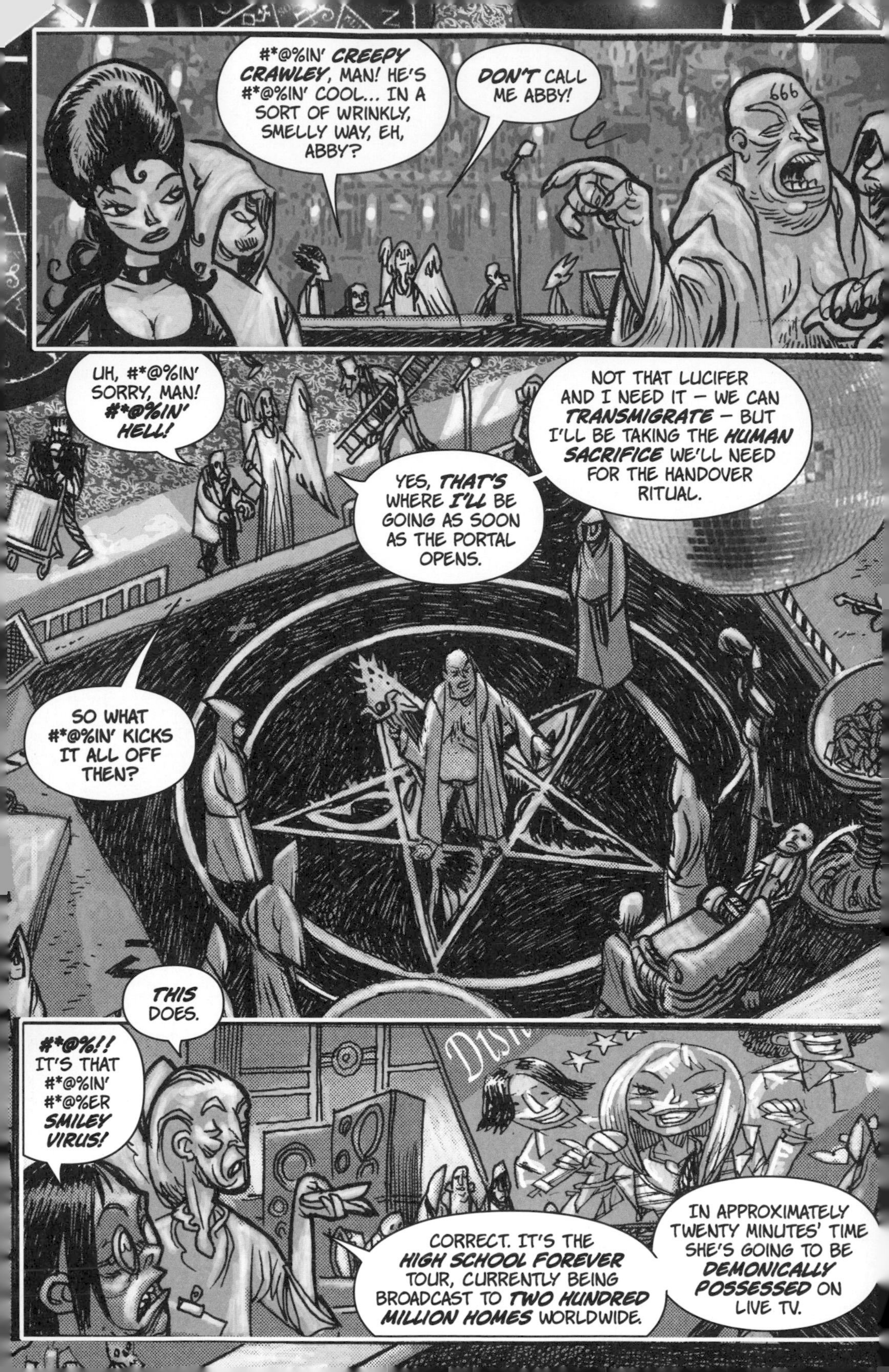
#*@%IN' CREEPY CRAWLEY, MAN! HE'S #*@%IN' COOL... IN A SORT OF WRINKLY, SMELLY WAY, EH, ABBY?
DON'T CALL ME ABBY!
UH, #*@%IN' SORRY, MAN! #*@%IN' HELL!
YES, THAT'S WHERE I'LL BE GOING AS SOON AS THE PORTAL OPENS.
NOT THAT LUCIFER AND I NEED IT — WE CAN TRANSMIGRATE — BUT I'LL BE TAKING THE HUMAN SACRIFICE WE'LL NEED FOR THE HANDOVER RITUAL.
SO WHAT #*@%IN' KICKS IT ALL OFF THEN?
THIS DOES.
#*@%!! IT'S THAT #*@%IN' #*@%ER SMILEY VIRUS!
CORRECT. IT'S THE HIGH SCHOOL FOREVER TOUR, CURRENTLY BEING BROADCAST TO TWO HUNDRED MILLION HOMES WORLDWIDE.
IN APPROXIMATELY TWENTY MINUTES' TIME SHE'S GOING TO BE DEMONICALLY POSSESSED ON LIVE TV.

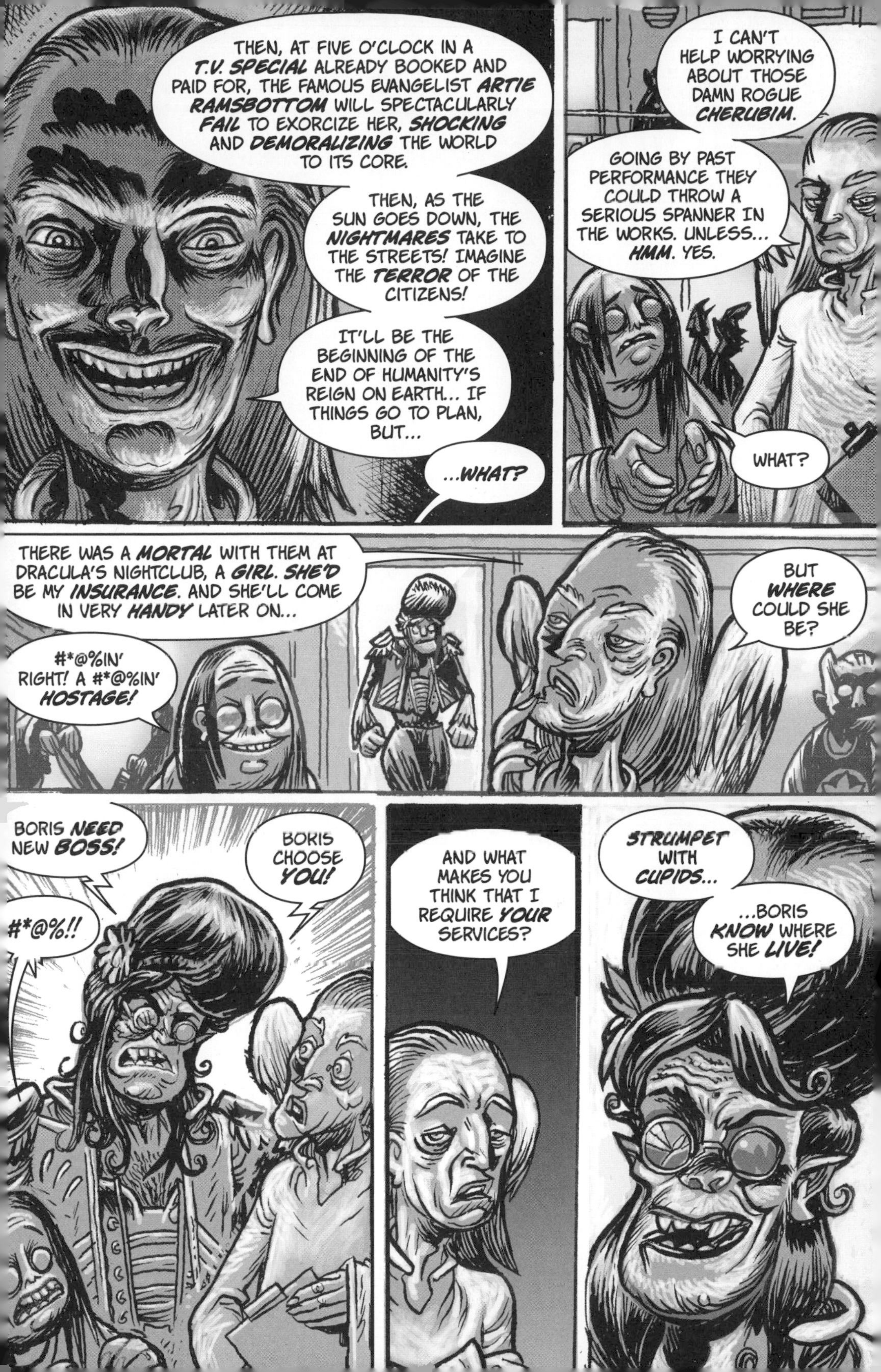
THEN, AT FIVE O'CLOCK IN A T.V. SPECIAL ALREADY BOOKED AND PAID FOR, THE FAMOUS EVANGELIST ARTIE RAMSBOTTOM WILL SPECTACULARLY FAIL TO EXORCIZE HER, SHOCKING AND DEMORALIZING THE WORLD TO ITS CORE.
THEN, AS THE SUN GOES DOWN, THE NIGHTMARES TAKE TO THE STREETS! IMAGINE THE TERROR OF THE CITIZENS!
IT'LL BE THE BEGINNING OF THE END OF HUMANITY'S REIGN ON EARTH... IF THINGS GO TO PLAN, BUT...
...WHAT?
I CAN'T HELP WORRYING ABOUT THOSE DAMN ROGUE CHERUBIM.
GOING BY PAST PERFORMANCE THEY COULD THROW A SERIOUS SPANNER IN THE WORKS. UNLESS... HMM. YES.
WHAT?
THERE WAS A MORTAL WITH THEM AT DRACULA'S NIGHTCLUB, A GIRL. SHE'D BE MY INSURANCE. AND SHE'LL COME IN VERY HANDY LATER ON...
BUT WHERE COULD SHE BE?
#*@%IN' RIGHT! A #*@%IN' HOSTAGE!
BORIS NEED NEW BOSS!
BORIS CHOOSE YOU!
#*@%!!
AND WHAT MAKES YOU THINK THAT I REQUIRE YOUR SERVICES?
STRUMPET WITH CUPIDS...
...BORIS KNOW WHERE SHE LIVE!

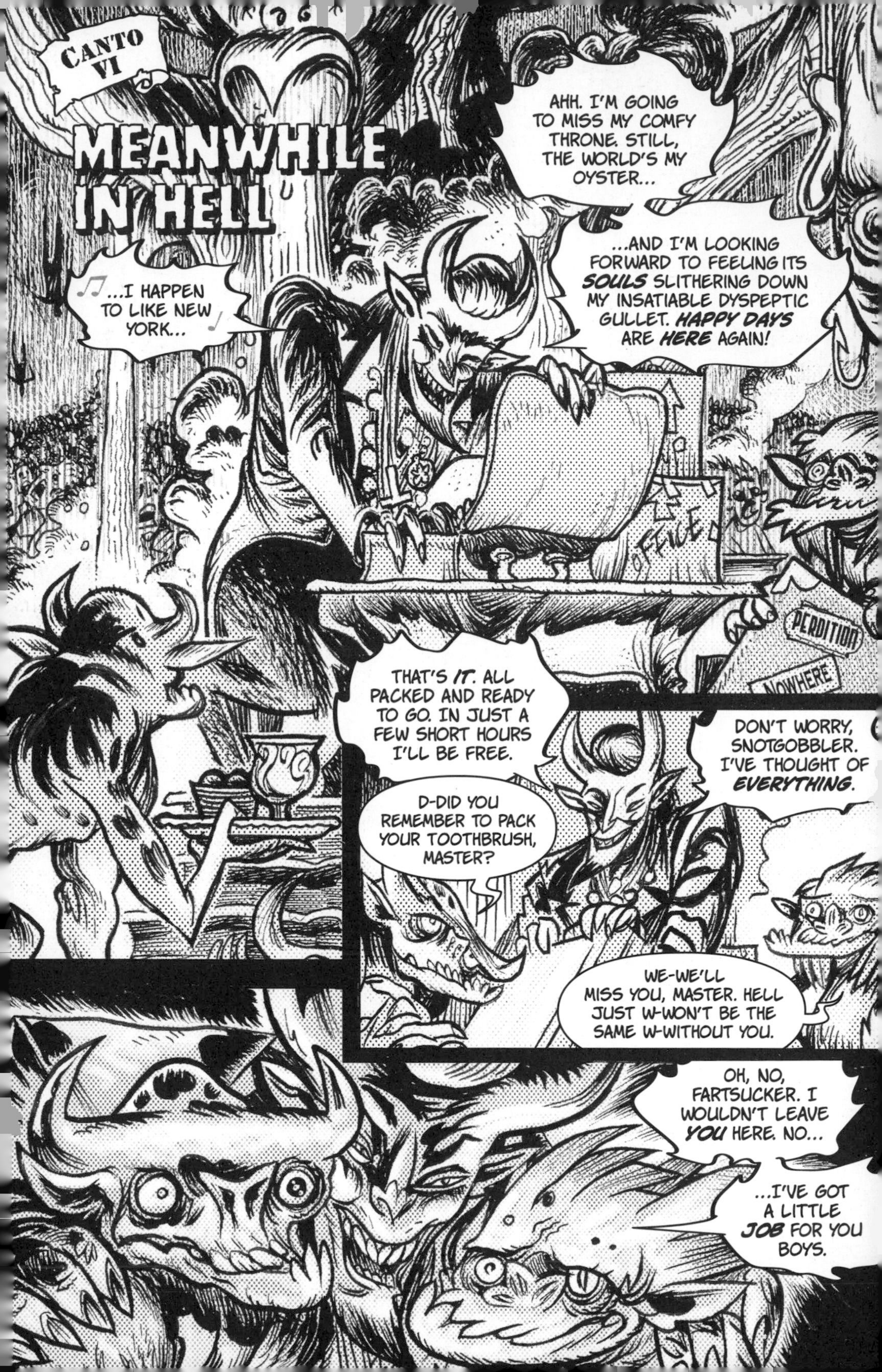

CANTO VI
MEANWHILE IN HELL
AHH. I'M GOING TO MISS MY COMFY THRONE. STILL, THE WORLD'S MY OYSTER...
...I HAPPEN TO LIKE NEW YORK...
...AND I'M LOOKING FORWARD TO FEELING ITS SOULS SLITHERING DOWN MY INSATIABLE DYSPEPTIC GULLET. HAPPY DAYS ARE HERE AGAIN!
OFFICE
PERDITION
NOWHERE
THAT'S IT. ALL PACKED AND READY TO GO. IN JUST A FEW SHORT HOURS I'LL BE FREE.
D-DID YOU REMEMBER TO PACK YOUR TOOTHBRUSH, MASTER?
DON'T WORRY, SNOTGOBBLER. I'VE THOUGHT OF EVERYTHING.
WE-WE'LL MISS YOU, MASTER. HELL JUST W-WON'T BE THE SAME W-WITHOUT YOU.
OH, NO, FARTSUCKER. I WOULDN'T LEAVE YOU HERE. NO...
...I'VE GOT A LITTLE JOB FOR YOU BOYS.

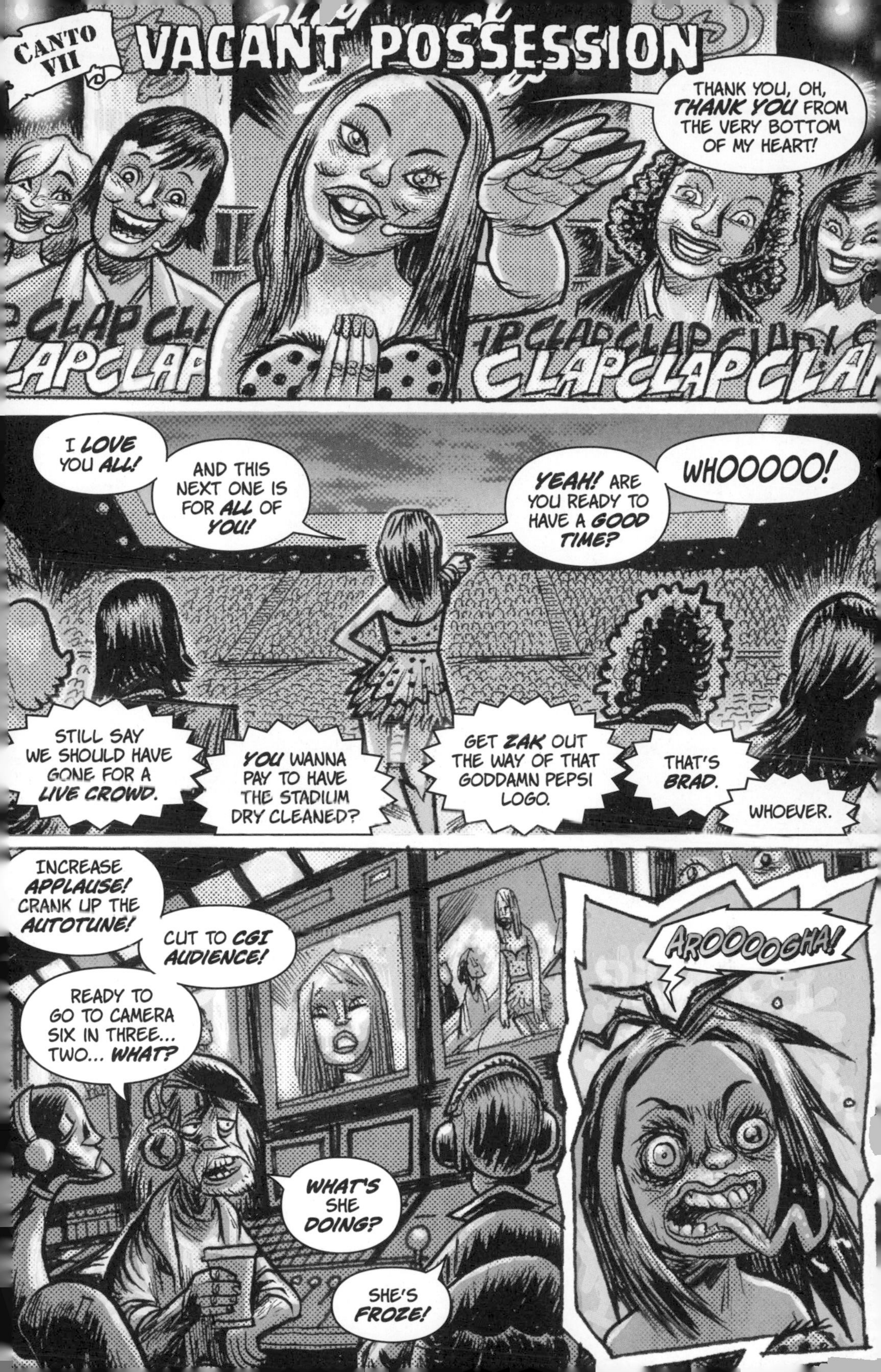
CANTO VII
VACANT POSSESSION
THANK YOU, OH, THANK YOU FROM THE VERY BOTTOM OF MY HEART!
CLAP CLAP CLAP CLAP CLAP CLAP CLAP
I LOVE YOU ALL!
AND THIS NEXT ONE IS FOR ALL OF YOU!
YEAH! ARE YOU READY TO HAVE A GOOD TIME?
WHOOOOO!
STILL SAY WE SHOULD HAVE GONE FOR A LIVE CROWD.
YOU WANNA PAY TO HAVE THE STADIUM DRY CLEANED?
GET ZAK OUT THE WAY OF THAT GODDAMN PEPSI LOGO.
THAT'S BRAD.
WHOEVER.
INCREASE APPLAUSE! CRANK UP THE AUTOTUNE!
CUT TO CGI AUDIENCE!
READY TO GO TO CAMERA SIX IN THREE... TWO... WHAT?
AROOOOOGHA!
WHAT'S SHE DOING?
SHE'S FROZE!

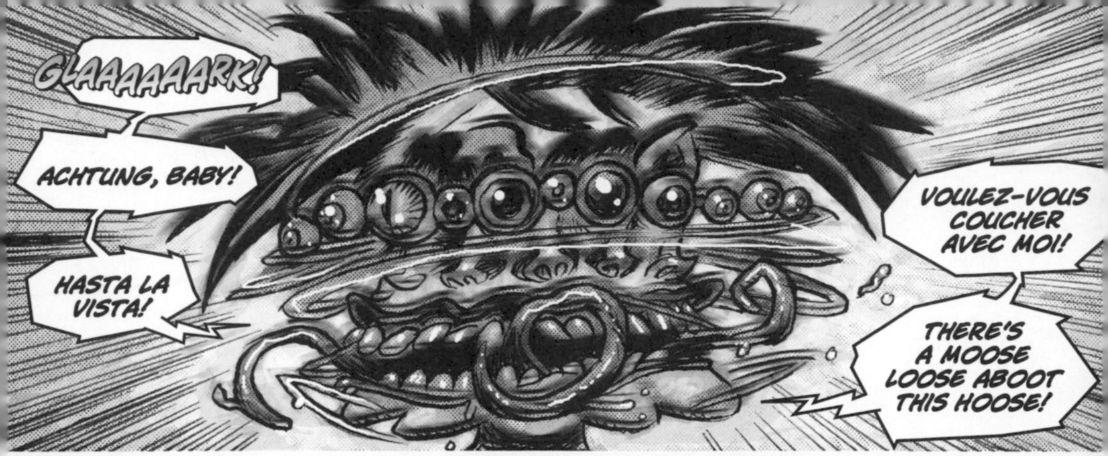
GLAAAAAARK!
ACHTUNG, BABY!
HASTA LA VISTA!
VOULEZ-VOUS COUCHER AVEC MOI!
THERE'S A MOOSE LOOSE ABOOT THIS HOOSE!

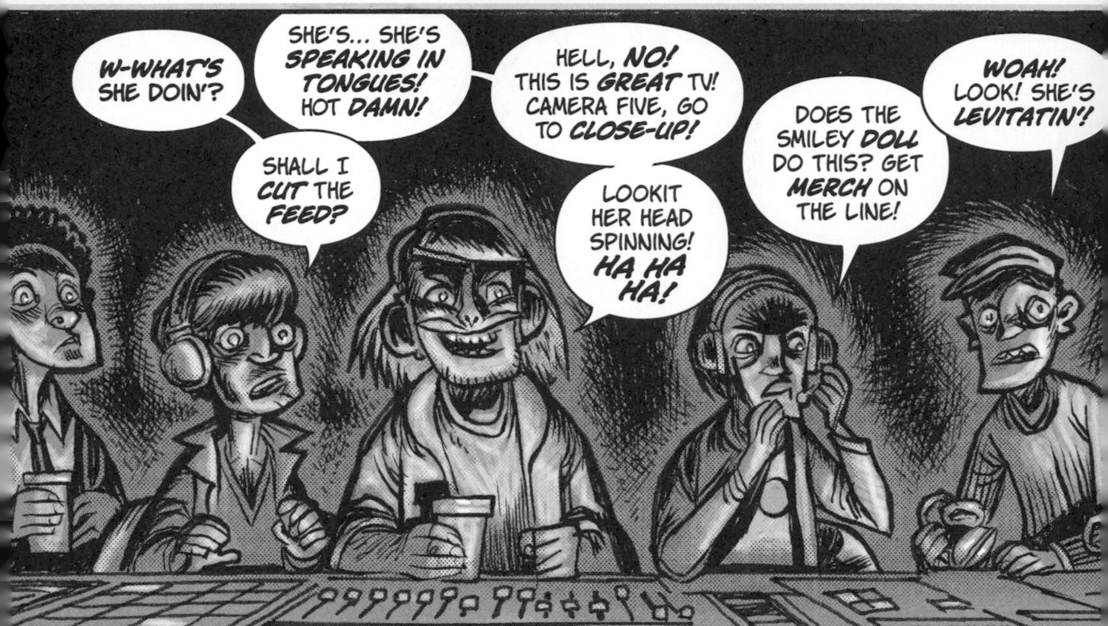
W-WHAT'S SHE DOIN'?
SHE'S... SHE'S SPEAKING IN TONGUES! HOT DAMN!
SHALL I CUT THE FEED?
HELL, NO! THIS IS GREAT TV! CAMERA FIVE, GO TO CLOSE-UP!
LOOKIT HER HEAD SPINNING! HA HA HA!
DOES THE SMILEY DOLL DO THIS? GET MERCH ON THE LINE!
WOAH! LOOK! SHE'S LEVITATIN'!

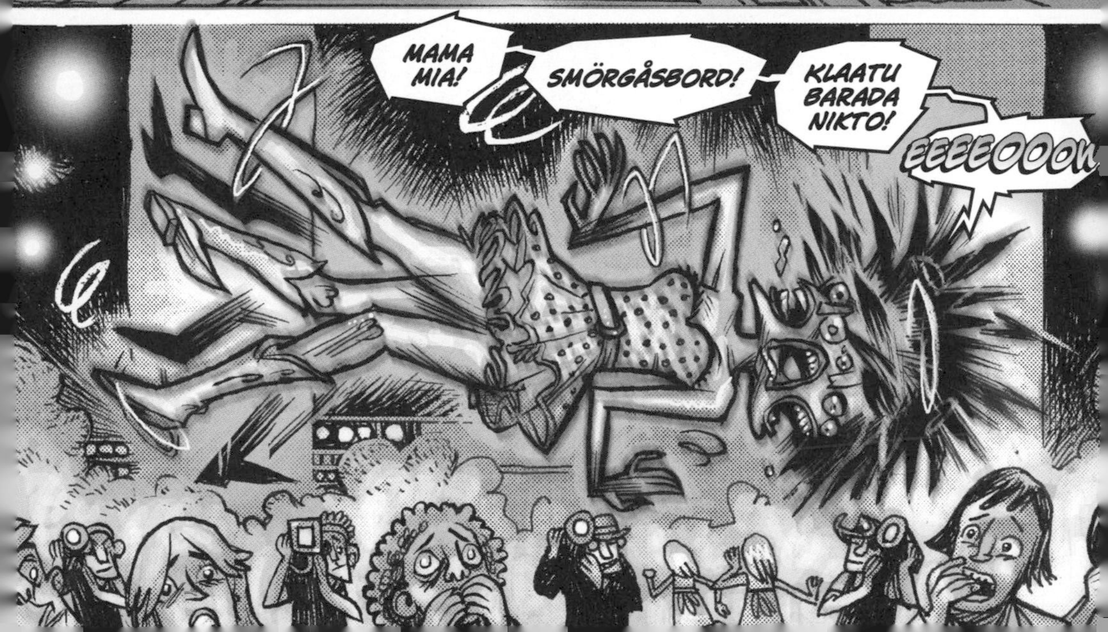
MAMA MIA!
SMÖRGÅSBORD!
KLAATU BARADA NIKTO!
EEEEOOOW

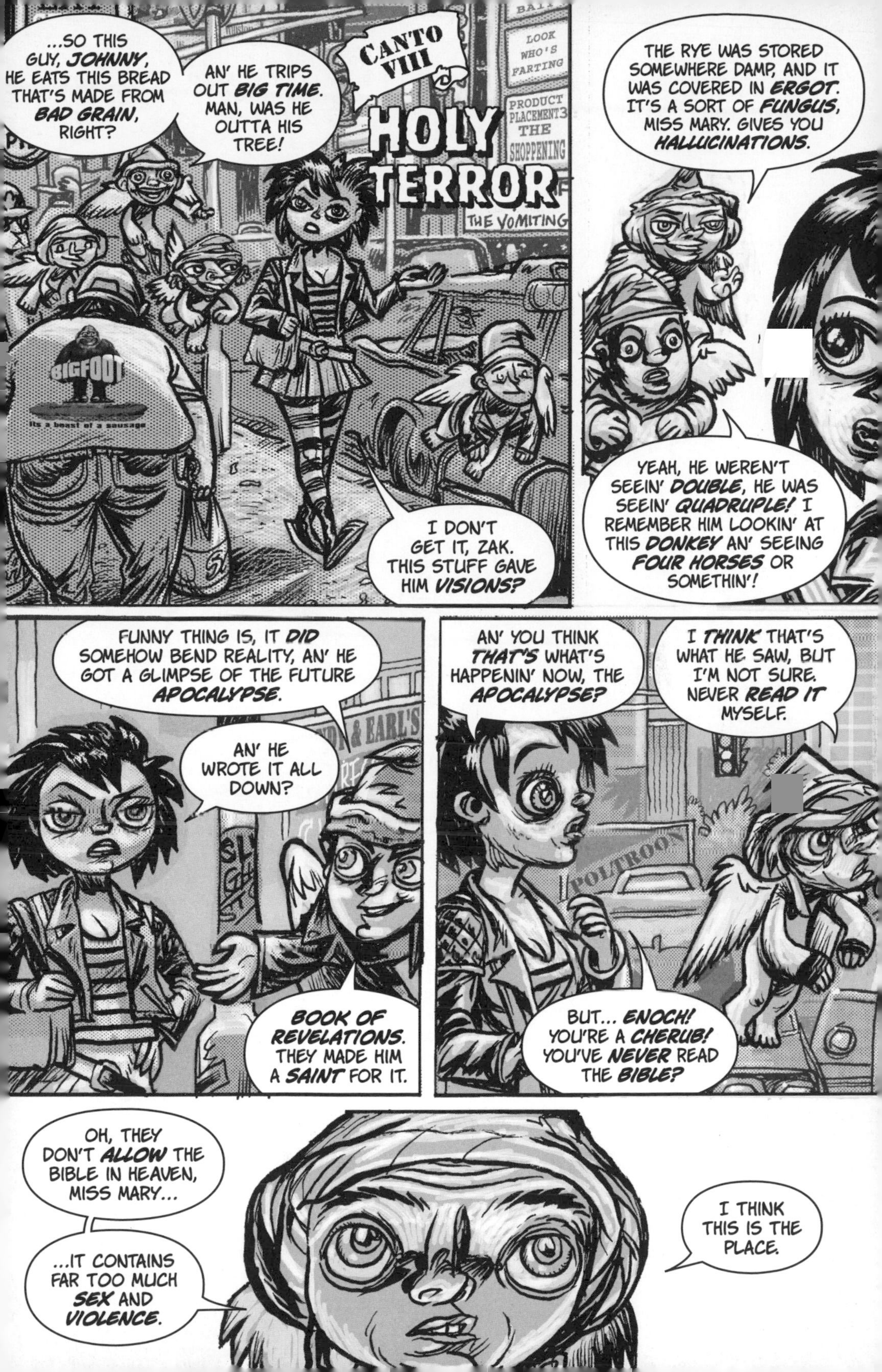
CANTO VIII
HOLY TERROR
...SO THIS GUY, JOHNNY, HE EATS THIS BREAD THAT'S MADE FROM BAD GRAIN, RIGHT?
AN' HE TRIPS OUT BIG TIME. MAN, WAS HE OUTTA HIS TREE!
I DON'T GET IT, ZAK. THIS STUFF GAVE HIM VISIONS?
THE RYE WAS STORED SOMEWHERE DAMP, AND IT WAS COVERED IN ERGOT. IT'S A SORT OF FUNGUS, MISS MARY. GIVES YOU HALLUCINATIONS.
YEAH, HE WEREN'T SEEIN' DOUBLE, HE WAS SEEIN' QUADRUPLE! I REMEMBER HIM LOOKIN' AT THIS DONKEY AN' SEEING FOUR HORSES OR SOMETHIN'!
FUNNY THING IS, IT DID SOMEHOW BEND REALITY, AN' HE GOT A GLIMPSE OF THE FUTURE APOCALYPSE.
AN' HE WROTE IT ALL DOWN?
BOOK OF REVELATIONS. THEY MADE HIM A SAINT FOR IT.
AN' YOU THINK THAT'S WHAT'S HAPPENIN' NOW, THE APOCALYPSE?
I THINK THAT'S WHAT HE SAW, BUT I'M NOT SURE. NEVER READ IT MYSELF.
BUT... ENOCH! YOU'RE A CHERUB! YOU'VE NEVER READ THE BIBLE?
OH, THEY DON'T ALLOW THE BIBLE IN HEAVEN, MISS MARY...
...IT CONTAINS FAR TOO MUCH SEX AND VIOLENCE.
I THINK THIS IS THE PLACE.

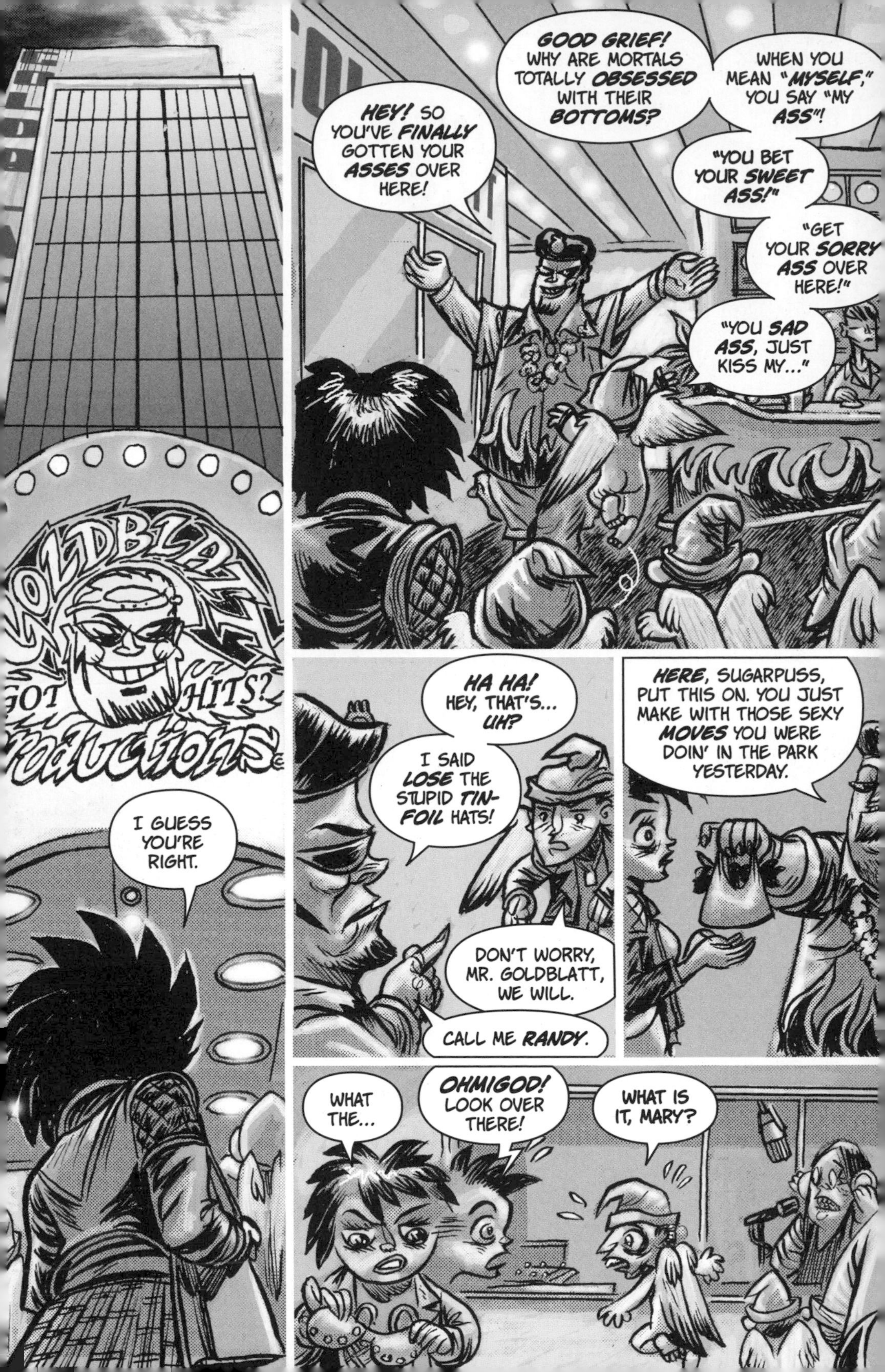
GOLDBLATT GOT HITS? Productions
I GUESS YOU'RE RIGHT.
HEY! SO YOU'VE FINALLY GOTTEN YOUR ASSES OVER HERE!
GOOD GRIEF! WHY ARE MORTALS TOTALLY OBSESSED WITH THEIR BOTTOMS?
WHEN YOU MEAN "MYSELF," YOU SAY "MY ASS"!
"YOU BET YOUR SWEET ASS!"
"GET YOUR SORRY ASS OVER HERE!"
"YOU SAD ASS, JUST KISS MY..."
HA HA! HEY, THAT'S... UH?
I SAID LOSE THE STUPID TIN-FOIL HATS!
DON'T WORRY, MR. GOLDBLATT, WE WILL.
CALL ME RANDY.
HERE, SUGARPUSS, PUT THIS ON. YOU JUST MAKE WITH THOSE SEXY MOVES YOU WERE DOIN' IN THE PARK YESTERDAY.
WHAT THE...
OHMIGOD! LOOK OVER THERE!
WHAT IS IT, MARY?

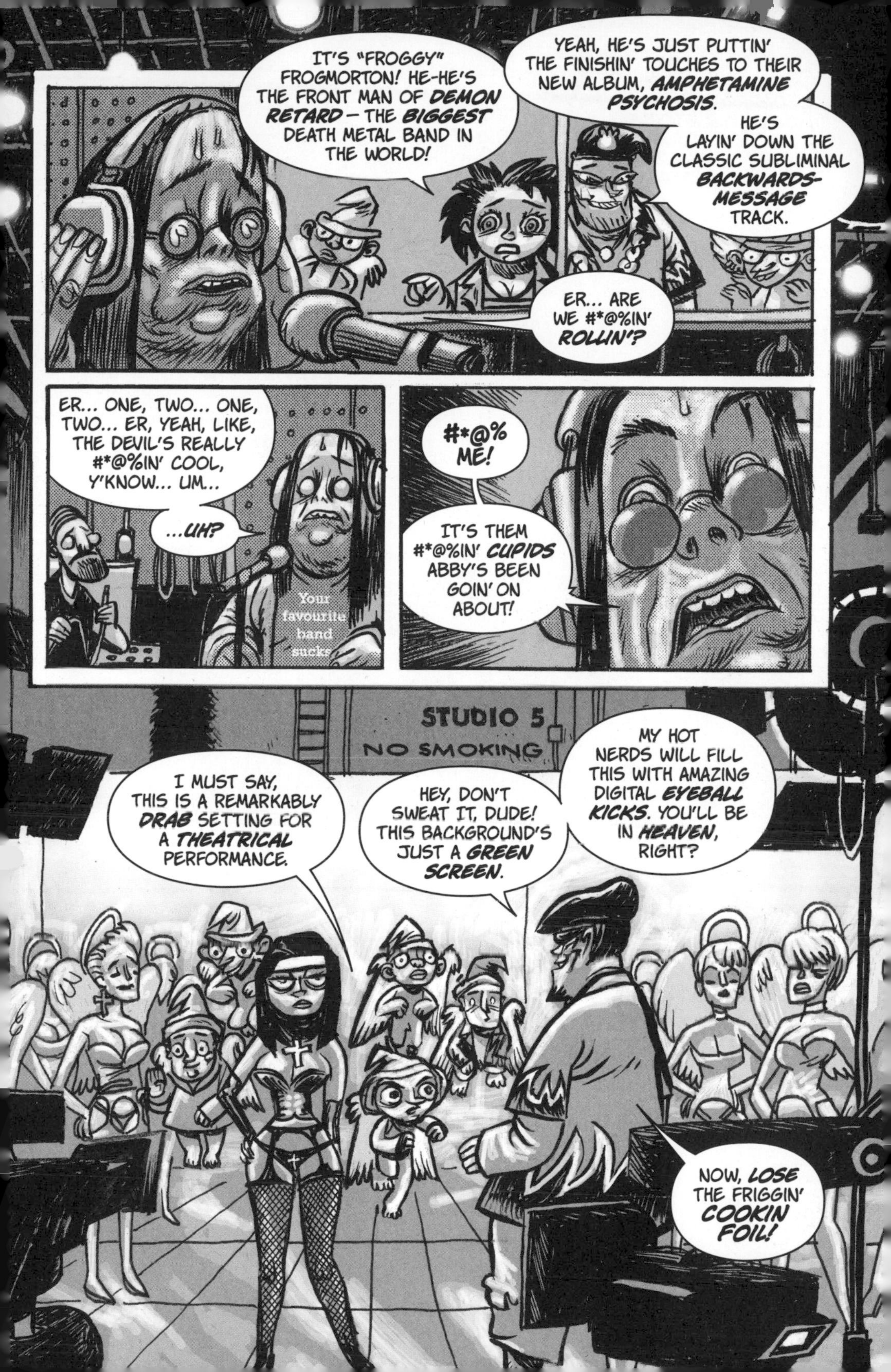
IT'S "FROGGY" FROGMORTON! HE-HE'S THE FRONT MAN OF DEMON RETARD – THE BIGGEST DEATH METAL BAND IN THE WORLD!
YEAH, HE'S JUST PUTTIN' THE FINISHIN' TOUCHES TO THEIR NEW ALBUM, AMPHETAMINE PSYCHOSIS.
HE'S LAYIN' DOWN THE CLASSIC SUBLIMINAL BACKWARDS-MESSAGE TRACK.
ER... ARE WE #*@%IN' ROLLIN'?
ER... ONE, TWO... ONE, TWO... ER, YEAH, LIKE, THE DEVIL'S REALLY #*@%IN' COOL, Y'KNOW... UM...
...UH?
Your favourite band sucks
#*@% ME!
IT'S THEM #*@%IN' CUPIDS ABBY'S BEEN GOIN' ON ABOUT!
STUDIO 5
NO SMOKING
I MUST SAY, THIS IS A REMARKABLY DRAB SETTING FOR A THEATRICAL PERFORMANCE.
HEY, DON'T SWEAT IT, DUDE! THIS BACKGROUND'S JUST A GREEN SCREEN.
MY HOT NERDS WILL FILL THIS WITH AMAZING DIGITAL EYEBALL KICKS. YOU'LL BE IN HEAVEN, RIGHT?
NOW, LOSE THE FRIGGIN' COOKIN FOIL!

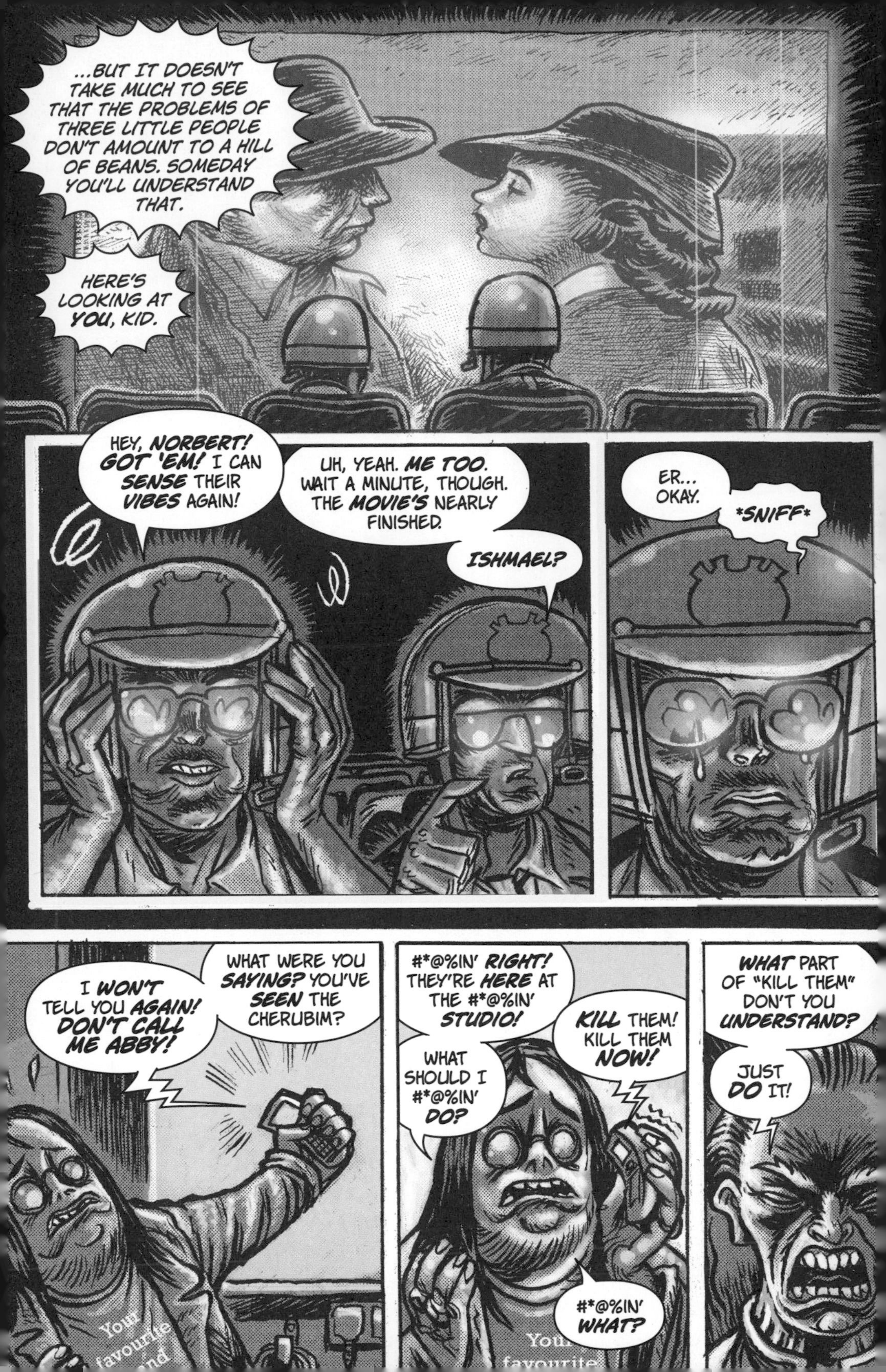
...BUT IT DOESN'T TAKE MUCH TO SEE THAT THE PROBLEMS OF THREE LITTLE PEOPLE DON'T AMOUNT TO A HILL OF BEANS. SOMEDAY YOU'LL UNDERSTAND THAT.
HERE'S LOOKING AT YOU, KID.
HEY, NORBERT! GOT 'EM! I CAN SENSE THEIR VIBES AGAIN!
UH, YEAH. ME TOO. WAIT A MINUTE, THOUGH. THE MOVIE'S NEARLY FINISHED.
ISHMAEL?
ER... OKAY.
SNIFF
I WON'T TELL YOU AGAIN! DON'T CALL ME ABBY!
WHAT WERE YOU SAYING? YOU'VE SEEN THE CHERUBIM?
#*@%IN' RIGHT! THEY'RE HERE AT THE #*@%IN' STUDIO!
WHAT SHOULD I #*@%IN' DO?
KILL THEM! KILL THEM NOW!
#*@%IN' WHAT?
WHAT PART OF "KILL THEM" DON'T YOU UNDERSTAND?
JUST DO IT!
Your favourite

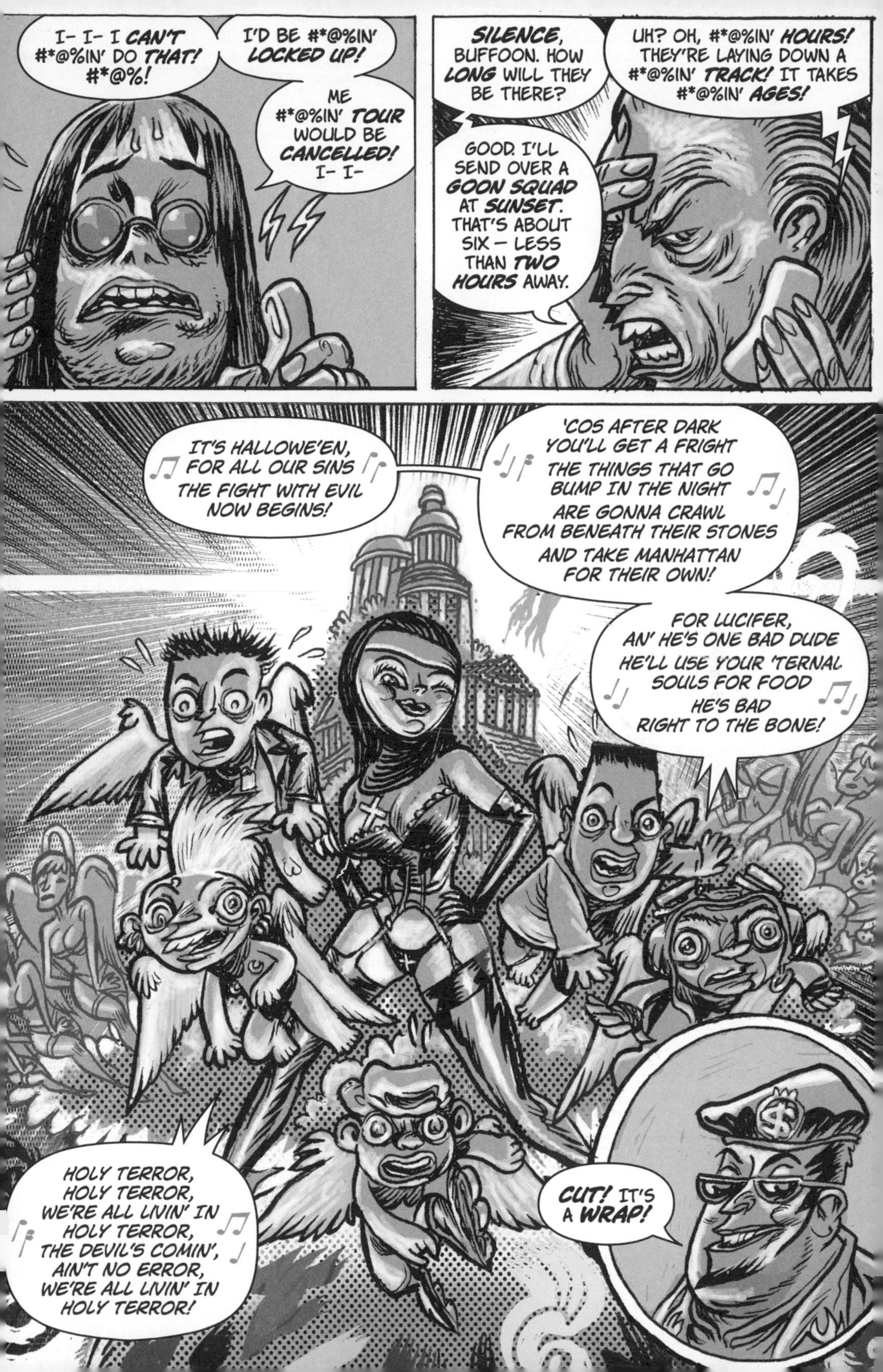
I- I- I CAN'T #*@%IN' DO THAT! #*@%!
I'D BE #*@%IN' LOCKED UP!
ME #*@%IN' TOUR WOULD BE CANCELLED! I- I-
SILENCE, BUFFOON. HOW LONG WILL THEY BE THERE?
UH? OH, #*@%IN' HOURS! THEY'RE LAYING DOWN A #*@%IN' TRACK! IT TAKES #*@%IN' AGES!
GOOD. I'LL SEND OVER A GOON SQUAD AT SUNSET. THAT'S ABOUT SIX — LESS THAN TWO HOURS AWAY.
IT'S HALLOWE'EN, FOR ALL OUR SINS THE FIGHT WITH EVIL NOW BEGINS!
'COS AFTER DARK YOU'LL GET A FRIGHT THE THINGS THAT GO BUMP IN THE NIGHT ARE GONNA CRAWL FROM BENEATH THEIR STONES AND TAKE MANHATTAN FOR THEIR OWN!
FOR LUCIFER, AN' HE'S ONE BAD DUDE HE'LL USE YOUR 'TERNAL SOULS FOR FOOD HE'S BAD RIGHT TO THE BONE!
HOLY TERROR, HOLY TERROR, WE'RE ALL LIVIN' IN HOLY TERROR, THE DEVIL'S COMIN', AIN'T NO ERROR, WE'RE ALL LIVIN' IN HOLY TERROR!
CUT! IT'S A WRAP!

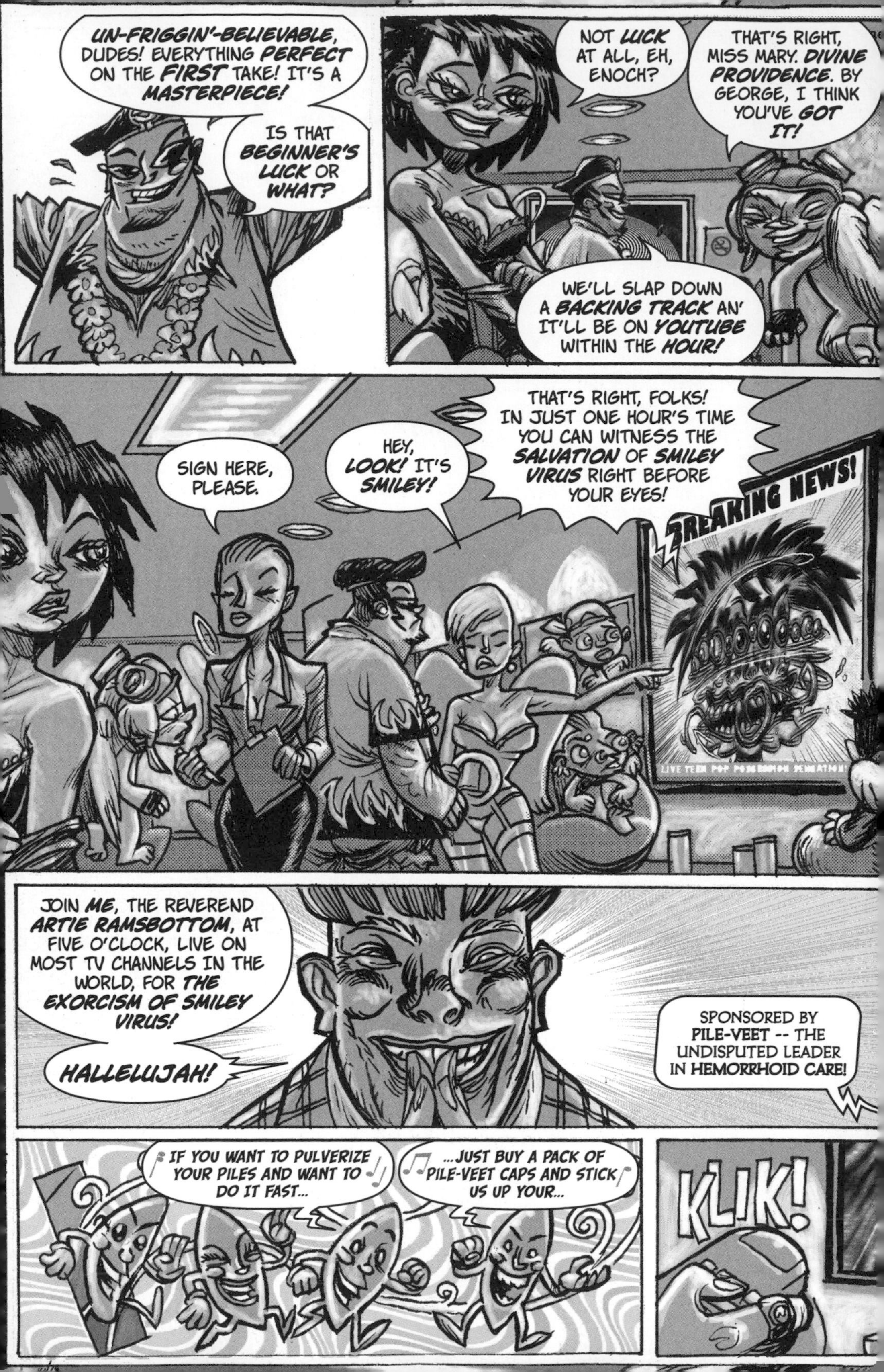

UN-FRIGGIN'-BELIEVABLE, DUDES! EVERYTHING PERFECT ON THE FIRST TAKE! IT'S A MASTERPIECE!
IS THAT BEGINNER'S LUCK OR WHAT?
NOT LUCK AT ALL, EH, ENOCH?
THAT'S RIGHT, MISS MARY. DIVINE PROVIDENCE. BY GEORGE, I THINK YOU'VE GOT IT!
WE'LL SLAP DOWN A BACKING TRACK AN' IT'LL BE ON YOUTUBE WITHIN THE HOUR!
SIGN HERE, PLEASE.
HEY, LOOK! IT'S SMILEY!
THAT'S RIGHT, FOLKS! IN JUST ONE HOUR'S TIME YOU CAN WITNESS THE SALVATION OF SMILEY VIRUS RIGHT BEFORE YOUR EYES!
BREAKING NEWS!
JOIN ME, THE REVEREND ARTIE RAMSBOTTOM, AT FIVE O'CLOCK, LIVE ON MOST TV CHANNELS IN THE WORLD, FOR THE EXORCISM OF SMILEY VIRUS!
HALLELUJAH!
SPONSORED BY PILE-VEET -- THE UNDISPUTED LEADER IN HEMORRHOID CARE!
IF YOU WANT TO PULVERIZE YOUR PILES AND WANT TO DO IT FAST...
...JUST BUY A PACK OF PILE-VEET CAPS AND STICK US UP YOUR...
KLIK!

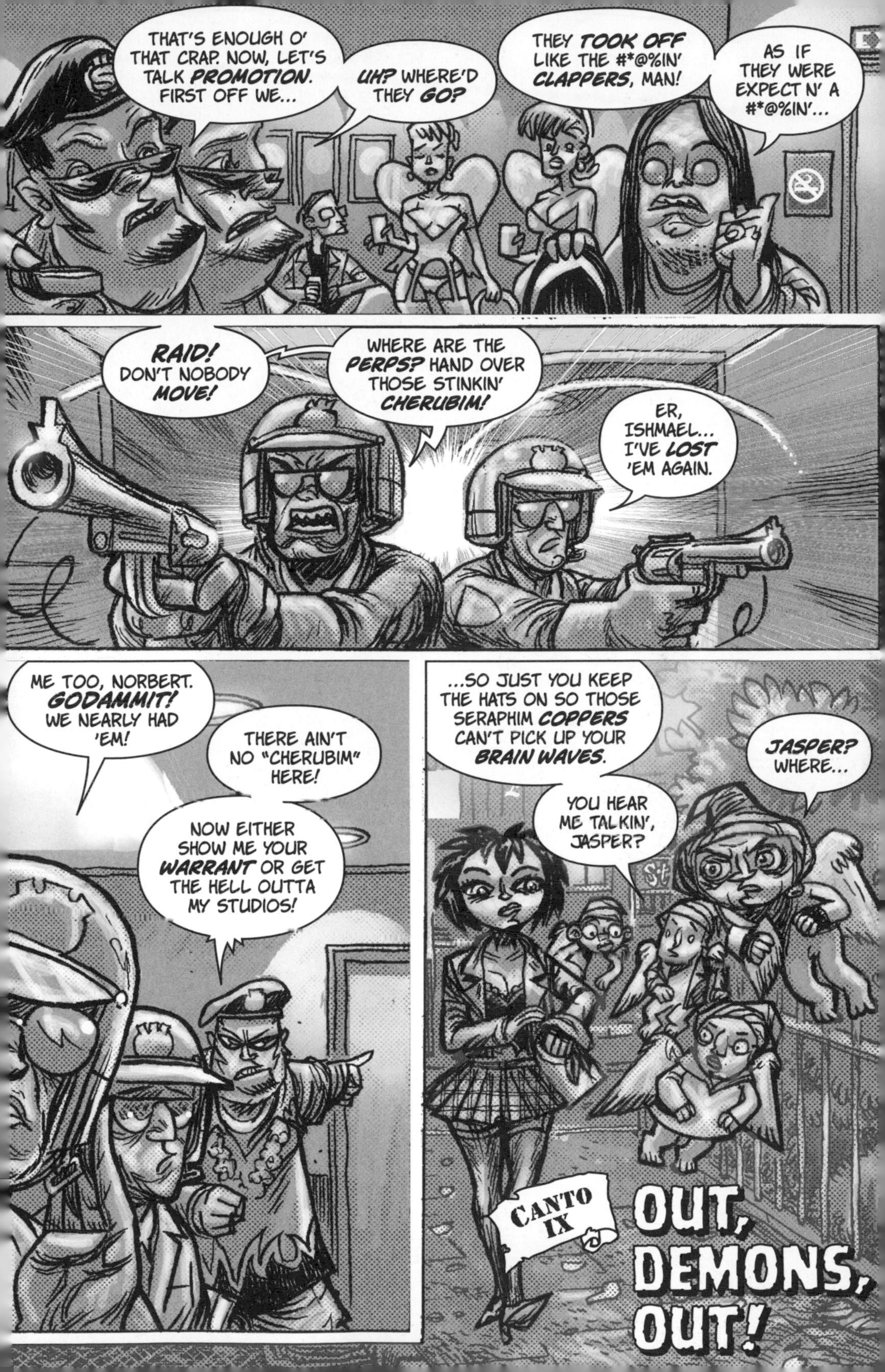
THAT'S ENOUGH O' THAT CRAP. NOW, LET'S TALK PROMOTION. FIRST OFF WE...
UH? WHERE'D THEY GO?
THEY TOOK OFF LIKE THE #*@%IN' CLAPPERS, MAN!
AS IF THEY WERE EXPECT N' A #*@%IN'...
RAID! DON'T NOBODY MOVE!
WHERE ARE THE PERPS? HAND OVER THOSE STINKIN' CHERUBIM!
ER, ISHMAEL... I'VE LOST 'EM AGAIN.
ME TOO, NORBERT. GODAMMIT! WE NEARLY HAD 'EM!
THERE AIN'T NO "CHERUBIM" HERE!
NOW EITHER SHOW ME YOUR WARRANT OR GET THE HELL OUTTA MY STUDIOS!
...SO JUST YOU KEEP THE HATS ON SO THOSE SERAPHIM COPPERS CAN'T PICK UP YOUR BRAIN WAVES.
YOU HEAR ME TALKIN', JASPER?
JASPER? WHERE...
CANTO IX
OUT, DEMONS, OUT!

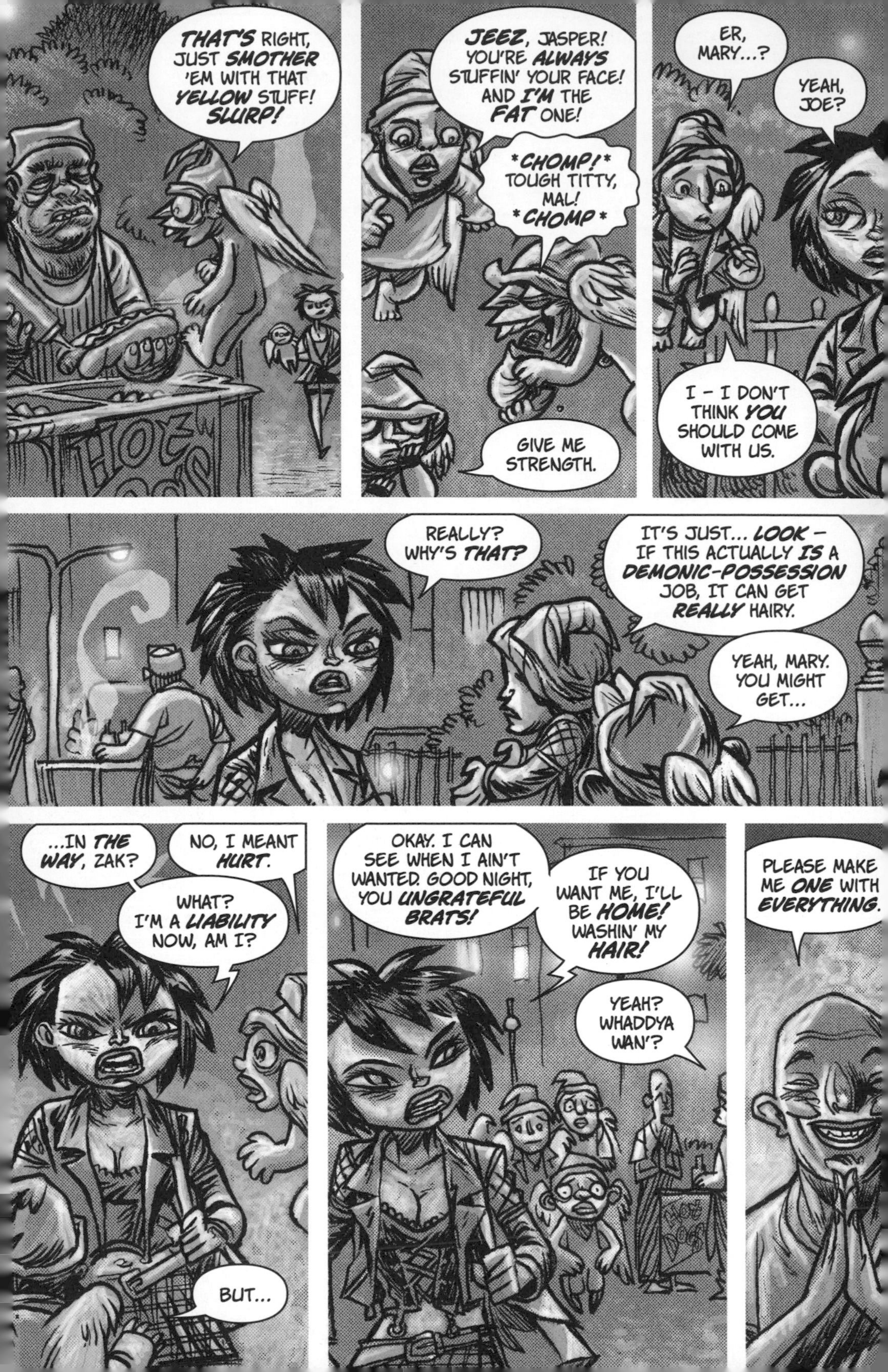
THAT'S RIGHT, JUST SMOTHER 'EM WITH THAT YELLOW STUFF! SLURP!
JEEZ, JASPER! YOU'RE ALWAYS STUFFIN' YOUR FACE! AND I'M THE FAT ONE!
CHOMP! TOUGH TITTY, MAL! *CHOMP*
GIVE ME STRENGTH.
ER, MARY...?
YEAH, JOE?
I – I DON'T THINK YOU SHOULD COME WITH US.
REALLY? WHY'S THAT?
IT'S JUST... LOOK – IF THIS ACTUALLY IS A DEMONIC-POSSESSION JOB, IT CAN GET REALLY HAIRY.
YEAH, MARY. YOU MIGHT GET...
...IN THE WAY, ZAK?
NO, I MEANT HURT.
WHAT? I'M A LIABILITY NOW, AM I?
BUT...
OKAY. I CAN SEE WHEN I AIN'T WANTED. GOOD NIGHT, YOU UNGRATEFUL BRATS!
IF YOU WANT ME, I'LL BE HOME! WASHIN' MY HAIR!
YEAH? WHADDYA WAN'?
PLEASE MAKE ME ONE WITH EVERYTHING.

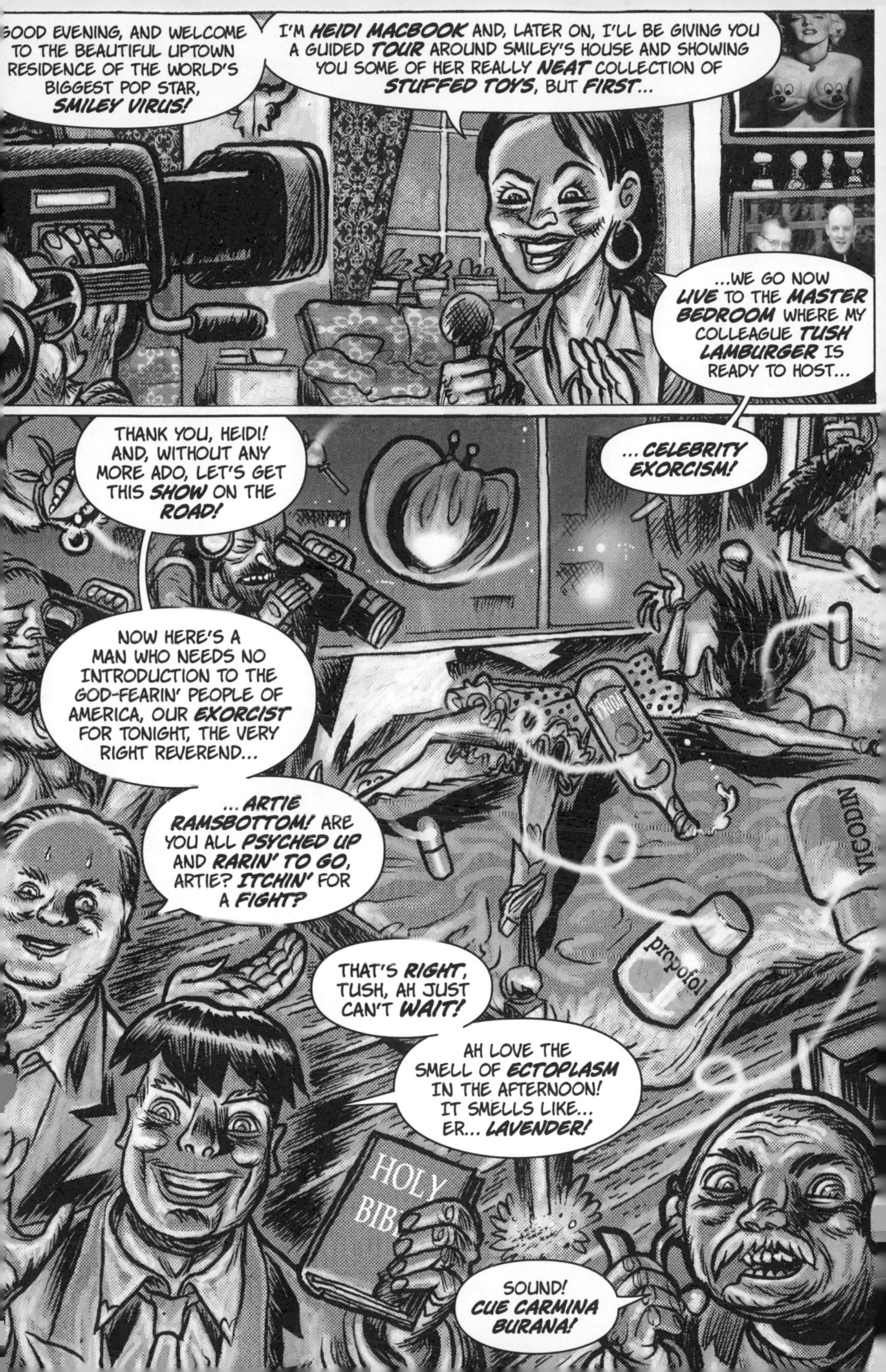
GOOD EVENING, AND WELCOME TO THE BEAUTIFUL UPTOWN RESIDENCE OF THE WORLD'S BIGGEST POP STAR, SMILEY VIRUS!
I'M HEIDI MACBOOK AND, LATER ON, I'LL BE GIVING YOU A GUIDED TOUR AROUND SMILEY'S HOUSE AND SHOWING YOU SOME OF HER REALLY NEAT COLLECTION OF STUFFED TOYS, BUT FIRST...
...WE GO NOW LIVE TO THE MASTER BEDROOM WHERE MY COLLEAGUE TUSH LAMBURGER IS READY TO HOST...
...CELEBRITY EXORCISM!
THANK YOU, HEIDI! AND, WITHOUT ANY MORE ADO, LET'S GET THIS SHOW ON THE ROAD!
NOW HERE'S A MAN WHO NEEDS NO INTRODUCTION TO THE GOD-FEARIN' PEOPLE OF AMERICA, OUR EXORCIST FOR TONIGHT, THE VERY RIGHT REVEREND...
...ARTIE RAMSBOTTOM! ARE YOU ALL PSYCHED UP AND RARIN' TO GO, ARTIE? ITCHIN' FOR A FIGHT?
VICODIN
propofol
THAT'S RIGHT, TUSH, AH JUST CAN'T WAIT!
AH LOVE THE SMELL OF ECTOPLASM IN THE AFTERNOON! IT SMELLS LIKE... ER... LAVENDER!
HOLY BIB
SOUND! CUE CARMINA BURANA!

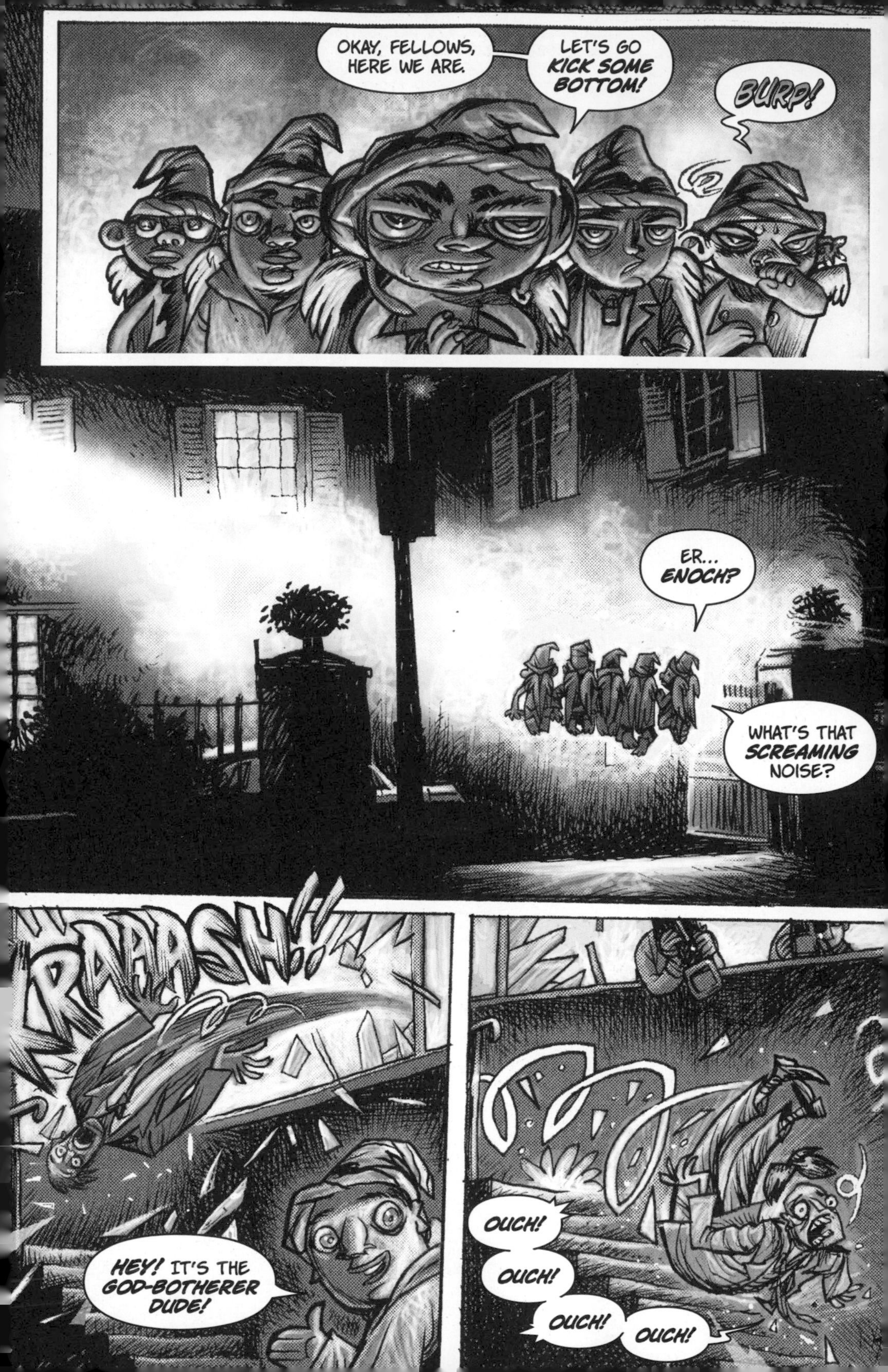

OKAY, FELLOWS, HERE WE ARE.
LET'S GO KICK SOME BOTTOM!
BURP!
ER... ENOCH?
WHAT'S THAT SCREAMING NOISE?
KRAASH!!
HEY! IT'S THE GOD-BOTHERER DUDE!
OUCH!
OUCH!
OUCH!
OUCH!

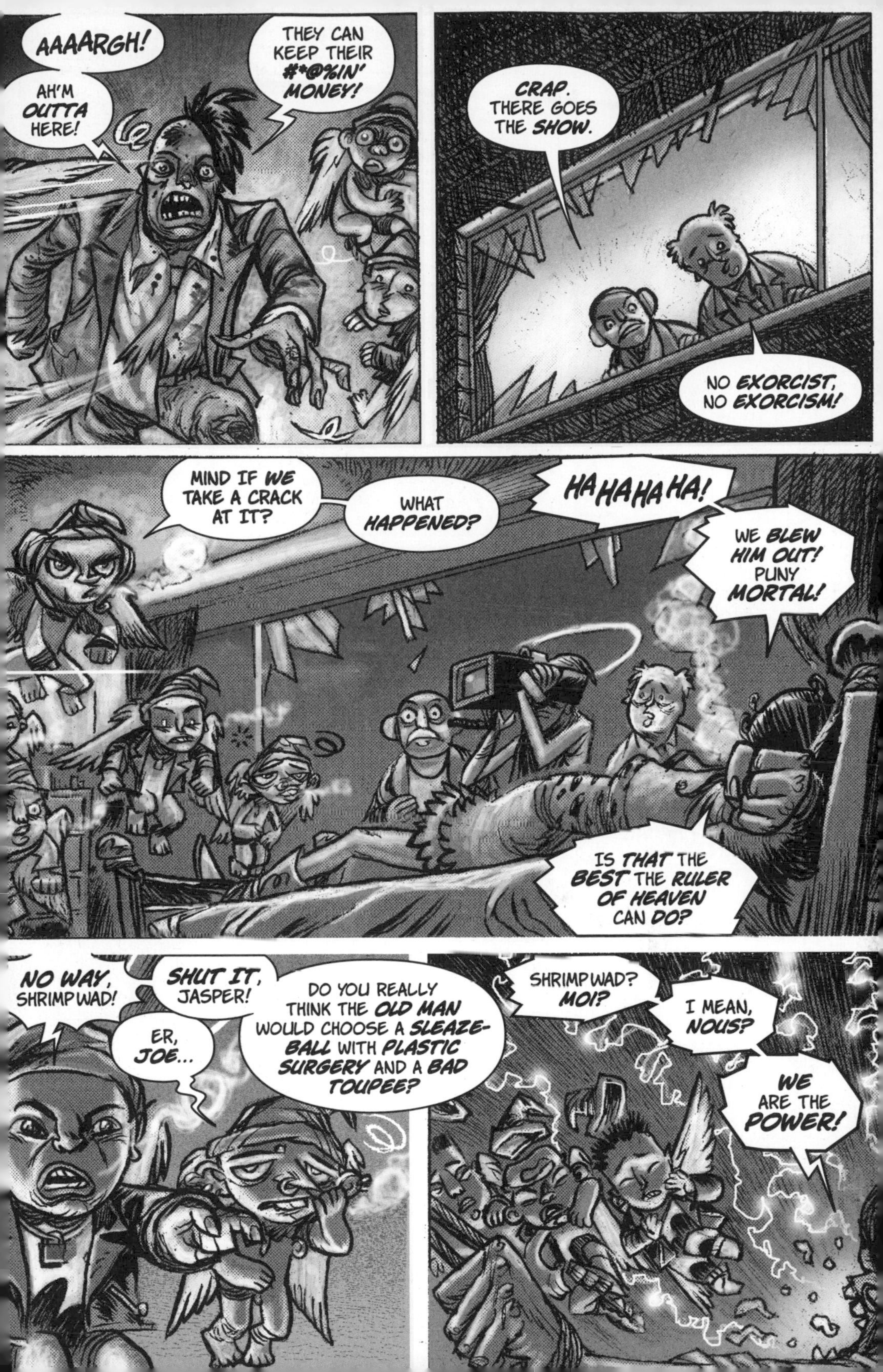
AAAARGH!
AH'M OUTTA HERE!
THEY CAN KEEP THEIR #*@%IN' MONEY!
CRAP. THERE GOES THE SHOW.
NO EXORCIST, NO EXORCISM!
MIND IF WE TAKE A CRACK AT IT?
WHAT HAPPENED?
HA HA HA HA HA!
WE BLEW HIM OUT! PUNY MORTAL!
IS THAT THE BEST THE RULER OF HEAVEN CAN DO?
NO WAY, SHRIMPWAD!
SHUT IT, JASPER!
ER, JOE...
DO YOU REALLY THINK THE OLD MAN WOULD CHOOSE A SLEAZE-BALL WITH PLASTIC SURGERY AND A BAD TOUPEE?
SHRIMPWAD? MOI?
I MEAN, NOUS?
WE ARE THE POWER!

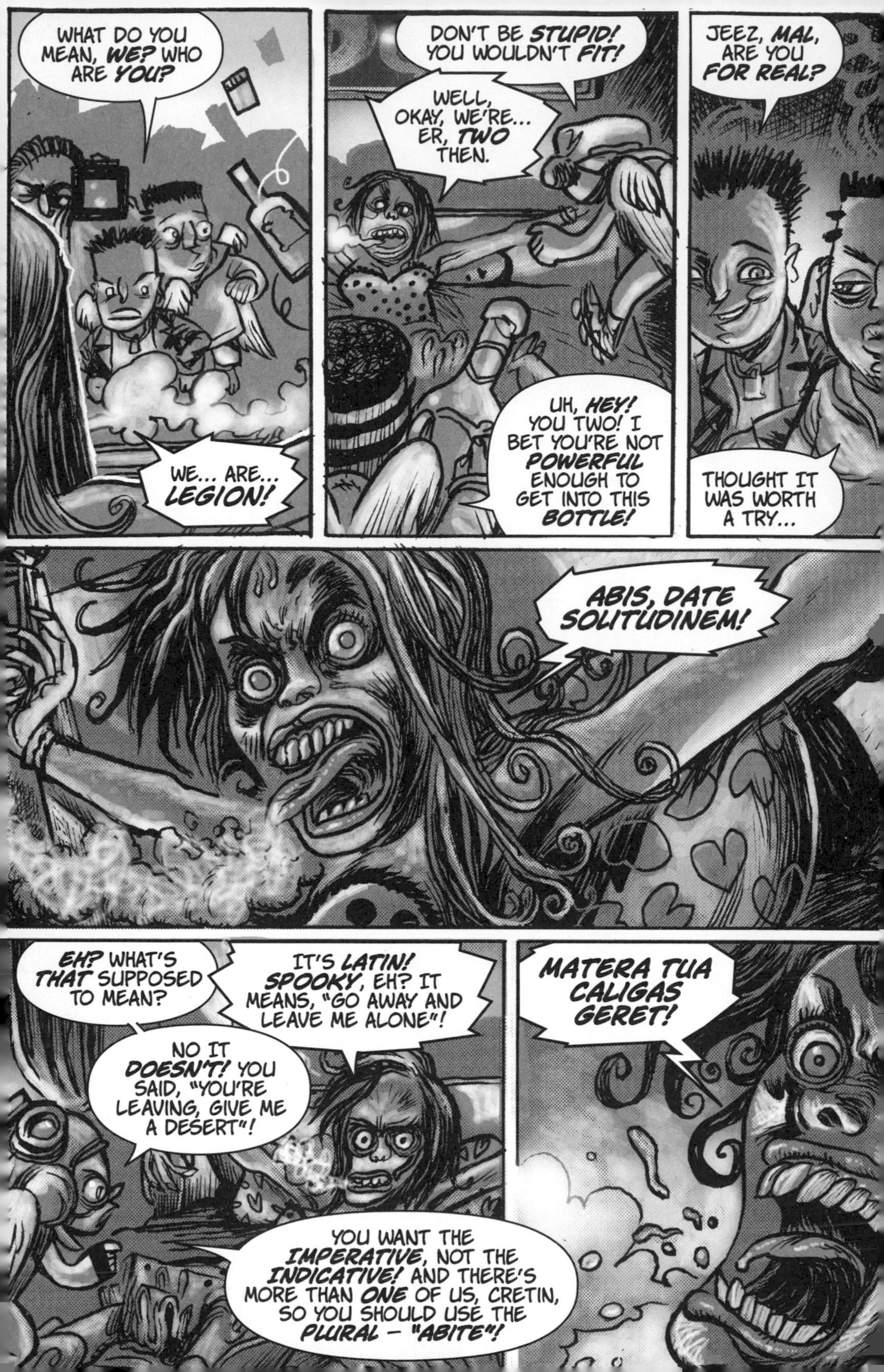
WHAT DO YOU MEAN, WE? WHO ARE YOU?
WE... ARE... LEGION!
DON'T BE STUPID! YOU WOULDN'T FIT!
WELL, OKAY, WE'RE... ER, TWO THEN.
UH, HEY! YOU TWO! I BET YOU'RE NOT POWERFUL ENOUGH TO GET INTO THIS BOTTLE!
JEEZ, MAL, ARE YOU FOR REAL?
THOUGHT IT WAS WORTH A TRY...
ABIS, DATE SOLITUDINEM!
EH? WHAT'S THAT SUPPOSED TO MEAN?
IT'S LATIN! SPOOKY, EH? IT MEANS, "GO AWAY AND LEAVE ME ALONE"!
NO IT DOESN'T! YOU SAID, "YOU'RE LEAVING, GIVE ME A DESERT"!
YOU WANT THE IMPERATIVE, NOT THE INDICATIVE! AND THERE'S MORE THAN ONE OF US, CRETIN, SO YOU SHOULD USE THE PLURAL – "ABITE"!
MATERA TUA CALIGAS GERET!

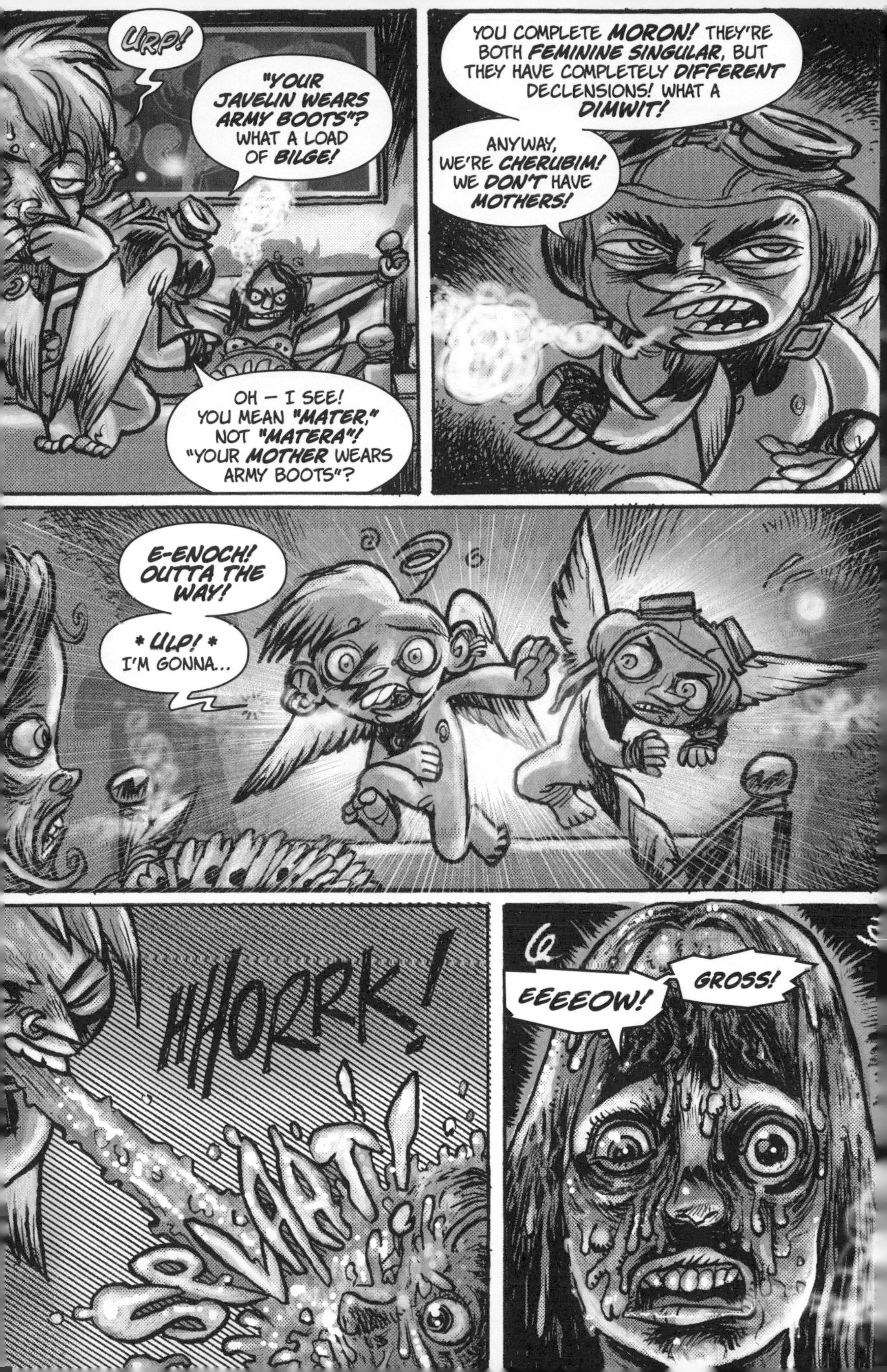

URP!
"YOUR JAVELIN WEARS ARMY BOOTS"? WHAT A LOAD OF BILGE!
OH — I SEE! YOU MEAN "MATER," NOT "MATERA"! "YOUR MOTHER WEARS ARMY BOOTS"?
YOU COMPLETE MORON! THEY'RE BOTH FEMININE SINGULAR, BUT THEY HAVE COMPLETELY DIFFERENT DECLENSIONS! WHAT A DIMWIT!
ANYWAY, WE'RE CHERUBIM! WE DON'T HAVE MOTHERS!
E-ENOCH! OUTTA THE WAY!
* ULP! * I'M GONNA...
HHORRK!
EEEEOW!
GROSS!

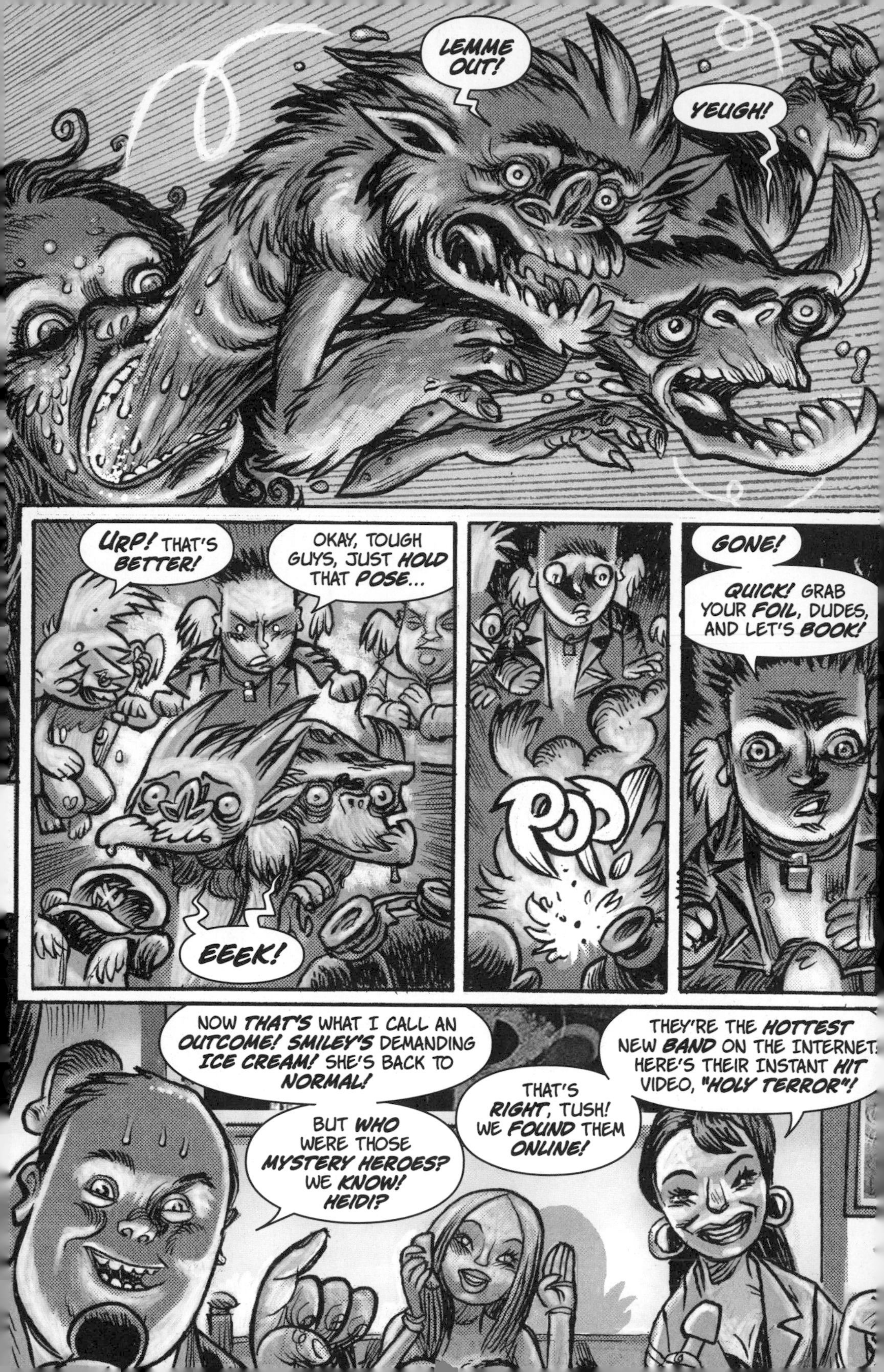
LEMME OUT!
YEUGH!
URP! THAT'S BETTER!
OKAY, TOUGH GUYS, JUST HOLD THAT POSE...
EEEK!
POP!
GONE!
QUICK! GRAB YOUR FOIL, DUDES, AND LET'S BOOK!
NOW THAT'S WHAT I CALL AN OUTCOME! SMILEY'S DEMANDING ICE CREAM! SHE'S BACK TO NORMAL!
BUT WHO WERE THOSE MYSTERY HEROES? WE KNOW! HEIDI?
THAT'S RIGHT, TUSH! WE FOUND THEM ONLINE!
THEY'RE THE HOTTEST NEW BAND ON THE INTERNET! HERE'S THEIR INSTANT HIT VIDEO, "HOLY TERROR"!

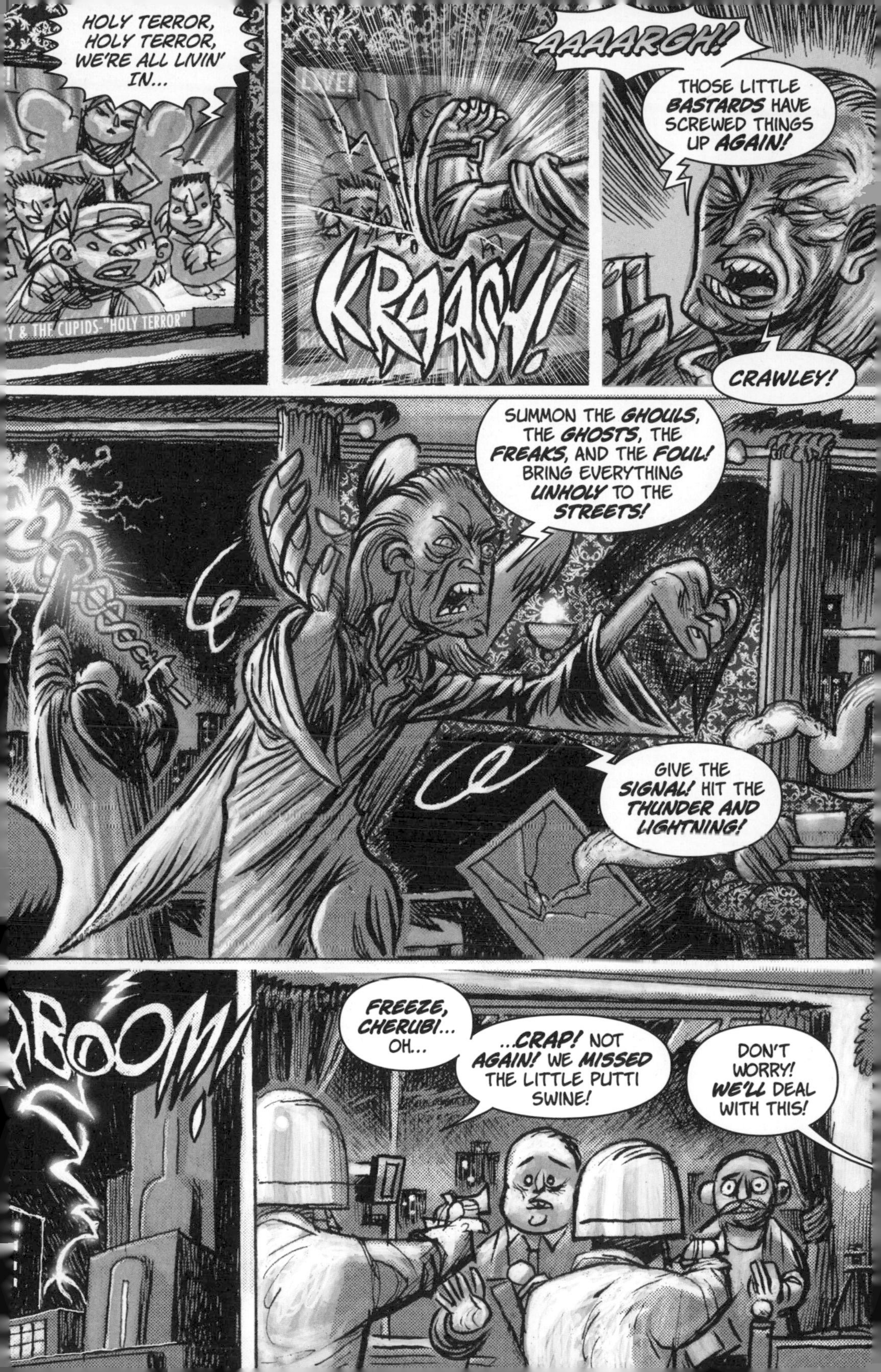
HOLY TERROR, HOLY TERROR, WE'RE ALL LIVIN' IN...
& THE CUPIDS-"HOLY TERROR"
AAAAARGH!
KRAASH!
THOSE LITTLE BASTARDS HAVE SCREWED THINGS UP AGAIN!
CRAWLEY!
SUMMON THE GHOULS, THE GHOSTS, THE FREAKS, AND THE FOUL! BRING EVERYTHING UNHOLY TO THE STREETS!
GIVE THE SIGNAL! HIT THE THUNDER AND LIGHTNING!
KABOOM!
FREEZE, CHERUBI... OH...
...CRAP! NOT AGAIN! WE MISSED THE LITTLE PUTTI SWINE!
DON'T WORRY! WE'LL DEAL WITH THIS!

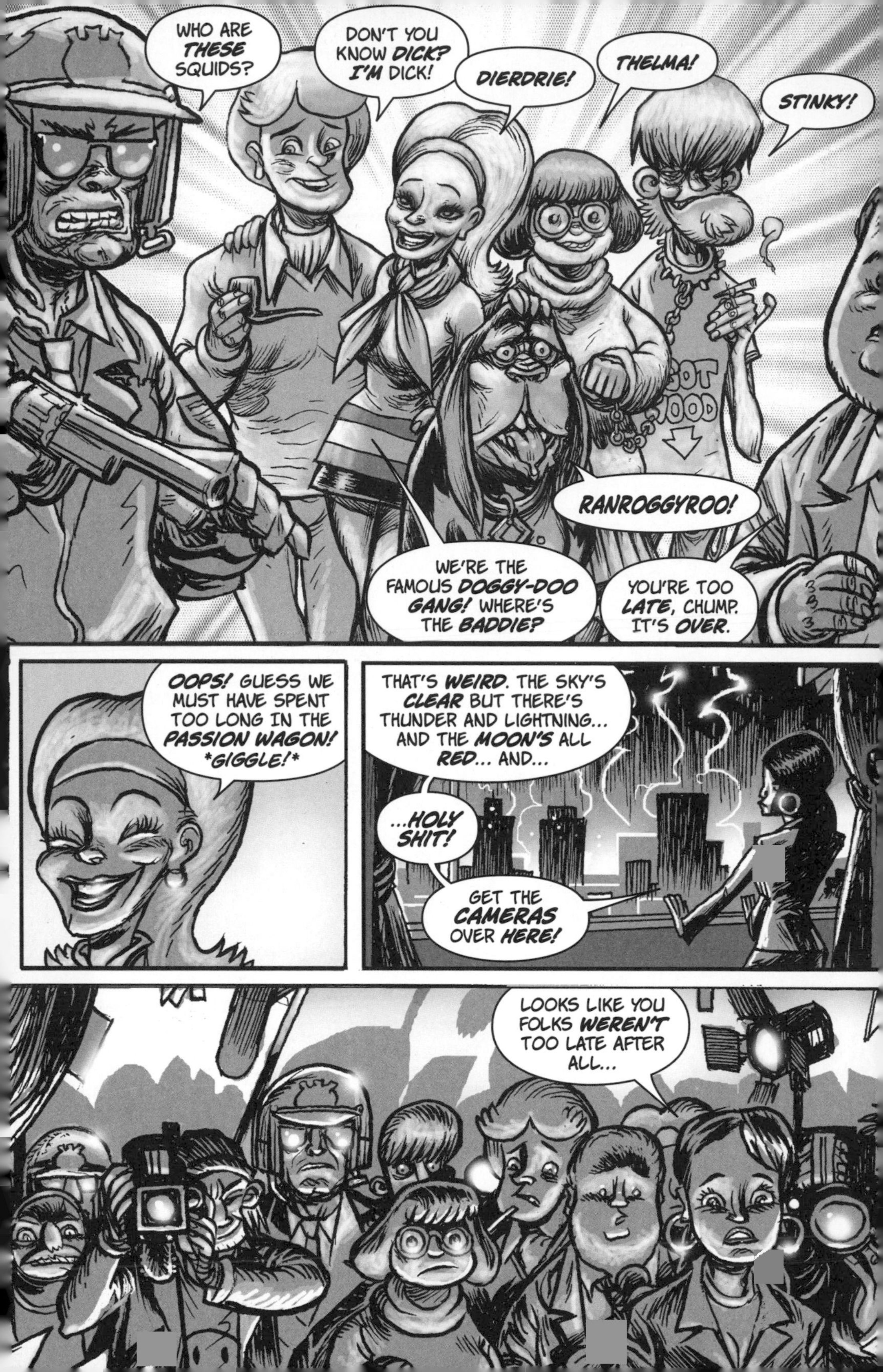
WHO ARE *THESE* SQUIDS?
DON'T YOU KNOW *DICK? I'M* DICK!
DIERDRIE!
THELMA!
STINKY!
RANROGGYROO!
WE'RE THE FAMOUS *DOGGY-DOO GANG!* WHERE'S THE *BADDIE?*
YOU'RE TOO *LATE*, CHUMP. IT'S *OVER*.
OOPS! GUESS WE MUST HAVE SPENT TOO LONG IN THE *PASSION WAGON!* *GIGGLE!*
THAT'S *WEIRD*. THE SKY'S *CLEAR* BUT THERE'S THUNDER AND LIGHTNING... AND THE *MOON'S* ALL *RED*... AND...
...HOLY SHIT!
GET THE *CAMERAS* OVER *HERE!*
LOOKS LIKE YOU FOLKS *WEREN'T* TOO LATE AFTER ALL...

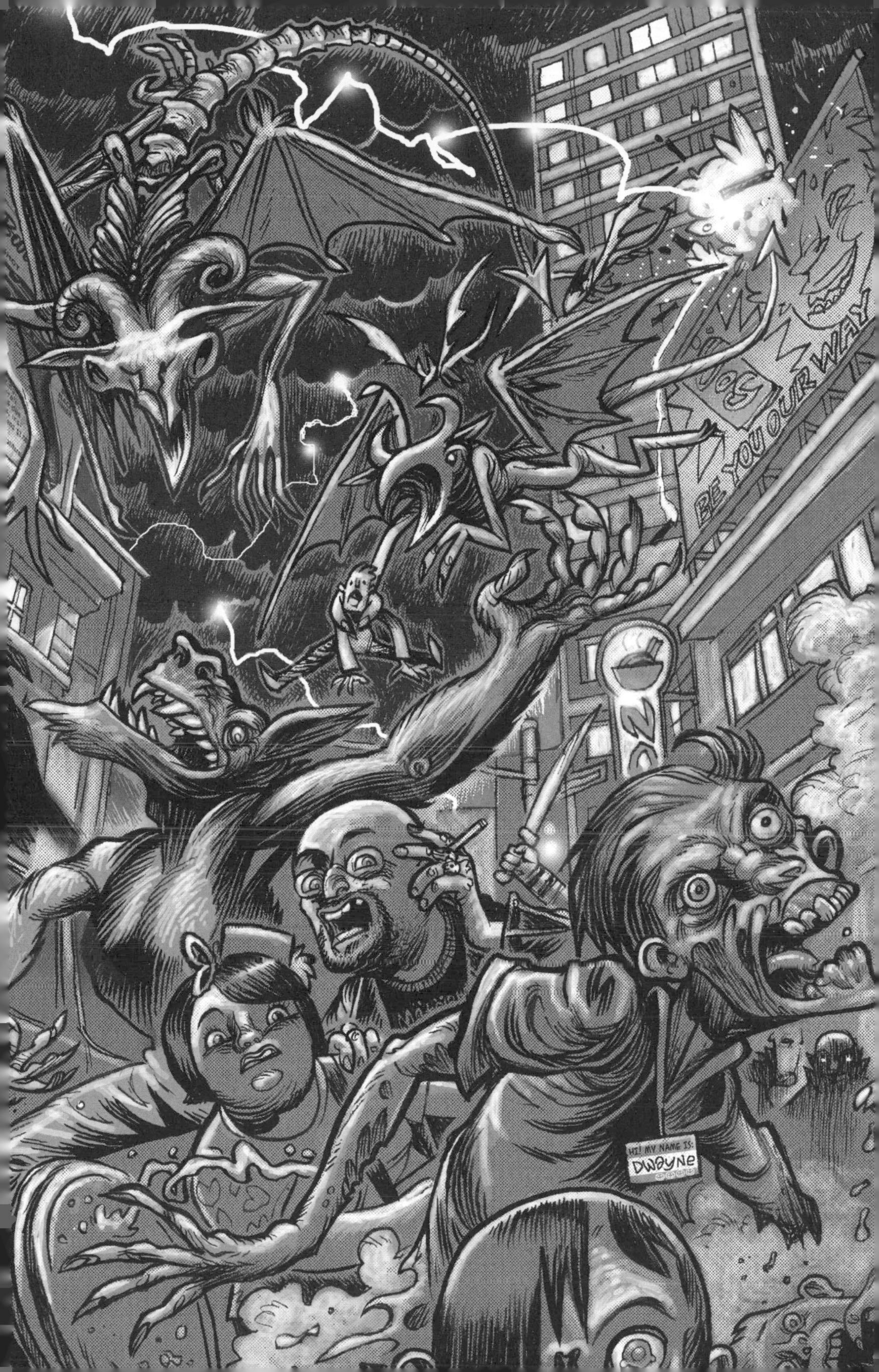
BE YOU OUR WAY
HI! MY NAME IS:
DWAYNE

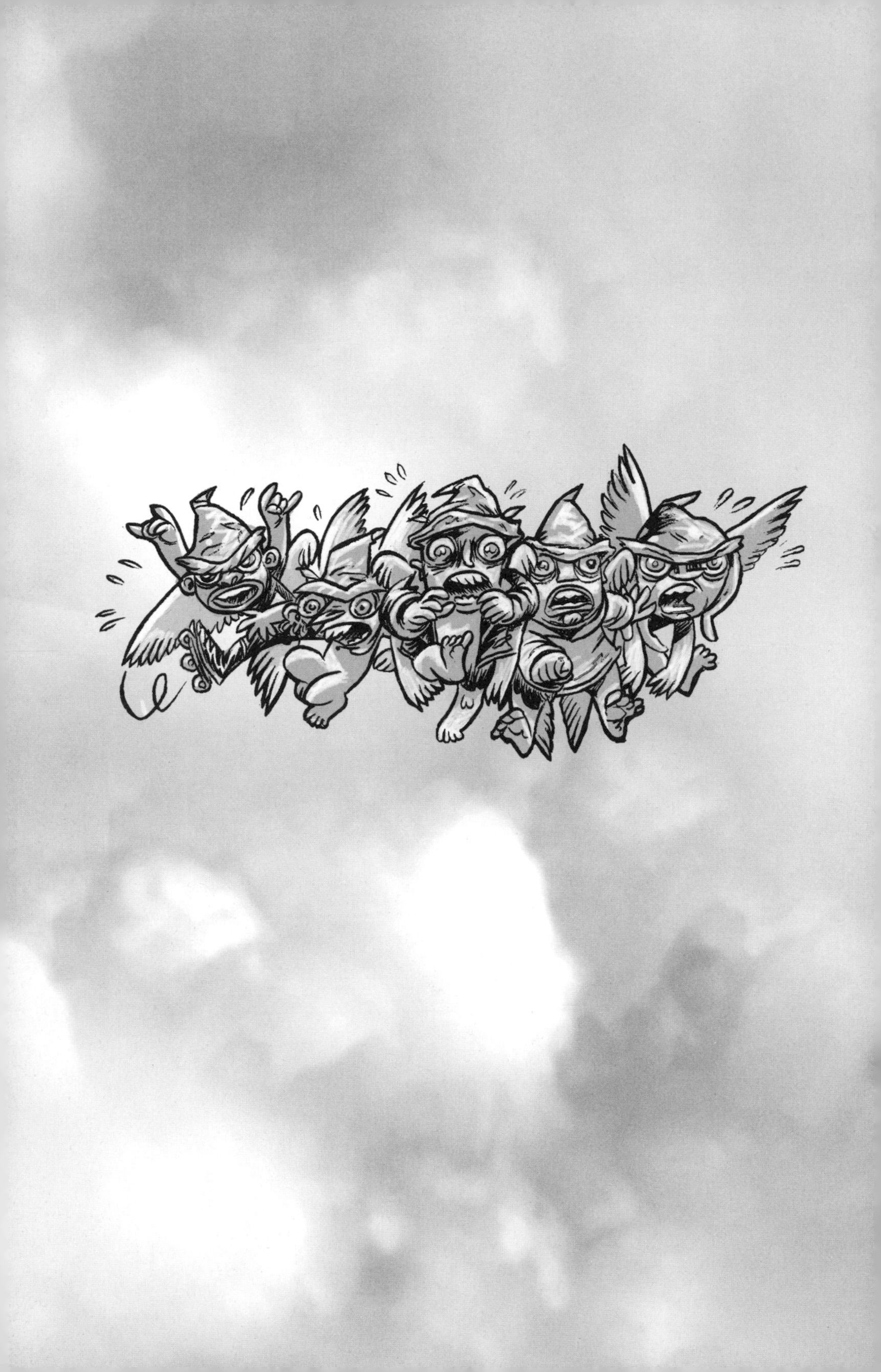

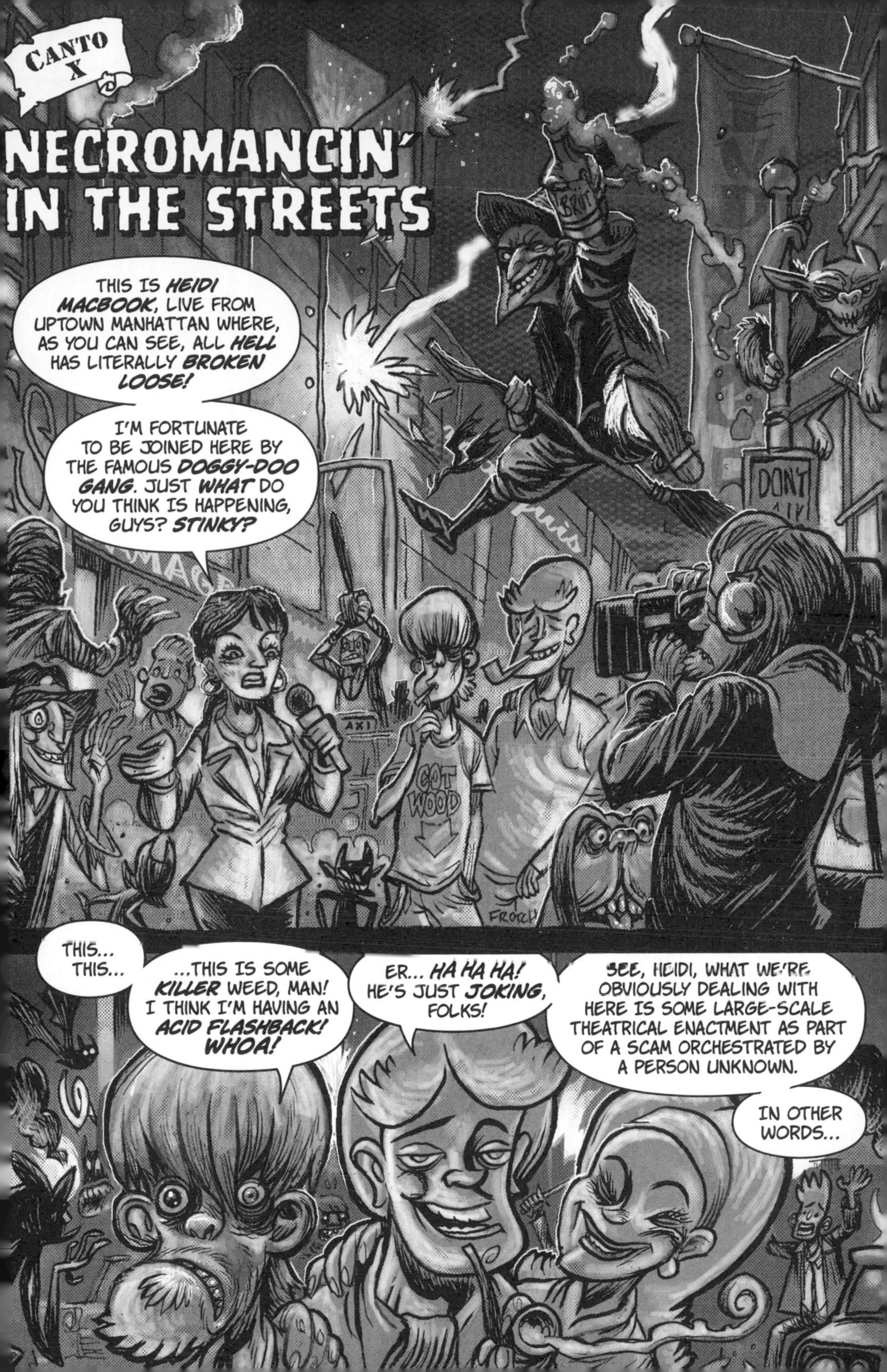
CANTO X
NECROMANCIN' IN THE STREETS
THIS IS HEIDI MACBOOK, LIVE FROM UPTOWN MANHATTAN WHERE, AS YOU CAN SEE, ALL HELL HAS LITERALLY BROKEN LOOSE!
I'M FORTUNATE TO BE JOINED HERE BY THE FAMOUS DOGGY-DOO GANG. JUST WHAT DO YOU THINK IS HAPPENING, GUYS? STINKY?
DON'T
GOT WOOD
FROCH
THIS... THIS...
...THIS IS SOME KILLER WEED, MAN! I THINK I'M HAVING AN ACID FLASHBACK! WHOA!
ER... HA HA HA! HE'S JUST JOKING, FOLKS!
SEE, HEIDI, WHAT WE'RE OBVIOUSLY DEALING WITH HERE IS SOME LARGE-SCALE THEATRICAL ENACTMENT AS PART OF A SCAM ORCHESTRATED BY A PERSON UNKNOWN.
IN OTHER WORDS...

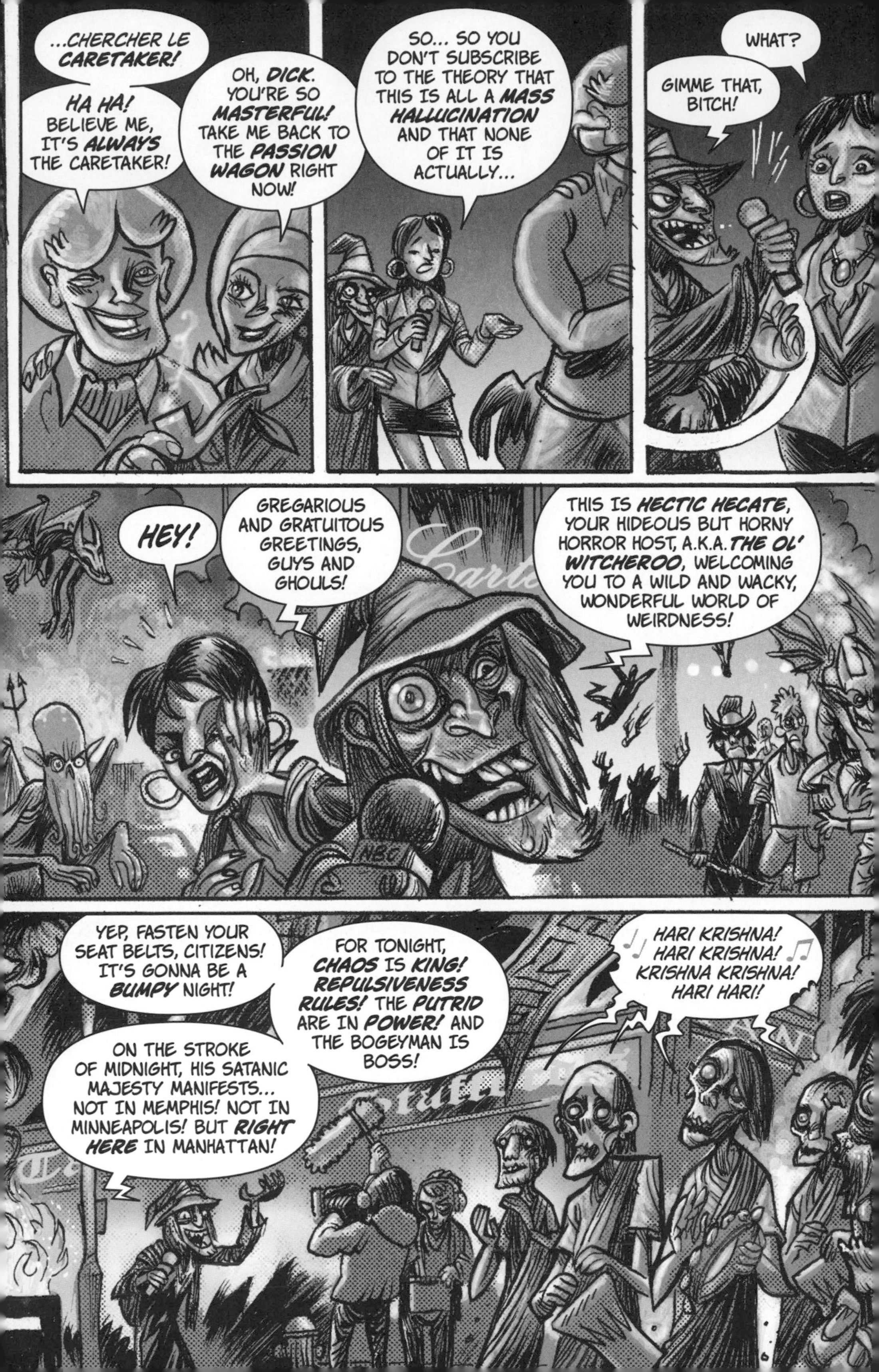
...CHERCHER LE CARETAKER!
HA HA! BELIEVE ME, IT'S ALWAYS THE CARETAKER!
OH, DICK. YOU'RE SO MASTERFUL! TAKE ME BACK TO THE PASSION WAGON RIGHT NOW!
SO... SO YOU DON'T SUBSCRIBE TO THE THEORY THAT THIS IS ALL A MASS HALLUCINATION AND THAT NONE OF IT IS ACTUALLY...
WHAT?
GIMME THAT, BITCH!
HEY!
GREGARIOUS AND GRATUITOUS GREETINGS, GUYS AND GHOULS!
THIS IS HECTIC HECATE, YOUR HIDEOUS BUT HORNY HORROR HOST, A.K.A. THE OL' WITCHEROO, WELCOMING YOU TO A WILD AND WACKY, WONDERFUL WORLD OF WEIRDNESS!
NBC
YEP, FASTEN YOUR SEAT BELTS, CITIZENS! IT'S GONNA BE A BUMPY NIGHT!
ON THE STROKE OF MIDNIGHT, HIS SATANIC MAJESTY MANIFESTS... NOT IN MEMPHIS! NOT IN MINNEAPOLIS! BUT RIGHT HERE IN MANHATTAN!
FOR TONIGHT, CHAOS IS KING! REPULSIVENESS RULES! THE PUTRID ARE IN POWER! AND THE BOGEYMAN IS BOSS!
HARI KRISHNA! HARI KRISHNA! KRISHNA KRISHNA! HARI HARI!

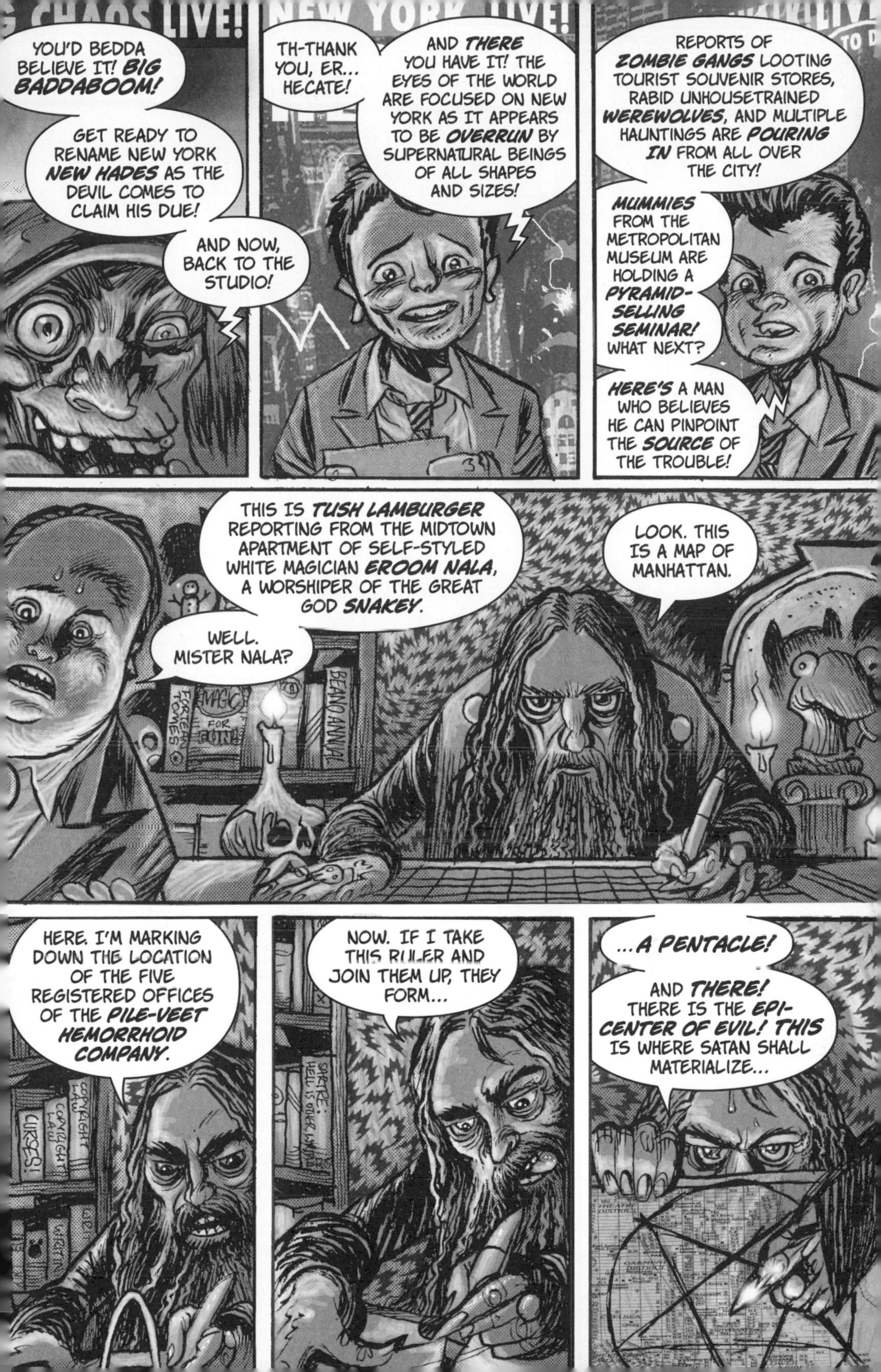
YOU'D BEDDA BELIEVE IT! BIG BADDABOOM!
GET READY TO RENAME NEW YORK NEW HADES AS THE DEVIL COMES TO CLAIM HIS DUE!
AND NOW, BACK TO THE STUDIO!
TH-THANK YOU, ER... HECATE!
AND THERE YOU HAVE IT! THE EYES OF THE WORLD ARE FOCUSED ON NEW YORK AS IT APPEARS TO BE OVERRUN BY SUPERNATURAL BEINGS OF ALL SHAPES AND SIZES!
REPORTS OF ZOMBIE GANGS LOOTING TOURIST SOUVENIR STORES, RABID UNHOUSETRAINED WEREWOLVES, AND MULTIPLE HAUNTINGS ARE POURING IN FROM ALL OVER THE CITY!
MUMMIES FROM THE METROPOLITAN MUSEUM ARE HOLDING A PYRAMID-SELLING SEMINAR! WHAT NEXT?
HERE'S A MAN WHO BELIEVES HE CAN PINPOINT THE SOURCE OF THE TROUBLE!
THIS IS TUSH LAMBURGER REPORTING FROM THE MIDTOWN APARTMENT OF SELF-STYLED WHITE MAGICIAN EROOM NALA, A WORSHIPER OF THE GREAT GOD SNAKEY.
WELL. MISTER NALA?
LOOK. THIS IS A MAP OF MANHATTAN.
FORTEAN TOMES
MAGIC FOR FUN!
BEANO ANNUAL
HERE. I'M MARKING DOWN THE LOCATION OF THE FIVE REGISTERED OFFICES OF THE PILE-VEET HEMORRHOID COMPANY.
CURSES!
COPYRIGHT LAW
NOW. IF I TAKE THIS RULER AND JOIN THEM UP, THEY FORM...
...A PENTACLE!
AND THERE! THERE IS THE EPI-CENTER OF EVIL! THIS IS WHERE SATAN SHALL MATERIALIZE...

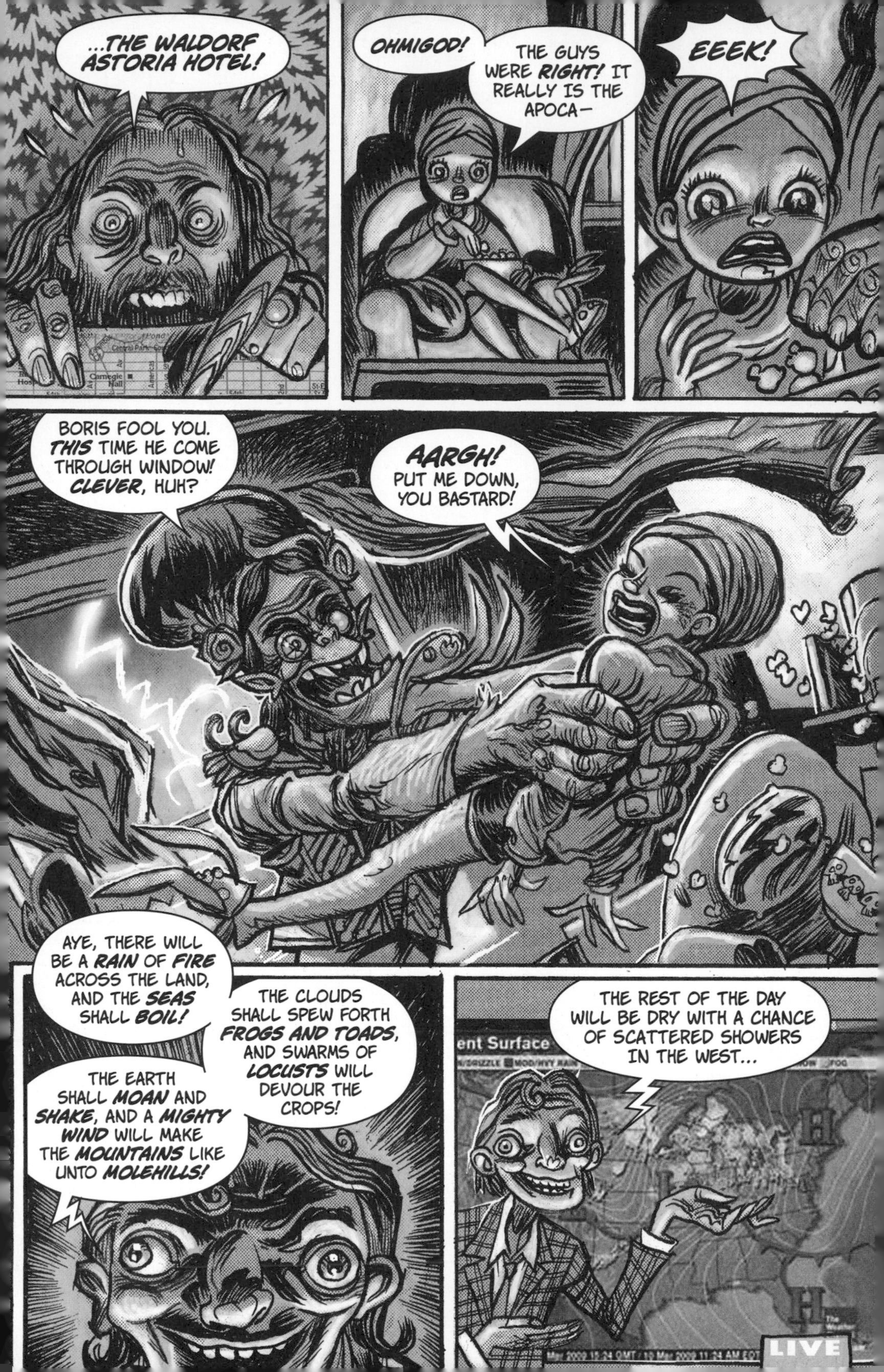
...THE WALDORF ASTORIA HOTEL!
OHMIGOD!
THE GUYS WERE RIGHT! IT REALLY IS THE APOCA—
EEEK!
BORIS FOOL YOU. THIS TIME HE COME THROUGH WINDOW! CLEVER, HUH?
AARGH! PUT ME DOWN, YOU BASTARD!
AYE, THERE WILL BE A RAIN OF FIRE ACROSS THE LAND, AND THE SEAS SHALL BOIL!
THE CLOUDS SHALL SPEW FORTH FROGS AND TOADS, AND SWARMS OF LOCUSTS WILL DEVOUR THE CROPS!
THE EARTH SHALL MOAN AND SHAKE, AND A MIGHTY WIND WILL MAKE THE MOUNTAINS LIKE UNTO MOLEHILLS!
THE REST OF THE DAY WILL BE DRY WITH A CHANCE OF SCATTERED SHOWERS IN THE WEST...
LIVE

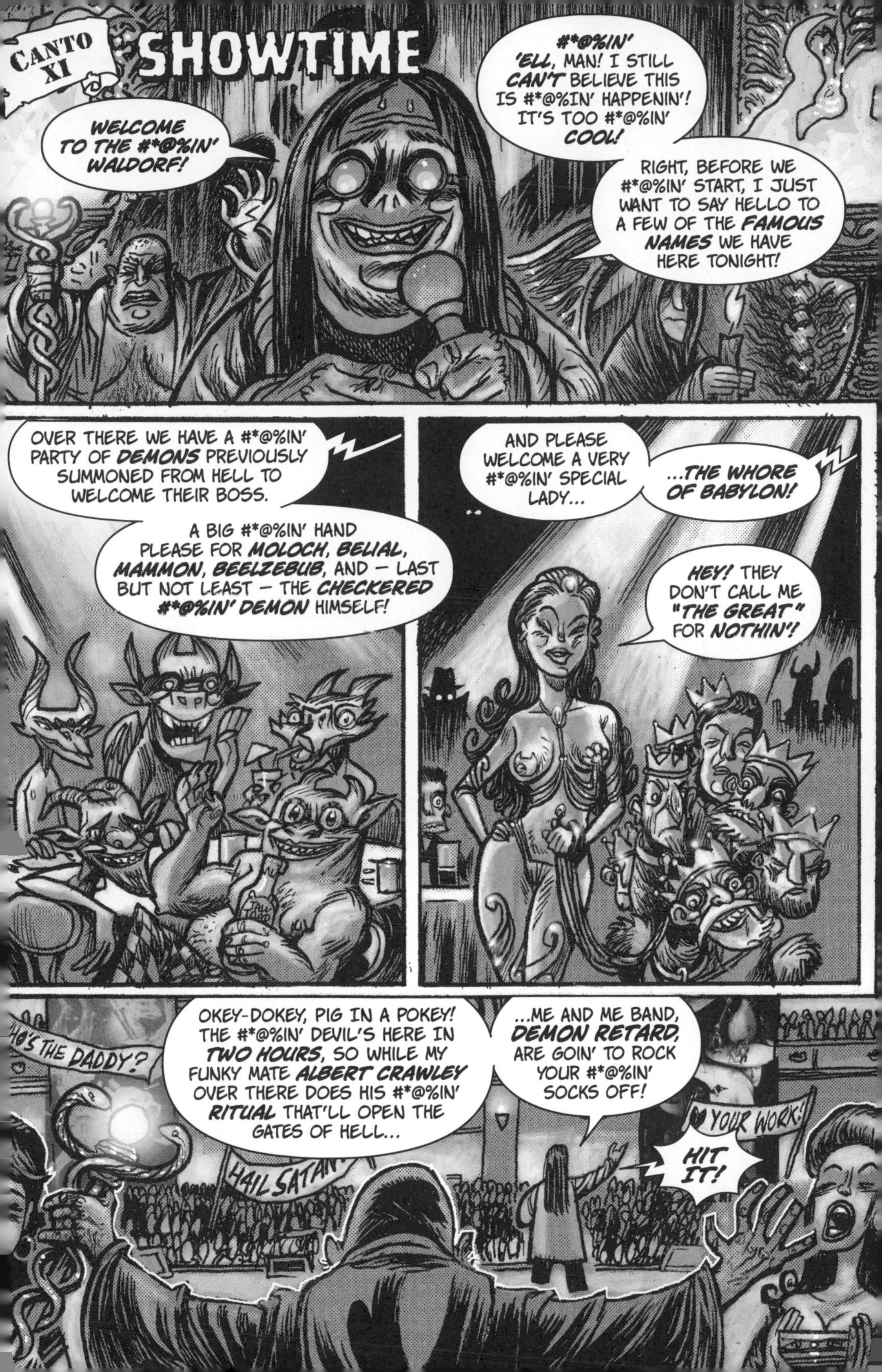
CANTO XI
SHOWTIME
WELCOME TO THE #*@%IN' WALDORF!
#*@%IN' 'ELL, MAN! I STILL CAN'T BELIEVE THIS IS #*@%IN' HAPPENIN'! IT'S TOO #*@%IN' COOL!
RIGHT, BEFORE WE #*@%IN' START, I JUST WANT TO SAY HELLO TO A FEW OF THE FAMOUS NAMES WE HAVE HERE TONIGHT!
OVER THERE WE HAVE A #*@%IN' PARTY OF DEMONS PREVIOUSLY SUMMONED FROM HELL TO WELCOME THEIR BOSS.
A BIG #*@%IN' HAND PLEASE FOR MOLOCH, BELIAL, MAMMON, BEELZEBUB, AND — LAST BUT NOT LEAST — THE CHECKERED #*@%IN' DEMON HIMSELF!
AND PLEASE WELCOME A VERY #*@%IN' SPECIAL LADY...
...THE WHORE OF BABYLON!
HEY! THEY DON'T CALL ME "THE GREAT" FOR NOTHIN'!
HO'S THE DADDY?
OKEY-DOKEY, PIG IN A POKEY! THE #*@%IN' DEVIL'S HERE IN TWO HOURS, SO WHILE MY FUNKY MATE ALBERT CRAWLEY OVER THERE DOES HIS #*@%IN' RITUAL THAT'LL OPEN THE GATES OF HELL...
...ME AND ME BAND, DEMON RETARD, ARE GOIN' TO ROCK YOUR #*@%IN' SOCKS OFF!
YOUR WORK!
HAIL SATAN
HIT IT!

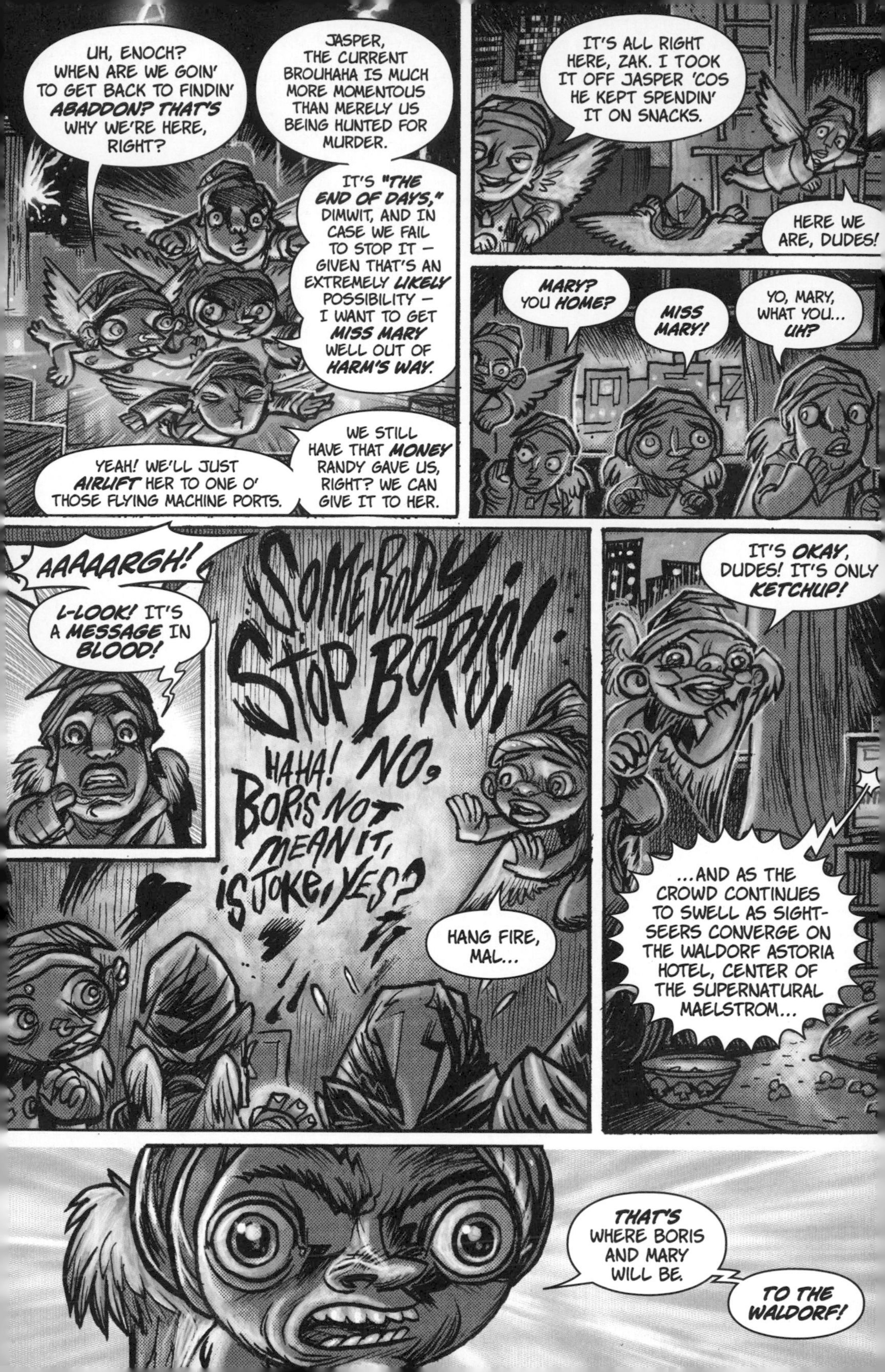
UH, ENOCH? WHEN ARE WE GOIN' TO GET BACK TO FINDIN' ABADDON? THAT'S WHY WE'RE HERE, RIGHT?
JASPER, THE CURRENT BROUHAHA IS MUCH MORE MOMENTOUS THAN MERELY US BEING HUNTED FOR MURDER.
IT'S "THE END OF DAYS," DIMWIT, AND IN CASE WE FAIL TO STOP IT — GIVEN THAT'S AN EXTREMELY LIKELY POSSIBILITY — I WANT TO GET MISS MARY WELL OUT OF HARM'S WAY.
YEAH! WE'LL JUST AIRLIFT HER TO ONE O' THOSE FLYING MACHINE PORTS.
WE STILL HAVE THAT MONEY RANDY GAVE US, RIGHT? WE CAN GIVE IT TO HER.
IT'S ALL RIGHT HERE, ZAK. I TOOK IT OFF JASPER 'COS HE KEPT SPENDIN' IT ON SNACKS.
HERE WE ARE, DUDES!
MARY? YOU HOME?
MISS MARY!
YO, MARY, WHAT YOU... UH?
AAAAARGH!
L-LOOK! IT'S A MESSAGE IN BLOOD!
SOMEBODY STOP BORIS!
HAHA! NO, BORIS NOT MEAN IT, IS JOKE, YES?
HANG FIRE, MAL...
IT'S OKAY, DUDES! IT'S ONLY KETCHUP!
...AND AS THE CROWD CONTINUES TO SWELL AS SIGHT-SEERS CONVERGE ON THE WALDORF ASTORIA HOTEL, CENTER OF THE SUPERNATURAL MAELSTROM...
THAT'S WHERE BORIS AND MARY WILL BE.
TO THE WALDORF!

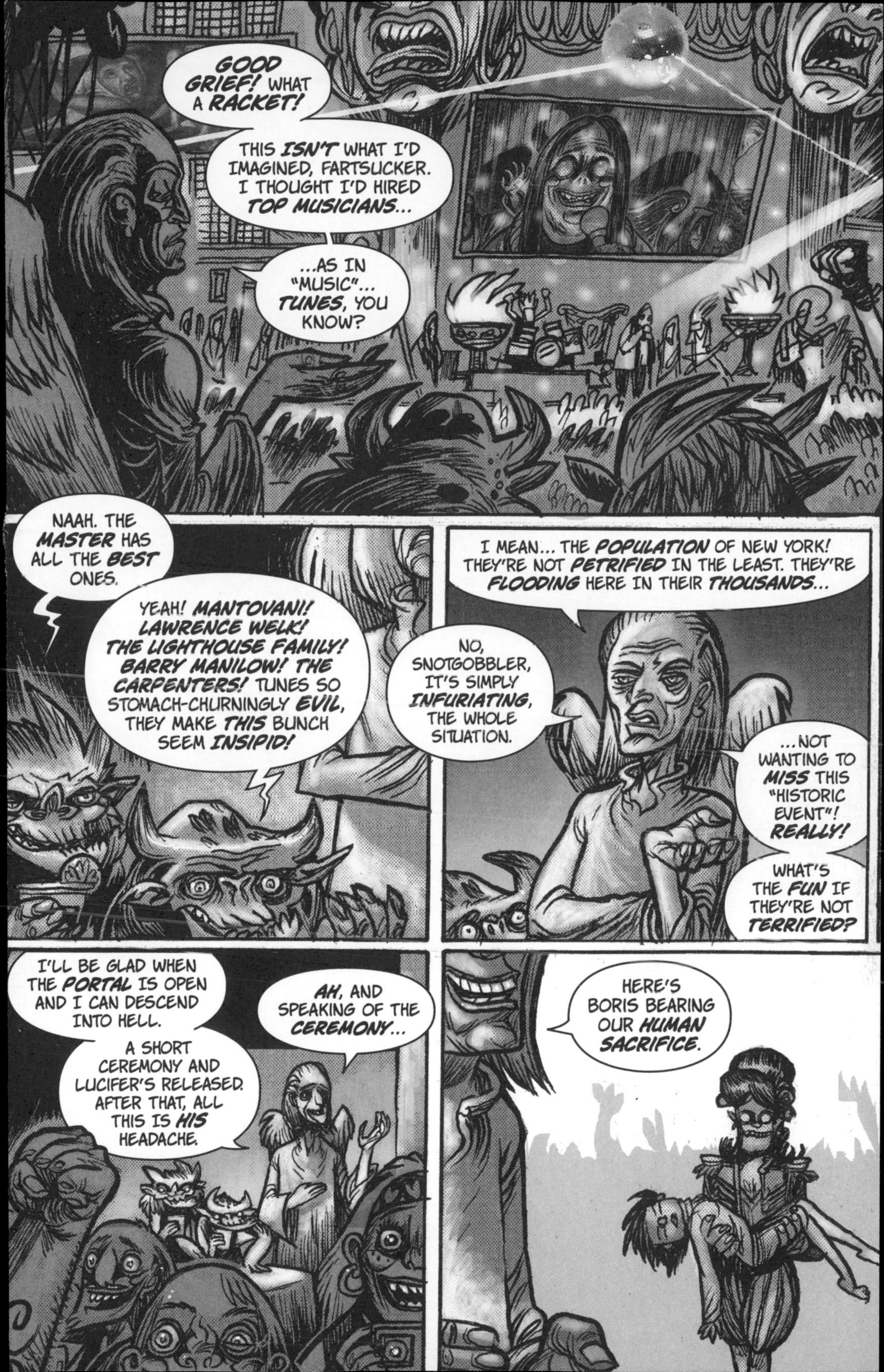
GOOD GRIEF! WHAT A RACKET!
THIS ISN'T WHAT I'D IMAGINED, FARTSUCKER. I THOUGHT I'D HIRED TOP MUSICIANS...
...AS IN "MUSIC"... TUNES, YOU KNOW?
NAAH. THE MASTER HAS ALL THE BEST ONES.
YEAH! MANTOVANI! LAWRENCE WELK! THE LIGHTHOUSE FAMILY! BARRY MANILOW! THE CARPENTERS! TUNES SO STOMACH-CHURNINGLY EVIL, THEY MAKE THIS BUNCH SEEM INSIPID!
I MEAN... THE POPULATION OF NEW YORK! THEY'RE NOT PETRIFIED IN THE LEAST. THEY'RE FLOODING HERE IN THEIR THOUSANDS...
NO, SNOTGOBBLER, IT'S SIMPLY INFURIATING, THE WHOLE SITUATION.
...NOT WANTING TO MISS THIS "HISTORIC EVENT"! REALLY!
WHAT'S THE FUN IF THEY'RE NOT TERRIFIED?
I'LL BE GLAD WHEN THE PORTAL IS OPEN AND I CAN DESCEND INTO HELL.
A SHORT CEREMONY AND LUCIFER'S RELEASED. AFTER THAT, ALL THIS IS HIS HEADACHE.
AH, AND SPEAKING OF THE CEREMONY...
HERE'S BORIS BEARING OUR HUMAN SACRIFICE.

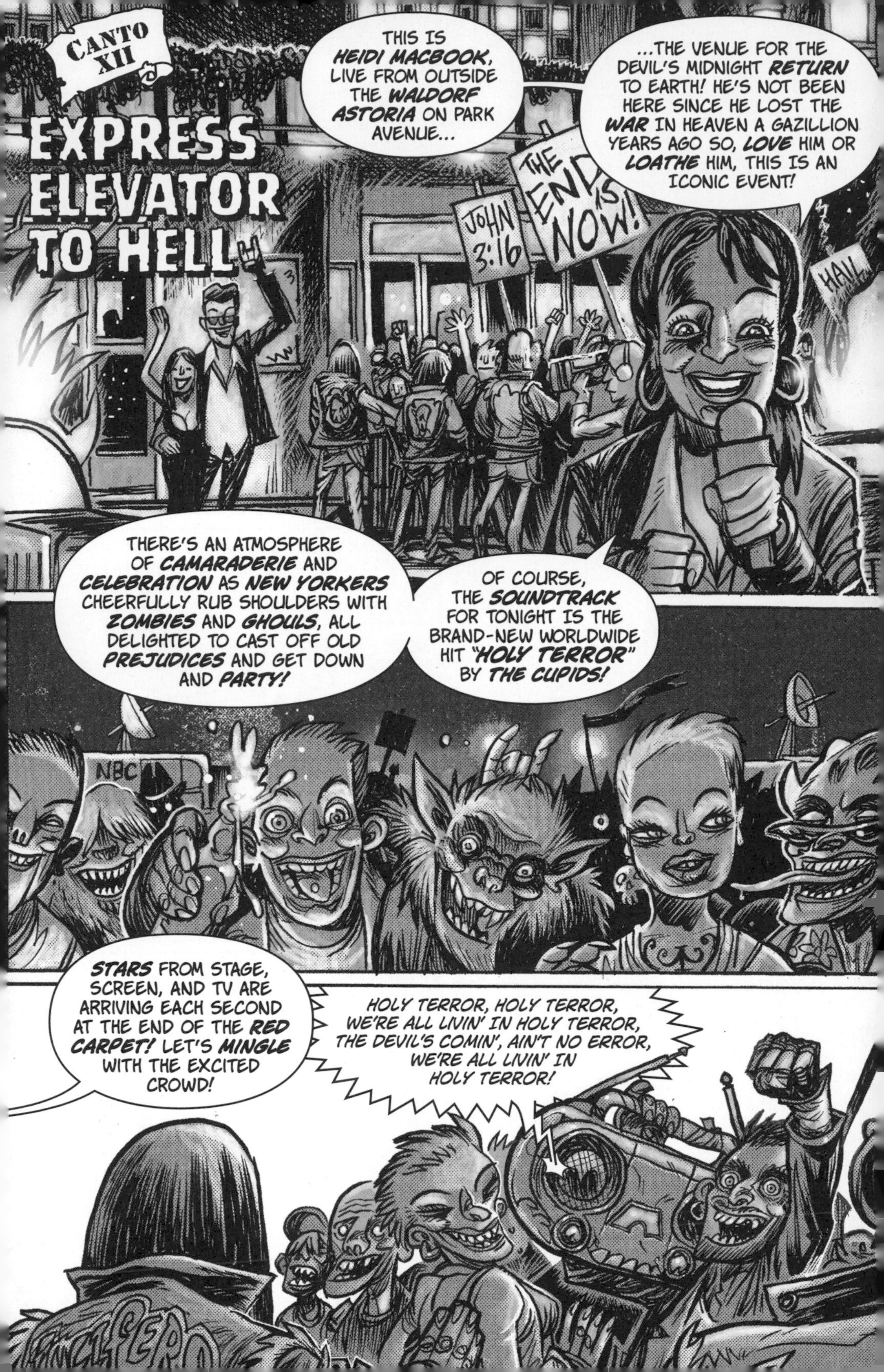
CANTO XII
EXPRESS ELEVATOR TO HELL
THIS IS HEIDI MACBOOK, LIVE FROM OUTSIDE THE WALDORF ASTORIA ON PARK AVENUE...
...THE VENUE FOR THE DEVIL'S MIDNIGHT RETURN TO EARTH! HE'S NOT BEEN HERE SINCE HE LOST THE WAR IN HEAVEN A GAZILLION YEARS AGO SO, LOVE HIM OR LOATHE HIM, THIS IS AN ICONIC EVENT!
JOHN 3:16
THE END IS NOW!
HAIL
THERE'S AN ATMOSPHERE OF CAMARADERIE AND CELEBRATION AS NEW YORKERS CHEERFULLY RUB SHOULDERS WITH ZOMBIES AND GHOULS, ALL DELIGHTED TO CAST OFF OLD PREJUDICES AND GET DOWN AND PARTY!
OF COURSE, THE SOUNDTRACK FOR TONIGHT IS THE BRAND-NEW WORLDWIDE HIT "HOLY TERROR" BY THE CUPIDS!
NBC
STARS FROM STAGE, SCREEN, AND TV ARE ARRIVING EACH SECOND AT THE END OF THE RED CARPET! LET'S MINGLE WITH THE EXCITED CROWD!
HOLY TERROR, HOLY TERROR, WE'RE ALL LIVIN' IN HOLY TERROR, THE DEVIL'S COMIN', AIN'T NO ERROR, WE'RE ALL LIVIN' IN HOLY TERROR!

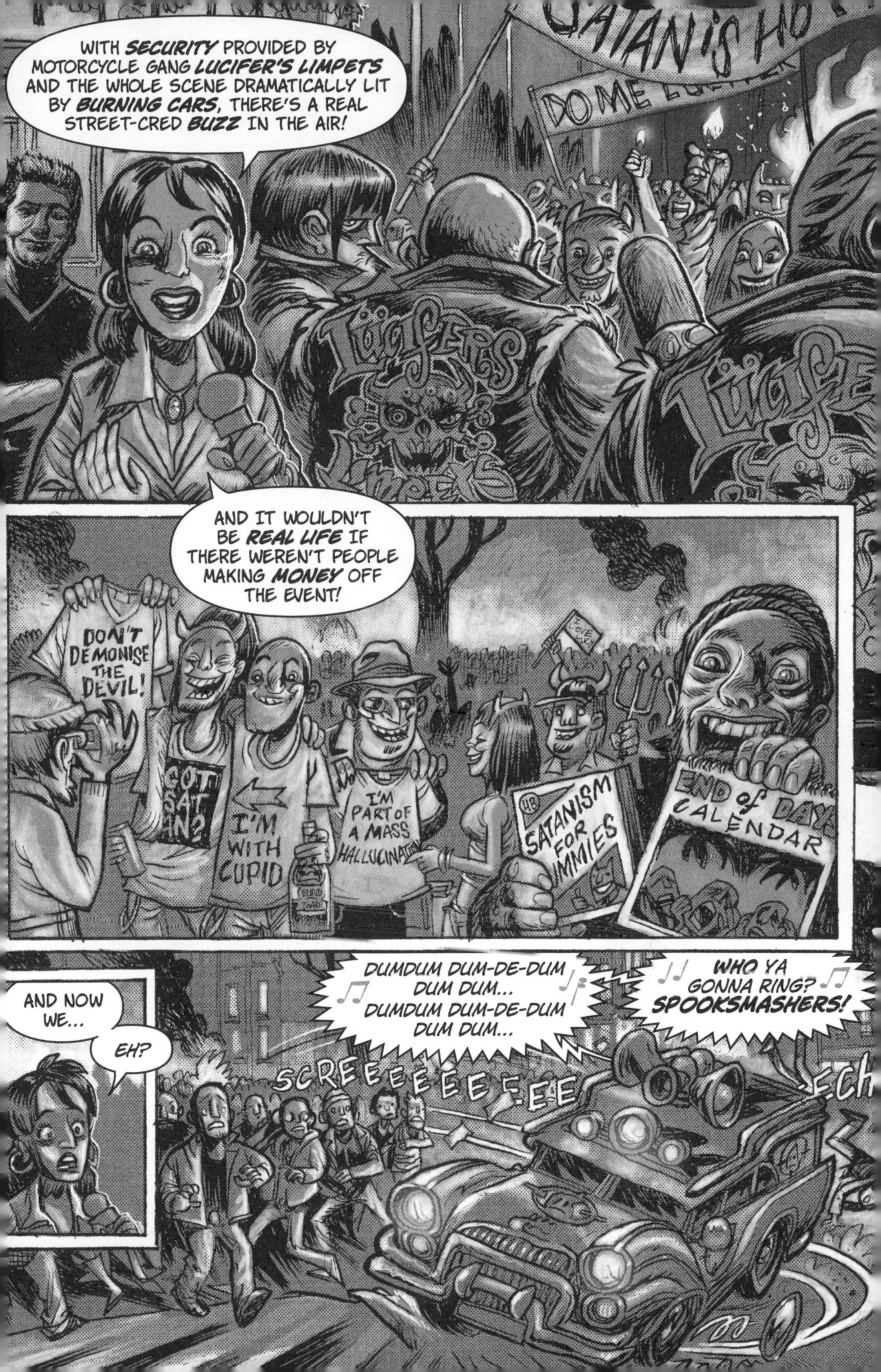
WITH SECURITY PROVIDED BY MOTORCYCLE GANG LUCIFER'S LIMPETS AND THE WHOLE SCENE DRAMATICALLY LIT BY BURNING CARS, THERE'S A REAL STREET-CRED BUZZ IN THE AIR!
AND IT WOULDN'T BE REAL LIFE IF THERE WEREN'T PEOPLE MAKING MONEY OFF THE EVENT!
DON'T DEMONISE THE DEVIL!
GOT SATAN?
I'M WITH CUPID
I'M PART OF A MASS
SATANISM FOR
CALENDAR
AND NOW WE...
EH?
DUMDUM DUM-DE-DUM DUM DUM... DUMDUM DUM-DE-DUM DUM DUM...
WHO YA GONNA RING? SPOOKSMASHERS!
SCREEEEEEEEEEEE

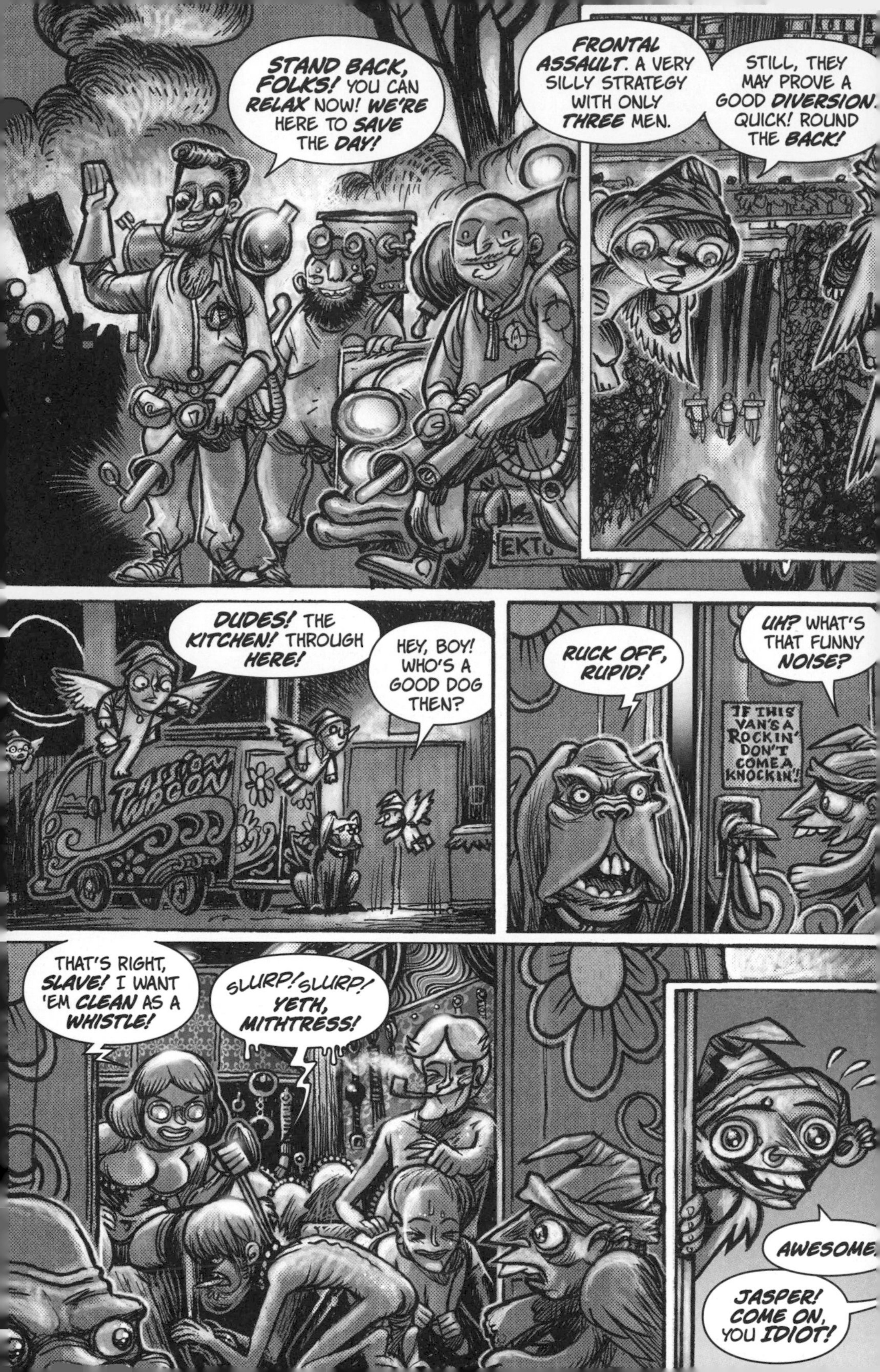
STAND BACK, FOLKS! YOU CAN RELAX NOW! WE'RE HERE TO SAVE THE DAY!
FRONTAL ASSAULT. A VERY SILLY STRATEGY WITH ONLY THREE MEN.
STILL, THEY MAY PROVE A GOOD DIVERSION. QUICK! ROUND THE BACK!
EKT
DUDES! THE KITCHEN! THROUGH HERE!
HEY, BOY! WHO'S A GOOD DOG THEN?
RUCK OFF, RUPID!
UH? WHAT'S THAT FUNNY NOISE?
IF THIS VAN'S A ROCKIN' DON'T COME A KNOCKIN'!
THAT'S RIGHT, SLAVE! I WANT 'EM CLEAN AS A WHISTLE!
SLURP! SLURP! YETH, MITHTRESS!
AWESOME.
JASPER! COME ON, YOU IDIOT!

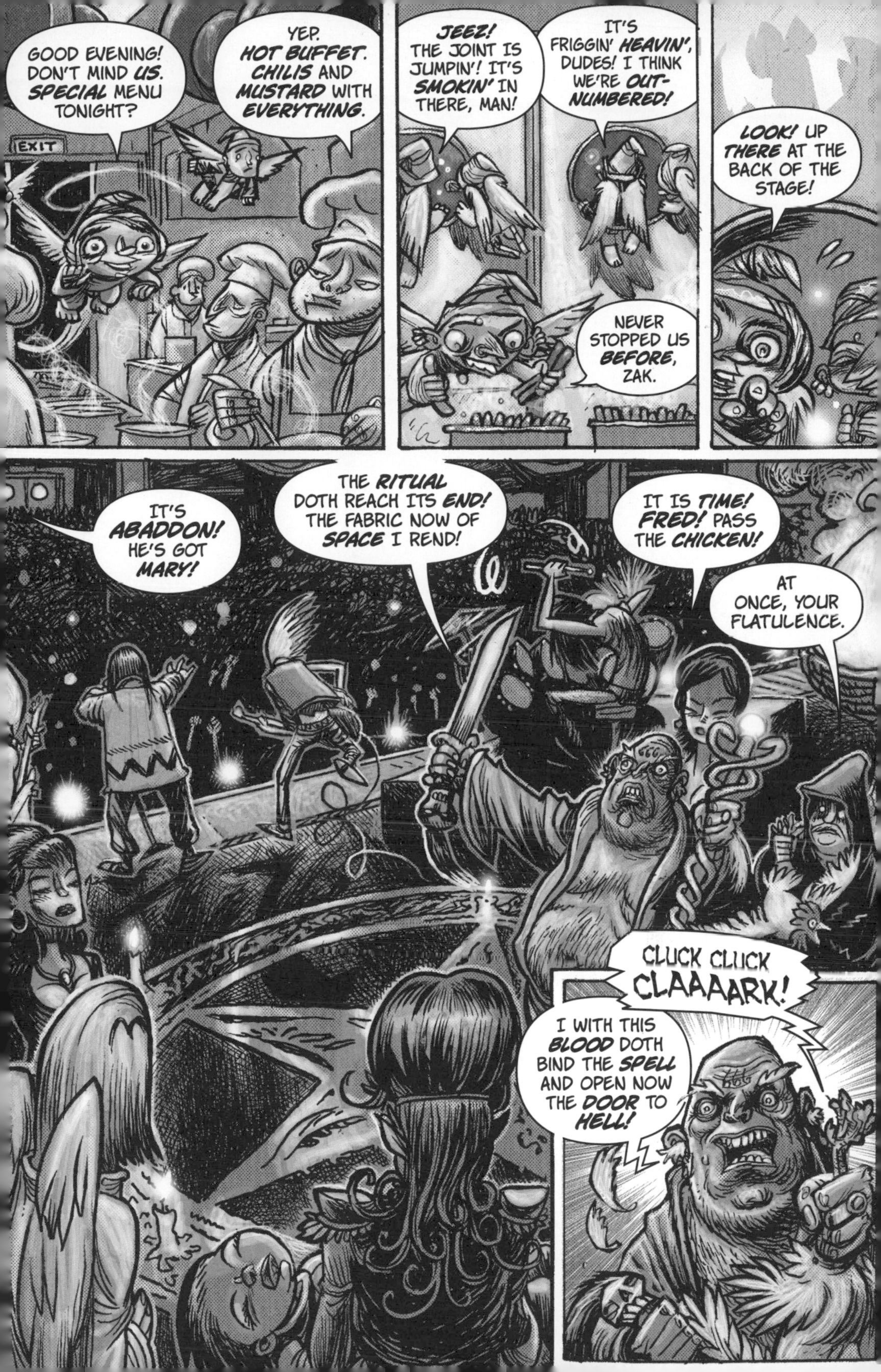
GOOD EVENING! DON'T MIND US. SPECIAL MENU TONIGHT?
YEP. HOT BUFFET. CHILIS AND MUSTARD WITH EVERYTHING.
EXIT
JEEZ! THE JOINT IS JUMPIN'! IT'S SMOKIN' IN THERE, MAN!
IT'S FRIGGIN' HEAVIN', DUDES! I THINK WE'RE OUT-NUMBERED!
NEVER STOPPED US BEFORE, ZAK.
LOOK! UP THERE AT THE BACK OF THE STAGE!
IT'S ABADDON! HE'S GOT MARY!
THE RITUAL DOTH REACH ITS END! THE FABRIC NOW OF SPACE I REND!
IT IS TIME! FRED! PASS THE CHICKEN!
AT ONCE, YOUR FLATULENCE.
CLUCK CLUCK CLAAAARK!
I WITH THIS BLOOD DOTH BIND THE SPELL AND OPEN NOW THE DOOR TO HELL!

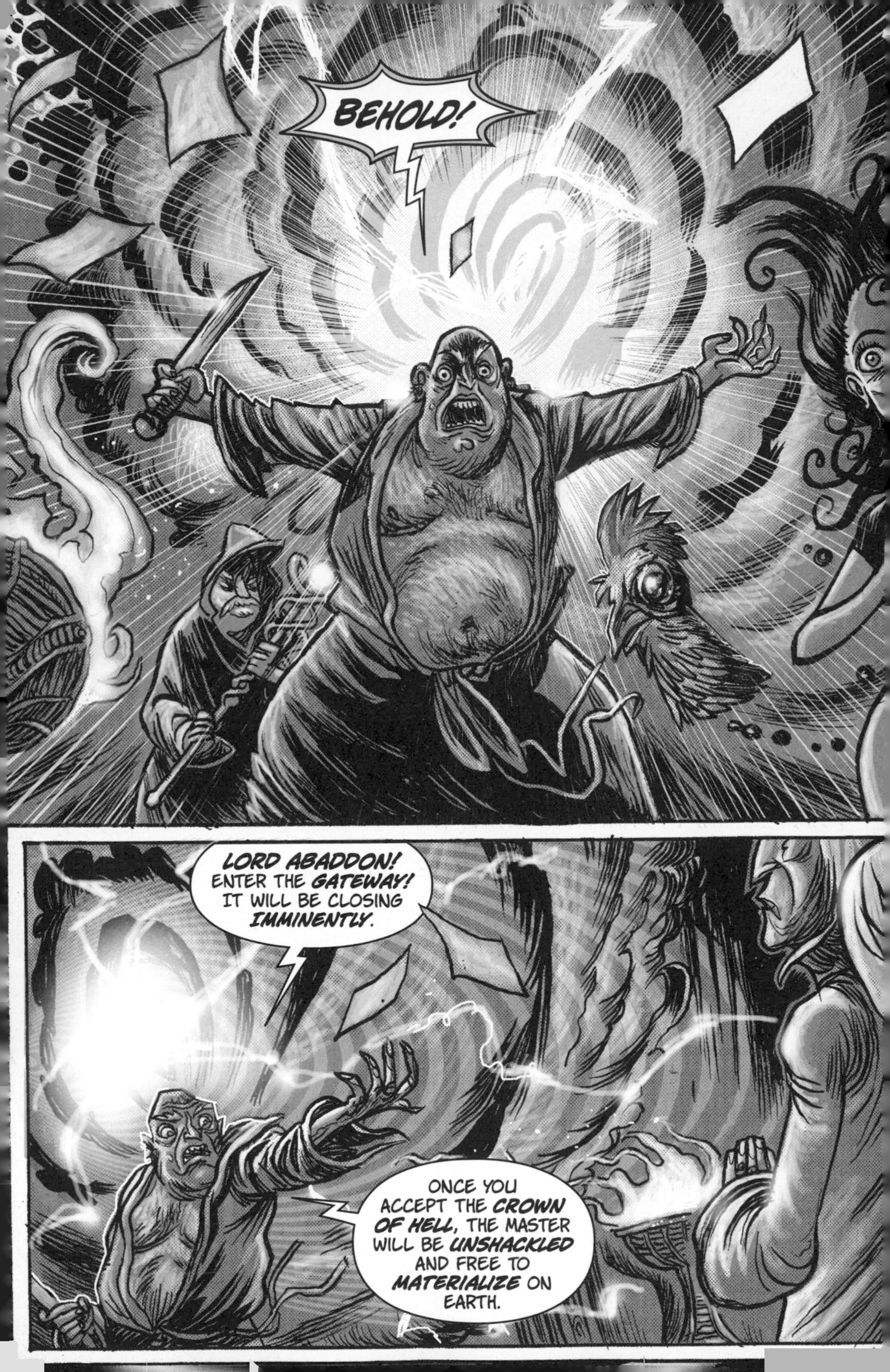
BEHOLD!
LORD ABADDON! ENTER THE GATEWAY! IT WILL BE CLOSING IMMINENTLY.
ONCE YOU ACCEPT THE CROWN OF HELL, THE MASTER WILL BE UNSHACKLED AND FREE TO MATERIALIZE ON EARTH.

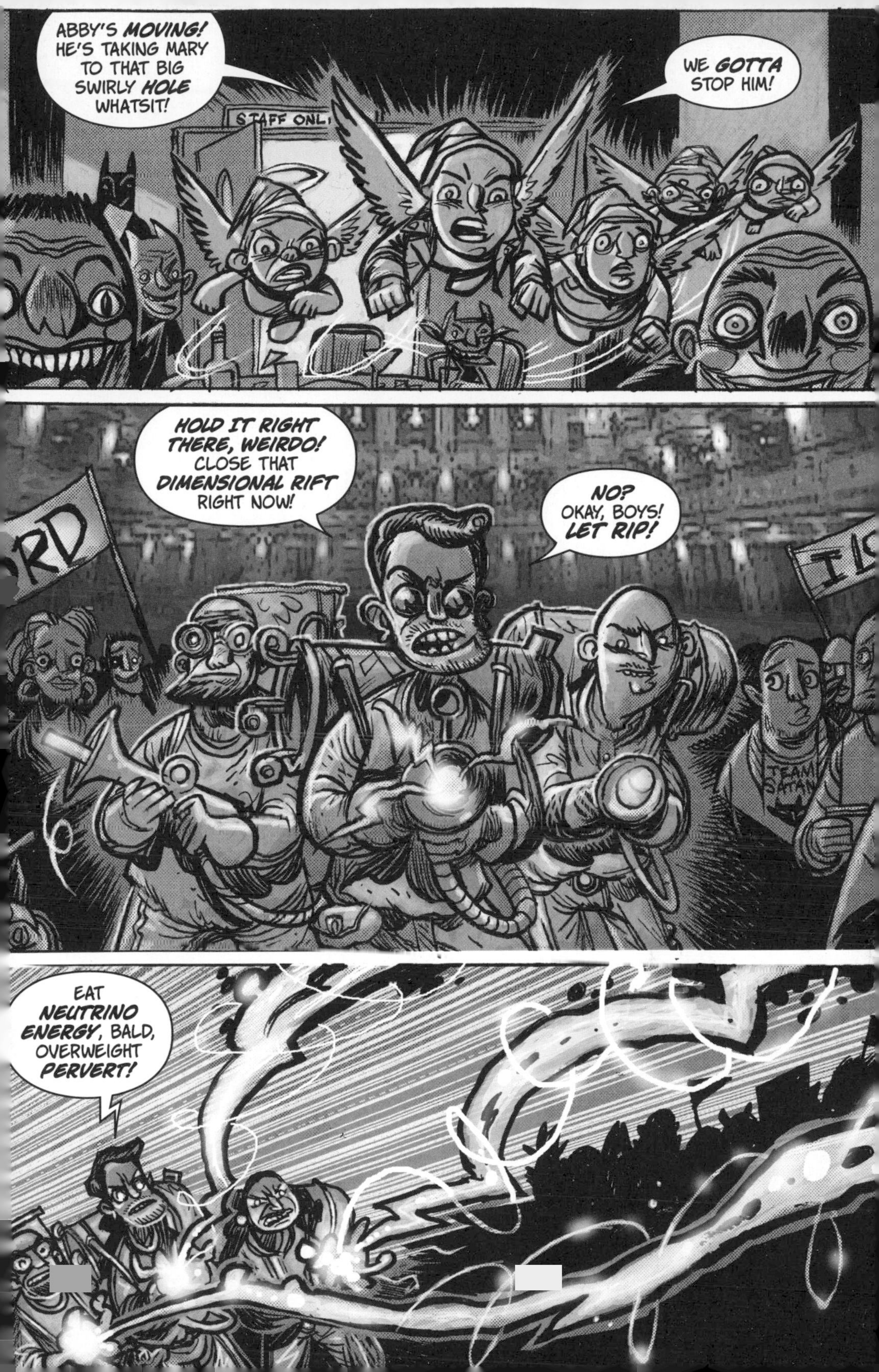
ABBY'S MOVING! HE'S TAKING MARY TO THAT BIG SWIRLY HOLE WHATSIT!
WE GOTTA STOP HIM!
STAFF ONL
HOLD IT RIGHT THERE, WEIRDO! CLOSE THAT DIMENSIONAL RIFT RIGHT NOW!
NO? OKAY, BOYS! LET RIP!
RD
TEAM SATAN
EAT NEUTRINO ENERGY, BALD, OVERWEIGHT PERVERT!

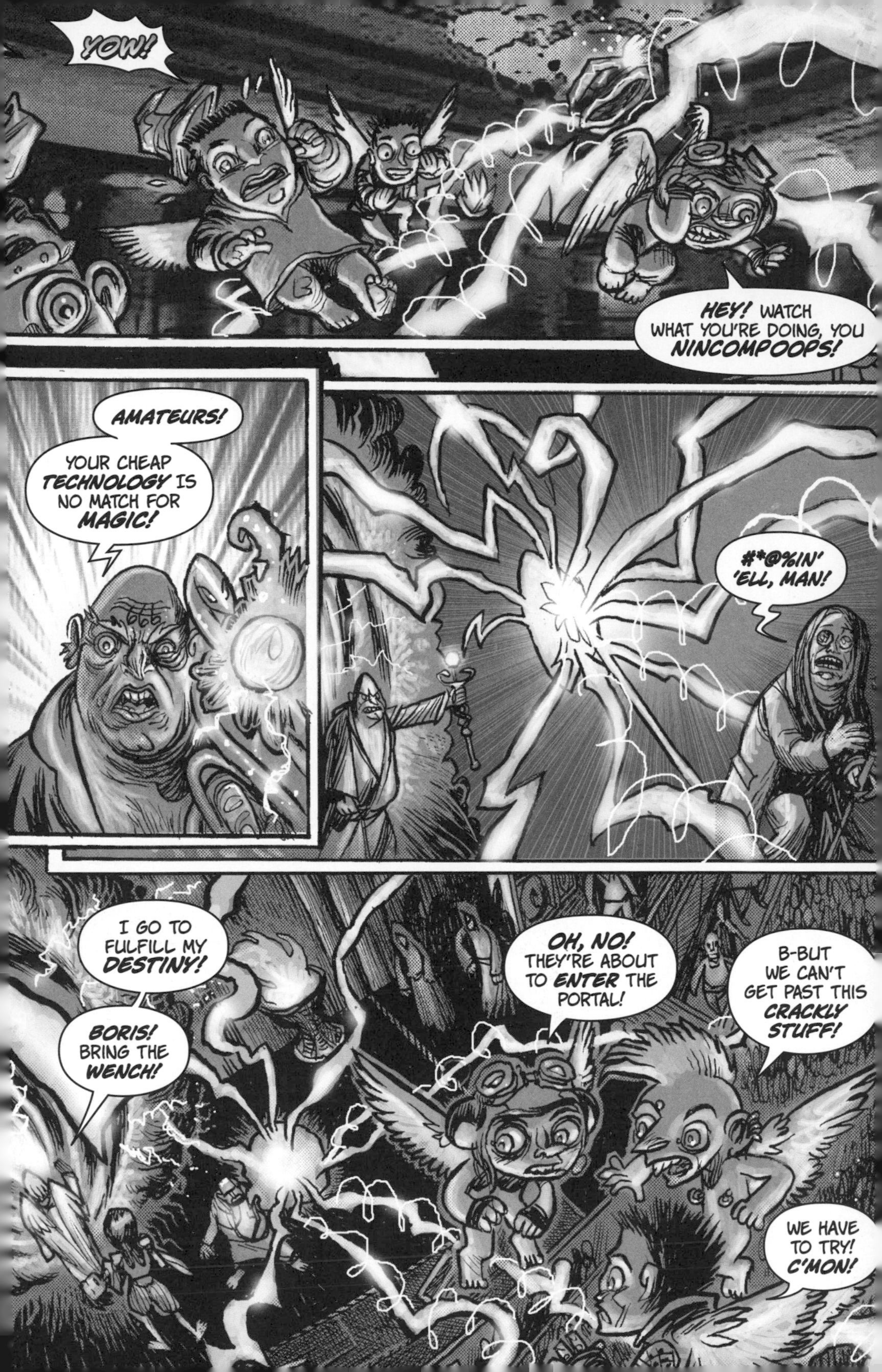
YOW!
HEY! WATCH WHAT YOU'RE DOING, YOU NINCOMPOOPS!
AMATEURS!
YOUR CHEAP TECHNOLOGY IS NO MATCH FOR MAGIC!
#*@%IN' 'ELL, MAN!
I GO TO FULFILL MY DESTINY!
BORIS! BRING THE WENCH!
OH, NO! THEY'RE ABOUT TO ENTER THE PORTAL!
B-BUT WE CAN'T GET PAST THIS CRACKLY STUFF!
WE HAVE TO TRY! C'MON!

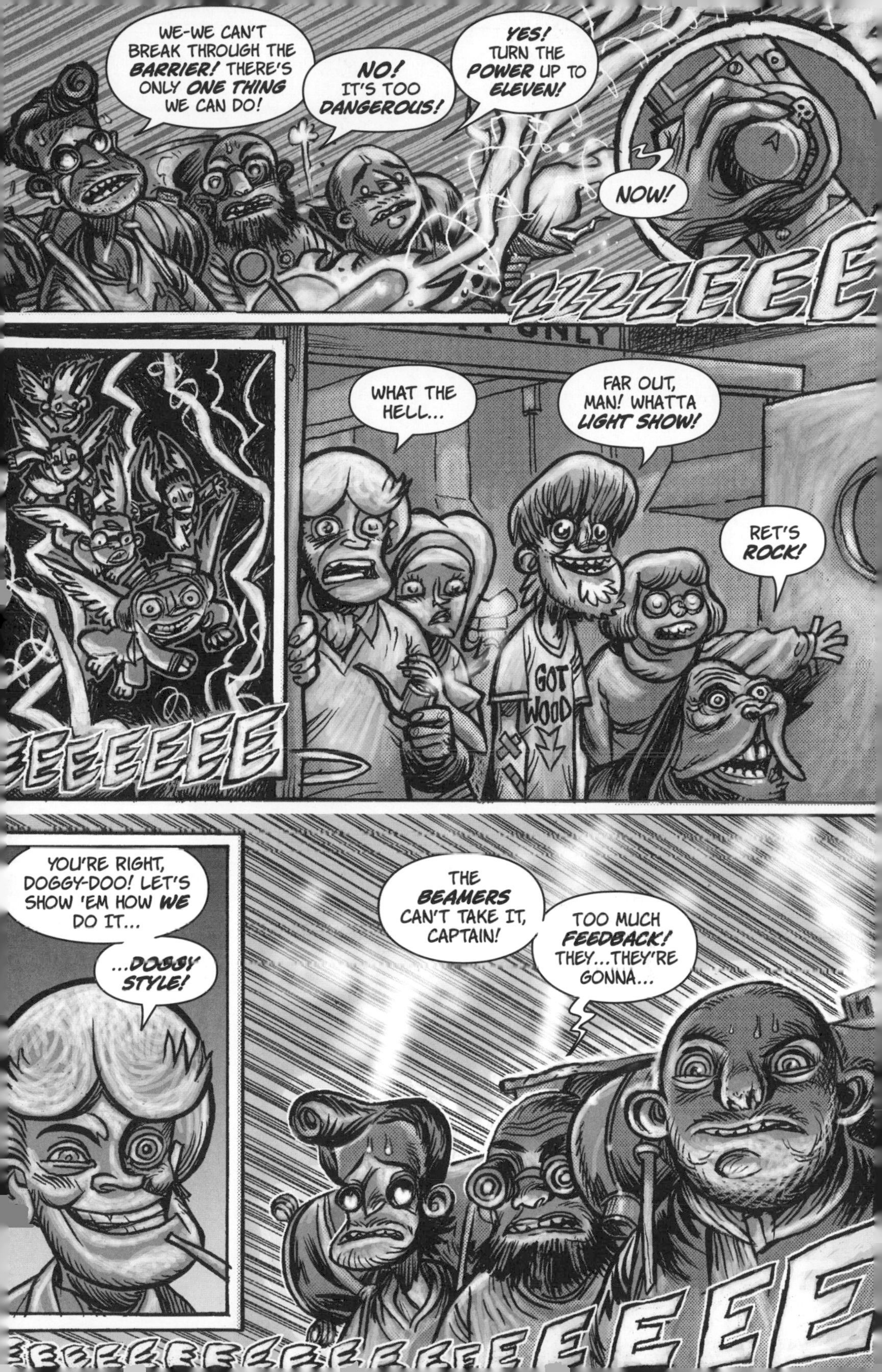

WE-WE CAN'T BREAK THROUGH THE BARRIER! THERE'S ONLY ONE THING WE CAN DO!
NO! IT'S TOO DANGEROUS!
YES! TURN THE POWER UP TO ELEVEN!
NOW!
ZZZZZEEE
EEEEEEE
ONLY
WHAT THE HELL...
FAR OUT, MAN! WHATTA LIGHT SHOW!
RET'S ROCK!
GOT WOOD
YOU'RE RIGHT, DOGGY-DOO! LET'S SHOW 'EM HOW WE DO IT...
...DOGGY STYLE!
THE BEAMERS CAN'T TAKE IT, CAPTAIN!
TOO MUCH FEEDBACK! THEY...THEY'RE GONNA...
EEEEEEEEEEEEEEEEEE

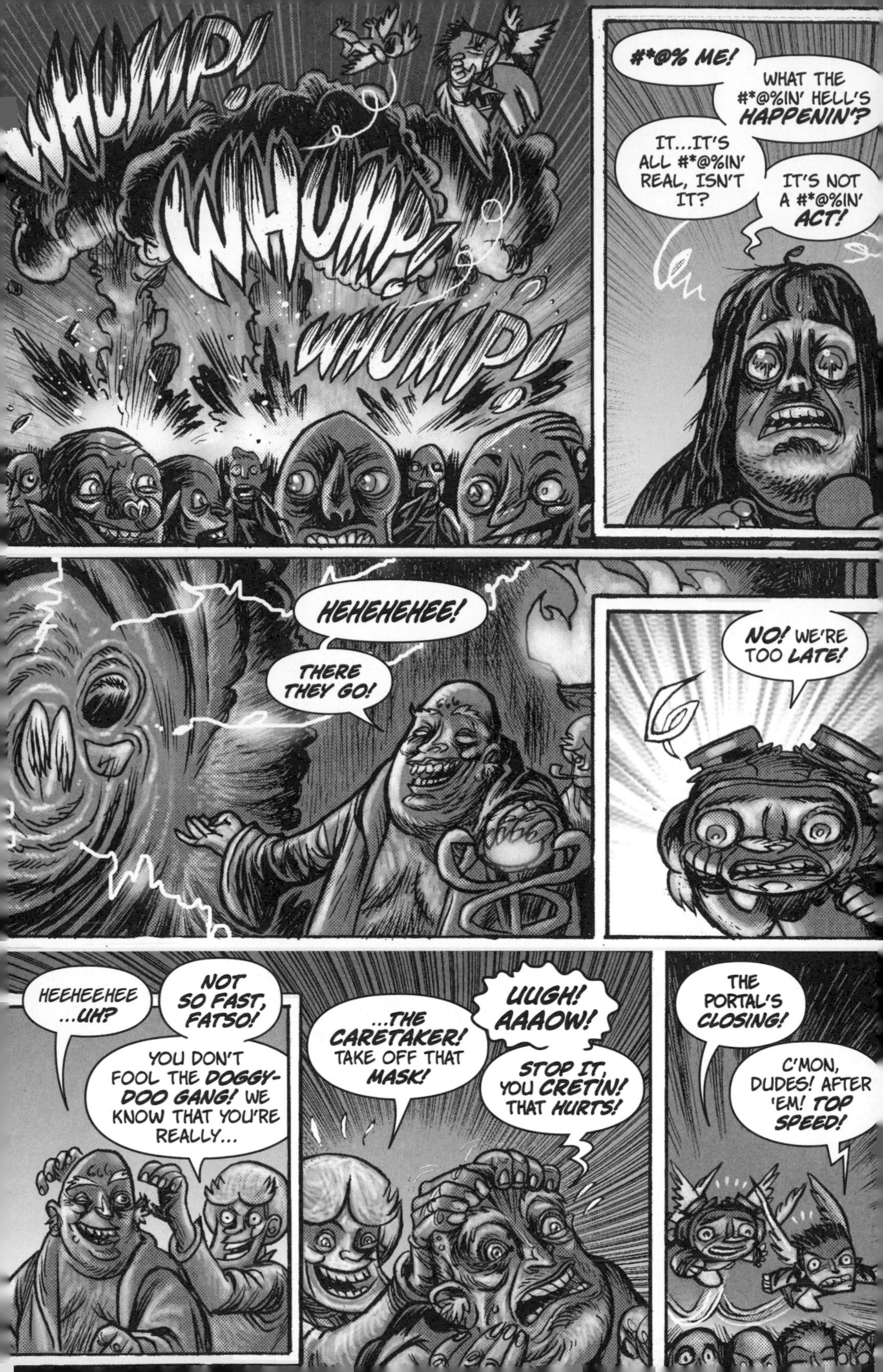

WHUMP!
WHUMP!
WHUMP!
#*@% ME!
WHAT THE #*@%IN' HELL'S HAPPENIN'?
IT...IT'S ALL #*@%IN' REAL, ISN'T IT?
IT'S NOT A #*@%IN' ACT!
HEHEHEHEE!
THERE THEY GO!
NO! WE'RE TOO LATE!
HEEHEEHEE ...UH?
NOT SO FAST, FATSO!
YOU DON'T FOOL THE DOGGY-DOO GANG! WE KNOW THAT YOU'RE REALLY...
...THE CARETAKER! TAKE OFF THAT MASK!
UUGH! AAAOW!
STOP IT, YOU CRETIN! THAT HURTS!
THE PORTAL'S CLOSING!
C'MON, DUDES! AFTER 'EM! TOP SPEED!

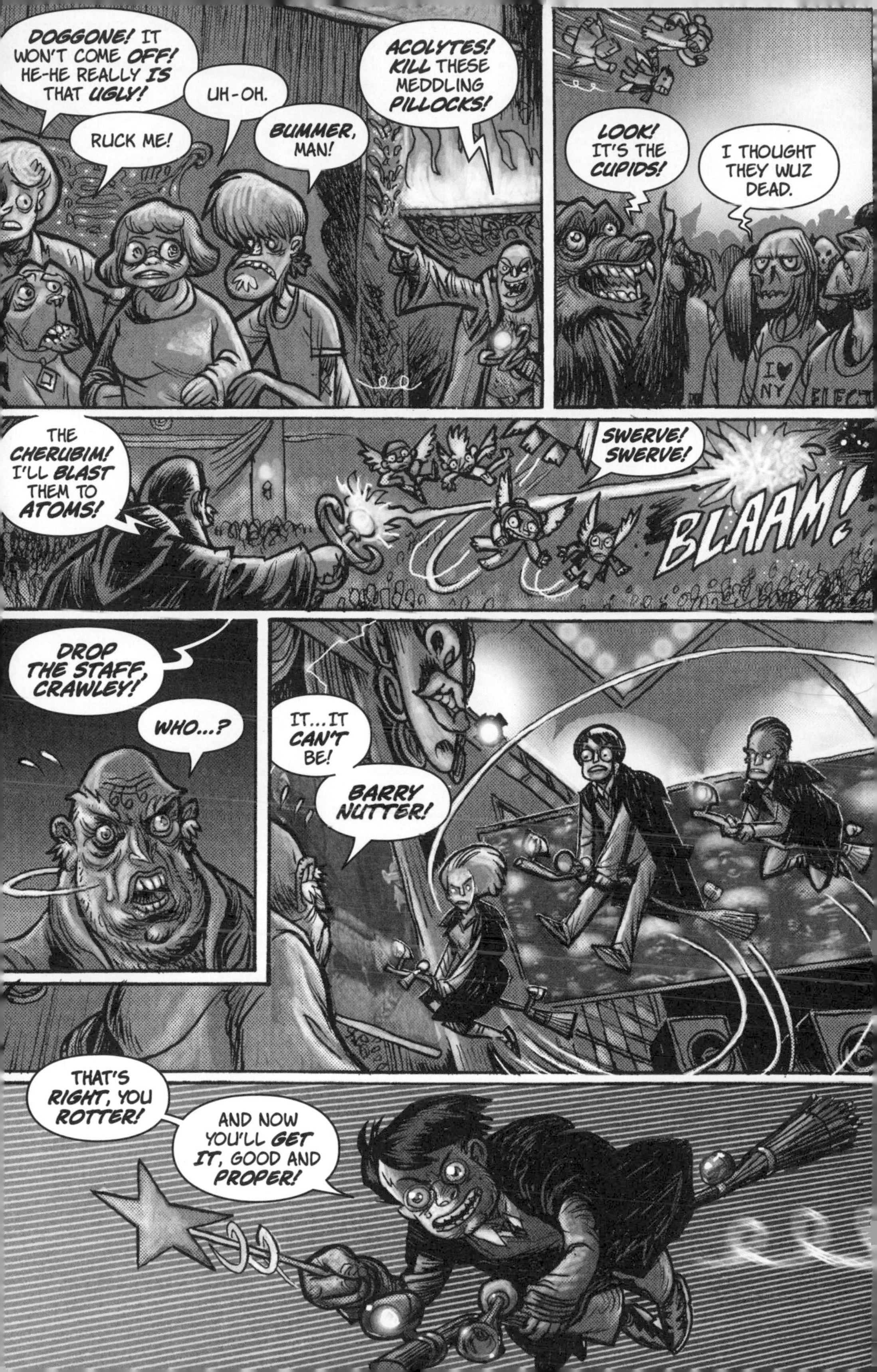

DOGGONE! IT WON'T COME OFF! HE-HE REALLY IS THAT UGLY!
RUCK ME!
UH-OH.
BUMMER, MAN!
ACOLYTES! KILL THESE MEDDLING PILLOCKS!
LOOK! IT'S THE CUPIDS!
I THOUGHT THEY WUZ DEAD.
I ♥ NY
THE CHERUBIM! I'LL BLAST THEM TO ATOMS!
SWERVE! SWERVE!
BLAAM!
DROP THE STAFF, CRAWLEY!
WHO...?
IT...IT CAN'T BE!
BARRY NUTTER!
THAT'S RIGHT, YOU ROTTER!
AND NOW YOU'LL GET IT, GOOD AND PROPER!

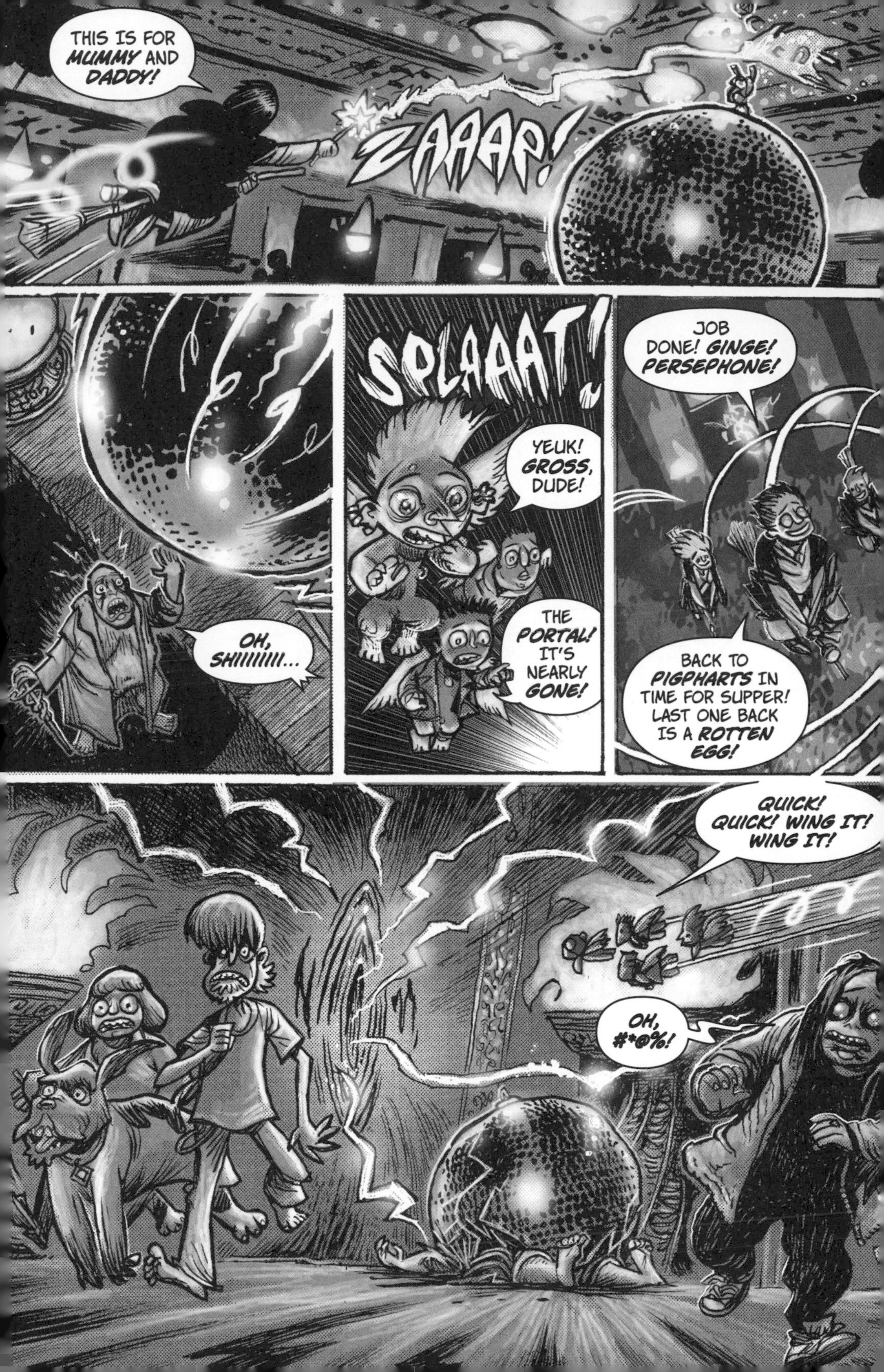
THIS IS FOR MUMMY AND DADDY!
ZAAAP!
OH, SHIIIIIIII...
SPLAAAT!
YEUK! GROSS, DUDE!
THE PORTAL! IT'S NEARLY GONE!
JOB DONE! GINGE! PERSEPHONE!
BACK TO PIGPHARTS IN TIME FOR SUPPER! LAST ONE BACK IS A ROTTEN EGG!
QUICK! QUICK! WING IT! WING IT!
OH, #*@%!

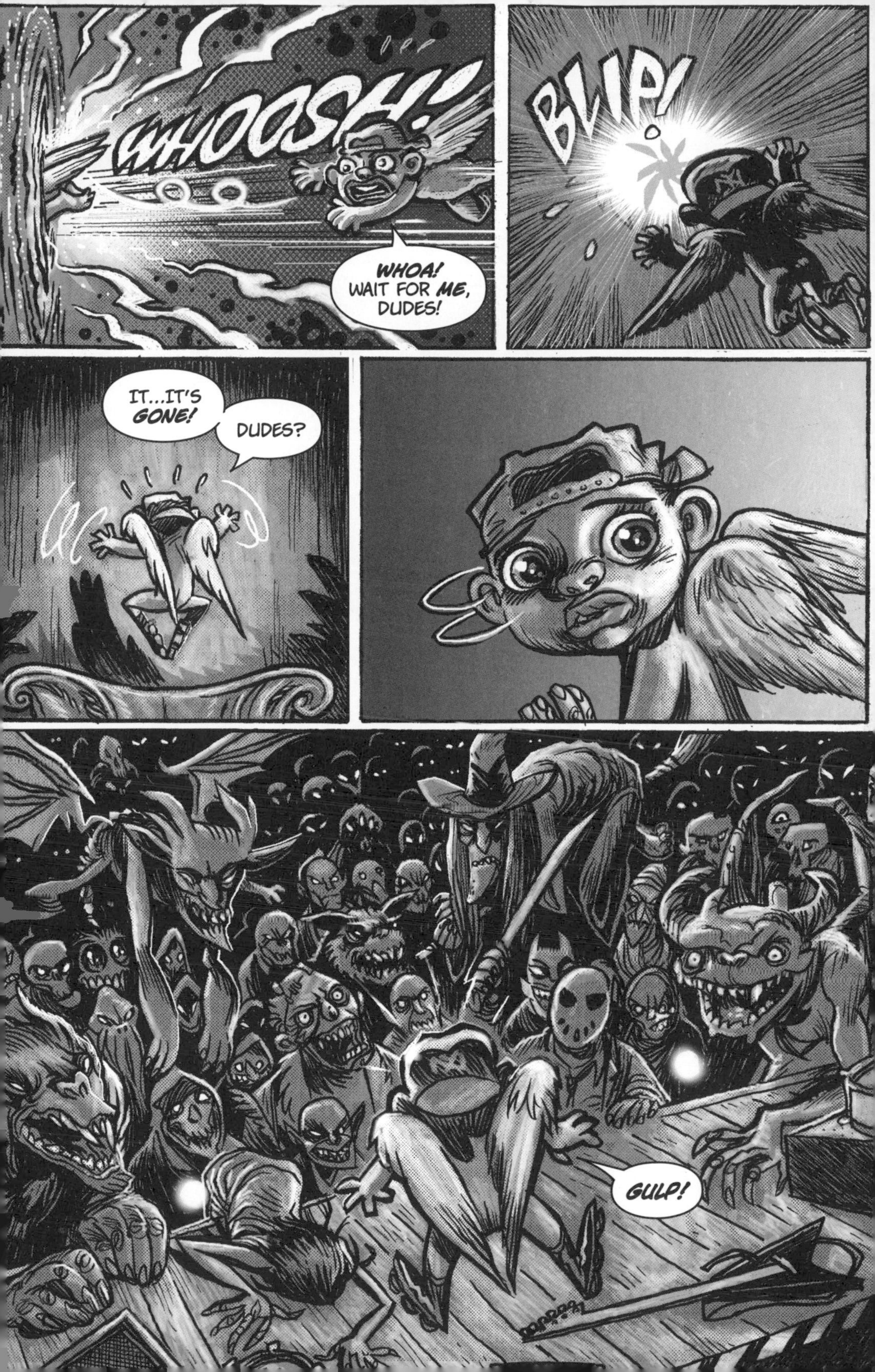
WHOOSH!
WHOA! WAIT FOR ME, DUDES!
BLIP!
IT...IT'S GONE!
DUDES?
GULP!

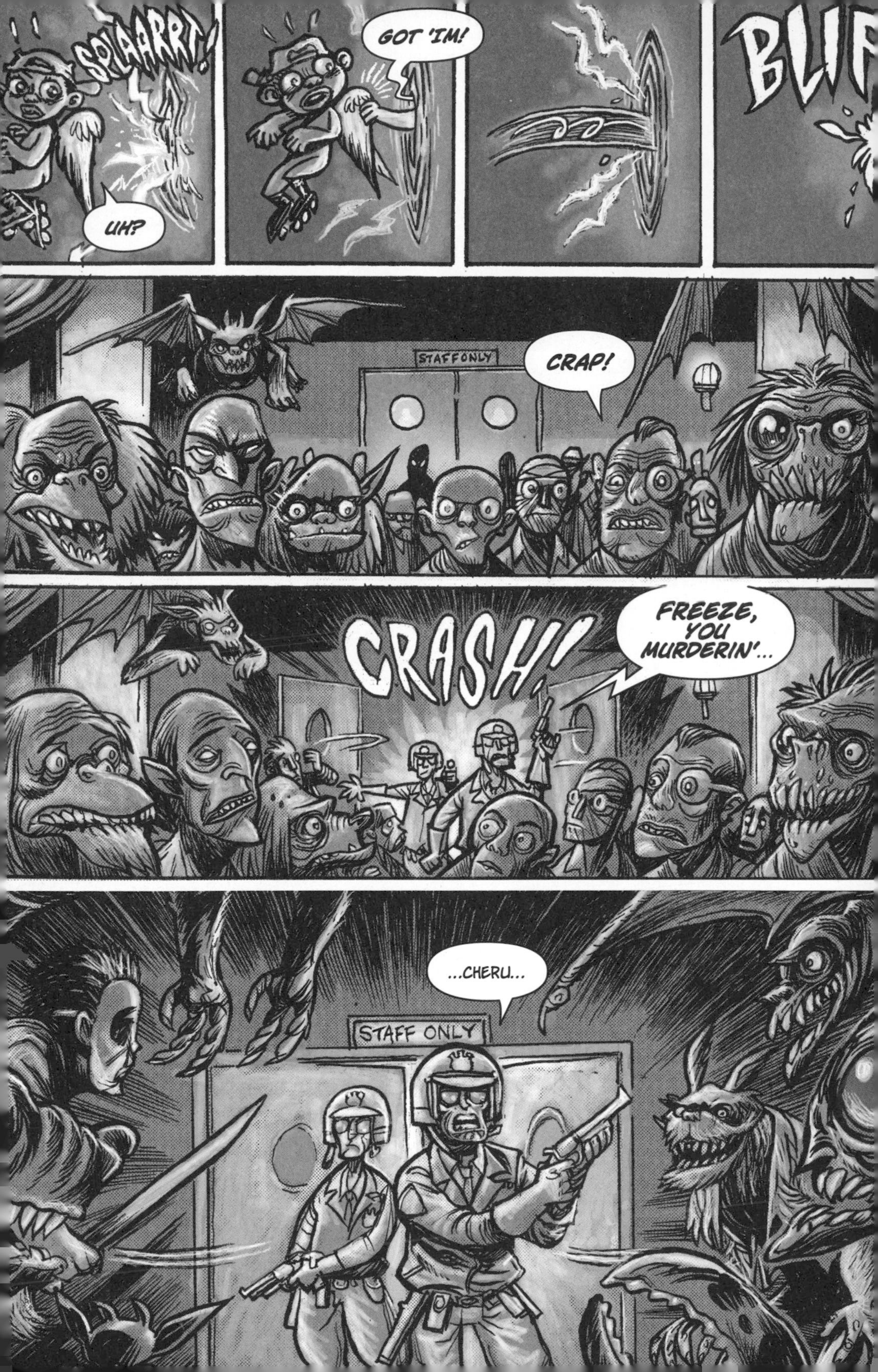
SPLAARRT!
UH?
GOT 'IM!
BLIF
STAFF ONLY
CRAP!
CRASH!
FREEZE, YOU MURDERIN'...
...CHERU...
STAFF ONLY

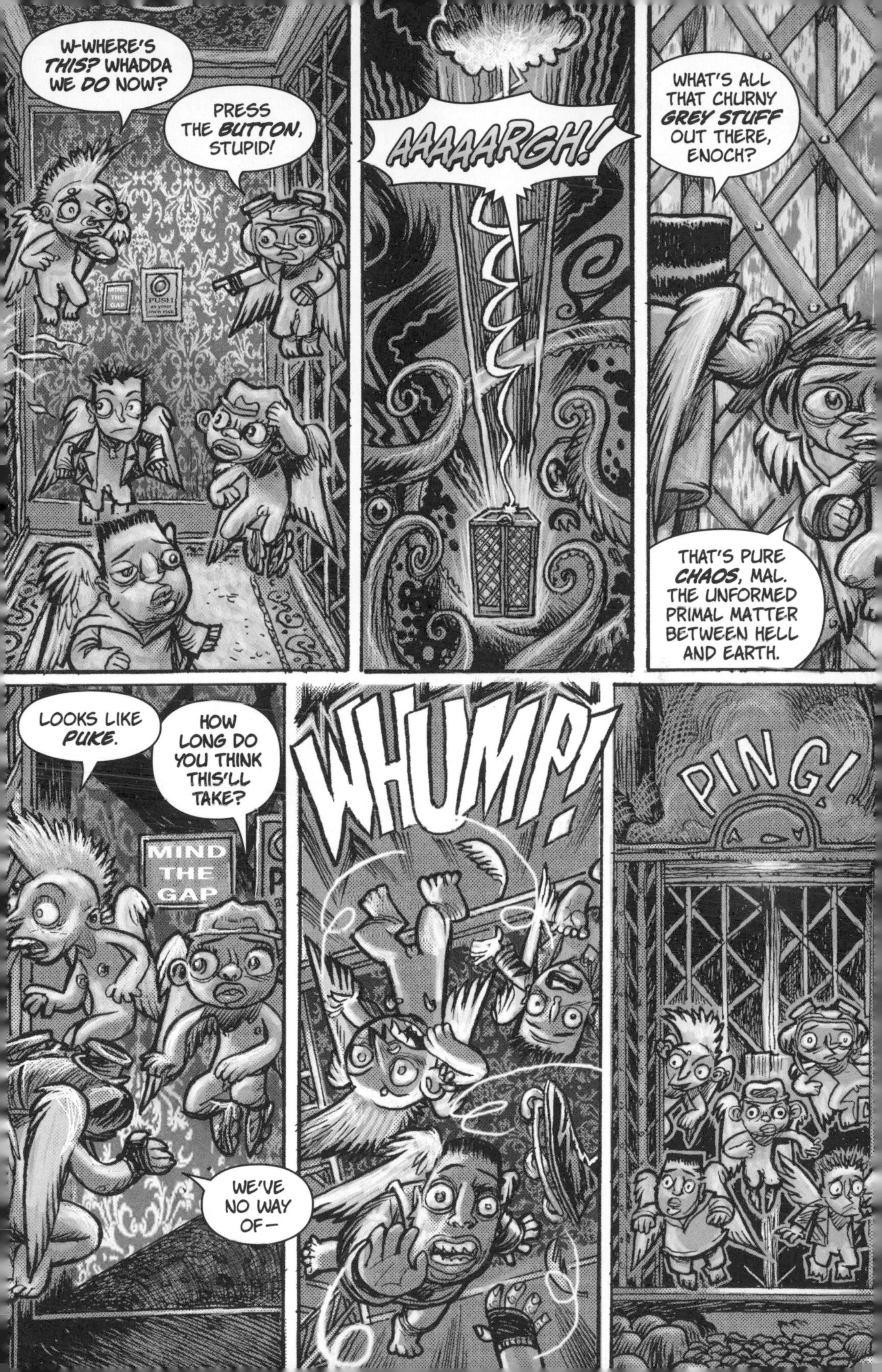
W-WHERE'S *THIS?* WHADDA WE *DO* NOW?
PRESS THE *BUTTON*, STUPID!
MIND THE GAP
PUSH at your own risk
AAAAARGH!
WHAT'S ALL THAT CHURNY *GREY STUFF* OUT THERE, ENOCH?
THAT'S PURE *CHAOS*, MAL. THE UNFORMED PRIMAL MATTER BETWEEN HELL AND EARTH.
LOOKS LIKE *PUKE*.
HOW LONG DO YOU THINK THIS'LL TAKE?
MIND THE GAP
WE'VE NO WAY OF—
WHUMP!
PING!

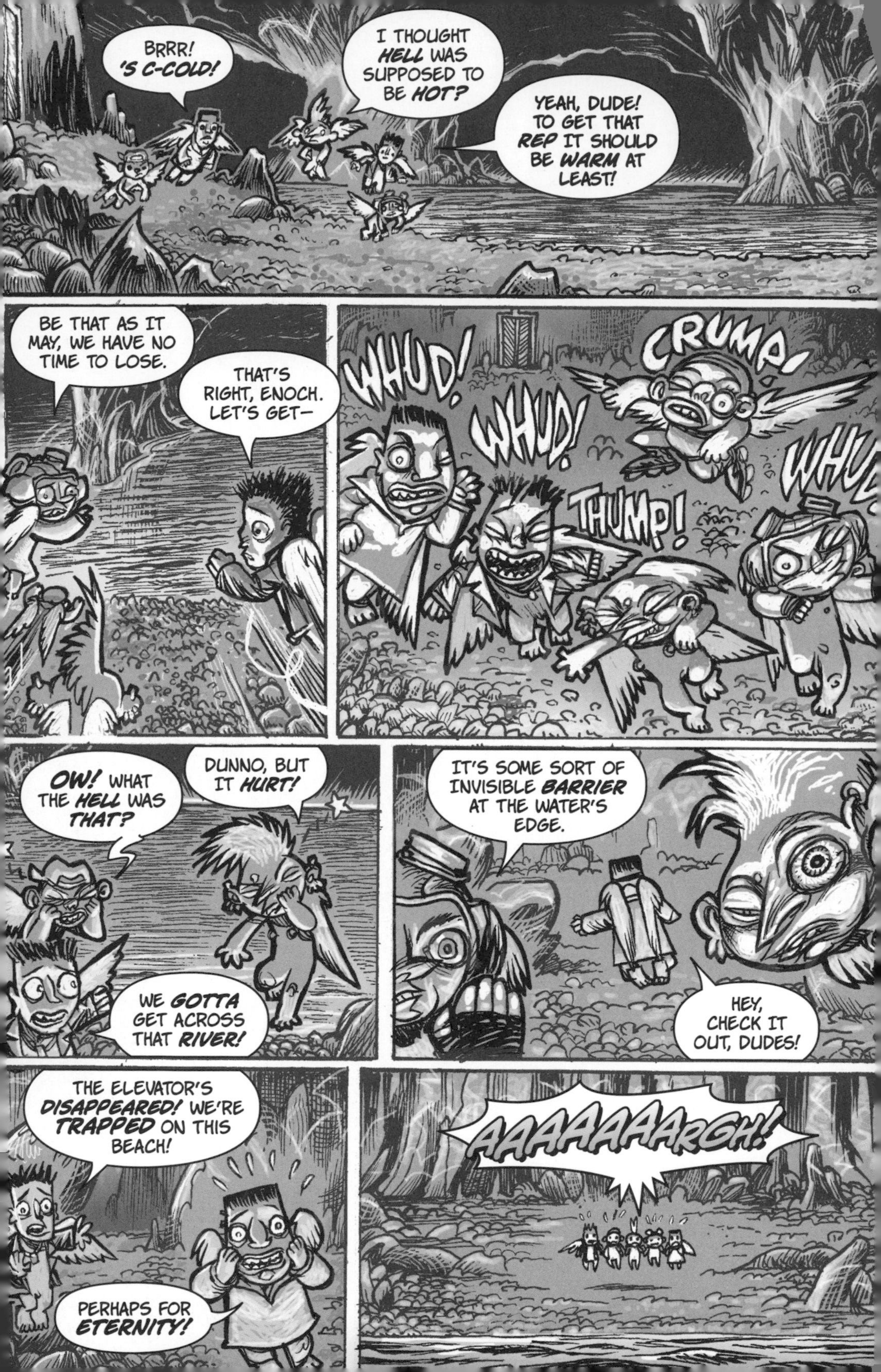
BRRR! 'S C-COLD!
I THOUGHT HELL WAS SUPPOSED TO BE HOT?
YEAH, DUDE! TO GET THAT REP IT SHOULD BE WARM AT LEAST!
BE THAT AS IT MAY, WE HAVE NO TIME TO LOSE.
THAT'S RIGHT, ENOCH. LET'S GET—
WHUD!
WHUD!
CRUMP!
THUMP!
OW! WHAT THE HELL WAS THAT?
DUNNO, BUT IT HURT!
WE GOTTA GET ACROSS THAT RIVER!
IT'S SOME SORT OF INVISIBLE BARRIER AT THE WATER'S EDGE.
HEY, CHECK IT OUT, DUDES!
THE ELEVATOR'S DISAPPEARED! WE'RE TRAPPED ON THIS BEACH!
PERHAPS FOR ETERNITY!
AAAAAAARGH!

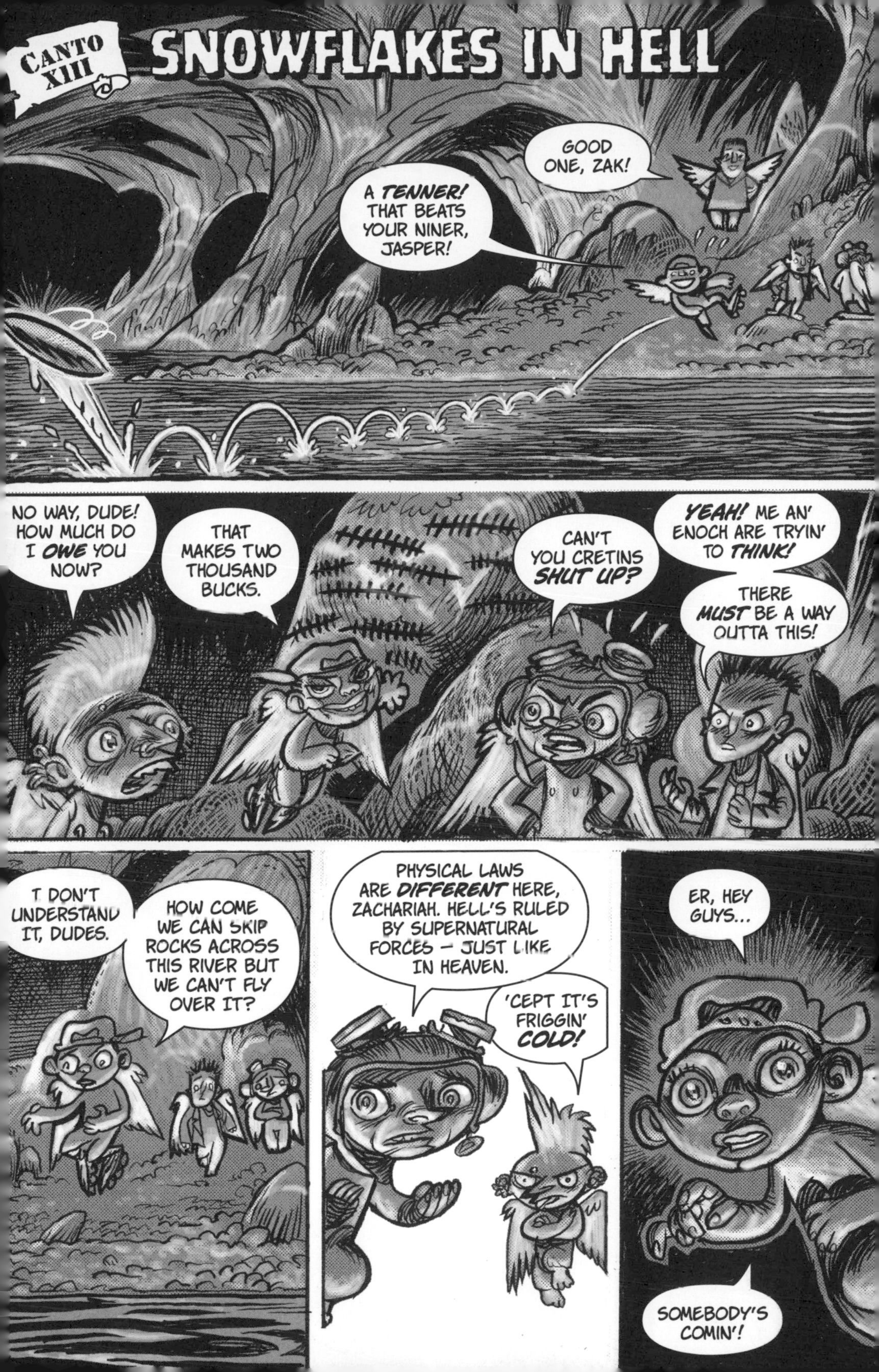
CANTO XIII
SNOWFLAKES IN HELL
GOOD ONE, ZAK!
A TENNER! THAT BEATS YOUR NINER, JASPER!
NO WAY, DUDE! HOW MUCH DO I OWE YOU NOW?
THAT MAKES TWO THOUSAND BUCKS.
CAN'T YOU CRETINS SHUT UP?
YEAH! ME AN' ENOCH ARE TRYIN' TO THINK!
THERE MUST BE A WAY OUTTA THIS!
I DON'T UNDERSTAND IT, DUDES.
HOW COME WE CAN SKIP ROCKS ACROSS THIS RIVER BUT WE CAN'T FLY OVER IT?
PHYSICAL LAWS ARE DIFFERENT HERE, ZACHARIAH. HELL'S RULED BY SUPERNATURAL FORCES — JUST LIKE IN HEAVEN.
'CEPT IT'S FRIGGIN' COLD!
ER, HEY GUYS...
SOMEBODY'S COMIN'!

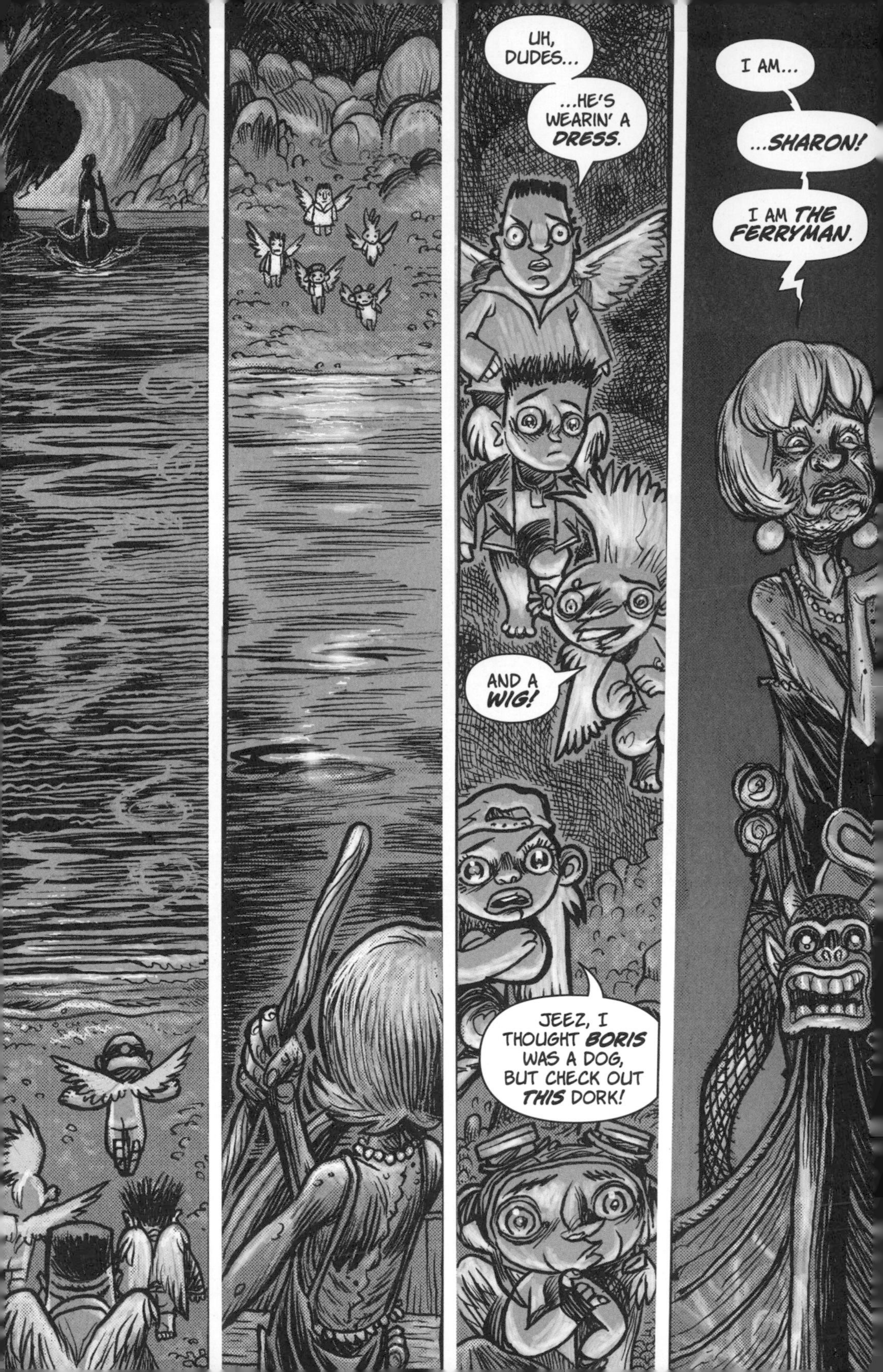
UH, DUDES...
...HE'S WEARIN' A DRESS.
AND A WIG!
JEEZ, I THOUGHT BORIS WAS A DOG, BUT CHECK OUT THIS DORK!
I AM...
...SHARON!
I AM THE FERRYMAN.

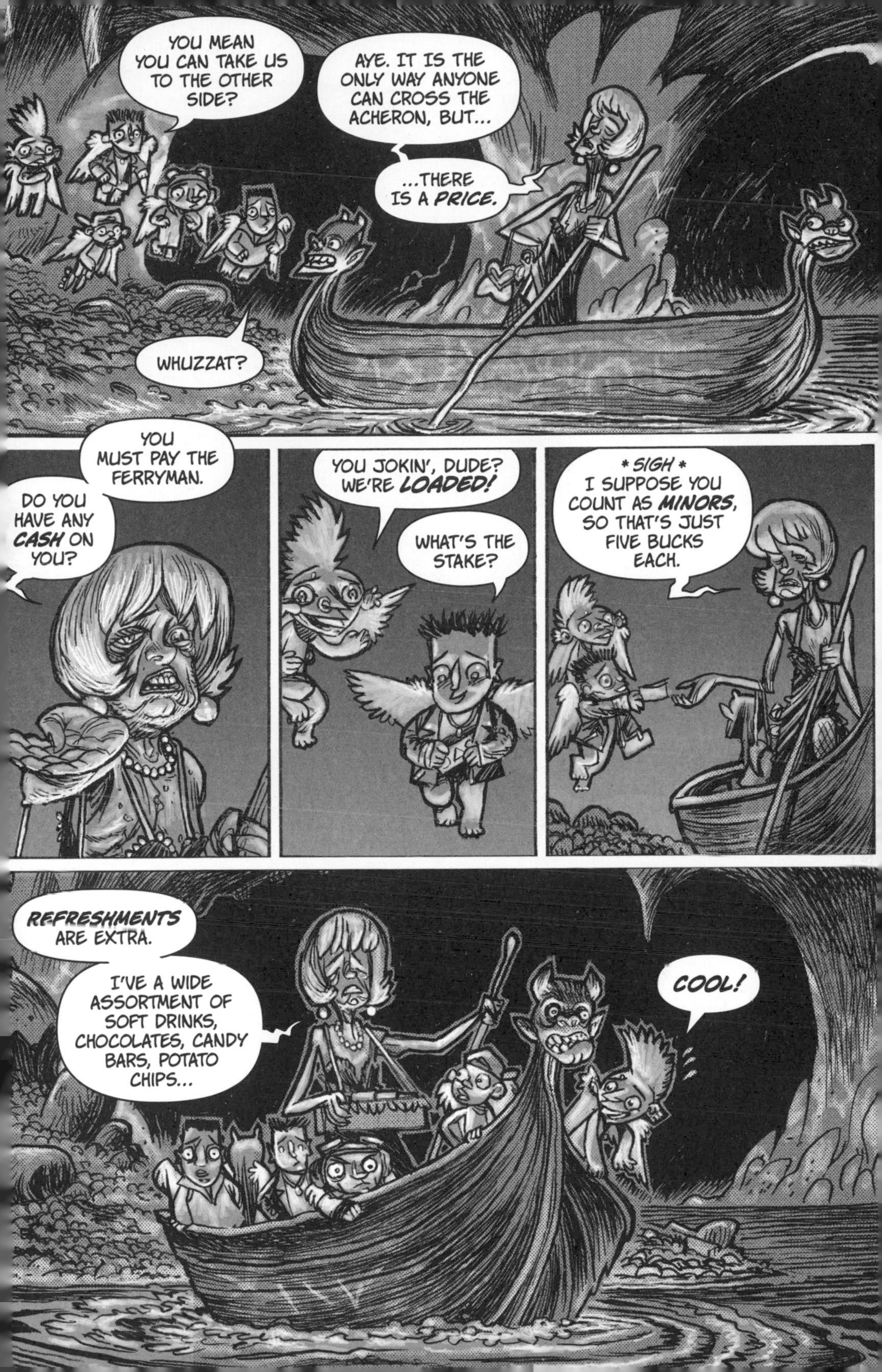
YOU MEAN YOU CAN TAKE US TO THE OTHER SIDE?
AYE. IT IS THE ONLY WAY ANYONE CAN CROSS THE ACHERON, BUT...
...THERE IS A PRICE.
WHUZZAT?
YOU MUST PAY THE FERRYMAN.
DO YOU HAVE ANY CASH ON YOU?
YOU JOKIN', DUDE? WE'RE LOADED!
WHAT'S THE STAKE?
* SIGH * I SUPPOSE YOU COUNT AS MINORS, SO THAT'S JUST FIVE BUCKS EACH.
REFRESHMENTS ARE EXTRA.
I'VE A WIDE ASSORTMENT OF SOFT DRINKS, CHOCOLATES, CANDY BARS, POTATO CHIPS...
COOL!

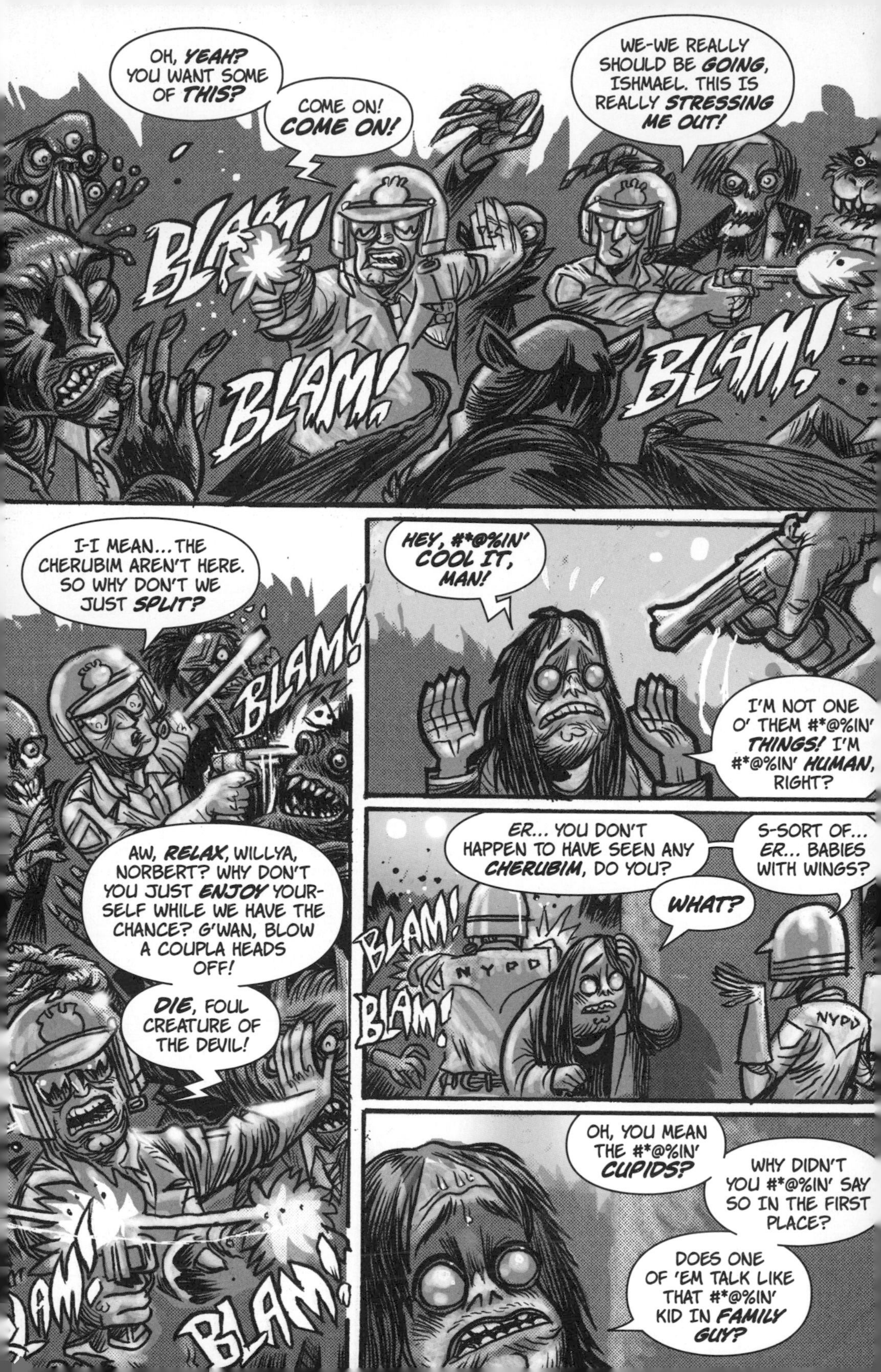
OH, YEAH? YOU WANT SOME OF THIS?
COME ON! COME ON!
WE-WE REALLY SHOULD BE GOING, ISHMAEL. THIS IS REALLY STRESSING ME OUT!
BLAM!
BLAM!
BLAM!
I-I MEAN... THE CHERUBIM AREN'T HERE. SO WHY DON'T WE JUST SPLIT?
BLAM!
AW, RELAX, WILLYA, NORBERT? WHY DON'T YOU JUST ENJOY YOURSELF WHILE WE HAVE THE CHANCE? G'WAN, BLOW A COUPLA HEADS OFF!
DIE, FOUL CREATURE OF THE DEVIL!
BLAM!
BLAM!
HEY, #*@%IN' COOL IT, MAN!
I'M NOT ONE O' THEM #*@%IN' THINGS! I'M #*@%IN' HUMAN, RIGHT?
ER... YOU DON'T HAPPEN TO HAVE SEEN ANY CHERUBIM, DO YOU?
S-SORT OF... ER... BABIES WITH WINGS?
WHAT?
BLAM!
BLAM!
NYPD
NYPD
OH, YOU MEAN THE #*@%IN' CUPIDS?
WHY DIDN'T YOU #*@%IN' SAY SO IN THE FIRST PLACE?
DOES ONE OF 'EM TALK LIKE THAT #*@%IN' KID IN FAMILY GUY?

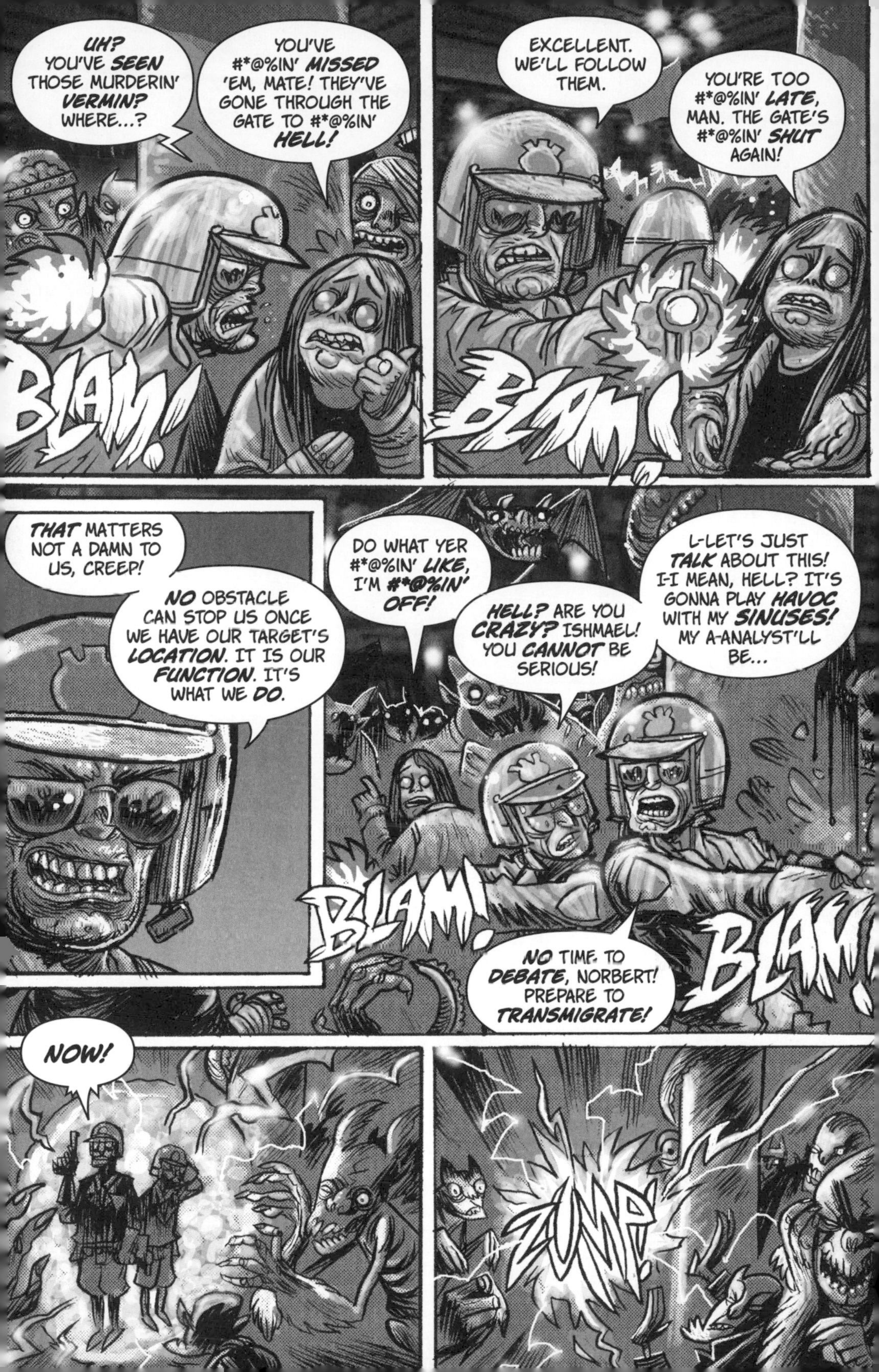
UH? YOU'VE SEEN THOSE MURDERIN' VERMIN? WHERE...?
YOU'VE #*@%IN' MISSED 'EM, MATE! THEY'VE GONE THROUGH THE GATE TO #*@%IN' HELL!
BLAM!
EXCELLENT. WE'LL FOLLOW THEM.
YOU'RE TOO #*@%IN' LATE, MAN. THE GATE'S #*@%IN' SHUT AGAIN!
BLAM!
THAT MATTERS NOT A DAMN TO US, CREEP!
NO OBSTACLE CAN STOP US ONCE WE HAVE OUR TARGET'S LOCATION. IT IS OUR FUNCTION. IT'S WHAT WE DO.
DO WHAT YER #*@%IN' LIKE, I'M #*@%IN' OFF!
HELL? ARE YOU CRAZY? ISHMAEL! YOU CANNOT BE SERIOUS!
L-LET'S JUST TALK ABOUT THIS! I-I MEAN, HELL? IT'S GONNA PLAY HAVOC WITH MY SINUSES! MY A-ANALYST'LL BE...
BLAM!
BLAM!
NO TIME TO DEBATE, NORBERT! PREPARE TO TRANSMIGRATE!
NOW!
ZUMP!

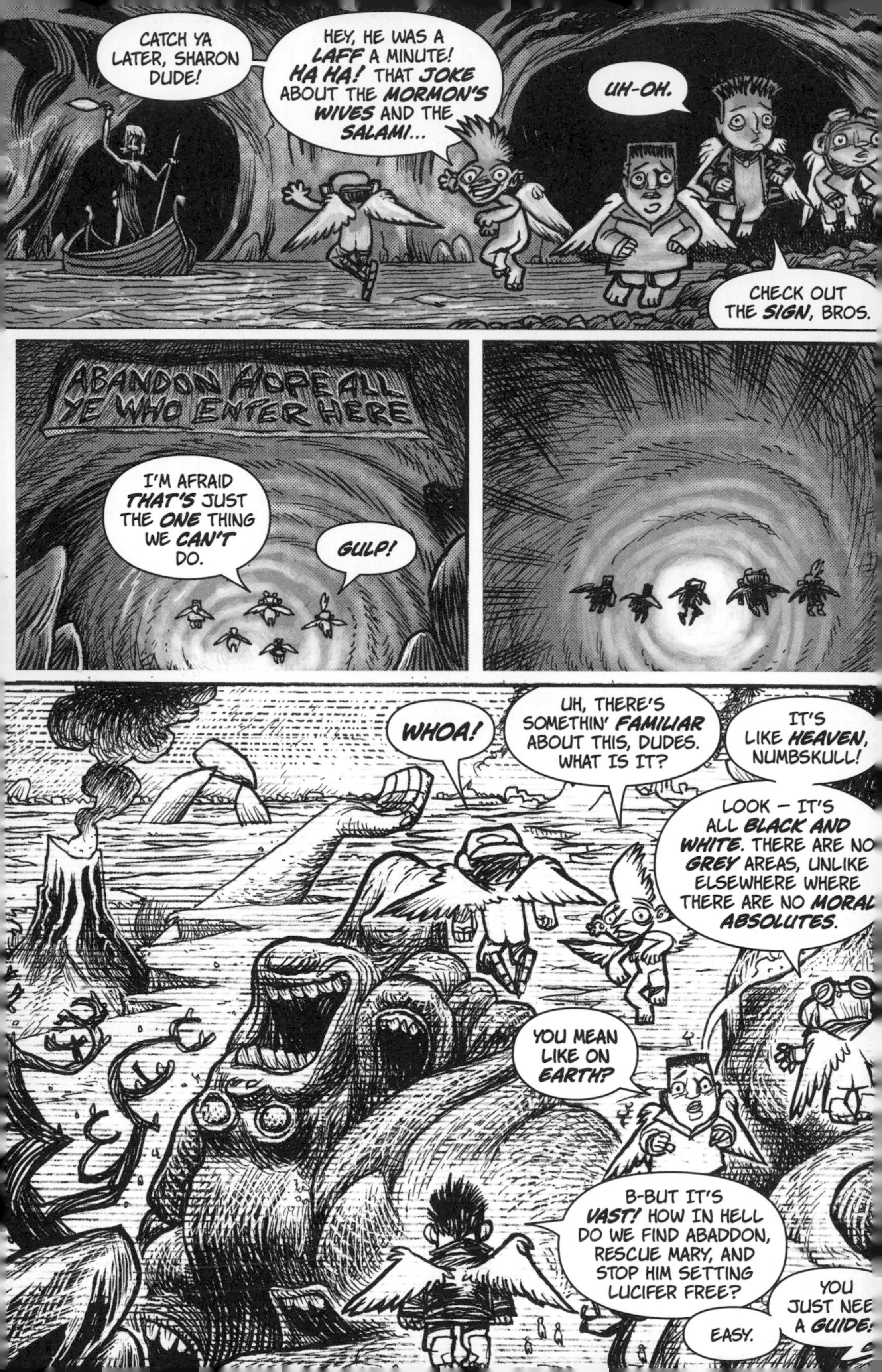
CATCH YA LATER, SHARON DUDE!
HEY, HE WAS A LAFF A MINUTE! HA HA! THAT JOKE ABOUT THE MORMON'S WIVES AND THE SALAMI...
UH-OH.
CHECK OUT THE SIGN, BROS.
ABANDON HOPE ALL YE WHO ENTER HERE
I'M AFRAID THAT'S JUST THE ONE THING WE CAN'T DO.
GULP!
WHOA!
UH, THERE'S SOMETHIN' FAMILIAR ABOUT THIS, DUDES. WHAT IS IT?
IT'S LIKE HEAVEN, NUMBSKULL!
LOOK — IT'S ALL BLACK AND WHITE. THERE ARE NO GREY AREAS, UNLIKE ELSEWHERE WHERE THERE ARE NO MORAL ABSOLUTES.
YOU MEAN LIKE ON EARTH?
B-BUT IT'S VAST! HOW IN HELL DO WE FIND ABADDON, RESCUE MARY, AND STOP HIM SETTING LUCIFER FREE?
EASY.
YOU JUST NEE A GUIDE!

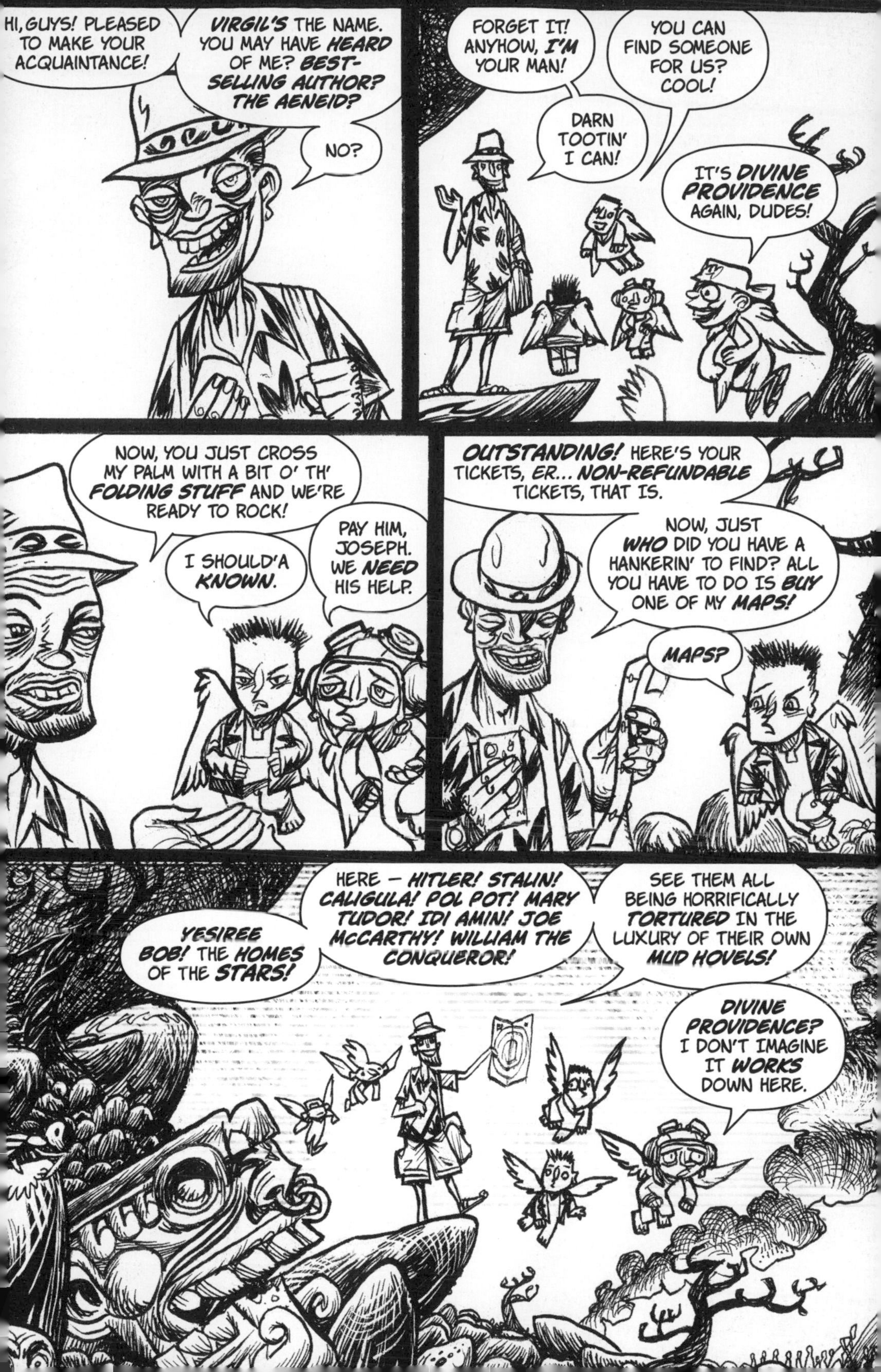
HI, GUYS! PLEASED TO MAKE YOUR ACQUAINTANCE!
VIRGIL'S THE NAME. YOU MAY HAVE HEARD OF ME? BEST-SELLING AUTHOR? THE AENEID?
NO?
FORGET IT! ANYHOW, I'M YOUR MAN!
DARN TOOTIN' I CAN!
YOU CAN FIND SOMEONE FOR US? COOL!
IT'S DIVINE PROVIDENCE AGAIN, DUDES!
NOW, YOU JUST CROSS MY PALM WITH A BIT O' TH' FOLDING STUFF AND WE'RE READY TO ROCK!
I SHOULD'A KNOWN.
PAY HIM, JOSEPH. WE NEED HIS HELP.
OUTSTANDING! HERE'S YOUR TICKETS, ER... NON-REFUNDABLE TICKETS, THAT IS.
NOW, JUST WHO DID YOU HAVE A HANKERIN' TO FIND? ALL YOU HAVE TO DO IS BUY ONE OF MY MAPS!
MAPS?
YESIREE BOB! THE HOMES OF THE STARS!
HERE – HITLER! STALIN! CALIGULA! POL POT! MARY TUDOR! IDI AMIN! JOE McCARTHY! WILLIAM THE CONQUEROR!
SEE THEM ALL BEING HORRIFICALLY TORTURED IN THE LUXURY OF THEIR OWN MUD HOVELS!
DIVINE PROVIDENCE? I DON'T IMAGINE IT WORKS DOWN HERE.

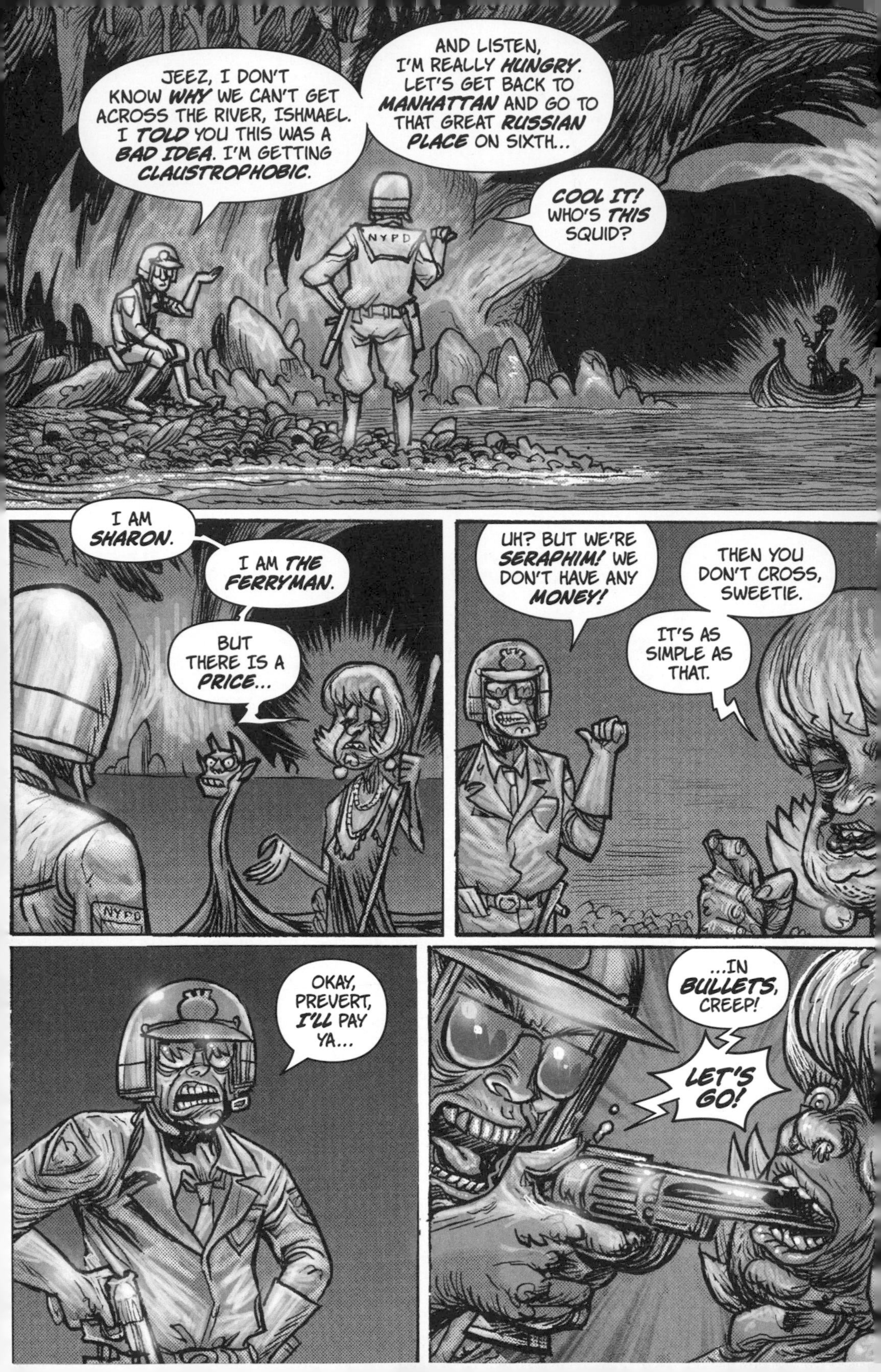
JEEZ, I DON'T KNOW WHY WE CAN'T GET ACROSS THE RIVER, ISHMAEL. I TOLD YOU THIS WAS A BAD IDEA. I'M GETTING CLAUSTROPHOBIC.
AND LISTEN, I'M REALLY HUNGRY. LET'S GET BACK TO MANHATTAN AND GO TO THAT GREAT RUSSIAN PLACE ON SIXTH...
NYPD
COOL IT! WHO'S THIS SQUID?
I AM SHARON.
I AM THE FERRYMAN.
BUT THERE IS A PRICE...
NYPD
UH? BUT WE'RE SERAPHIM! WE DON'T HAVE ANY MONEY!
THEN YOU DON'T CROSS, SWEETIE.
IT'S AS SIMPLE AS THAT.
OKAY, PREVERT, I'LL PAY YA...
...IN BULLETS, CREEP!
LET'S GO!

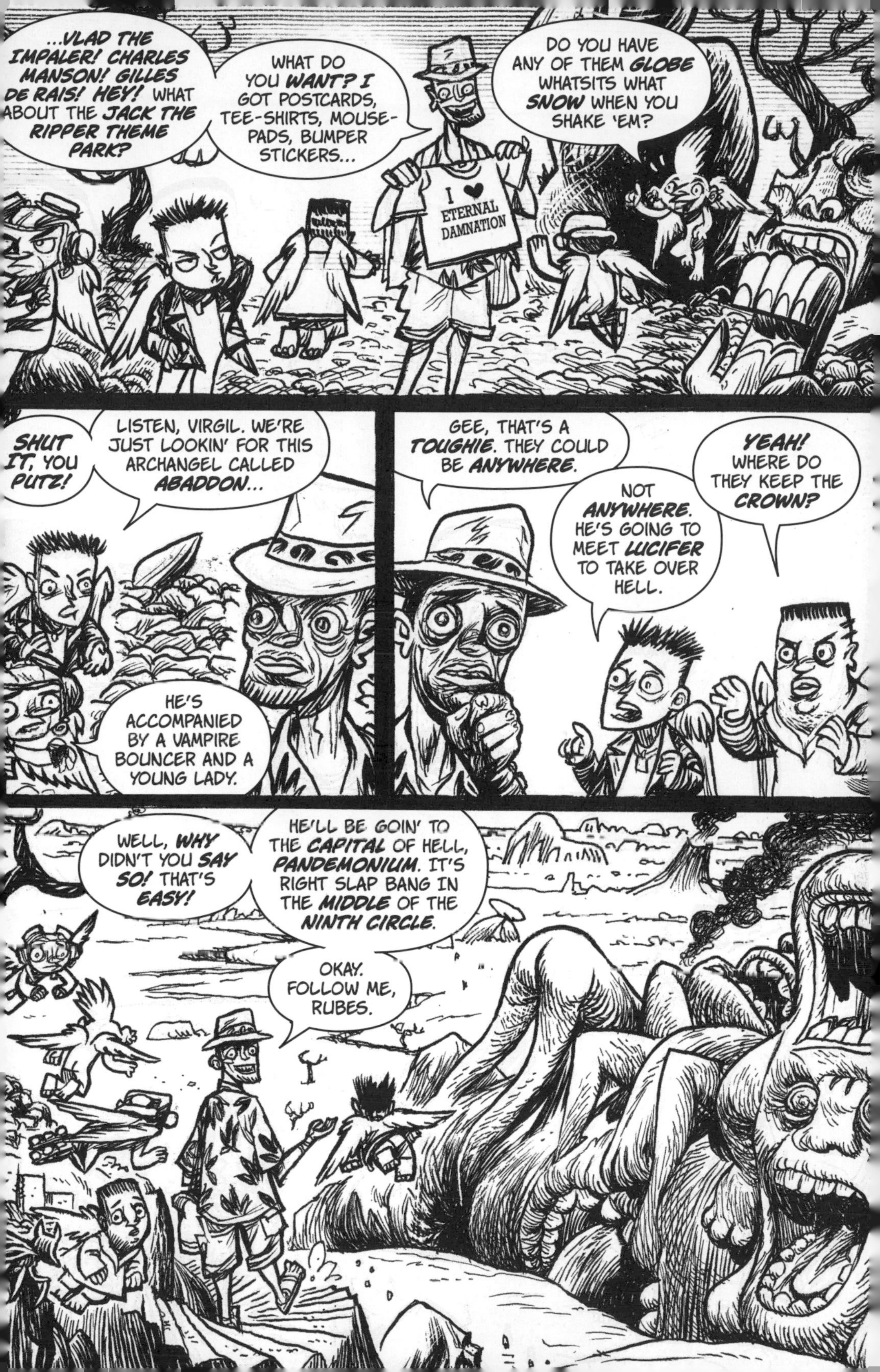
...VLAD THE IMPALER! CHARLES MANSON! GILLES DE RAIS! HEY! WHAT ABOUT THE JACK THE RIPPER THEME PARK?
WHAT DO YOU WANT? I GOT POSTCARDS, TEE-SHIRTS, MOUSE-PADS, BUMPER STICKERS...
DO YOU HAVE ANY OF THEM GLOBE WHATSITS WHAT SNOW WHEN YOU SHAKE 'EM?
I ♥ ETERNAL DAMNATION
SHUT IT, YOU PUTZ!
LISTEN, VIRGIL. WE'RE JUST LOOKIN' FOR THIS ARCHANGEL CALLED ABADDON...
HE'S ACCOMPANIED BY A VAMPIRE BOUNCER AND A YOUNG LADY.
GEE, THAT'S A TOUGHIE. THEY COULD BE ANYWHERE.
NOT ANYWHERE. HE'S GOING TO MEET LUCIFER TO TAKE OVER HELL.
YEAH! WHERE DO THEY KEEP THE CROWN?
WELL, WHY DIDN'T YOU SAY SO! THAT'S EASY!
HE'LL BE GOIN' TO THE CAPITAL OF HELL, PANDEMONIUM. IT'S RIGHT SLAP BANG IN THE MIDDLE OF THE NINTH CIRCLE.
OKAY. FOLLOW ME, RUBES.

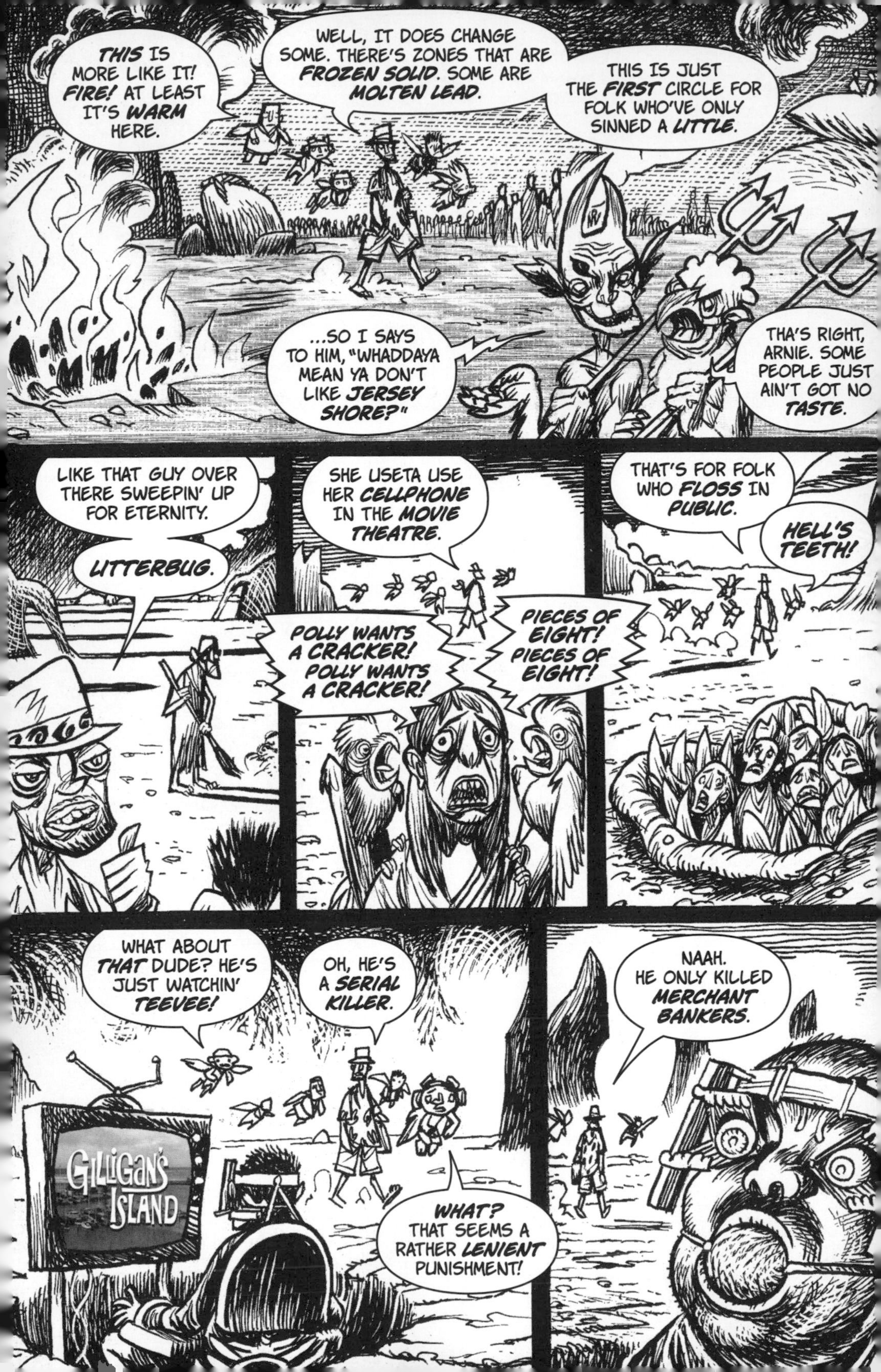
THIS IS MORE LIKE IT! FIRE! AT LEAST IT'S WARM HERE.
WELL, IT DOES CHANGE SOME. THERE'S ZONES THAT ARE FROZEN SOLID. SOME ARE MOLTEN LEAD.
THIS IS JUST THE FIRST CIRCLE FOR FOLK WHO'VE ONLY SINNED A LITTLE.
...SO I SAYS TO HIM, "WHADDAYA MEAN YA DON'T LIKE JERSEY SHORE?"
THA'S RIGHT, ARNIE. SOME PEOPLE JUST AIN'T GOT NO TASTE.
LIKE THAT GUY OVER THERE SWEEPIN' UP FOR ETERNITY.
LITTERBUG.
SHE USETA USE HER CELLPHONE IN THE MOVIE THEATRE.
POLLY WANTS A CRACKER! POLLY WANTS A CRACKER!
PIECES OF EIGHT! PIECES OF EIGHT!
THAT'S FOR FOLK WHO FLOSS IN PUBLIC.
HELL'S TEETH!
WHAT ABOUT THAT DUDE? HE'S JUST WATCHIN' TEEVEE!
OH, HE'S A SERIAL KILLER.
GILLIGAN'S ISLAND
WHAT? THAT SEEMS A RATHER LENIENT PUNISHMENT!
NAAH. HE ONLY KILLED MERCHANT BANKERS.

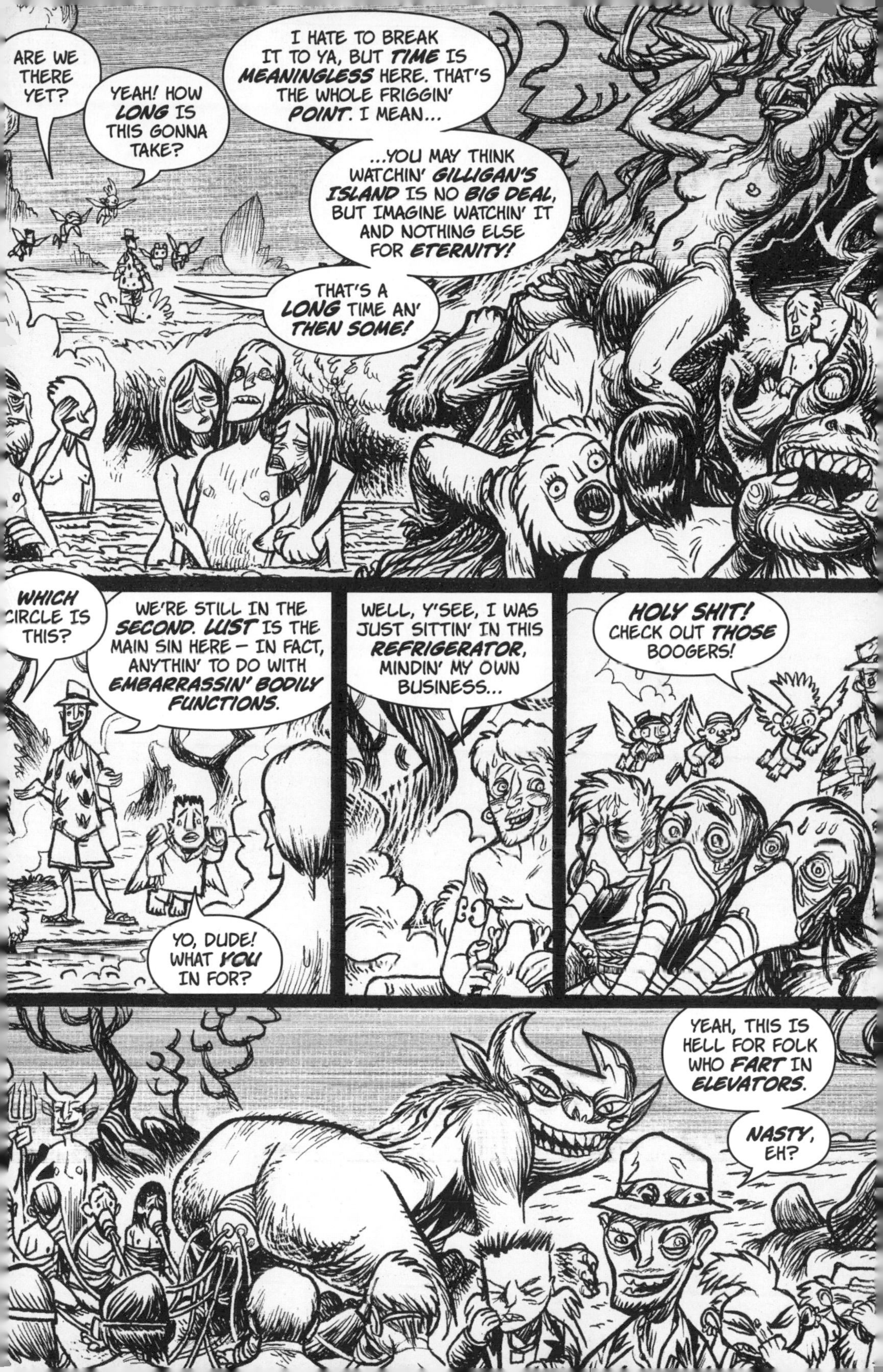
ARE WE THERE YET?
YEAH! HOW LONG IS THIS GONNA TAKE?
I HATE TO BREAK IT TO YA, BUT TIME IS MEANINGLESS HERE. THAT'S THE WHOLE FRIGGIN' POINT. I MEAN...
...YOU MAY THINK WATCHIN' GILLIGAN'S ISLAND IS NO BIG DEAL, BUT IMAGINE WATCHIN' IT AND NOTHING ELSE FOR ETERNITY!
THAT'S A LONG TIME AN' THEN SOME!
WHICH CIRCLE IS THIS?
WE'RE STILL IN THE SECOND. LUST IS THE MAIN SIN HERE — IN FACT, ANYTHIN' TO DO WITH EMBARRASSIN' BODILY FUNCTIONS.
YO, DUDE! WHAT YOU IN FOR?
WELL, Y'SEE, I WAS JUST SITTIN' IN THIS REFRIGERATOR, MINDIN' MY OWN BUSINESS...
HOLY SHIT! CHECK OUT THOSE BOOGERS!
YEAH, THIS IS HELL FOR FOLK WHO FART IN ELEVATORS.
NASTY, EH?

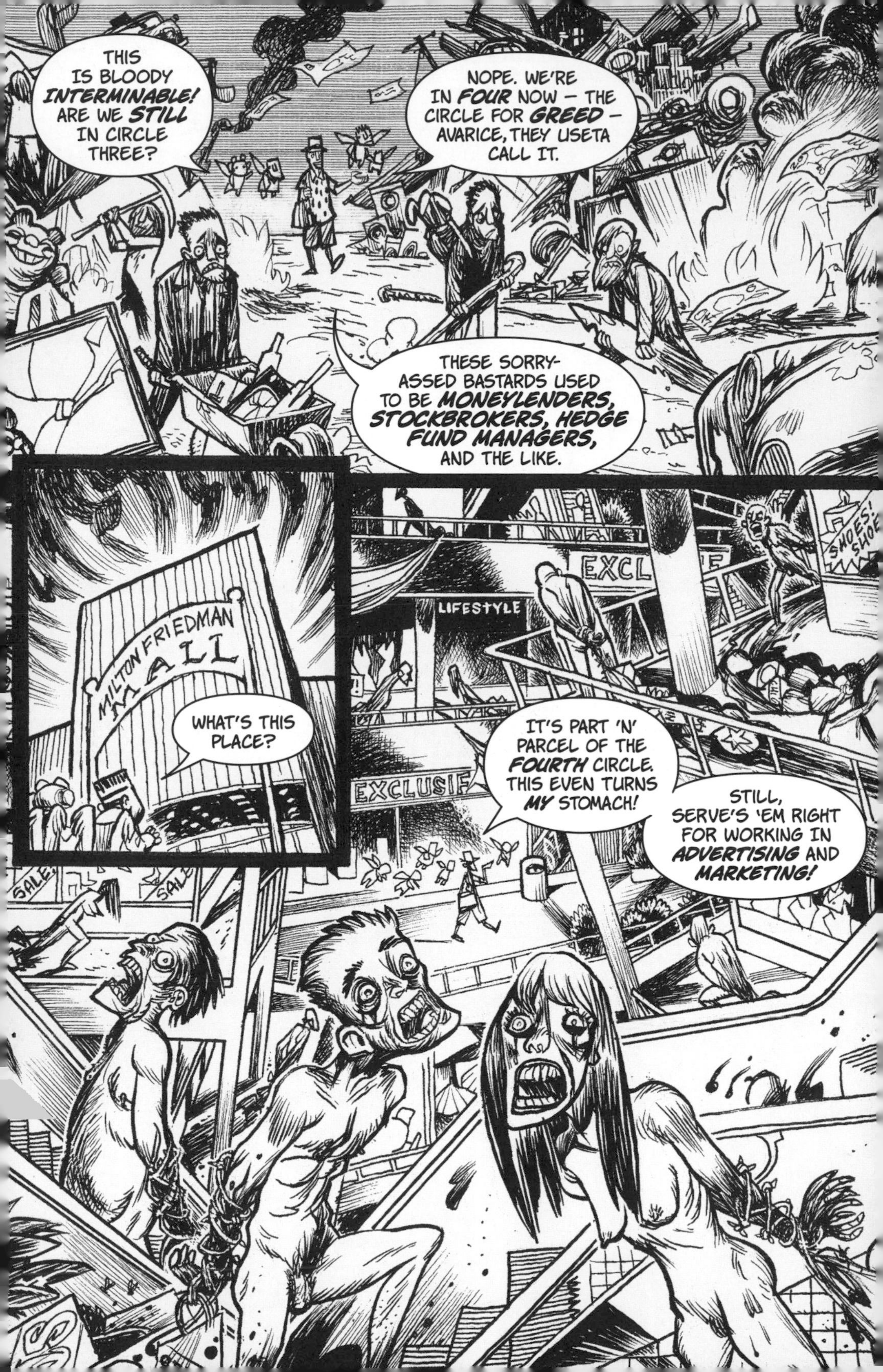
THIS IS BLOODY INTERMINABLE! ARE WE STILL IN CIRCLE THREE?
NOPE. WE'RE IN FOUR NOW — THE CIRCLE FOR GREED — AVARICE, THEY USETA CALL IT.
THESE SORRY-ASSED BASTARDS USED TO BE MONEYLENDERS, STOCKBROKERS, HEDGE FUND MANAGERS, AND THE LIKE.
MILTON FRIEDMAN MALL
WHAT'S THIS PLACE?
LIFESTYLE
EXCLUSIF
IT'S PART 'N' PARCEL OF THE FOURTH CIRCLE. THIS EVEN TURNS MY STOMACH!
STILL, SERVE'S 'EM RIGHT FOR WORKING IN ADVERTISING AND MARKETING!

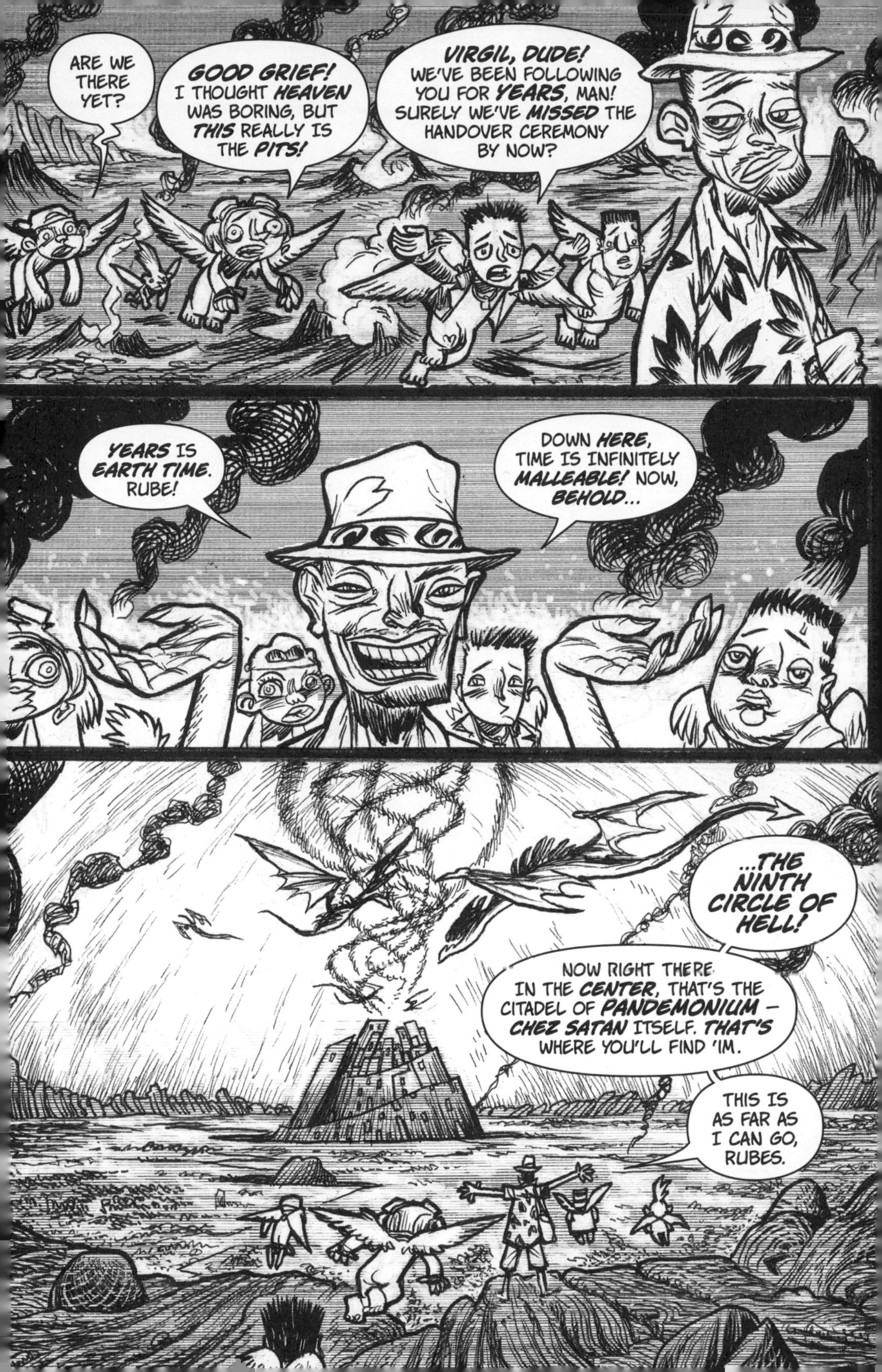
ARE WE THERE YET?
GOOD GRIEF! I THOUGHT HEAVEN WAS BORING, BUT THIS REALLY IS THE PITS!
VIRGIL, DUDE! WE'VE BEEN FOLLOWING YOU FOR YEARS, MAN! SURELY WE'VE MISSED THE HANDOVER CEREMONY BY NOW?
YEARS IS EARTH TIME. RUBE!
DOWN HERE, TIME IS INFINITELY MALLEABLE! NOW, BEHOLD...
...THE NINTH CIRCLE OF HELL!
NOW RIGHT THERE IN THE CENTER, THAT'S THE CITADEL OF PANDEMONIUM – CHEZ SATAN ITSELF. THAT'S WHERE YOU'LL FIND 'IM.
THIS IS AS FAR AS I CAN GO, RUBES.

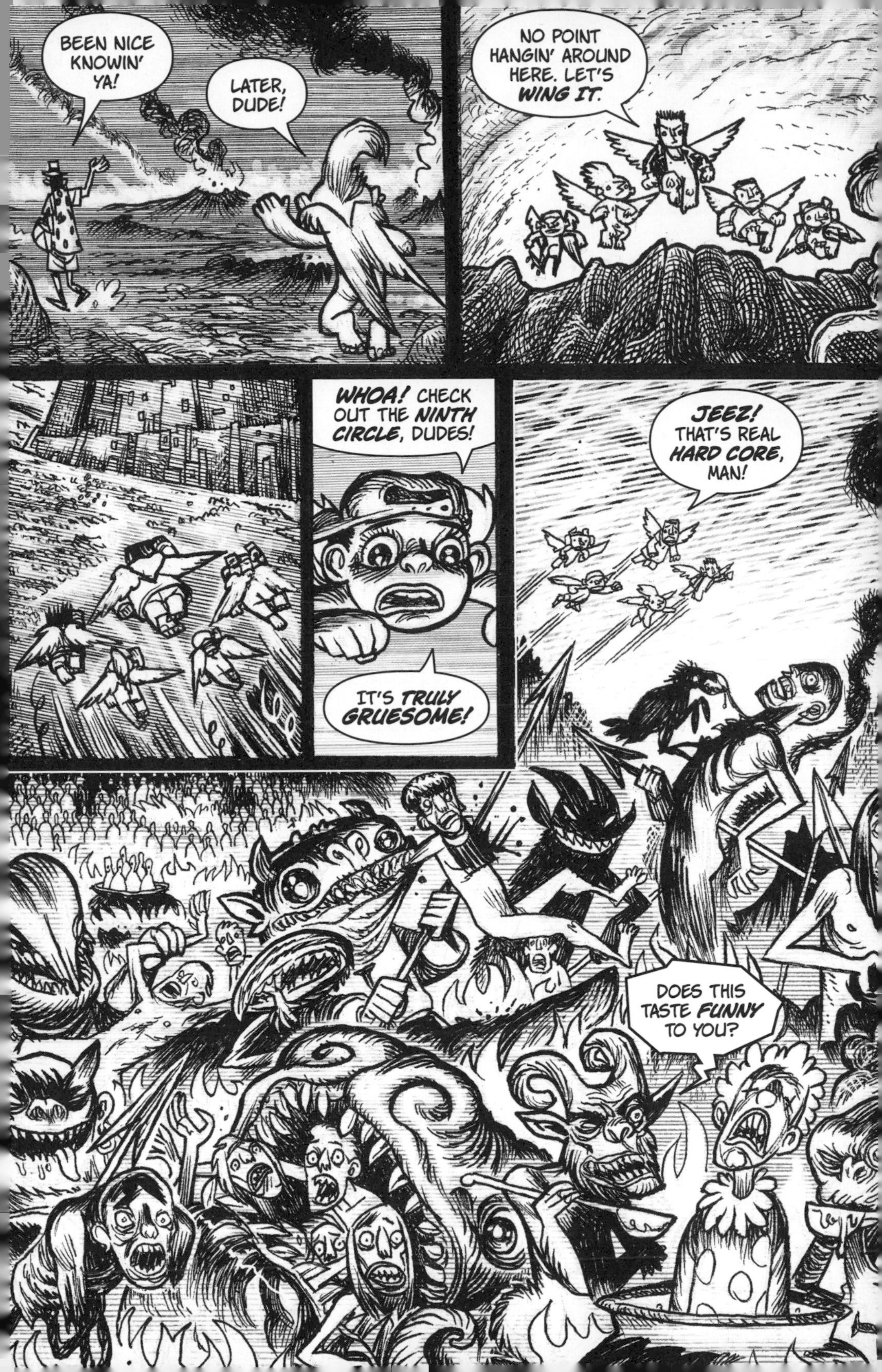
BEEN NICE KNOWIN' YA!
LATER, DUDE!
NO POINT HANGIN' AROUND HERE. LET'S WING IT.
WHOA! CHECK OUT THE NINTH CIRCLE, DUDES!
IT'S TRULY GRUESOME!
JEEZ! THAT'S REAL HARD CORE, MAN!
DOES THIS TASTE FUNNY TO YOU?

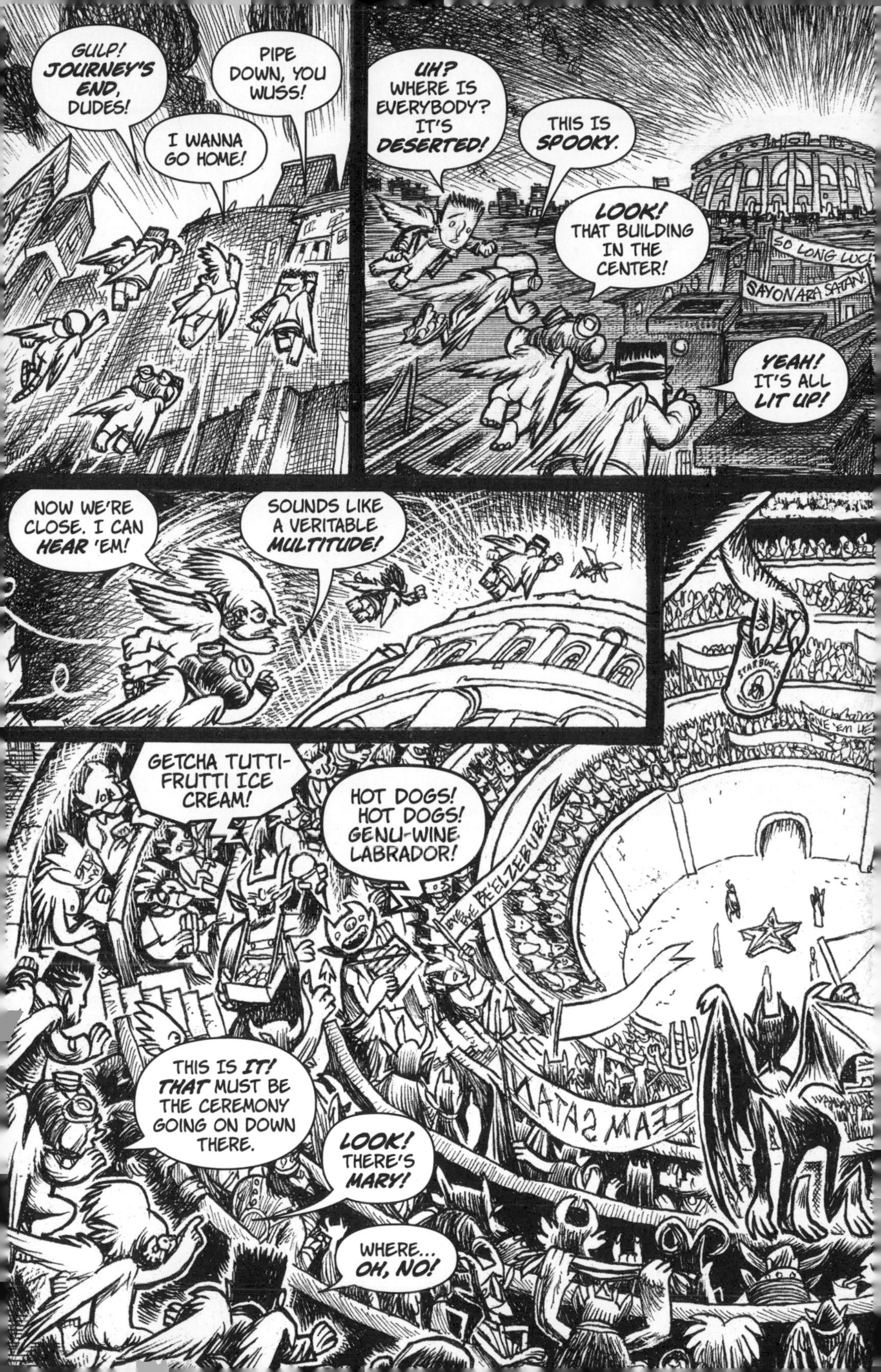
GULP! JOURNEY'S END, DUDES!
PIPE DOWN, YOU WUSS!
I WANNA GO HOME!
UH? WHERE IS EVERYBODY? IT'S DESERTED!
THIS IS SPOOKY.
LOOK! THAT BUILDING IN THE CENTER!
SO LONG LUC
SAYONARA SATAN
YEAH! IT'S ALL LIT UP!
NOW WE'RE CLOSE. I CAN HEAR 'EM!
SOUNDS LIKE A VERITABLE MULTITUDE!
STARBUCKS
GETCHA TUTTI-FRUTTI ICE CREAM!
HOT DOGS! HOT DOGS! GENU-WINE LABRADOR!
BYE BYE BEELZEBUB!!
THIS IS IT! THAT MUST BE THE CEREMONY GOING ON DOWN THERE.
TEAM SATAN
LOOK! THERE'S MARY!
WHERE... OH, NO!

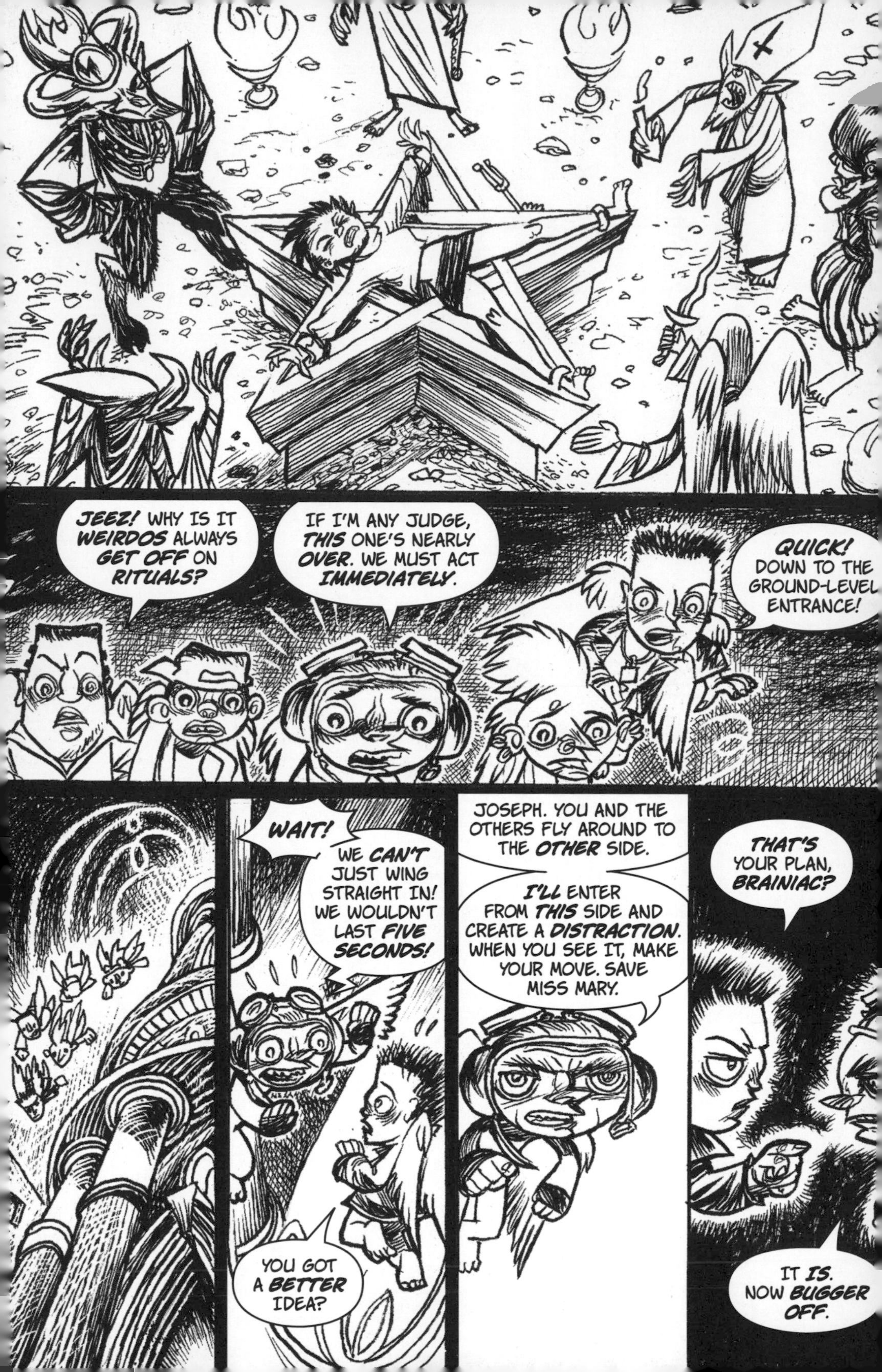
JEEZ! WHY IS IT WEIRDOS ALWAYS GET OFF ON RITUALS?
IF I'M ANY JUDGE, THIS ONE'S NEARLY OVER. WE MUST ACT IMMEDIATELY.
QUICK! DOWN TO THE GROUND-LEVEL ENTRANCE!
WAIT!
WE CAN'T JUST WING STRAIGHT IN! WE WOULDN'T LAST FIVE SECONDS!
YOU GOT A BETTER IDEA?
JOSEPH. YOU AND THE OTHERS FLY AROUND TO THE OTHER SIDE.
I'LL ENTER FROM THIS SIDE AND CREATE A DISTRACTION. WHEN YOU SEE IT, MAKE YOUR MOVE. SAVE MISS MARY.
THAT'S YOUR PLAN, BRAINIAC?
IT IS. NOW BUGGER OFF.

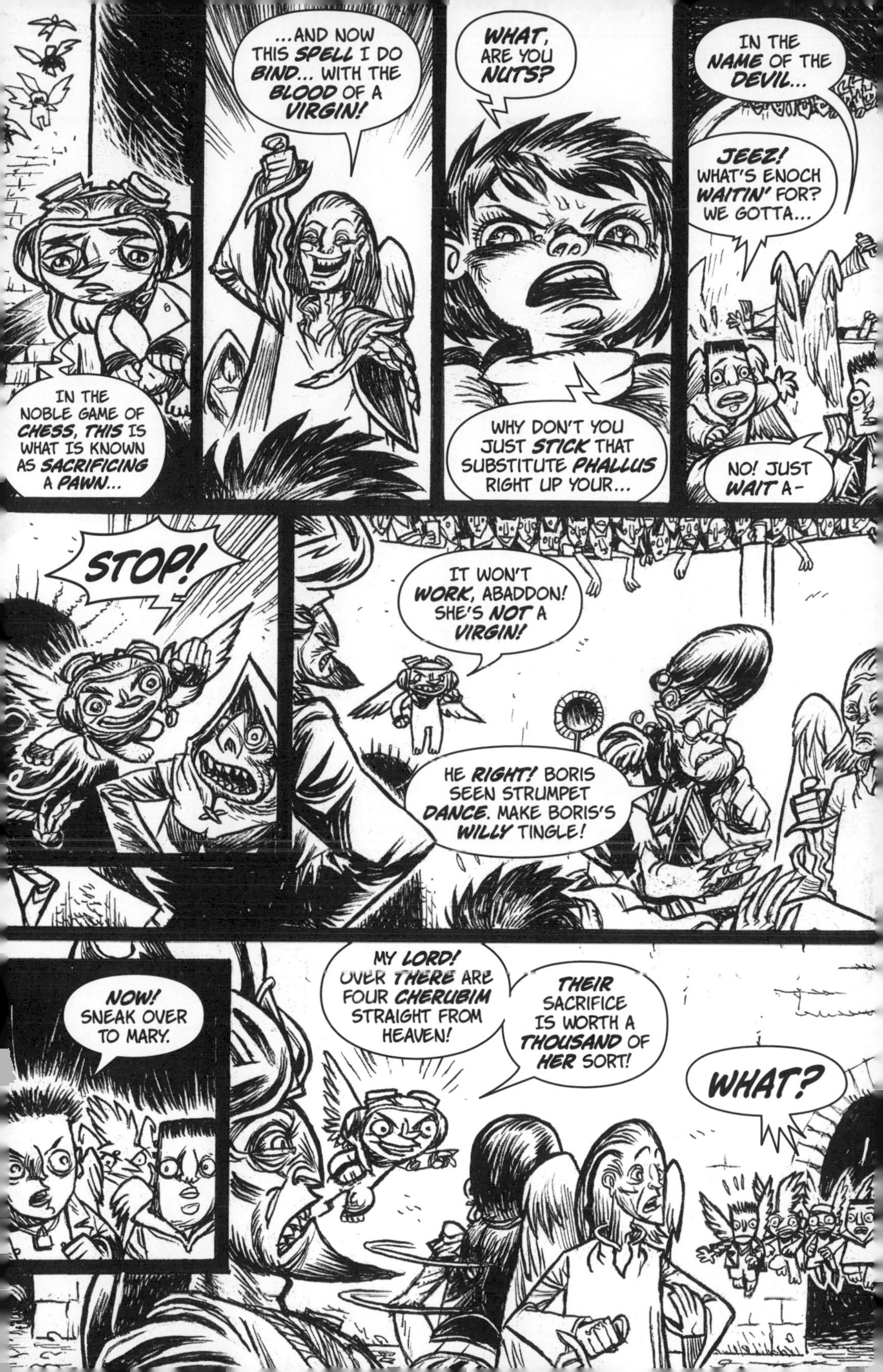

IN THE NOBLE GAME OF CHESS, THIS IS WHAT IS KNOWN AS SACRIFICING A PAWN...
...AND NOW THIS SPELL I DO BIND... WITH THE BLOOD OF A VIRGIN!
WHAT, ARE YOU NUTS?
WHY DON'T YOU JUST STICK THAT SUBSTITUTE PHALLUS RIGHT UP YOUR...
IN THE NAME OF THE DEVIL...
JEEZ! WHAT'S ENOCH WAITIN' FOR? WE GOTTA...
NO! JUST WAIT A-
STOP!
IT WON'T WORK, ABADDON! SHE'S NOT A VIRGIN!
HE RIGHT! BORIS SEEN STRUMPET DANCE. MAKE BORIS'S WILLY TINGLE!
NOW! SNEAK OVER TO MARY.
MY LORD! OVER THERE ARE FOUR CHERUBIM STRAIGHT FROM HEAVEN!
THEIR SACRIFICE IS WORTH A THOUSAND OF HER SORT!
WHAT?

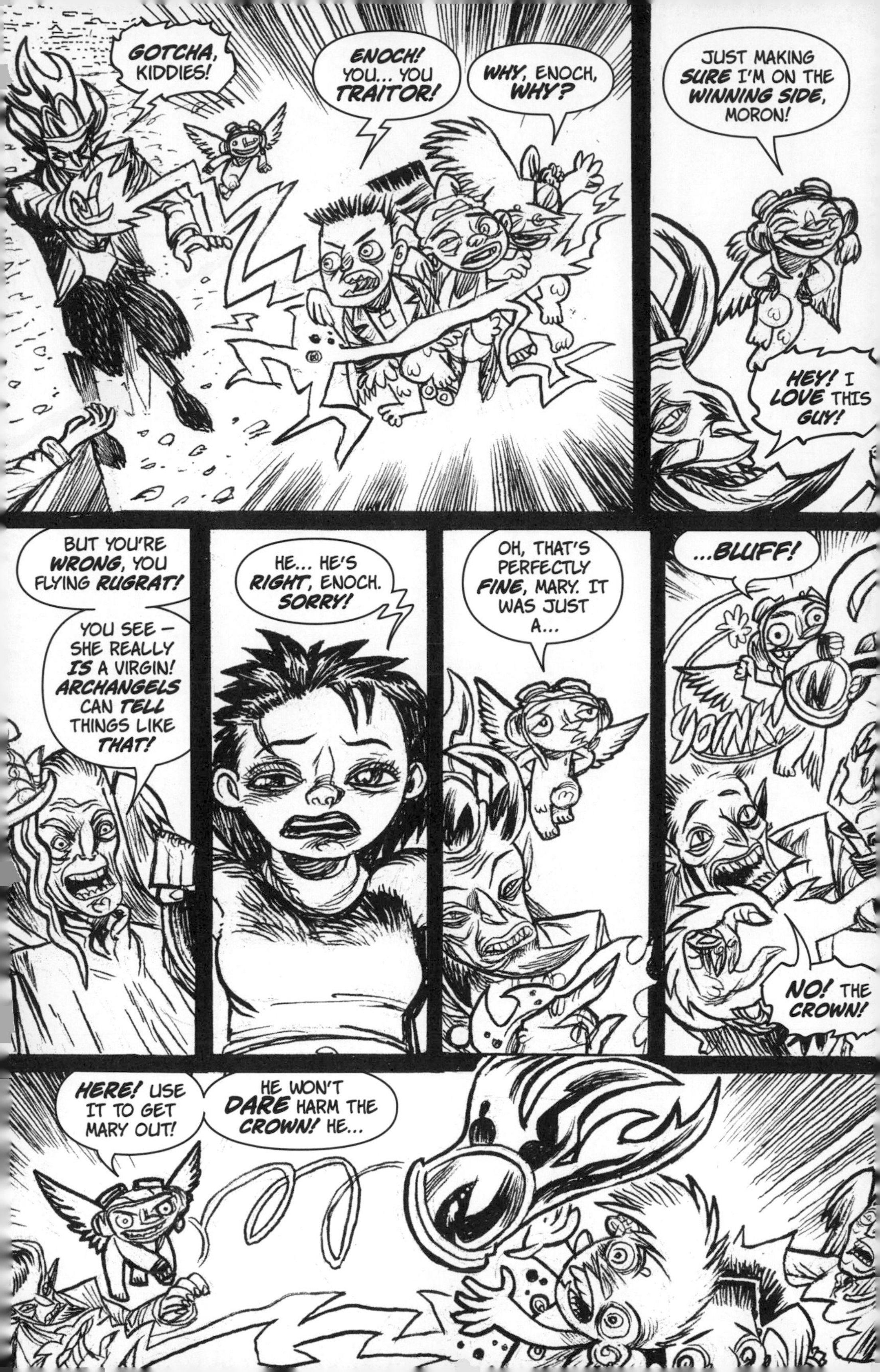
GOTCHA, KIDDIES!
ENOCH! YOU... YOU TRAITOR!
WHY, ENOCH, WHY?
JUST MAKING SURE I'M ON THE WINNING SIDE, MORON!
HEY! I LOVE THIS GUY!
BUT YOU'RE WRONG, YOU FLYING RUGRAT!
YOU SEE — SHE REALLY IS A VIRGIN! ARCHANGELS CAN TELL THINGS LIKE THAT!
HE... HE'S RIGHT, ENOCH. SORRY!
OH, THAT'S PERFECTLY FINE, MARY. IT WAS JUST A...
...BLUFF!
YOINK
NO! THE CROWN!
HERE! USE IT TO GET MARY OUT!
HE WON'T DARE HARM THE CROWN! HE...

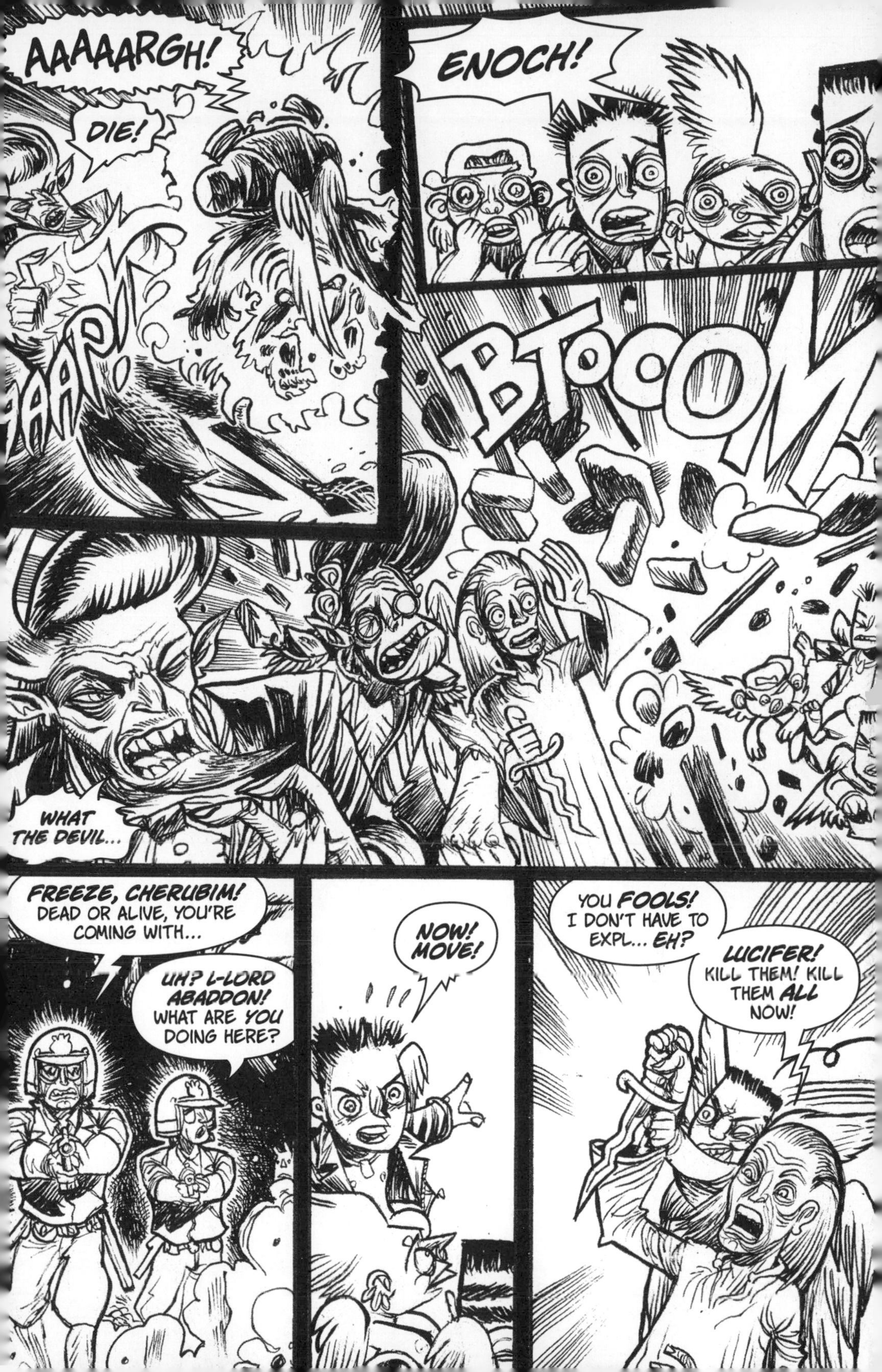
AAAAARGH!
DIE!
AAAP!
ENOCH!
BTOOOM
WHAT THE DEVIL...
FREEZE, CHERUBIM! DEAD OR ALIVE, YOU'RE COMING WITH...
UH? L-LORD ABADDON! WHAT ARE YOU DOING HERE?
NOW! MOVE!
YOU FOOLS! I DON'T HAVE TO EXPL... EH?
LUCIFER! KILL THEM! KILL THEM ALL NOW!

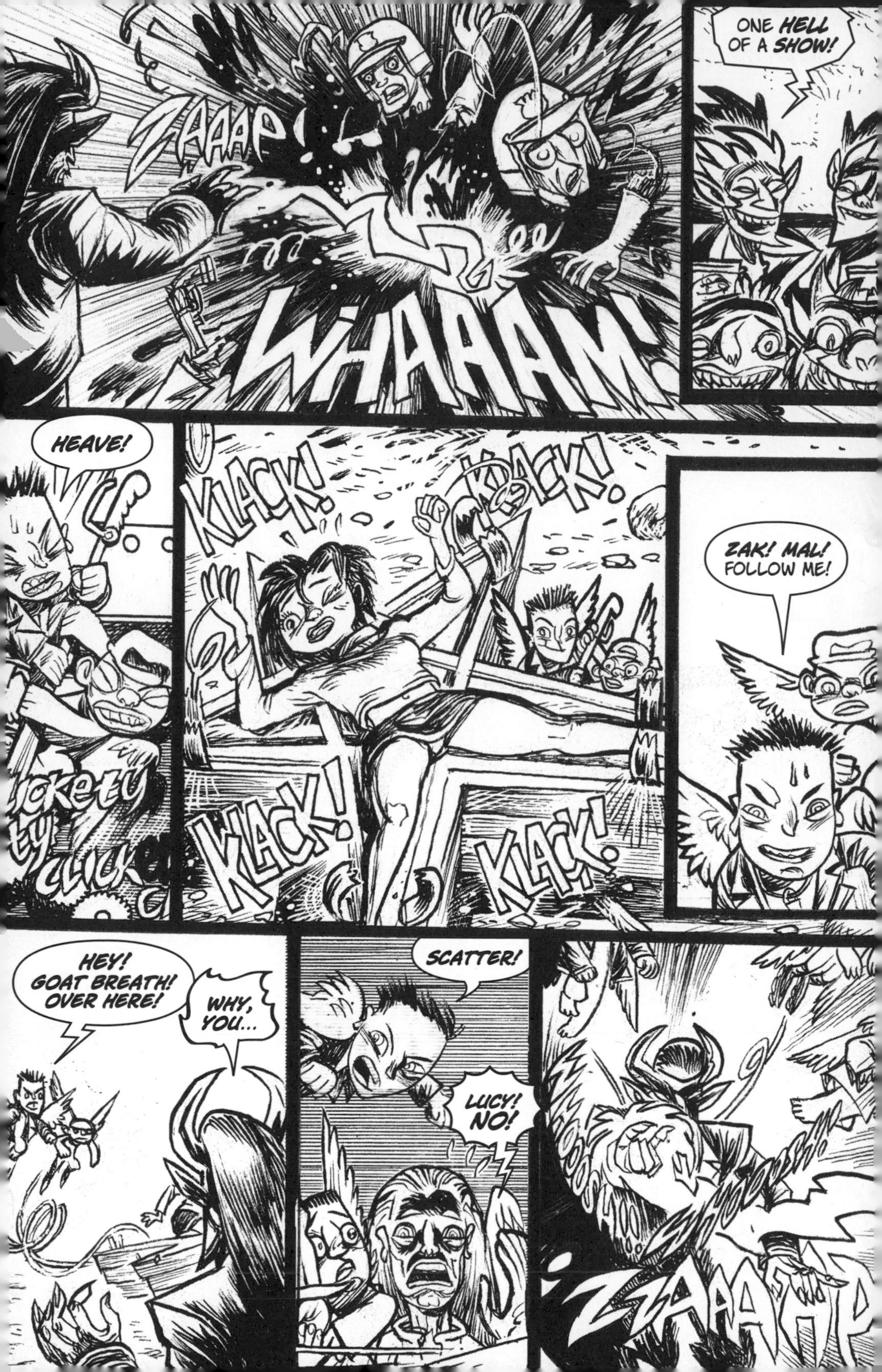
ZAAAP
WHAAAM!
ONE HELL OF A SHOW!
HEAVE!
KLACK!
KLACK!
ZAK! MAL! FOLLOW ME!
KLACK!
KLACK!
HEY! GOAT BREATH! OVER HERE!
WHY, YOU...
SCATTER!
LUCY! NO!

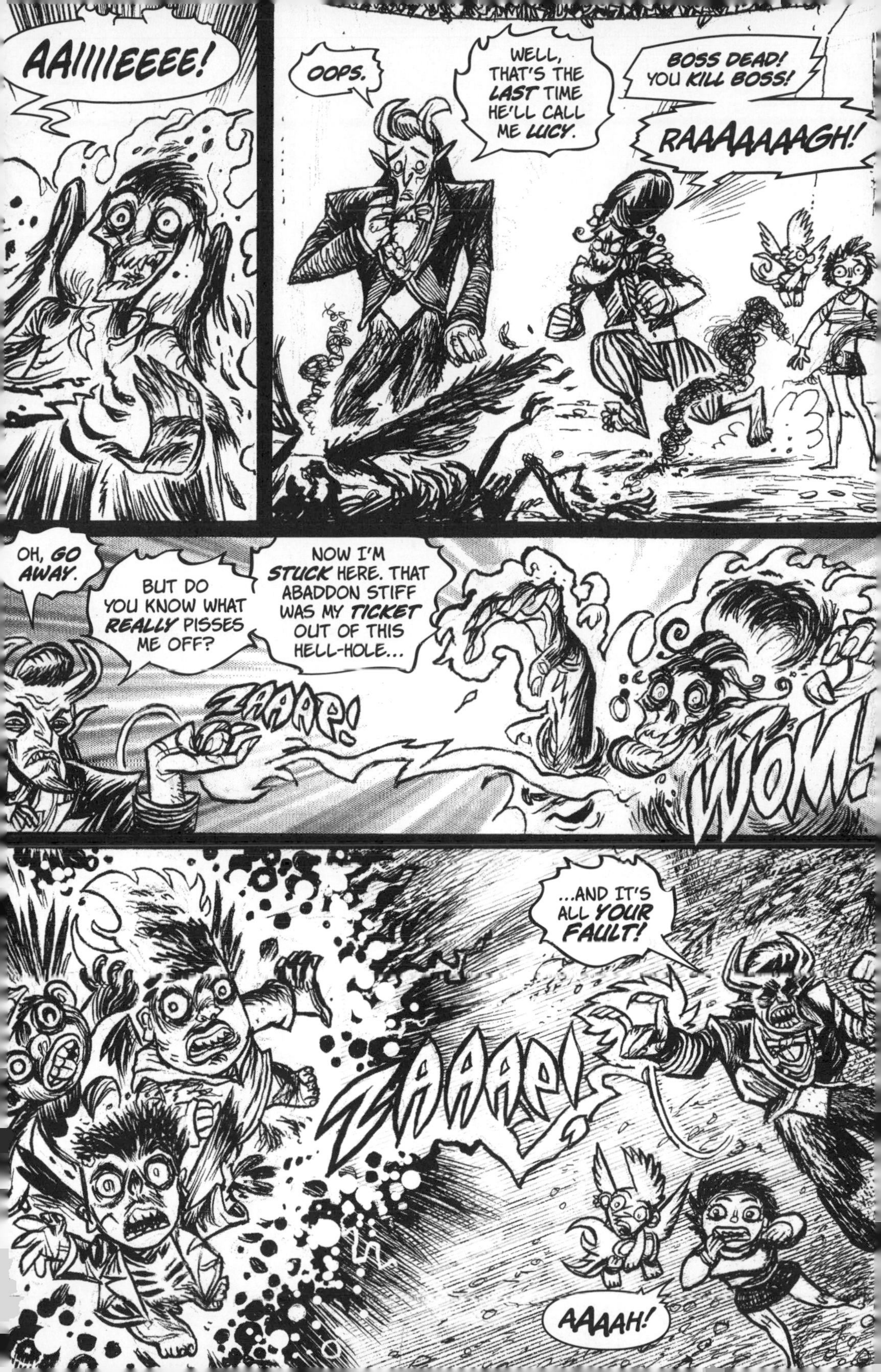
AAIIIIEEEE!
OOPS.
WELL, THAT'S THE LAST TIME HE'LL CALL ME LUCY.
BOSS DEAD! YOU KILL BOSS!
RAAAAAAAGH!
OH, GO AWAY.
BUT DO YOU KNOW WHAT REALLY PISSES ME OFF?
NOW I'M STUCK HERE. THAT ABADDON STIFF WAS MY TICKET OUT OF THIS HELL-HOLE...
ZAAAP!
WOM!
...AND IT'S ALL YOUR FAULT!
ZAAAP!
AAAAH!

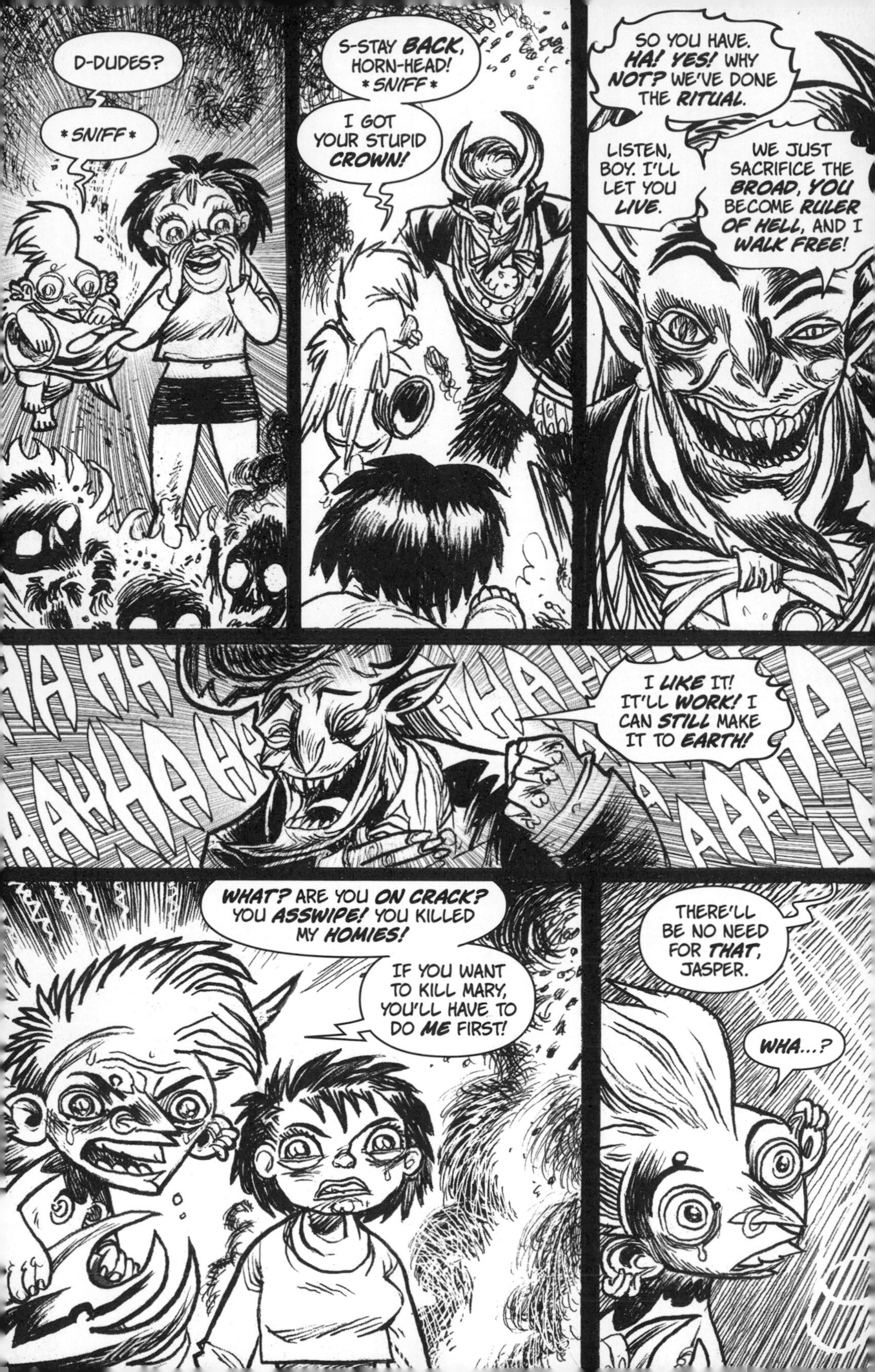
D-DUDES?
SNIFF
S-STAY BACK, HORN-HEAD! *SNIFF*
I GOT YOUR STUPID CROWN!
SO YOU HAVE. HA! YES! WHY NOT? WE'VE DONE THE RITUAL.
LISTEN, BOY. I'LL LET YOU LIVE.
WE JUST SACRIFICE THE BROAD, YOU BECOME RULER OF HELL, AND I WALK FREE!
I LIKE IT! IT'LL WORK! I CAN STILL MAKE IT TO EARTH!
WHAT? ARE YOU ON CRACK? YOU ASSWIPE! YOU KILLED MY HOMIES!
IF YOU WANT TO KILL MARY, YOU'LL HAVE TO DO ME FIRST!
THERE'LL BE NO NEED FOR THAT, JASPER.
WHA...?

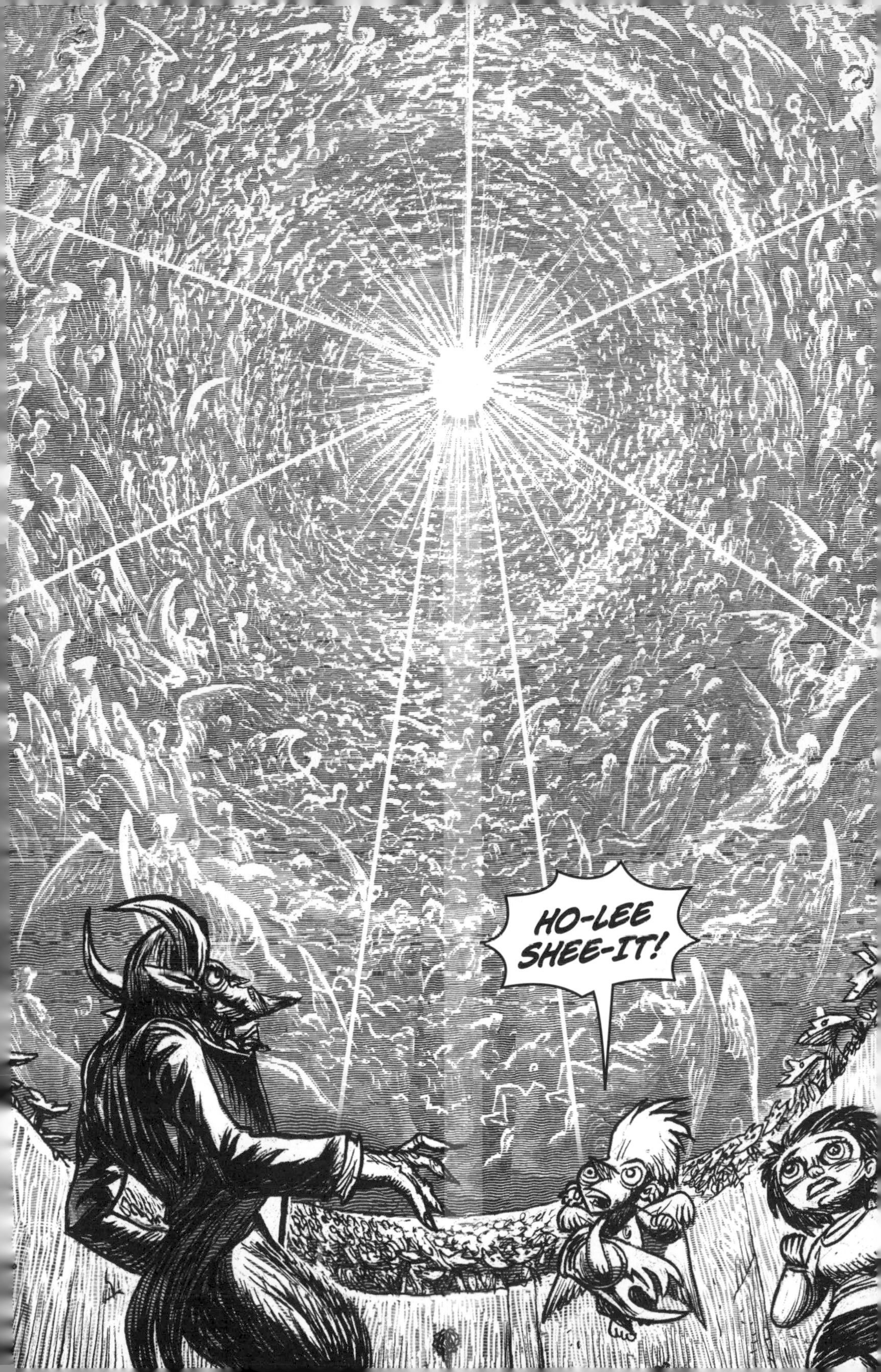
HO-LEE SHEE-IT!

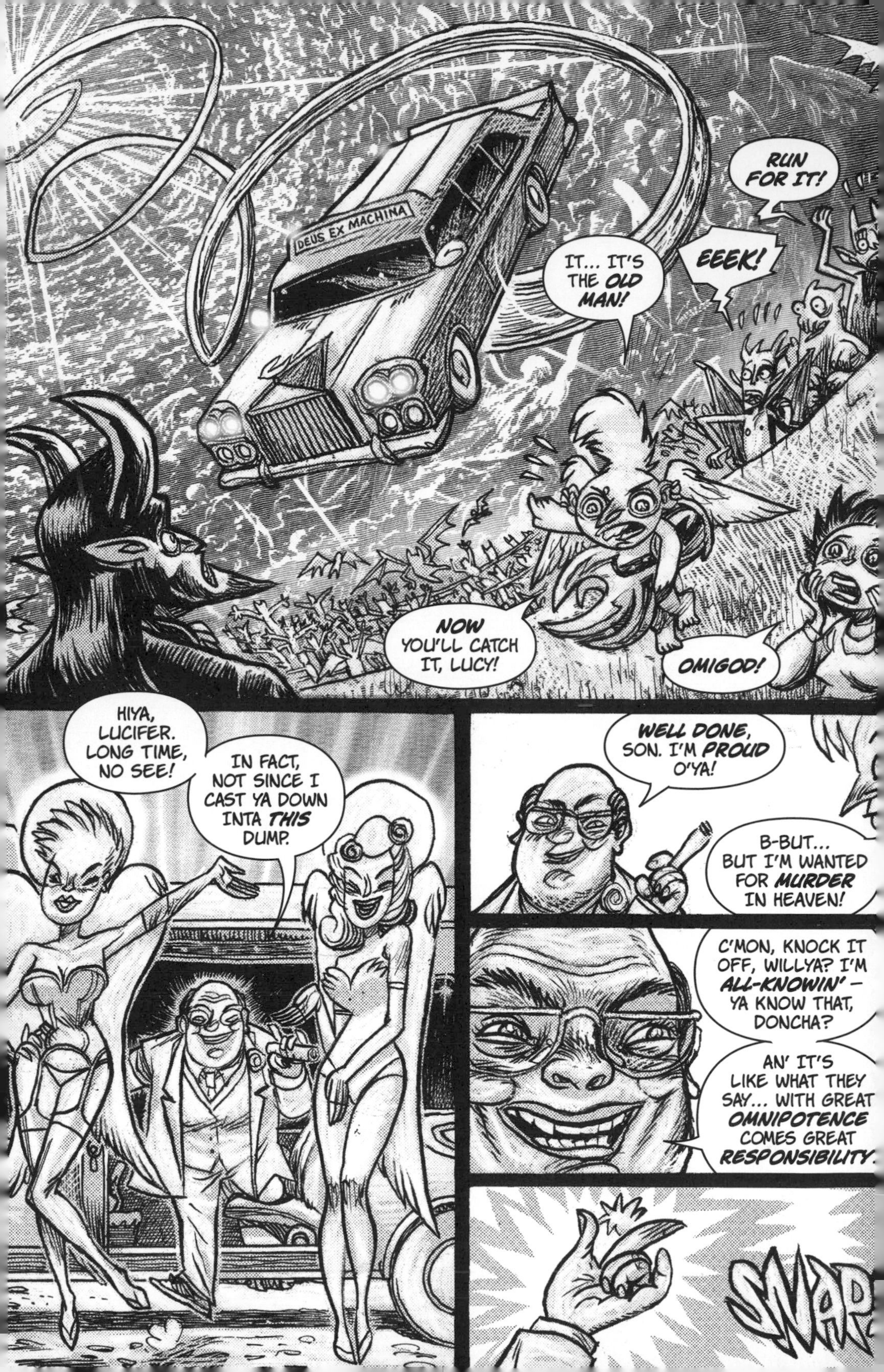
DEUS EX MACHINA
RUN FOR IT!
EEEK!
IT... IT'S THE OLD MAN!
NOW YOU'LL CATCH IT, LUCY!
OMIGOD!
HIYA, LUCIFER. LONG TIME, NO SEE!
IN FACT, NOT SINCE I CAST YA DOWN INTA THIS DUMP.
WELL DONE, SON. I'M PROUD O'YA!
B-BUT... BUT I'M WANTED FOR MURDER IN HEAVEN!
C'MON, KNOCK IT OFF, WILLYA? I'M ALL-KNOWIN' – YA KNOW THAT, DONCHA?
AN' IT'S LIKE WHAT THEY SAY... WITH GREAT OMNIPOTENCE COMES GREAT RESPONSIBILITY.
SNAP

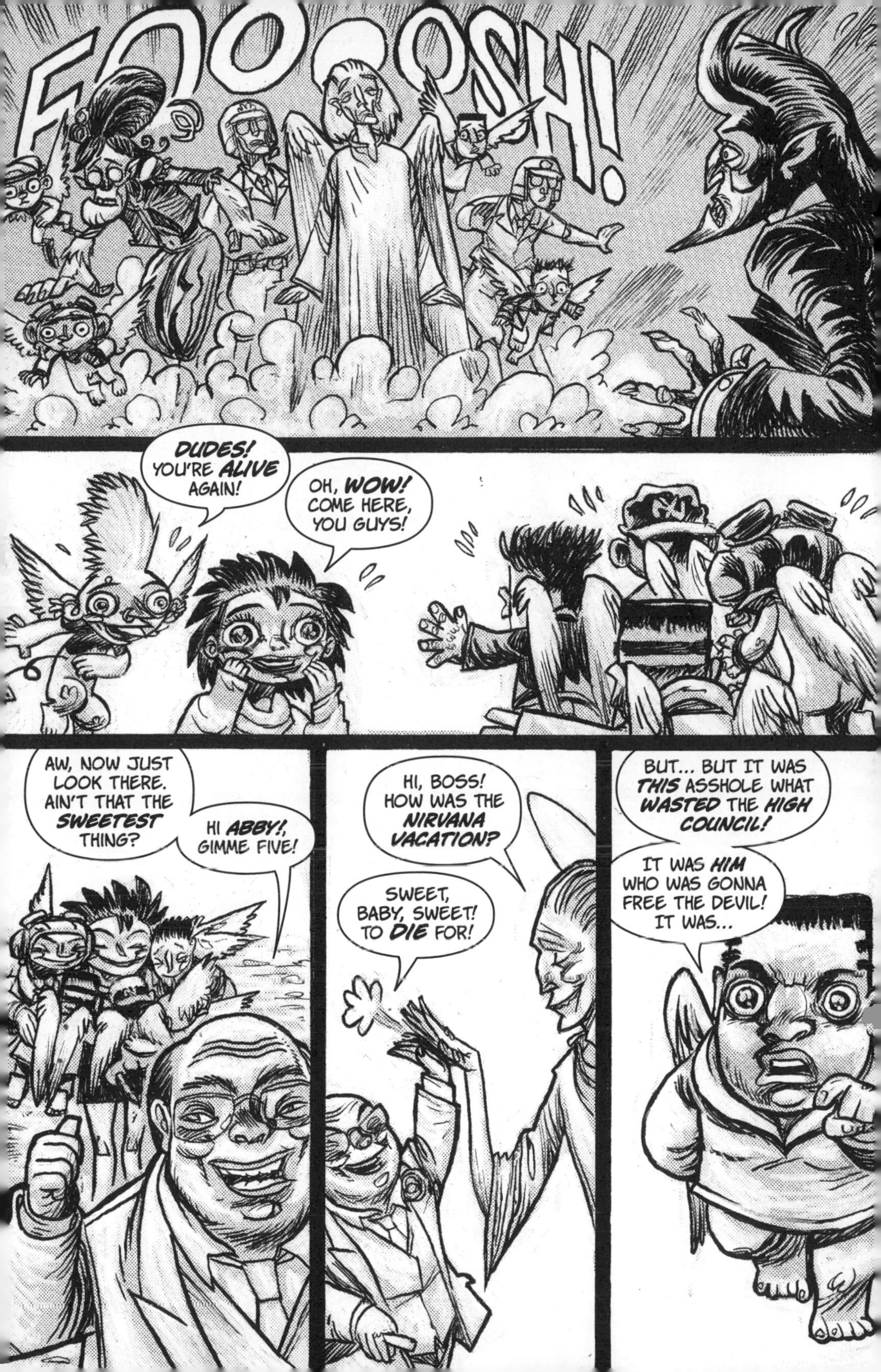
FOOOOOSH!
DUDES! YOU'RE ALIVE AGAIN!
OH, WOW! COME HERE, YOU GUYS!
AW, NOW JUST LOOK THERE. AIN'T THAT THE SWEETEST THING?
HI ABBY!, GIMME FIVE!
HI, BOSS! HOW WAS THE NIRVANA VACATION?
SWEET, BABY, SWEET! TO DIE FOR!
BUT... BUT IT WAS THIS ASSHOLE WHAT WASTED THE HIGH COUNCIL!
IT WAS HIM WHO WAS GONNA FREE THE DEVIL! IT WAS...

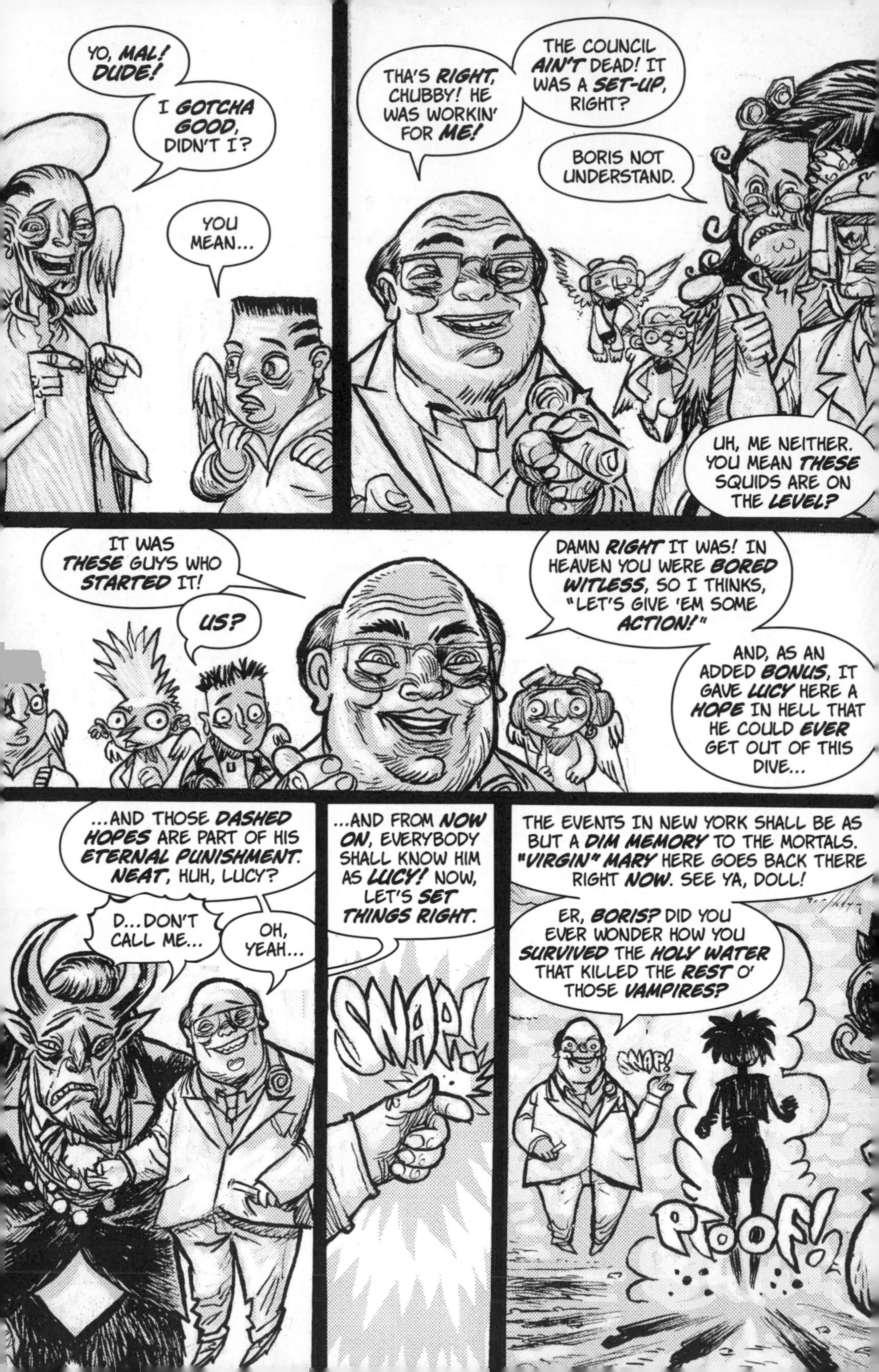
YO, MAL! DUDE!
I GOTCHA GOOD, DIDN'T I?
YOU MEAN...
THE COUNCIL AIN'T DEAD! IT WAS A SET-UP, RIGHT?
THA'S RIGHT, CHUBBY! HE WAS WORKIN' FOR ME!
BORIS NOT UNDERSTAND.
UH, ME NEITHER. YOU MEAN THESE SQUIDS ARE ON THE LEVEL?
IT WAS THESE GUYS WHO STARTED IT!
US?
DAMN RIGHT IT WAS! IN HEAVEN YOU WERE BORED WITLESS, SO I THINKS, "LET'S GIVE 'EM SOME ACTION!"
AND, AS AN ADDED BONUS, IT GAVE LUCY HERE A HOPE IN HELL THAT HE COULD EVER GET OUT OF THIS DIVE...
...AND THOSE DASHED HOPES ARE PART OF HIS ETERNAL PUNISHMENT. NEAT, HUH, LUCY?
D...DON'T CALL ME...
OH, YEAH...
...AND FROM NOW ON, EVERYBODY SHALL KNOW HIM AS LUCY! NOW, LET'S SET THINGS RIGHT.
SNAP!
THE EVENTS IN NEW YORK SHALL BE AS BUT A DIM MEMORY TO THE MORTALS. "VIRGIN" MARY HERE GOES BACK THERE RIGHT NOW. SEE YA, DOLL!
ER, BORIS? DID YOU EVER WONDER HOW YOU SURVIVED THE HOLY WATER THAT KILLED THE REST O' THOSE VAMPIRES?
SNAP!
POOF!

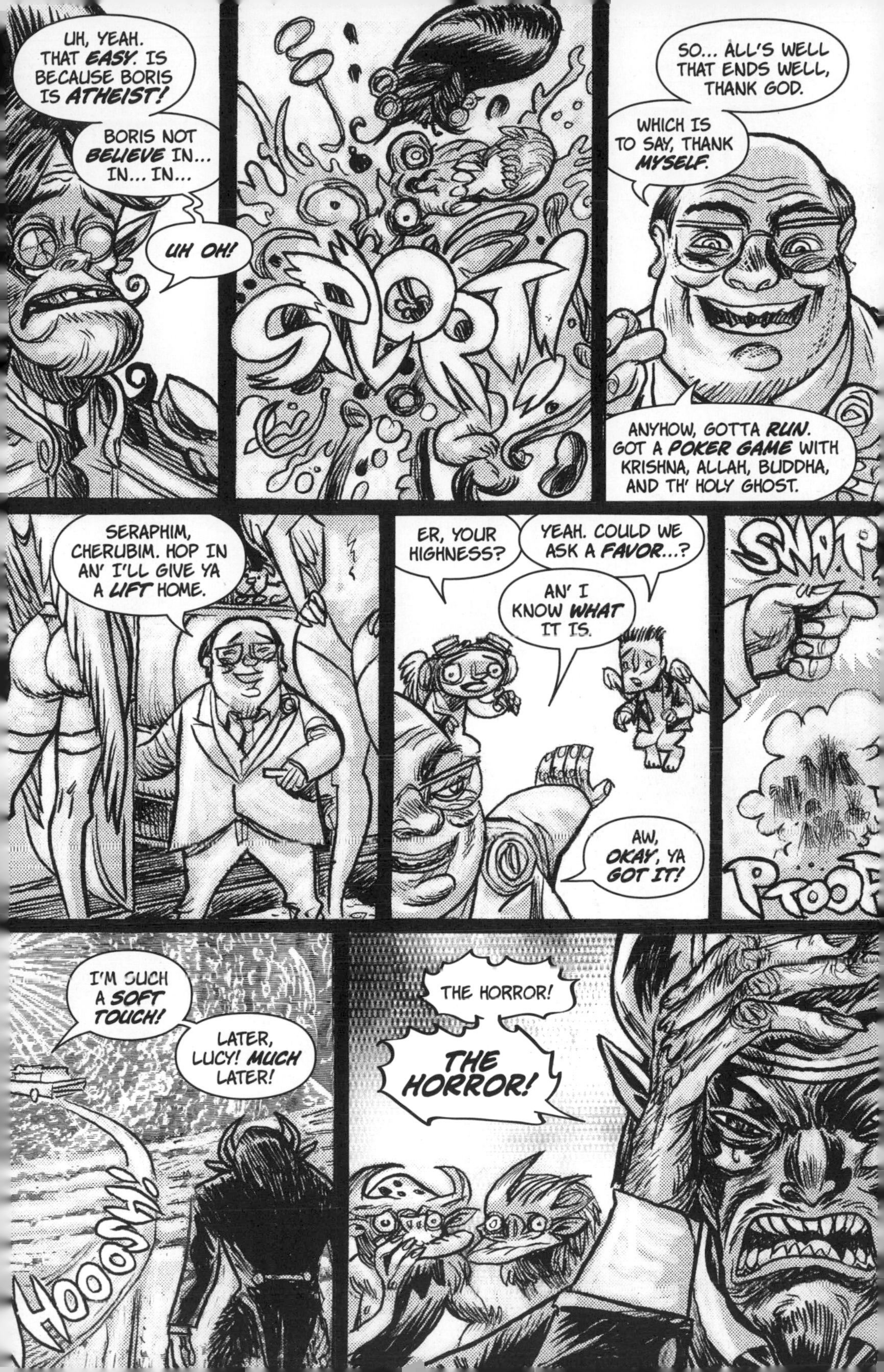

UH, YEAH. THAT EASY. IS BECAUSE BORIS IS ATHEIST!
BORIS NOT BELIEVE IN... IN... IN...
UH OH!
SPLORT
SO... ALL'S WELL THAT ENDS WELL, THANK GOD.
WHICH IS TO SAY, THANK MYSELF.
ANYHOW, GOTTA RUN. GOT A POKER GAME WITH KRISHNA, ALLAH, BUDDHA, AND TH' HOLY GHOST.
SERAPHIM, CHERUBIM. HOP IN AN' I'LL GIVE YA A LIFT HOME.
ER, YOUR HIGHNESS?
YEAH. COULD WE ASK A FAVOR...?
AN' I KNOW WHAT IT IS.
AW, OKAY, YA GOT IT!
SNAP
P-TOOF
I'M SUCH A SOFT TOUCH!
LATER, LUCY! MUCH LATER!
WHOOSH!
THE HORROR!
THE HORROR!

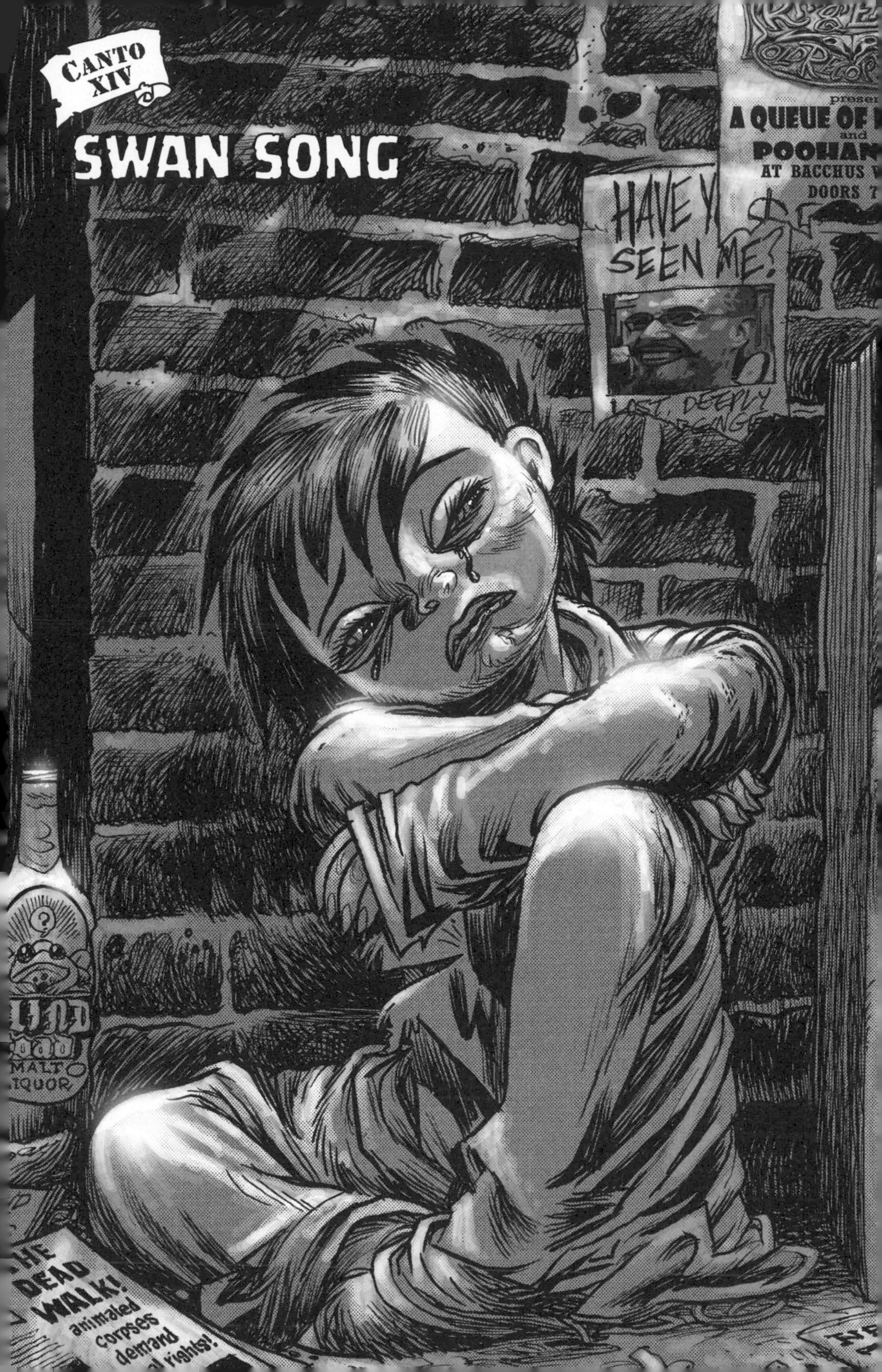
CANTO XIV
SWAN SONG
A QUEUE OF
and
AT BACCHUS
HAVE Y
SEEN ME?
DEAD
WALK!
animated
corpses
demand
rights!
MALT
LIQUOR

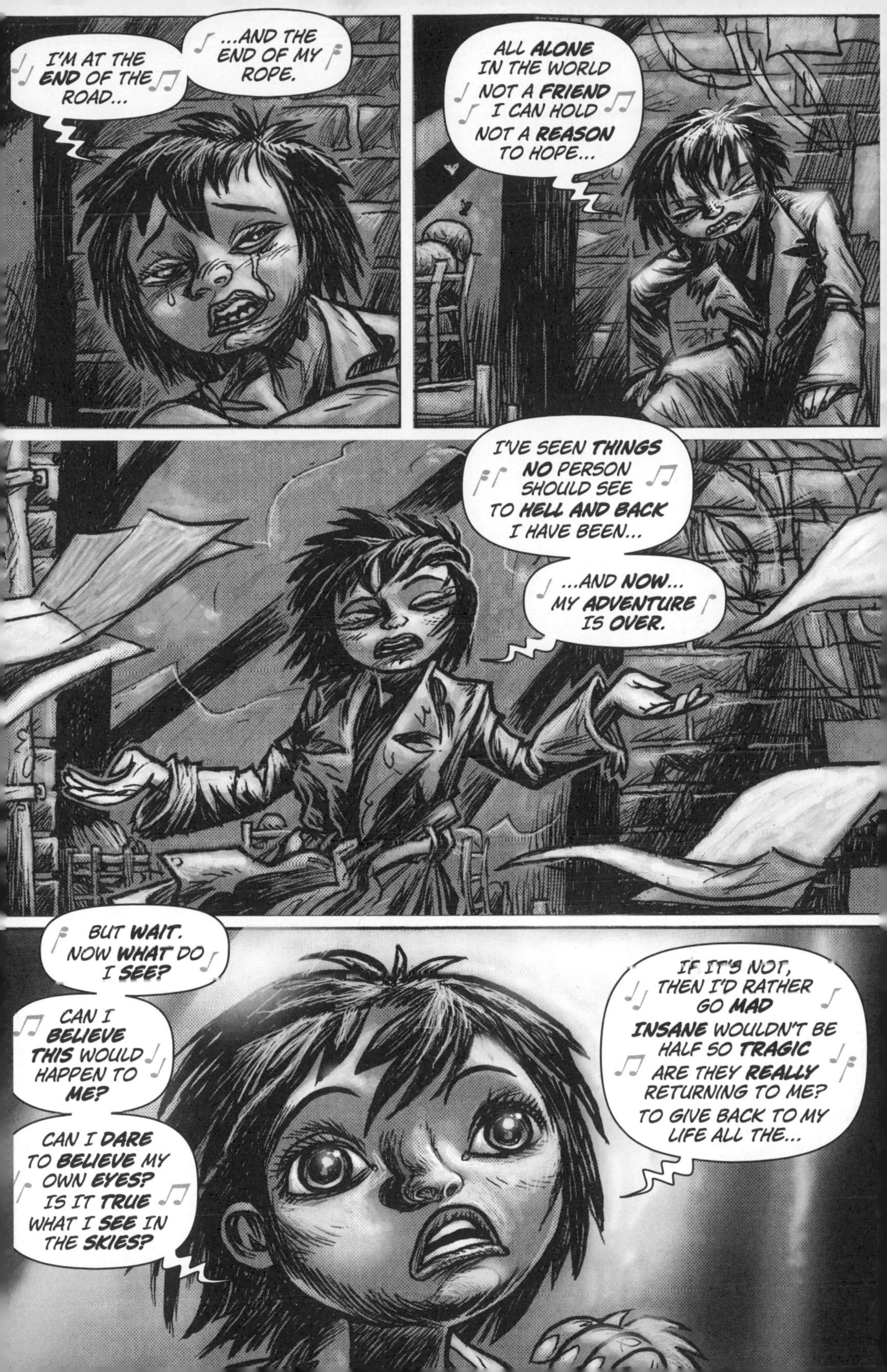
I'M AT THE END OF THE ROAD...
...AND THE END OF MY ROPE.
ALL ALONE IN THE WORLD NOT A FRIEND I CAN HOLD NOT A REASON TO HOPE...
I'VE SEEN THINGS NO PERSON SHOULD SEE TO HELL AND BACK I HAVE BEEN...
...AND NOW... MY ADVENTURE IS OVER.
BUT WAIT. NOW WHAT DO I SEE?
CAN I BELIEVE THIS WOULD HAPPEN TO ME?
CAN I DARE TO BELIEVE MY OWN EYES? IS IT TRUE WHAT I SEE IN THE SKIES?
IF IT'S NOT, THEN I'D RATHER GO MAD INSANE WOULDN'T BE HALF SO TRAGIC ARE THEY REALLY RETURNING TO ME? TO GIVE BACK TO MY LIFE ALL THE...

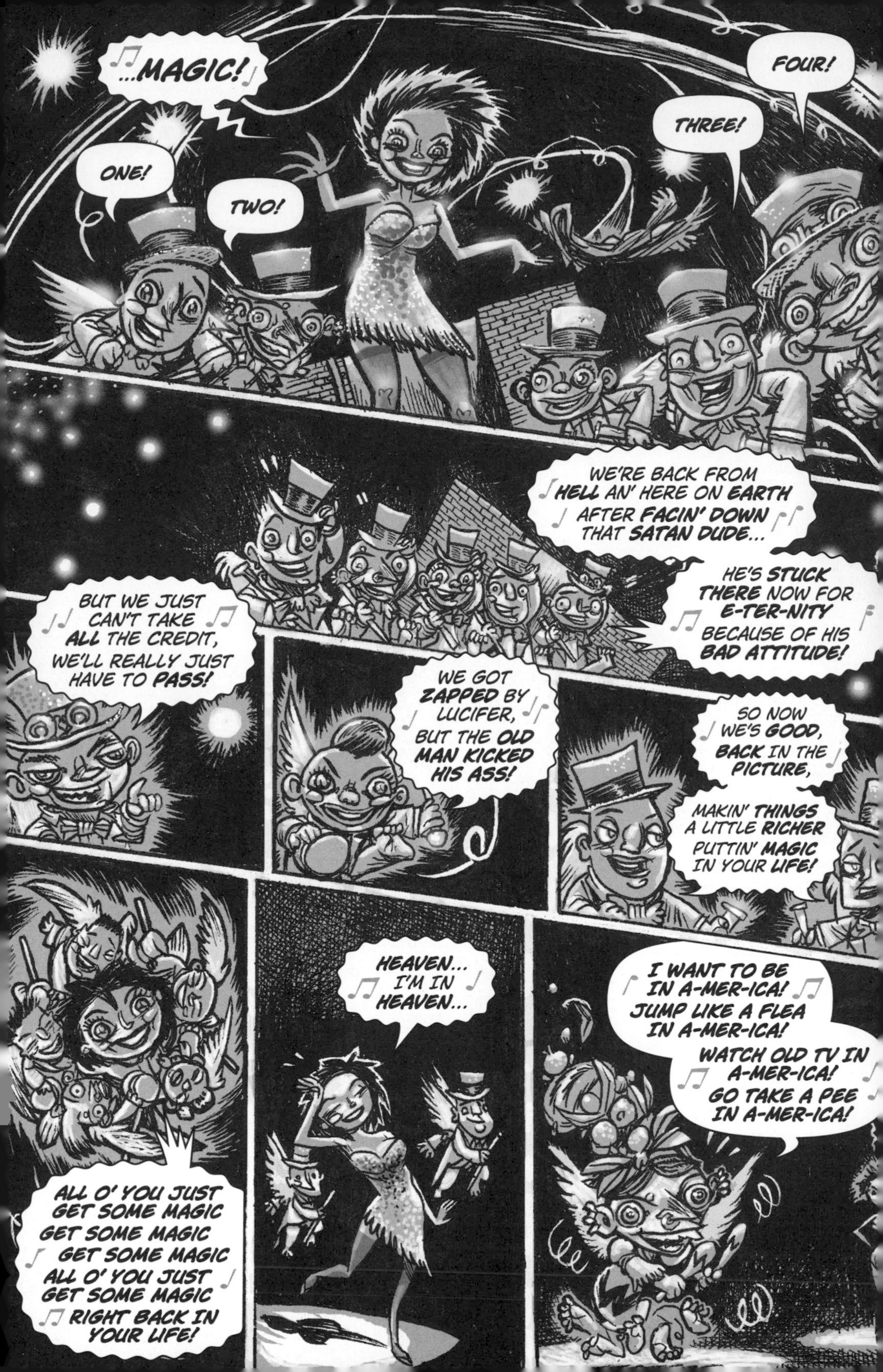
...MAGIC!
ONE!
TWO!
THREE!
FOUR!
WE'RE BACK FROM HELL AN' HERE ON EARTH AFTER FACIN' DOWN THAT SATAN DUDE...
HE'S STUCK THERE NOW FOR E-TER-NITY BECAUSE OF HIS BAD ATTITUDE!
BUT WE JUST CAN'T TAKE ALL THE CREDIT, WE'LL REALLY JUST HAVE TO PASS!
WE GOT ZAPPED BY LUCIFER, BUT THE OLD MAN KICKED HIS ASS!
SO NOW WE'S GOOD, BACK IN THE PICTURE,
MAKIN' THINGS A LITTLE RICHER PUTTIN' MAGIC IN YOUR LIFE!
ALL O' YOU JUST GET SOME MAGIC GET SOME MAGIC GET SOME MAGIC ALL O' YOU JUST GET SOME MAGIC RIGHT BACK IN YOUR LIFE!
HEAVEN... I'M IN HEAVEN...
I WANT TO BE IN A-MER-ICA! JUMP LIKE A FLEA IN A-MER-ICA!
WATCH OLD TV IN A-MER-ICA! GO TAKE A PEE IN A-MER-ICA!

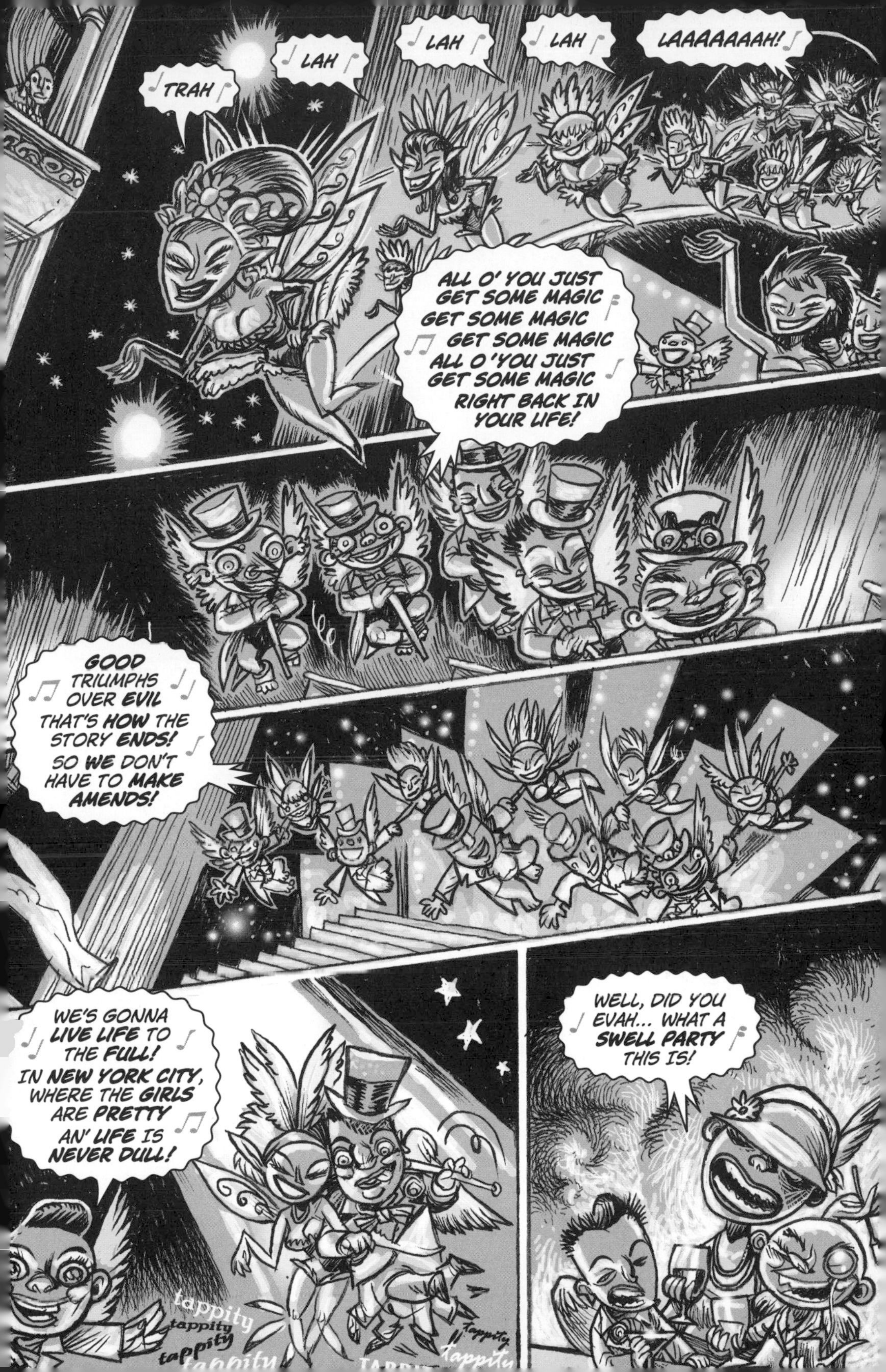
TRAH
LAH
LAH
LAH
LAAAAAAAH!
ALL O' YOU JUST GET SOME MAGIC GET SOME MAGIC GET SOME MAGIC ALL O' YOU JUST GET SOME MAGIC RIGHT BACK IN YOUR LIFE!
GOOD TRIUMPHS OVER EVIL THAT'S HOW THE STORY ENDS! SO WE DON'T HAVE TO MAKE AMENDS!
WE'S GONNA LIVE LIFE TO THE FULL! IN NEW YORK CITY, WHERE THE GIRLS ARE PRETTY AN' LIFE IS NEVER DULL!
tappity tappity tappity
tappity
tappity
WELL, DID YOU EVAH... WHAT A SWELL PARTY THIS IS!

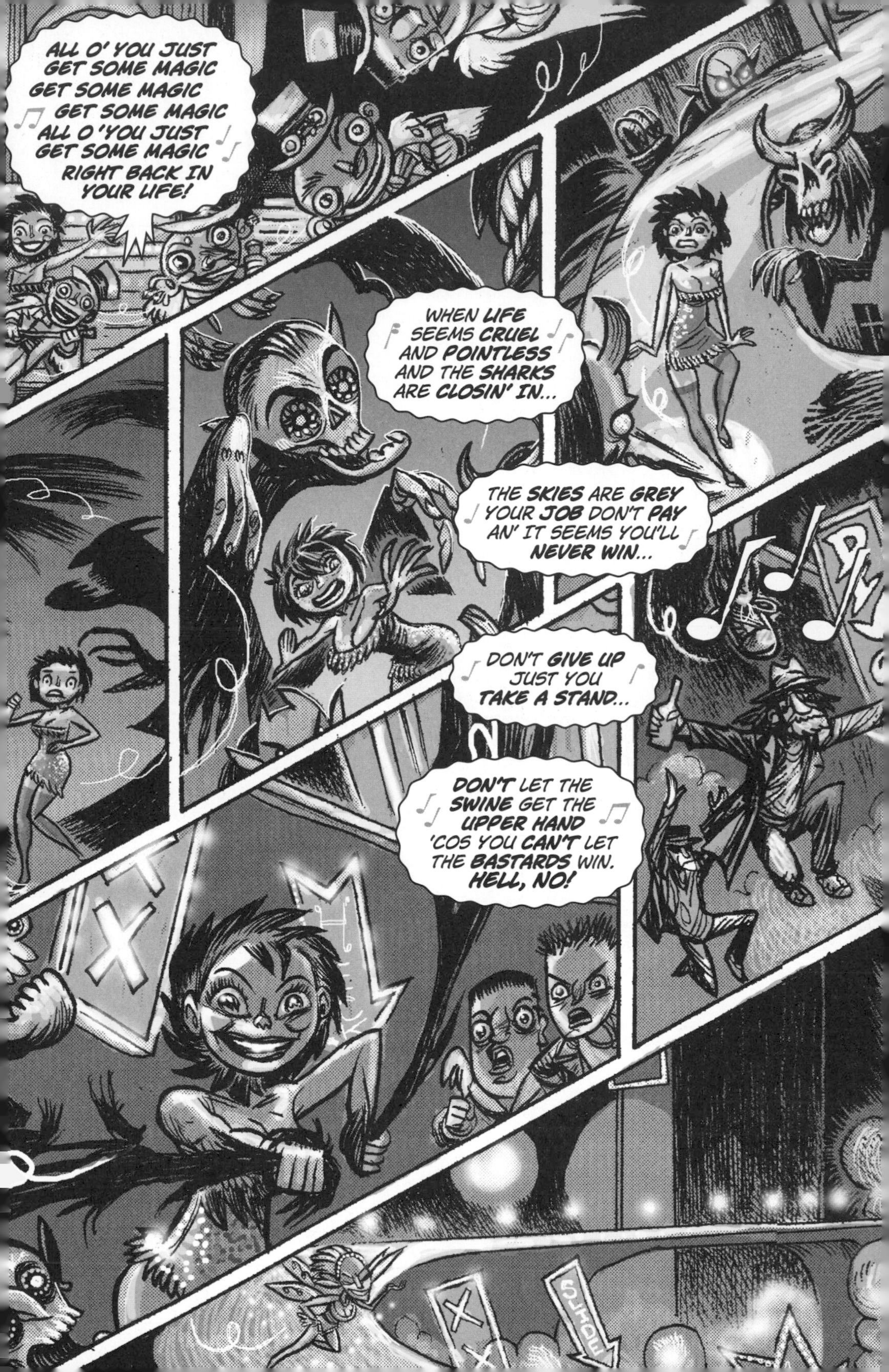
ALL O' YOU JUST GET SOME MAGIC GET SOME MAGIC GET SOME MAGIC ALL O'YOU JUST GET SOME MAGIC RIGHT BACK IN YOUR LIFE!
WHEN LIFE SEEMS CRUEL AND POINTLESS AND THE SHARKS ARE CLOSIN' IN...
THE SKIES ARE GREY YOUR JOB DON'T PAY AN' IT SEEMS YOU'LL NEVER WIN...
DON'T GIVE UP JUST YOU TAKE A STAND...
DON'T LET THE SWINE GET THE UPPER HAND 'COS YOU CAN'T LET THE BASTARDS WIN. HELL, NO!

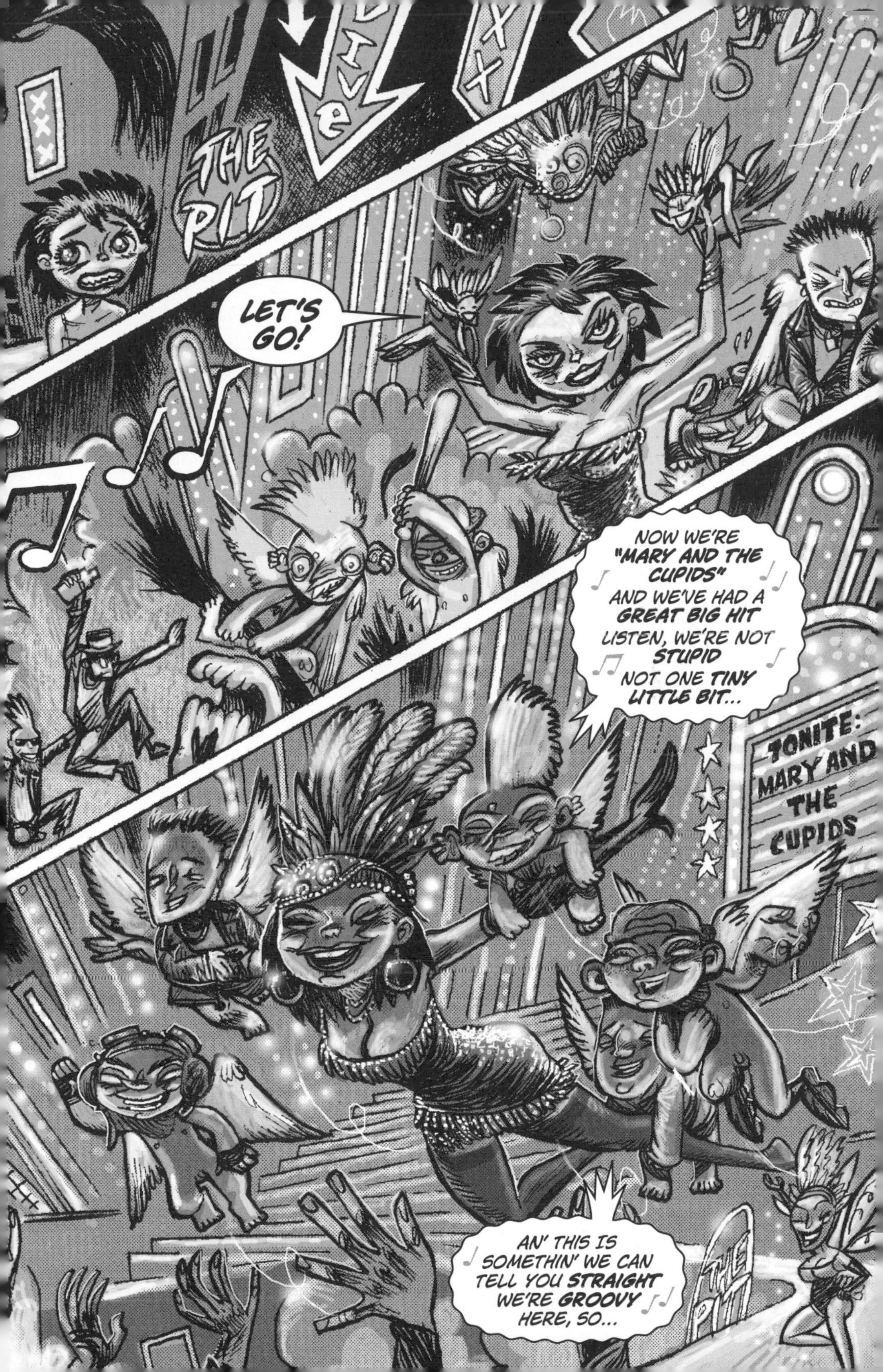

THE PIT
DIVE
XXX
LET'S GO!
NOW WE'RE "MARY AND THE CUPIDS" AND WE'VE HAD A GREAT BIG HIT LISTEN, WE'RE NOT STUPID NOT ONE TINY LITTLE BIT...
TONITE: MARY AND THE CUPIDS
AN' THIS IS SOMETHIN' WE CAN TELL YOU STRAIGHT WE'RE GROOVY HERE, SO...
THE PIT

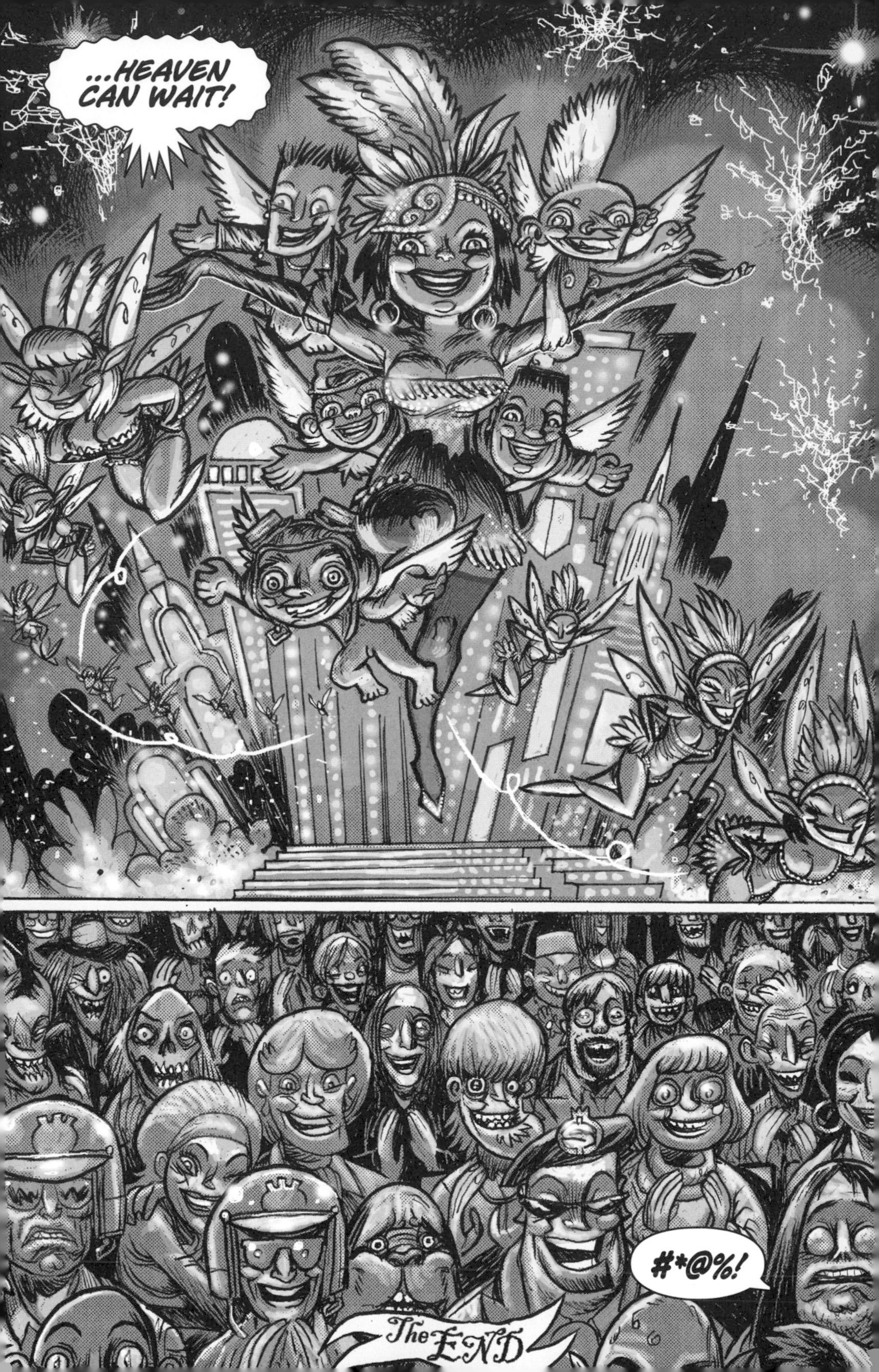
...HEAVEN CAN WAIT!
#*@%!
The END

AFTERWORD

*C*herubs! has a special—and even essential—quality in comics that might be called *turnability*—that exciting feeling when you can't help but keep turning the pages. This magical element is what makes the best comics something you want to return to again and again. We see it in works as diverse as Schulz's *Peanuts*, Morrison and Quitely's *All-Star Superman*, Mignola and Corben's *Hellboy* stories, Jodorowsky and Moebius doing *L'Incal*. The list is long, thank God, and we have many great comics for our shelves. And thank God no two can be made alike. The most successful comics are those you can't help but read once you start turning the pages. The best drag you into their ink and paper worlds, they seduce you into entertaining their balloon-festooned stories, they persuade you into living the story with the characters, panel by blocky panel. As for the unique book you are now holding, it is possible to isolate qualities in Mark Stafford's artwork that make you keep turning the page. It is possible to pinpoint key lines and cadences in the dialogue and direction of Bryan Talbot's writing that keep you reading. Each artist provides buoyancy for the other's strengths. For their many noteworthy skills as individual artists, it seems to me the quality of *readability* in this book is in the particular alchemy between these two creators as collaborators—a solid story coupled with solid drawing. Together, these two ink slingers produce a sum greater than the individual parts. It is hard to imagine this story existing without these two in tandem. Mark gives *Cherubs!* its flesh and telegraphs the maps for Bryan's feverish, ribald call-and-response to a great and dimly familiar history of literature concerned with questions theological and spiritual . . . John Milton filtered through the tongue-in-pierced-cheek of punk rock's double-digit salute to all things sacred and canonical. Even the logo of the book itself reflects this balance between high and low—the artists' names are presented in an almost gaudy, pompous script style; all croquill elegance and parchment flanking a distressed, stamplike "ransom note" type style that would do Vivienne Westwood proud. Bryan has peppered his script with many keen references to both works of Western high art and literature as well as more mundane (and knowingly) pop-cultural pap, with more than a couple of *roman à clef* characters to be found for those in the know. Mark's artwork has a sensibility that seems somewhere between Watterson's *Calvin and Hobbes* and Dave Cooper's *Weasel*, with a dash of Guy Davis thrown in for gritty measure. Foul-mouthed cherubim skirting back alleyways with a good-hearted stripper (for are there any other kind in fiction?), art-critic seraphim perplexing over a Jackson Pollock, lugubrious fallen angels as conniving business executives. Somehow, it all works.

Iggy Pop was once asked what he thought of the music of Nick Cave. "I listen to his albums and I go to his concerts. That's the highest praise I can give a musician." That would seem to me to define the quality of *listenability*. That always seemed like a proper benchmark for comics and literature as well: "I read his (or her) work." *Cherubs!* has that quality.

Turnability.

—Paul Pope
NYC, October 2012

CHERUBS!

sketches and such

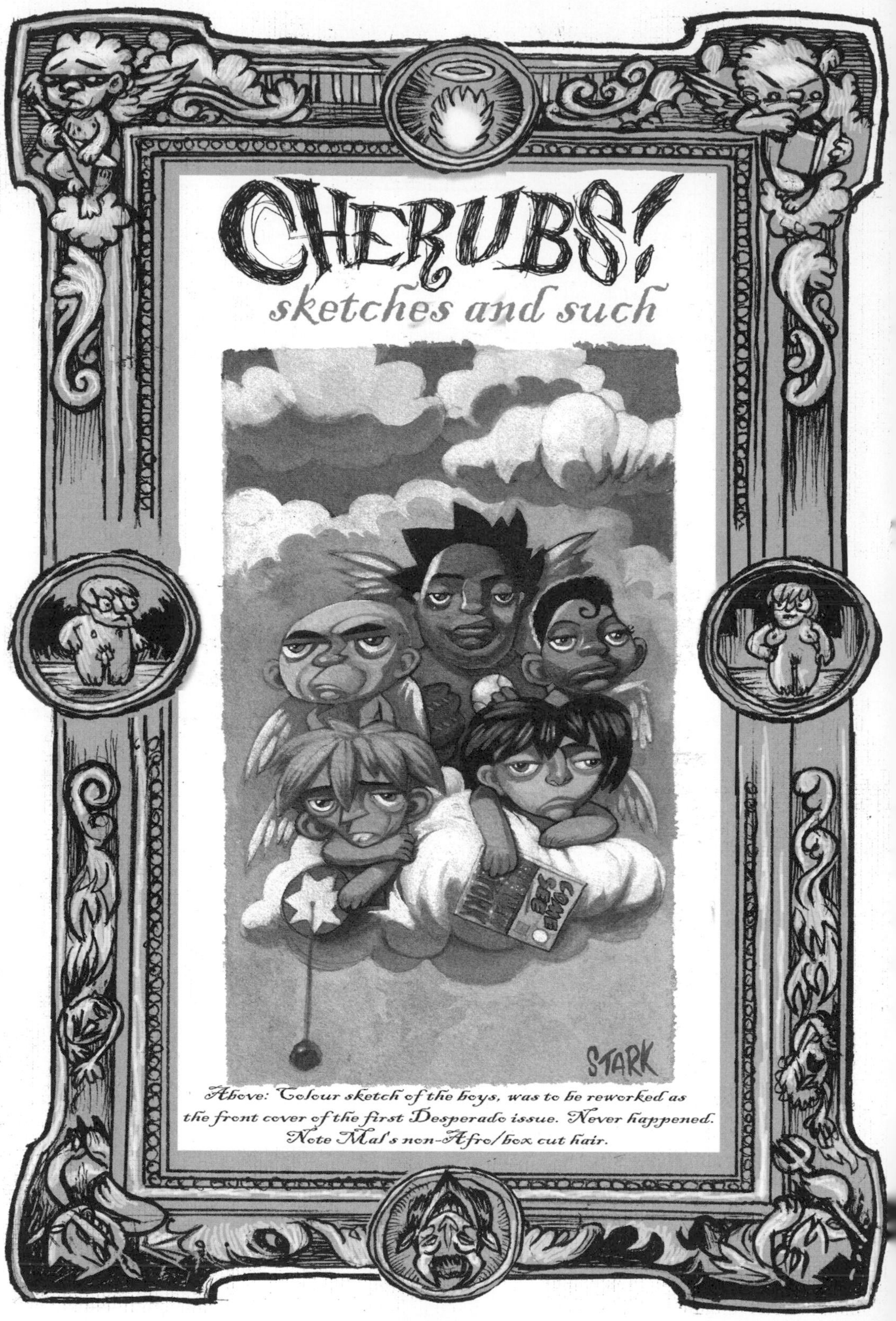
COME SEE
STARK

Above: Colour sketch of the boys, was to be reworked as the front cover of the first Desperado issue. Never happened. Note Mal's non-Afro/box cut hair.

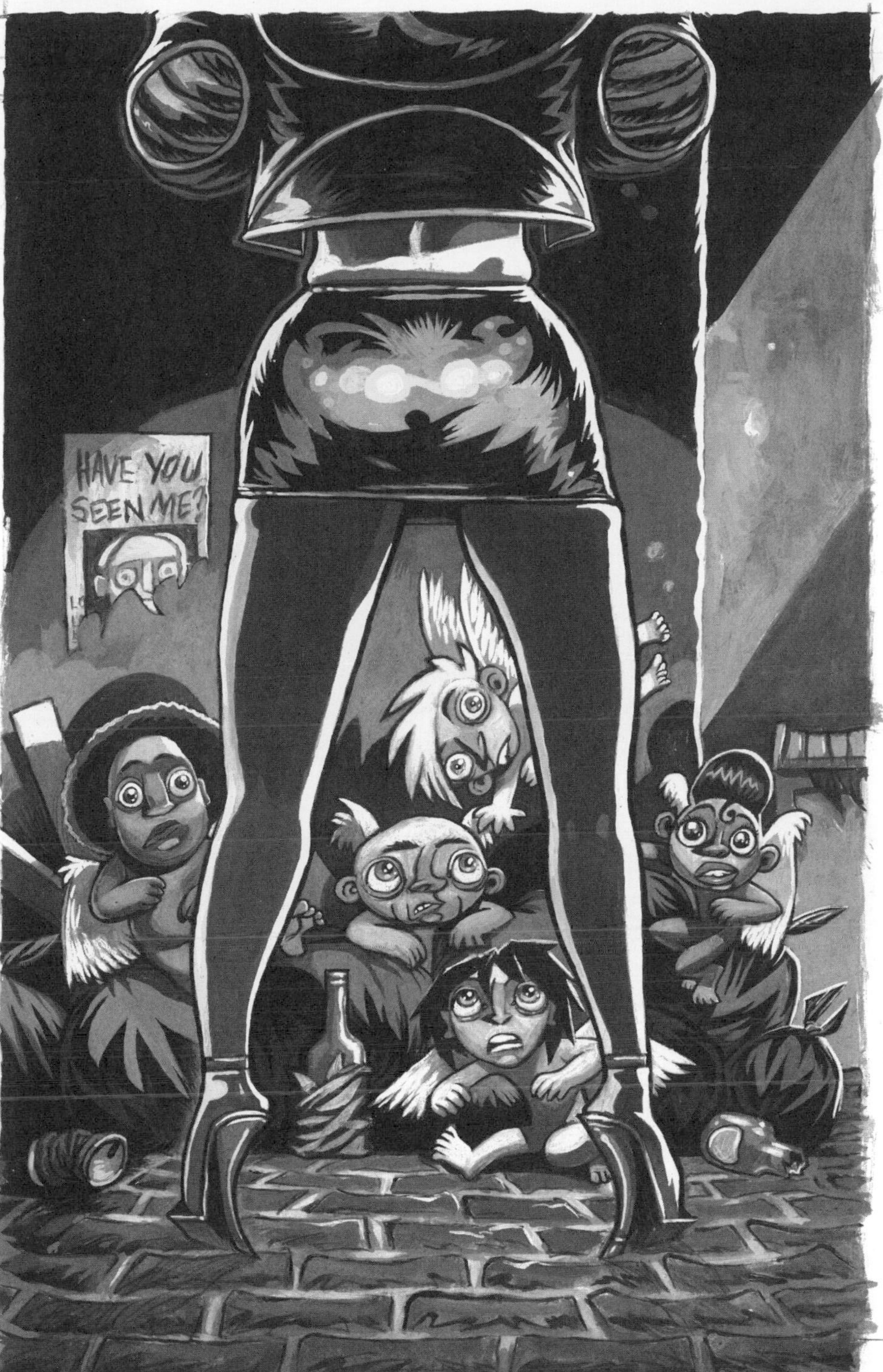
HAVE YOU SEEN ME?
STaRK

Raphael? Pah! His leather miniskirt work was mediocre at best. Would-be cover to issue 2, ended up as the back of the Desperado book. Ink on board. Lovely.

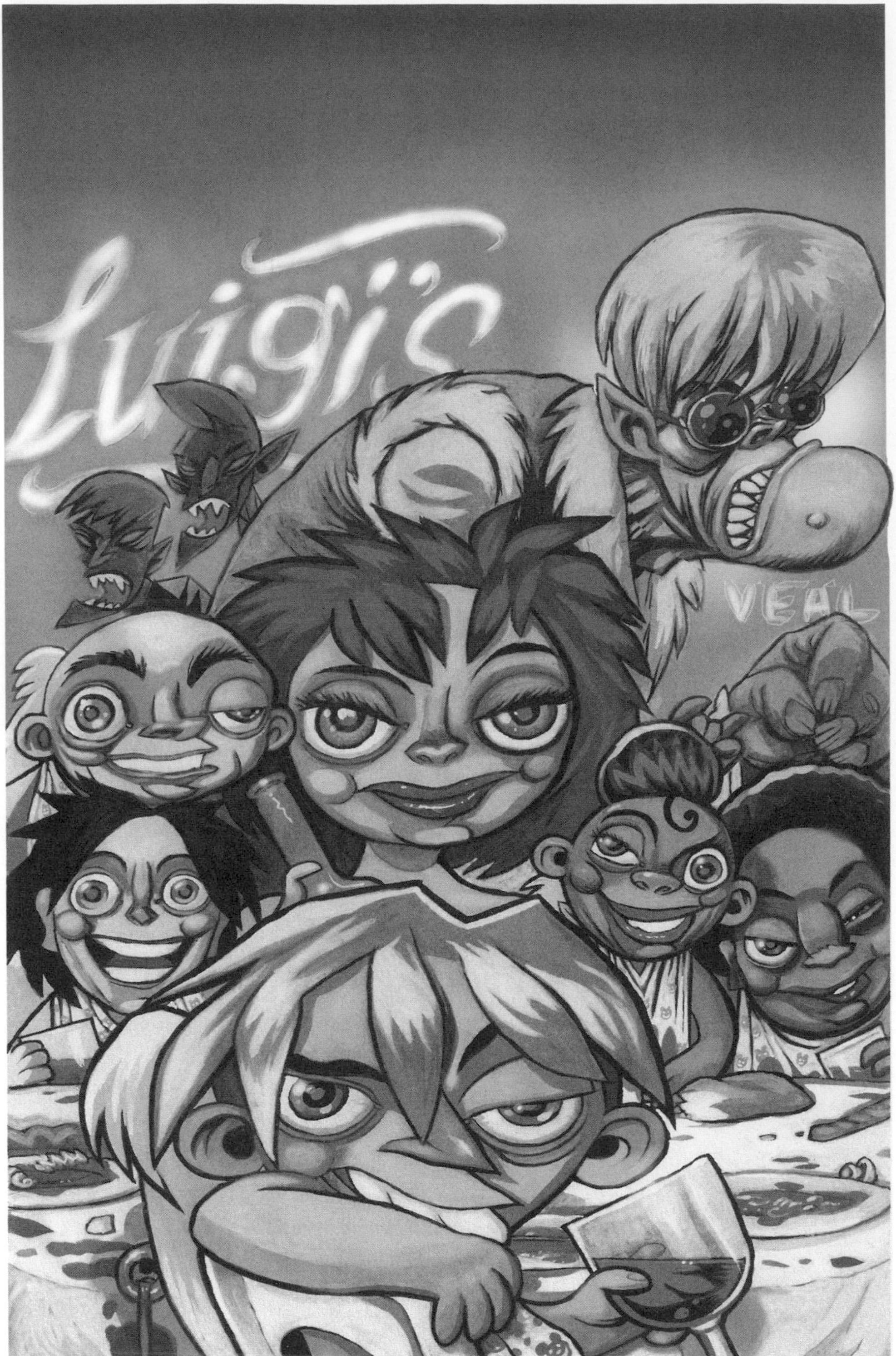
Luigi's
VEAL

Would-be cover to the third issue of book one, when Desperado were planning to issue it as four comics. Ink on bristol board.

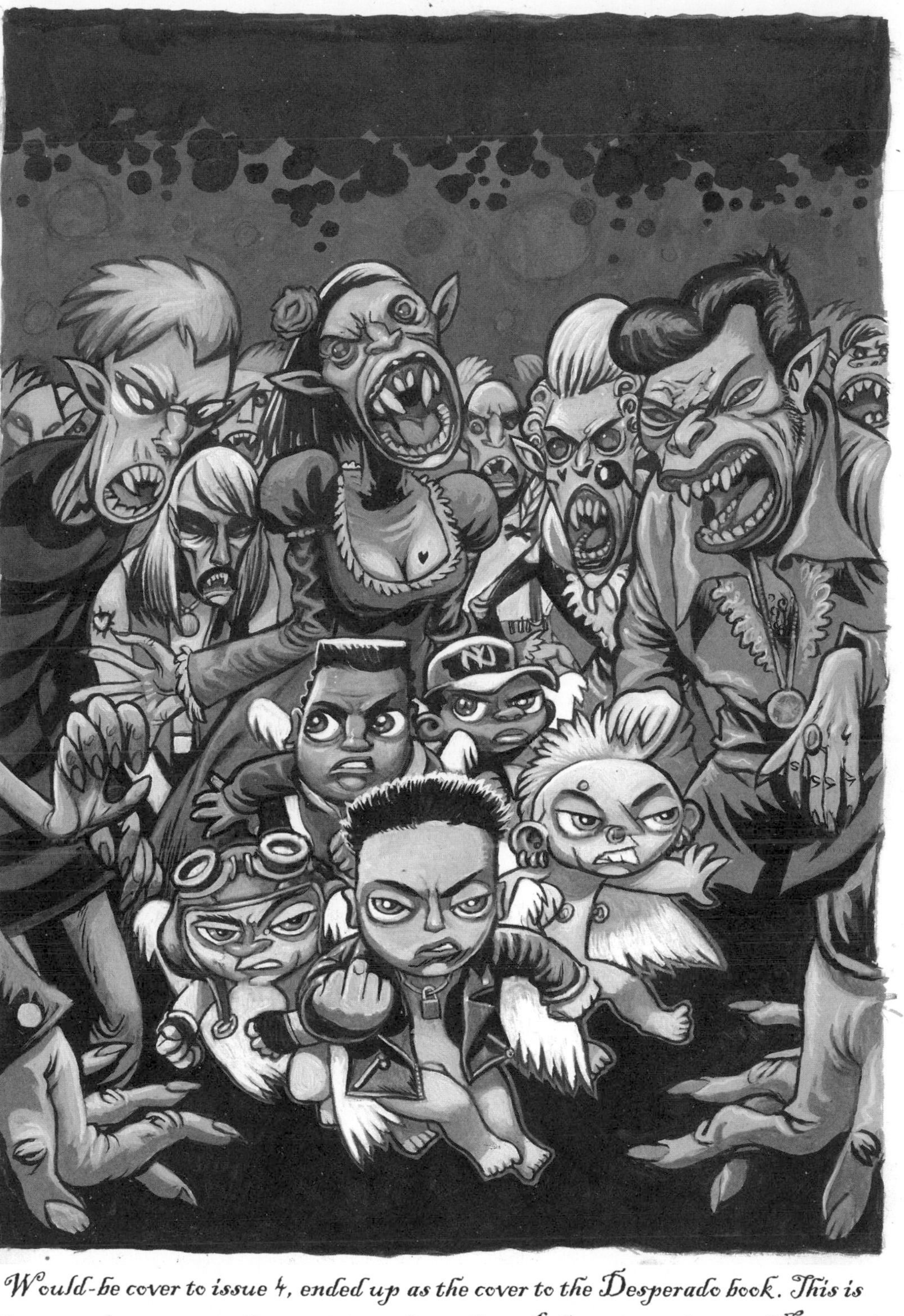

Would-be cover to issue 4, ended up as the cover to the Desperado book. This is the original, minus graphics and digital tweaking. Inks on bristol board. Notice that our vampires don't bloody sparkle.

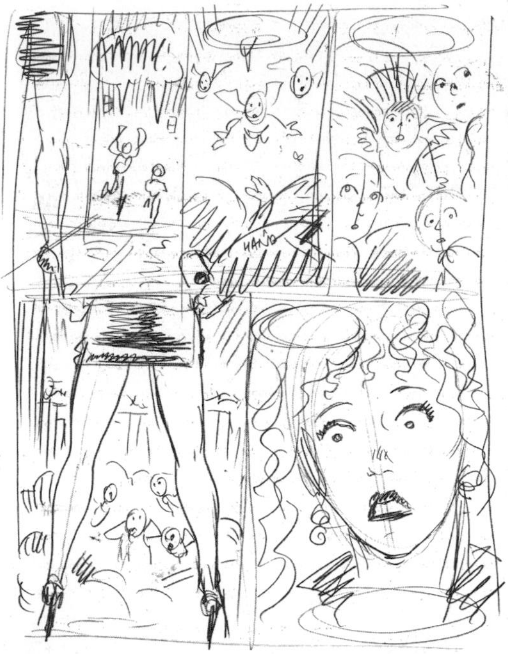

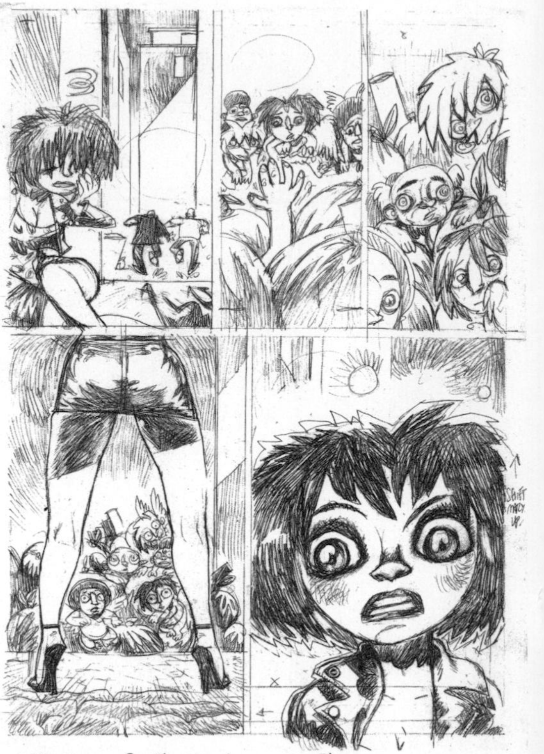

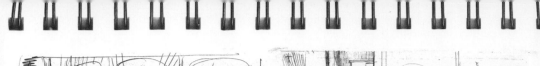

Bryan's layouts and my pencils from book one. Looking back, I was more than a little intimidated by the whole scale and ambition of the project at the outset. Most of my small-press stuff had been one or two pages long, and here was a sustained piece of storytelling, with a large cast of characters, heaven, hell, and New York. Thank gawd Bryan volunteered to provide thumbnails. I've learnt a hell of a lot.

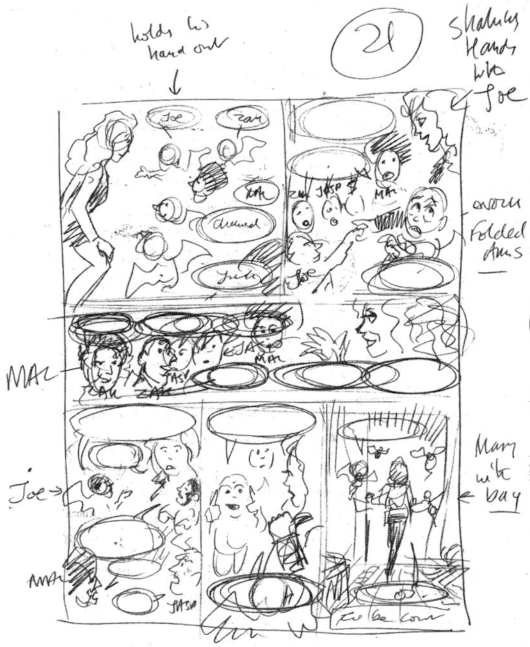
21
MAL
Joe

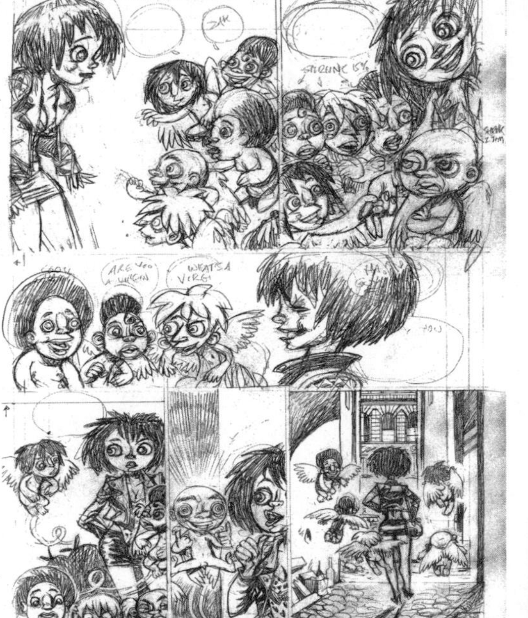

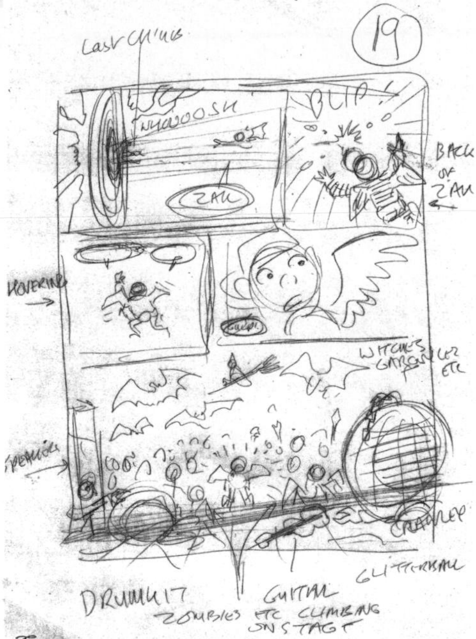
19
WHOOOOSH
BLIP!
BACK OF ZAK
ZAK
HOVERING
WITCHES GARGOYLES ETC
GLITTERBALL
DRUMKIT
GUITAR
ZOMBIES ETC CLIMBING ON STAGE

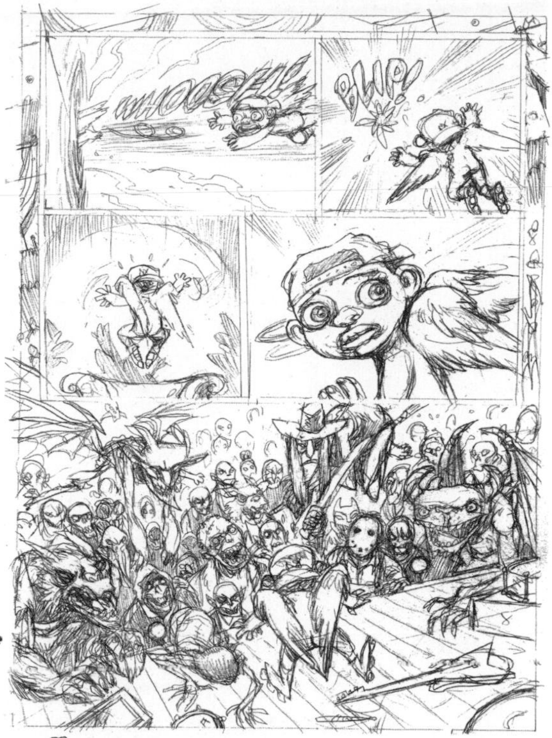
WHOOOSH!!
BLIP!

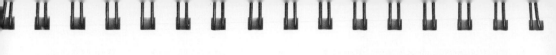

By the end of book two the layouts were getting looser and looser; we both now knew what we were after, and he could, for the most part, trust me to get on with it. But still, for all the tricky business with eye levels and balloon placement, the knowledge of what has to be in the panel, and all that other invisible and essential stuff, these scribbly buggers were invaluable.

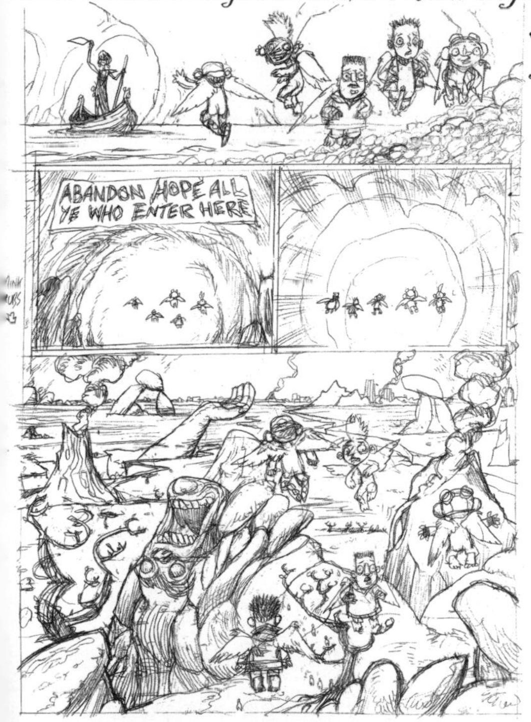
ABANDON HOPE ALL YE WHO ENTER HERE

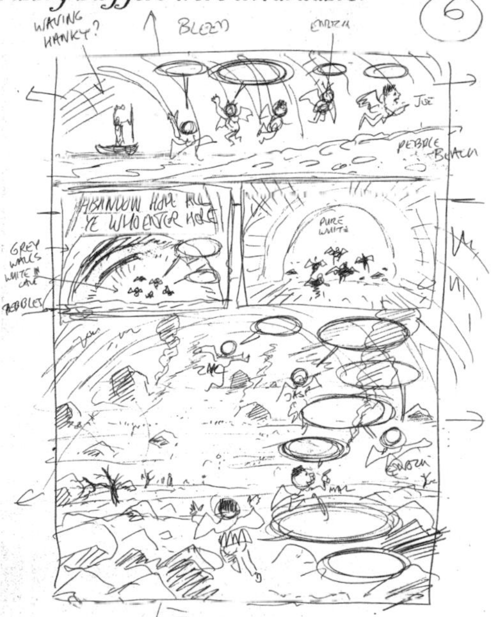
6
WAVING HANKY?
BLEED
JOE
PEBBLE BEACH
ABANDON HOPE ALL YE WHO ENTER HERE
GREY WALLS WHITE IN CAVE
PEBBLES
PURE WHITE
BLEED

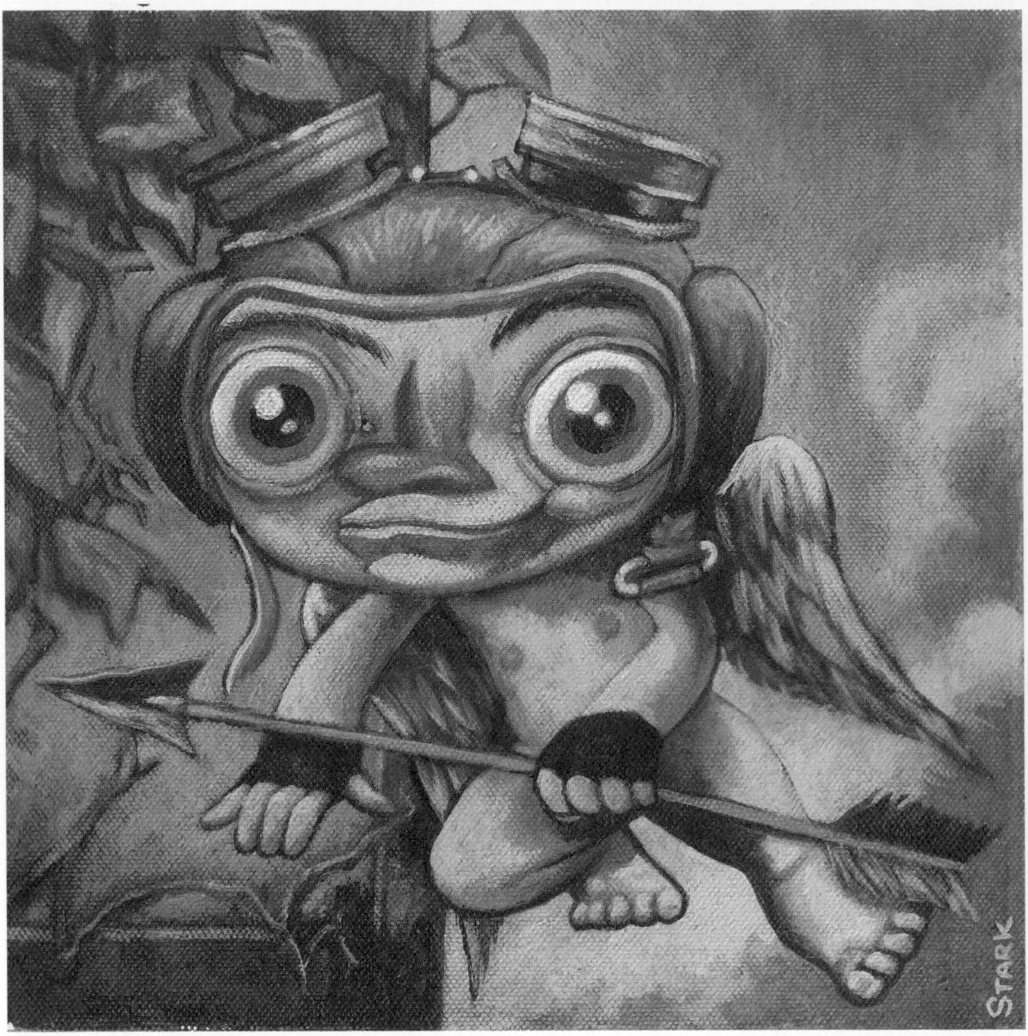
STARK

Above: Enoch! An acrylic on canvas painting, done for the hell of it, but shown as part of my 'Largely Unseen' show at Orbital Comics. Now property of Mr Talbot.
Below: Those logos, in full, decorate that jacket now.

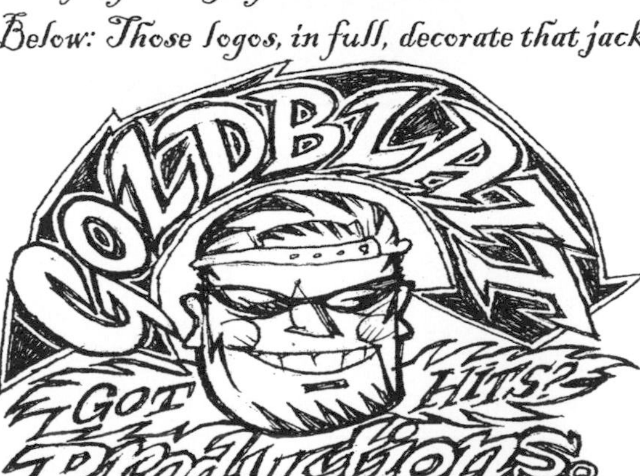
GOLDBLAZE
GOT HITS?
Productions.

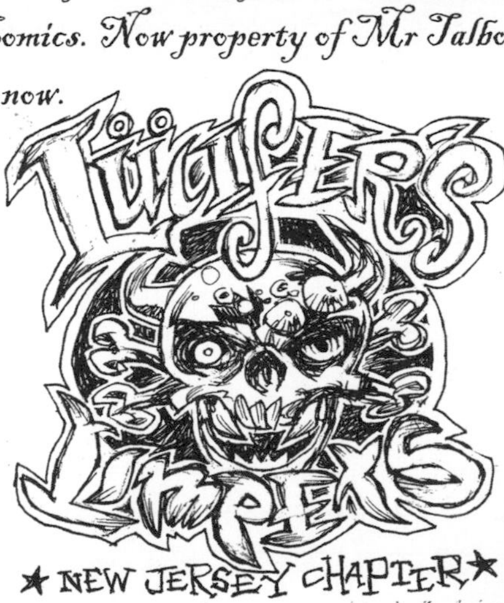
LUCIFER'S IMPERS
★ NEW JERSEY CHAPTER ★

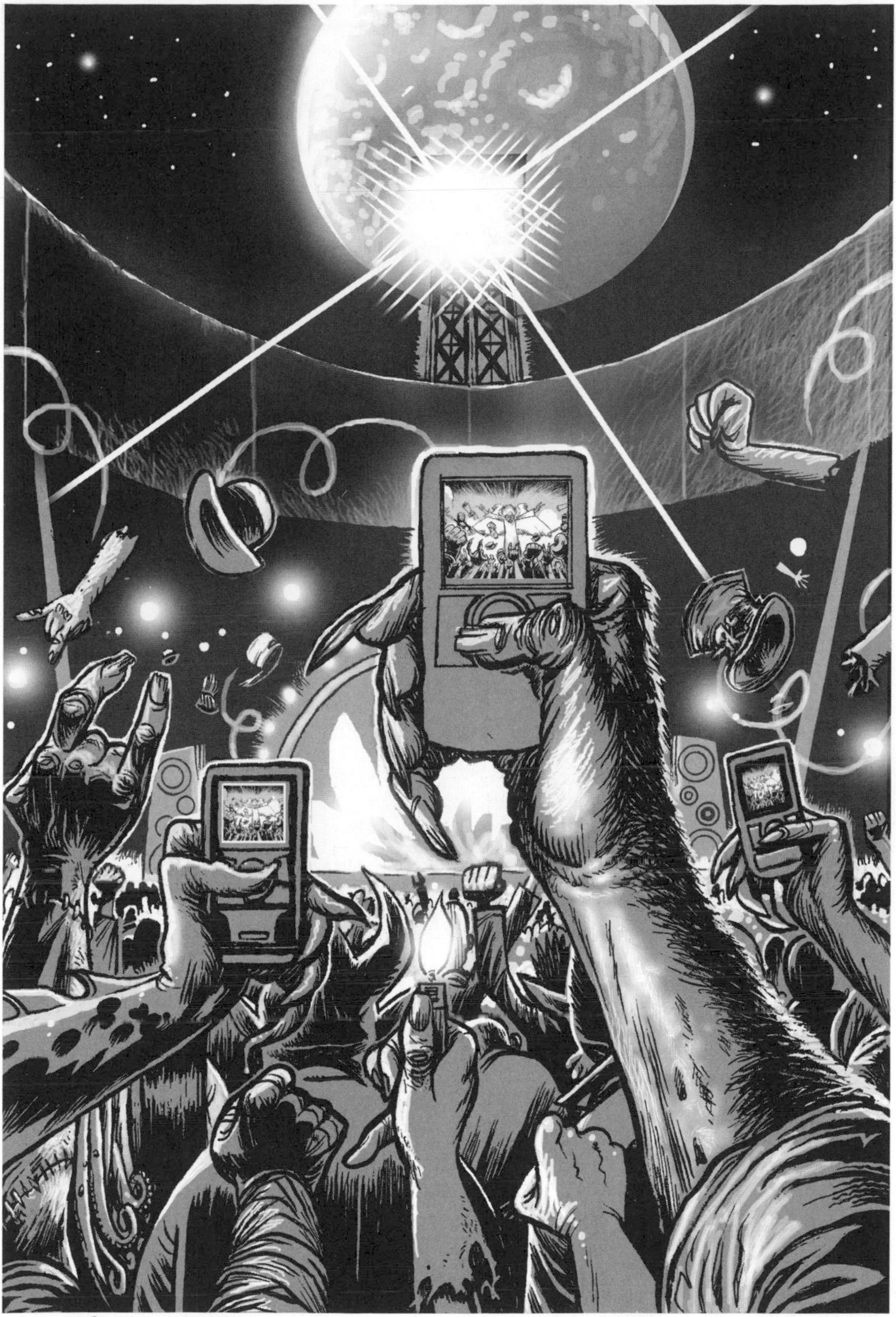

Did this page for my own amusement, and as a test of my abilities with monochrome computer shading, just wanted to emphasise the camera-phone gag, which doesn't come over that well in the story art. Guess you could insert it into chapter one of book two, with "Caaan you dig it?!" lettered over the top. Knock yourself out.

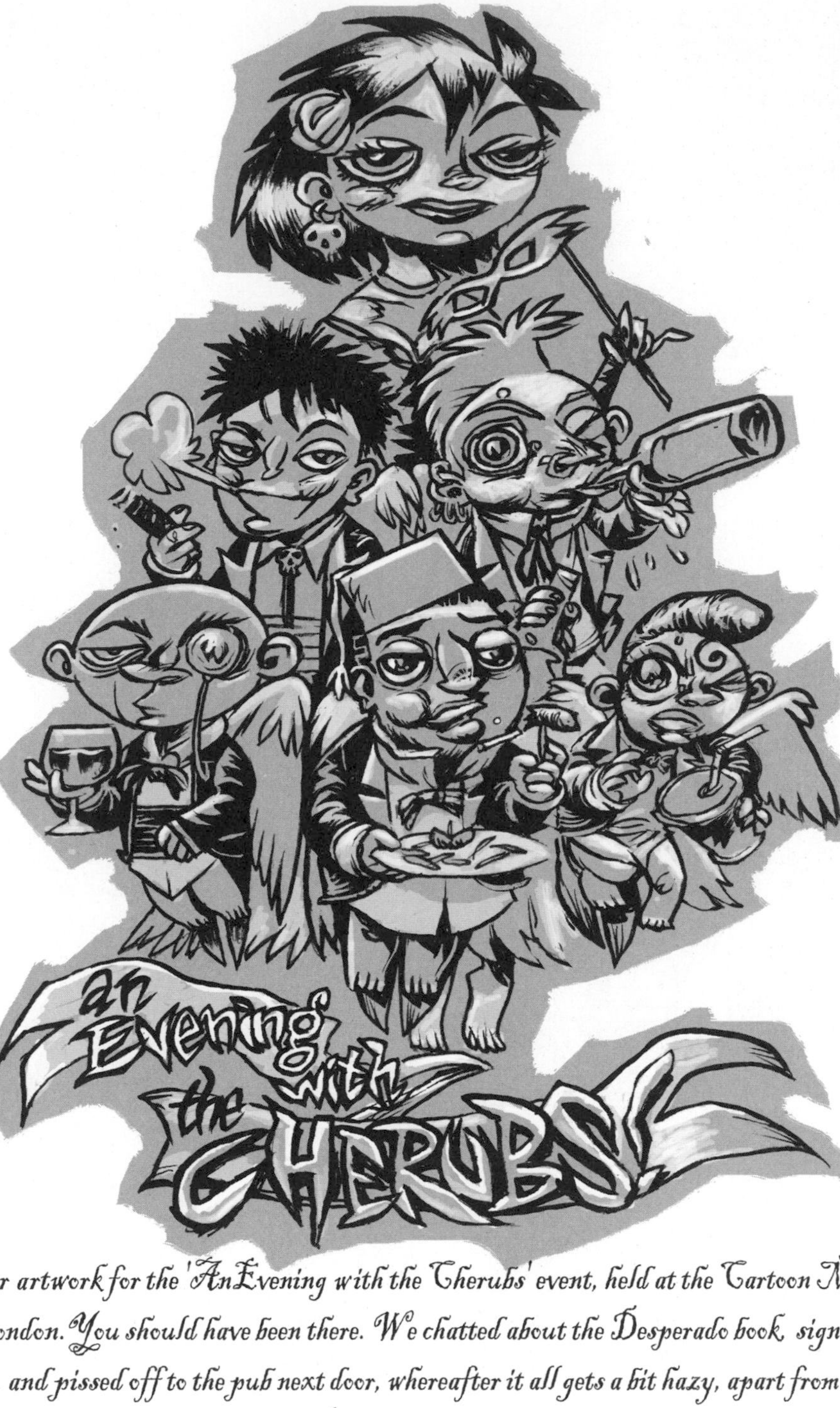
an Evening with the CHERUBS!

Flier artwork for the 'An Evening with the Cherubs' event, held at the Cartoon Museum in London. You should have been there. We chatted about the Desperado book, signed a few copies, and pissed off to the pub next door, whereafter it all gets a bit hazy, apart from Bryan's stellar rendition of the works of John Cooper Clarke, and the welcome reappearance of some much loved friends. Getting a bit emotional thinking about it. Pity the book sold bugger all..

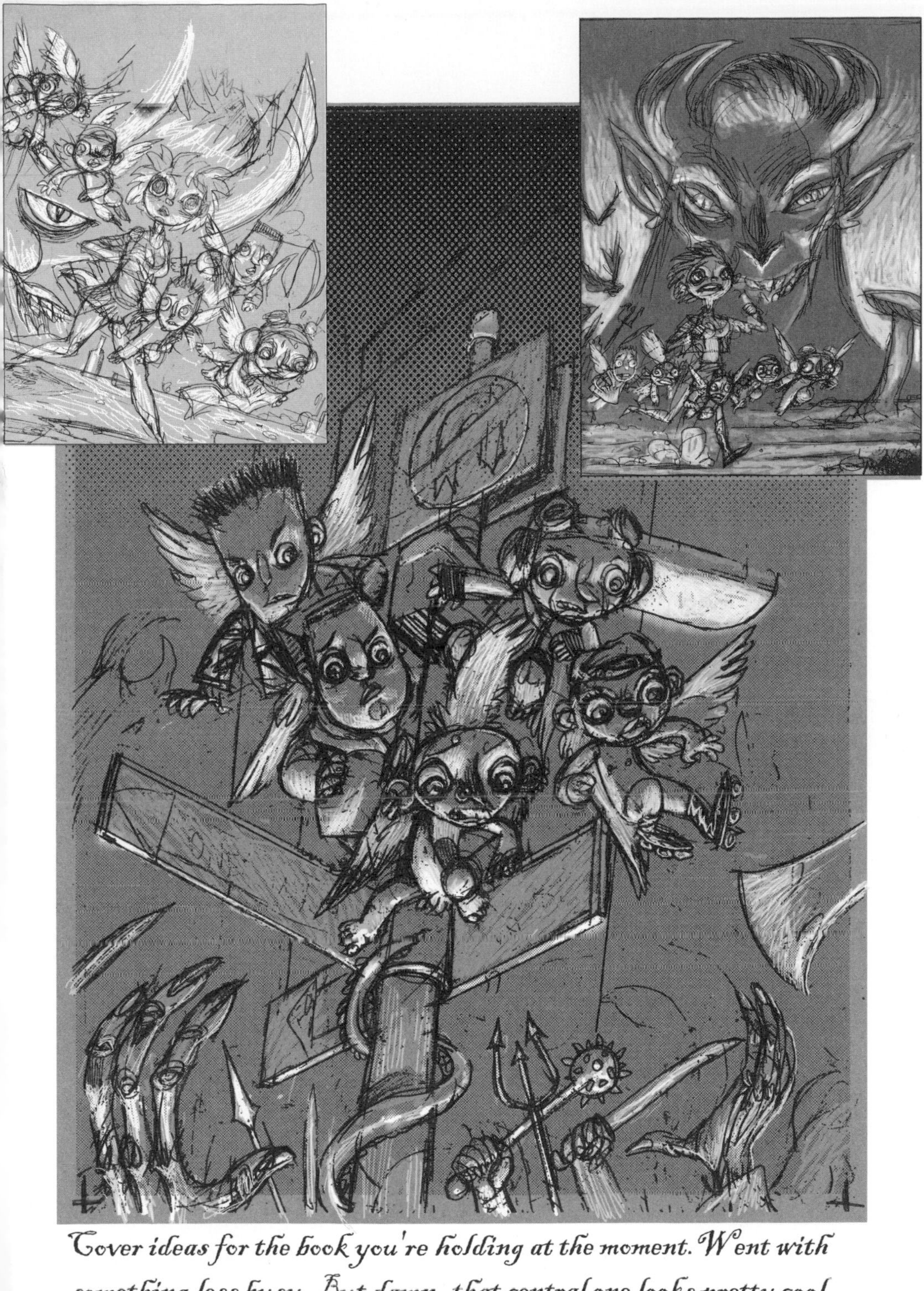

Cover ideas for the book you're holding at the moment. Went with something less busy. But damn, that central one looks pretty cool.

BRYAN TALBOT has written and drawn comics and graphic novels for over thirty years, including *Judge Dredd*, *Batman*, *Sandman*, *The Adventures of Luther Arkwright*, *The Tale of One Bad Rat*, *Heart of Empire*, *Alice in Sunderland*, and his recent *Grandville* series of steampunk detective thrillers. His most recent graphic novel is *Dotter of Her Father's Eyes*, written by his wife Mary Talbot. Bryan's work has been recognized with numerous industry awards, and he has been presented with honorary doctorates from both Sunderland University and Northumbria University. Bryan is the first British comics creator to be so honored twice. Visit Bryan's website at Bryan-Talbot.com.

MARK STAFFORD has been lurking around the fringes of London's overlapping comics/small press/underground art scenes for as long as he can remember. He's produced a lot of illustrations, a fair few paintings, and at least one mural over the years, as well as writing and drawing too few comics. He's been the semipermanent Cartoonist in Residence for the rather wonderful Cartoon Museum since 2006, and writes about cinema for *Electric Sheep* when he can. With the writer Dave Hine he's adapted Lovecraft's 'The Colour Out of Space,' and is working on Victor Hugo's *The Man Who Laughs*, both for SelfMadeHero. See Mark's stuff at Hocus-Baloney.com.

OTHER BOOKS BY BRYAN TALBOT

The Adventures of Luther Arkwright
ISBN 978-1-59307-725-9 $18.99

Heart of Empire: The Legacy of Luther Arkwright
ISBN 978-1-59307-726-6 $27.95

The Tale of One Bad Rat
ISBN 978-1-59582-493-6 $19.99

Alice in Sunderland
ISBN 978-1-59307-673-3 $29.99

Dotter of Her Father's Eyes
ISBN 978-1-59582-850-7 $14.99

Grandville
ISBN 978-1-59582-397-7 $19.99

Grandville Mon Amour
ISBN 978-1-59582-574-2 $19.99

Grandville Bête Noire
ISBN 978-1-59582-890-3 $19.99

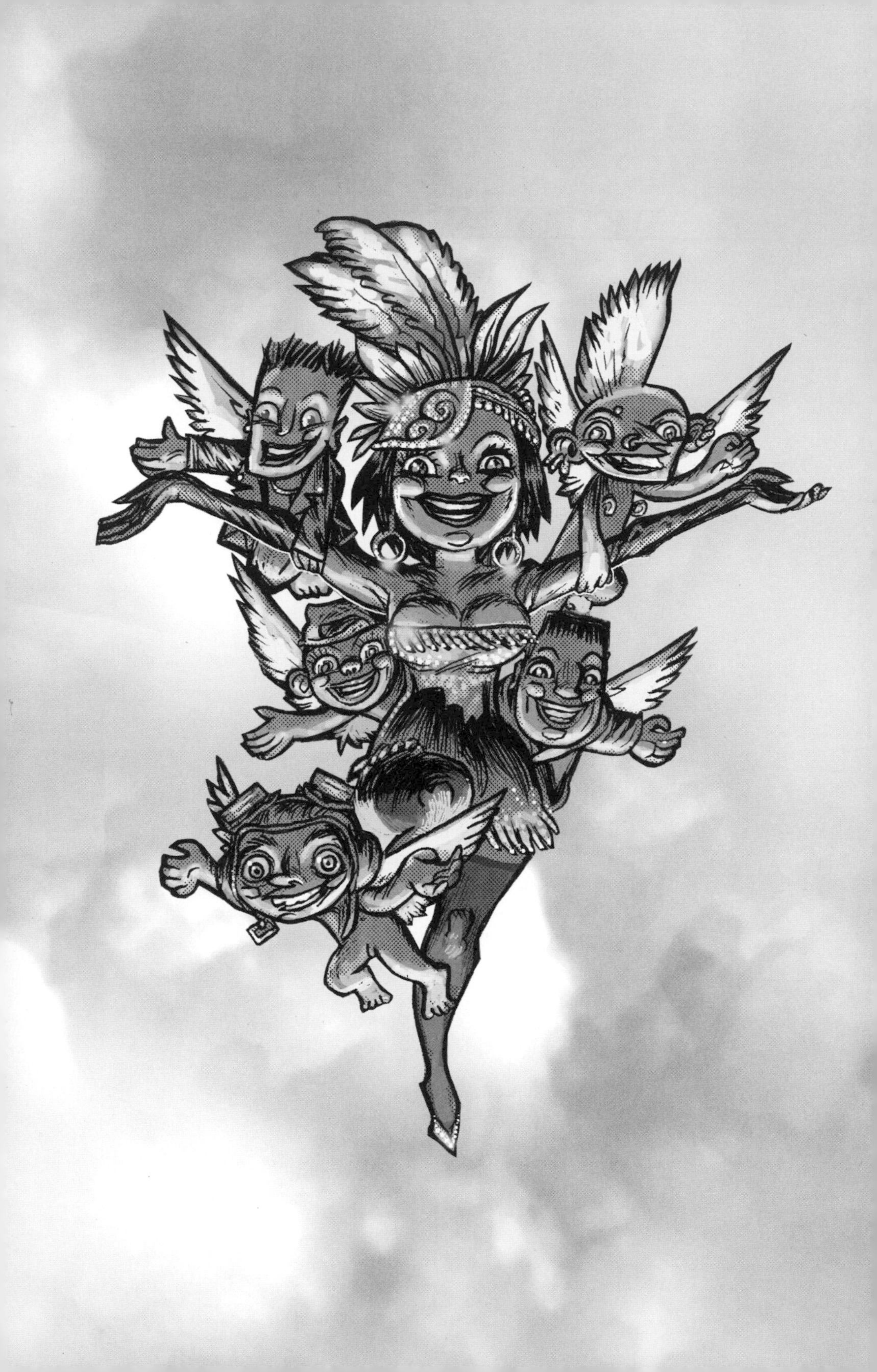

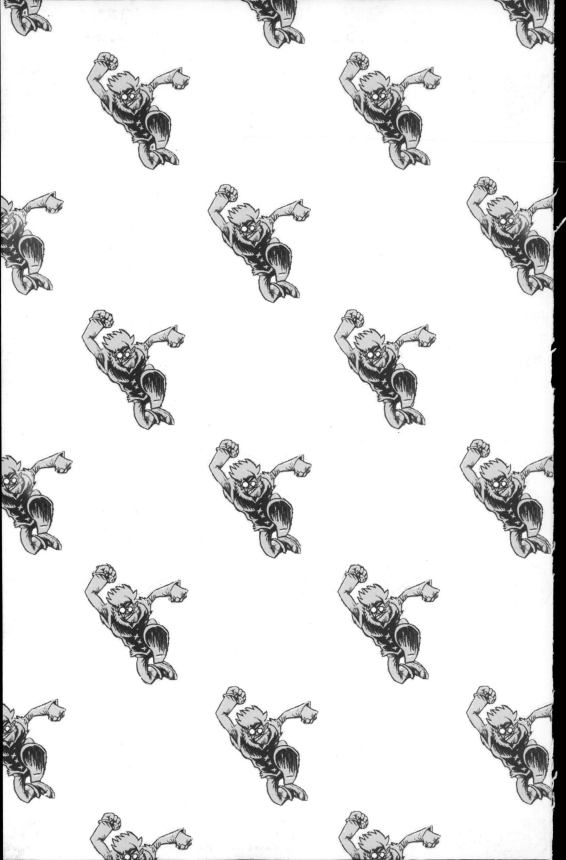